7/21/00

THEIR KINGDOM COME

THEIR KINGDOM COME
INSIDE THE SECRET WORLD OF OPUS DEI

Robert Hutchison

THOMAS DUNNE BOOKS

ST. MARTIN'S PRESS
NEW YORK

THOMAS DUNNE BOOKS.
An imprint of St. Martin's Press.

Library of Congress Cataloging-in-Publication Data

Hutchison, Robert A., 1938–
    Their kingdom come : inside the secret world of Opus Dei / Robert
Hutchison. – 1st U.S. ed.
        p. cm.
    "Thomas Dunne books."
    Includes bibliographical references and index.
    ISBN 0-312-19344-0
    1. Opus Dei (Society).   I. Title.
BX819.3.O68H87   1999
267'.182—dc21
                                                                99-19465
                                                                CIP

First published in Great Britain by Doubleday, a division of Transworld Publishers
Ltd.

First U.S. Edition: June 1999

10 9 8 7 6 5 4 3 2 1

For Lucia,
Dawne and Ian

ACKNOWLEDGEMENTS

THE SENSITIVITIES SURROUNDING OPUS DEI AND THE SHYNESS OF people who have been victims of religious sects mean that many whose experiences and comments helped structure this exposé of power and deceit within the Catholic Church have no wish to be named. Though not a Catholic myself, I was deeply touched by their faith and openness when talking with me, and without their testimony this book would never have come to life in the form it has taken. I am, therefore, grateful to all of them.

Among those to whom I owe special thanks, and who can be named, are my agent, Gillon Aitken, and my editor at Doubleday, Joanna Goldsworthy. Thanks also to Arthur Radley in London, who organized the UK research, and my daughter Tamara in Geneva, whose knowledge of languages I often put to good use.

With background documentation in five languages, the translation assistance of Didier Favre, Petra and José Sánchez and Hugo Valencia was especially appreciated. Also my thanks to Charles Raw, author of *The Moneychangers*, a model work of analysis and research on the Banco Ambrosiano affair, Carlo Calvi, who placed the Calvi family archives at my disposal, Godfrey Hodgson, whose file on the Pinay Group gave needed insight, Jeff Katz of Kroll Associates, Andrew Soane of Opus Dei in London, Fergal Bowers in Dublin, Professor Oldrich Fryc, head of the Department of Legal Medicine in Geneva, Marjorie Garvey of Our Lady and St Joseph in

Search of the Lost Child in New York, Father Gabriel Campo Villegas, historian of the Barbastro martyrs, and London solicitor Paul Terzeon, whose submission on the Calvi murder proved an excellent guide. Alberto Moncada, Javier Sainz Moreno, Pilar Navarro-Rubio and Francisco José de Saralegui in Madrid provided valuable counsel, and the kindness of María del Carmen Tapia of Santa Barbara, California, John Prewett in Fairbanks, Randy Engel and Suzanne Rini in Pittsburgh, Father Vladimir Felzmann of the Archdiocese of Westminster and Dr John Roche of Oxford also will not be forgotten.

Michael Walsh, author of *The Secret World of Opus Dei*, allowed me access to the library at Heythrop College, and José Luis, the librarian of *La Vanguardia*, provided assistance at his newspaper's offices in Barcelona.

In a special category come Thomson von Stein, of Washington D.C., Michael Bennett and Jacques Wittmer of Geneva. They know why, and no more need be said. Dan Urlich of Leysin mounted the computer systems used for data-basing and back-ups, and helped design the maps and graphs.

Leysin, September 1996

It is easy to get to know Opus Dei. It works in broad daylight in all countries, with the full juridical recognition of the civil and ecclesiastical authorities. The names of its directors are well known. Anyone who wants information can obtain it without difficulty.

Josemaría Escrivá de Balaguer
7 January 1966

CONTENTS

Introduction

THE POPE'S SECRET WARRIORS

Christians, even as they strive to resist and prevent every form of warfare ... have a right and even a duty to protect their existence and freedom by proportionate means against an unjust aggressor.

Pope John Paul II

A Muslim is not allowed to start violence, but he is allowed to answer back with violence if someone else starts.

Dr Hassan al-Turabi

IN FEBRUARY 1993, POPE JOHN PAUL II PAID A NINE-HOUR VISIT TO Khartoum, capital of Sudan, Africa's largest country, of which almost 80 per cent of the population – some 26 million souls – follow the Islamic faith. The Pope was on the last lap of his tenth African tour. After stooping to kiss the ground, he delivered a message to his Arab hosts that was starkly void of diplomacy: they must stop 'the terrible harvest of suffering' caused through their persecution of the Christian minority, and end the ten-year-old civil war that was turning the south of the country into a wasteland. Later, outside Khartoum Cathedral, where he celebrated Mass, he compared the plight of the Sudanese Christians to that of Jesus on the Cross: 'in this part of Africa, I see clearly a particular reproduction of Calvary in the lives of the majority of the Christian people.'[1]

His admonishments were directed at the Sudanese president, General Omar Hassan al-Bashir, who had seized power in a military coup almost four years before, and Dr Hassan al-Turabi, the regime's chief ideologist and real power behind the military council. As the secretary general of the National Islamic Front, Dr Turabi was one of the architects of a modern alliance between extremist Sunni and Shiite forces that had not been seen since the first centuries of Islam, when the followers of the Prophet conquered an empire that stretched from the Pamirs to the Pyrenees.

But who had counselled the Pope to make such a bold move, or, as some would call it, a 'no-win encounter'?

John Paul II's closest advisers were the men of Opus Dei – God's Work – a spiritual organization, which, through his help, had become the Church's only Personal Prelature, that is to say, a privileged bishopric without a territory. The confrontation between John Paul II and the leaders of radical Islam was part of Opus Dei's latest step in its twentieth-century Crusade. It was a double-handed strategy that was both cunning and simple: offer an olive branch, and strike with the rod. In other words, have dialogue with the more open face of Islam – an Islam that the West can live with and respect – while meeting radical Islam's militancy with an appropriate measure of Christian militancy, because to do otherwise would be to condemn Christendom to a sorry fate. It was a flexible strategy, and by the same measure more aggressive than any other branch of the Catholic Church was prepared to recommend. And it was high-risk.

If no *modus vivendi* was possible, Opus Dei wanted the West to be morally prepared for a showdown with Islam. Now we are not talking about Opus Dei as some fringe group, but a powerful organization that, since the mid-1980s, has been at the heart of the Vatican power structure – an organization every bit as fundamentalist on the Christian side of the Spiritual Curtain as Turabi and his followers are on the Islamic side. Its members include the Pope's personal secretary, his spokesman and certain of his ministers. Behind them stand the ranks of political and moral strategists at the Opus Dei

---

[1] Alan Cowell, 'The Pope's Plea to Sudan', New York Times Service, *International Herald Tribune*, 11 February 1993.

rigorously. To the non-initiated, this might seem unsettling. But Opus Dei seeks to reassure doubters by stressing, 'We have no aims outside the pastoral or doctrinal sphere. Specifically, we have no political or economic agenda, or any means of carrying one out.'[1]

In all objectivity I intend to demonstrate that this is not an accurate affirmation. But first let us trace the development of Opus Dei from its founding in 1928 to the present and seek to place the organization in a historical and social context, formulated without bias and free of the hagiography and admiring subjectivity of the 'official' documentation promoted by the Prelature.

One of the things that surprised me while researching this book was the fear expressed by some ex-members and their families when talking about 'the Work'. I was warned that by pushing my own enquiries too far I might place myself in jeopardy. Never, however, was I conscious of being menaced, and my relations with the Prelature remained courteous though distant. Nevertheless, I found myself wandering through a world of deceit and dissimulation, crowded with holy manipulators and regulated by unscrupulous interests. As the story unravelled, I found it punctuated by a score of sudden, untimely and often violent deaths: a Spanish Nationalist official who wanted to bring a charge of treason against one of the Founder's first disciples, a Swiss priest who threatened to expose the Vatican's financial misdealings, a former Spanish foreign minister, six bankers, a shadowy London antiques dealer, a Russian metropolitan suspected of being a KGB agent, a cardinal who opposed Opus Dei's transformation into a Personal Prelature and a pope who favoured artificial birth control. Some were apparently explainable, others not at all.

Now I am not a public prosecutor, and there are limits to which private citizens can pursue complex investigations. But I have heard the stories of families torn apart by the Prelature's recruiting practices and of former members who were harassed after leaving the organization and who suffered severe 'withdrawal' problems. The organization's attempts to explain away these cases were frankly unconvincing and frequently lacked compassion. The evidence and affidavits made available to me have left me with an uneasy feeling that Opus Dei, because it operates with lack of oversight and engages

---

[1] Andrew Soane, Director, Opus Dei Information Office UK, 24 March 1995.

in activities not commonly associated with religious organizations, constitutes a danger to the Church. People driven by fundamentalism have never been 'led by responsibility, by responsible love', but by strong, deeply felt emotions and a singleminded belief that they possess *all* the answers.

THEIR KINGDOM COME

PART ONE
VISION

CAUSES OF SAINTS

Behold, I send you out as sheep in the midst of wolves; so be wise as serpents and innocent as doves.

Matthew 10:16

ROME HAD RARELY SEEN ANYTHING LIKE THE MID-MAY 1992 INFLUX of pilgrims for a gala beatification that paralysed traffic for days, causing greater mayhem than usual in a city that often knows little else. All hotel rooms had been booked for months in advance. Charter flights landed at Fiumicino airport every few minutes carrying Catholics from sixty countries. More than 200 flights came from Spain alone. Meanwhile 2,500 buses from every corner of Europe converged on Via della Conciliazione, leading from Castel Sant'Angelo to St Peter's Square. And a pair of cruise ships had anchored off Ostia with a full complement of South American pilgrims who during one week were bussed up to Rome daily.

The size of the turnout for raising to the altars one of the Church's most dedicated servants had surprised even the experts, and for the Vatican's right wing it offered heartening evidence that conservative Catholicism was alive, indeed thriving, and certainly thronging. No gathering quite so large had been seen in front of St Peter's since June 1944, when Rome celebrated with delirium its liberation from

3

Hitler's legions. The current celebration was not for the *defensor urbis et salvator civitatis,* Pius XII, who died in 1958 and still had not been beatified, but for one of his lesser domestic prelates. His name was Josemaría Escrivá de Balaguer, the founder of Opus Dei. Escrivá had begun his lifetime of service to the Church as an ordinary Spanish priest. He died in 1975, when seventy-three, in his office at the Villa Tevere, across the Tiber in Viale Bruno Buozzi, less than five kilometres from the Vatican, and though not even a bishop he held more power than most cardinals.

On the third Sunday in May 1992, John Paul II would confer the rank of *Blessed* upon him, a distinction that placed the Spanish prelate in the waiting room of saints. Such a spiritual honour was cause for great rejoicing among Opus Dei's 80,000 members and the thousands of others – according to Opus Dei, they could be counted in the millions – from every walk of life who, thanks to the Founder, had encountered Christ. During his own lifetime, Escrivá had encouraged his followers to call him 'Father'. Now he was their Father in Heaven where, assured Bishop Alvaro del Portillo, Escrivá's successor as head of Opus Dei, 'he continues to concern himself with all his children'.[1]

Several ecclesiastic authorities have stated that this mystical and even thaumaturgical priest had done more to restore and strengthen the Catholic faith than any other since St Ignatius of Loyola. For these same authorities, it was a matter of grace that Josemaría Escrivá should be beatified in near record time – not quite seventeen years after his death – as even in death he continued through miracles to recast the aura of mystery enveloping the Catholic Church. Furthermore John Paul II was said to be determined to push through Escrivá's canonization during what remained of his pontificate. But why such haste? The record for speedy canonizations is held by Thomas Becket, the Archbishop of Canterbury who was murdered in 1170 and made a saint twenty-six months later. 'But that was a political job if ever there was,' commented Professor Terence Morris of Winchester, a student of fast sainthoods. The same could be said of the Escrivá affair. It was another 'political job'.

John Paul II believed without exaggeration that the Church of

[1] In his homily at a Requiem Mass for Father Escrivá on 26 July 1975, Monsignor del Portillo stated: 'Our Father is with God in our House in Heaven.' [Source: *Opus Dei Newsletter* No. 1, p. 4, published by the Vice-Postulator of Opus Dei in Britain, 1989].

Rome was confronted with its most serious crisis since the Protestant Reformation. Papal authority was under attack. He blamed much of the dissension on the Second Vatican Council. Ever since, there had been insubordination and rebellion among the clergy. Leftist-inspired Liberation Theology and notions of a Cosmic Christ were threatening the established orthodoxy. The Pope's authority to appoint the bishops he wanted was roundly contested in many of the more influential dioceses. The role of women was being re-examined against his will, the use of condoms openly recommended by some bishops, and the obligation of celibacy challenged. While dissension reigned within, from without he saw a threat in the worldwide reawakening of Islam.

Under these circumstances, Opus Dei was a valued ally. And so, John Paul II accepted the thesis that Escrivá had founded his *Obra* with divine assistance, the result of the Aragonese priest's ability to commune with God. The 'divine inspiration' had come in 1928, at a time when the social structure of Spain was facing dislocation. Ideologically, the inspiration was authoritarian. Opus Dei had thrived under Franco. Opus Dei's leadership, one is left to conclude, was only too aware that even the most guileful of strategies is of itself useless unless backed by power and authority to implement it. Opus Dei knows how to create an illusion and it has amassed considerable power. Beatification of the Founder – and hopefully his later canonization – was part of that illusion, for it demonstrated papal approbation and proved it was at the centre of power within the Church. It was understandable, therefore, that as preparations for the Sunday ceremony progressed towards their culmination, the mood at the Opus Dei headquarters in Viale Bruno Buozzi bordered on ecstasy. Only one worrisome hitch existed. The Italian police had been told that the military arm of ETA, the Basque separatist organization, was planning to kidnap the remains of Father Escrivá and hold them to ransom. ETA was the most experienced terrorist organization in Europe. But it was said to be short of funds and so Opus Dei, which it accused of flagrant ostentation, seemed a natural target.[1]

---

[1] Opus Dei denied knowledge of this incident. When asked if it had received such a warning, its UK information officer replied, 'the answer is *probably* [sic] that there was no such warning'.

The Italian police took the threat seriously. Although the list of ETA atrocities was long, its most spectacular act had been to place a bomb in the centre of Madrid, a few days before Christmas 1973, which blasted Admiral Luis Carrero Blanco, the Spanish premier, along with his car, clear over a five-storey building onto the balcony of another building in the next street, killing him, his chauffeur and his bodyguard. Carrero Blanco had been Opus Dei's protector, appointing ten of its members to his last cabinet, while another five of his nineteen ministers were known Opus Dei supporters. His assassination had curtailed – though not for long – Opus Dei's political influence, and this only months before General Franco was due to hand over the reins of state to the future king, Juan Carlos de Borbón.

Notwithstanding the new ETA threat, on the Thursday before the beatification ceremony the remains of the Founder were removed from the prelatic church in the Villa Tevere and transported to the imposing Basilica of Sant'Eugenio, at the western end of Viale Bruno Buozzi. The simple hardwood coffin, covered by a red mantle and surrounded by thickets of freshly cut roses, was placed on a catafalque in front of the altar where it was to remain on public view during the entire week of celebrations and afterwards returned in public procession to the Villa Tevere for its encasement inside a reliquary under the altar of the prelatic church. The ETA threat never materialized.

From dawn on the appointed Sunday, under a ceramic blue sky, the air scented with pinewood from the Vatican gardens, St Peter's Square began to fill with pilgrims. *L'Osservatore Romano*, the Vatican newspaper, estimated their number at 300,000. Raised six steps above the paving stones, the papal dais was covered by a golden canopy to provide shade for the frail Pope. No less than forty-six cardinals were on hand to assist him and more than 300 bishops. Among the pilgrims were Santiago Escrivá, the Founder's younger brother, Giulio Andreotti, the Italian senator-for-life who had been seven times premier, and Mother Teresa of Calcutta. The two-and-a-half hour ceremony was transmitted live by Italian television to networks in thirty countries, mainly in Latin America.

Beatified alongside Father Escrivá was a former slave woman, Josephine Bakhita, whose heroic virtues had been hitherto unknown to the world. She was a Dinka from southern Sudan, born in 1869.

At the age of ten she had been carried off by slave traders who sold her into a lifetime of misery. The last of her four masters, a Turkish army officer, had offered her as a gift to the Italian consul in Istanbul. The consul brought her to Venice where she became a nun, living in a convent until her death in 1947. At the very moment the Pope conferred the title of *Blessed* on them giant tapestries fixed to the façade of St Peter's were unfurled to reveal their larger-than-life portraits. A roar of applause broke out and spontaneously the crowd started singing *Christus vincit*.

Behind the pomp and ritual was an extremely serious message. Wherever the Church of Rome turned in search of new souls she was confronted by a rising Islam, whose leadership, though divided, was relatively rich and resolute. With 1,200 million adherents compared to 965 million Catholics, Islam was growing fast. It had become the second largest religion in France, Italy and Spain. Immigration and proselytizing was adding daily to its numbers throughout Europe and the Americas. More than 5 million Muslims lived in the United States, 5 million in France, 3.5 million in Germany, 2 million in Britain, 1 million in Italy. These figures, however, represented little more than informed guesswork as the flood of illegal aliens made it impossible for legislators to count accurately the number of Muslims moving into the heartlands of Europe and America.

The significance of the Vatican's message was in the identity of the two people chosen for beatification. Sister Josephine Bakhita had been converted by force to Islam and then, freedom restored, had chosen Christianity. Christians in southern Sudan, the Dinkas in particular, were being persecuted by Islamic fundamentalists from the north. News of her beatification was banned by Khartoum. Nevertheless, she became a symbol of hope for oppressed Christians and a warning to Khartoum that the 'harvest of suffering' in the south could turn against it. Nine months later, the Pope would make his visit to Khartoum.

As for Blessed Josemaría, after Communism he would have viewed Islam as the most serious threat to the Church. Coming from Upper Aragon, concern for the Moor was part of his heritage. Escrivá's successor, Alvaro del Portillo, had seen the outbreak of sectarian war in the Balkans as a sign that Islam was again surging westwards, edging Europe closer to the abyss.

7

Seen from another angle, hurrying the Founder down the road to sainthood fitted perfectly into John Paul II's preparations for the Great Jubilee he planned at the end of the second millennium. He believed that canonizations showed the vitality of the Church in modern times. Making Escrivá a saint was like presenting Christ with a trophy, proof that 2,000 years after His ascension there were still believers who followed His footsteps to the point of perfection. This was esoteric logic of a sort that not everyone could accept or comprehend. Indeed, to many outside the faith the custom of elevating departed servants to heavenly councils might seem a little strange, not to say unreal, and irrelevant to the worship of God. But inside the Vatican the making of saints is a serious business. Those raised to the honours of the altars – Vatican-speak for beatification – become icons of faith. At a time when the Church is losing priests icons of faith are sorely needed. During the previous twenty-four years, since 1969 in fact, more than 100,000 men had left the priesthood, with the result that by the early 1990s, 43 per cent of all Catholic parishes had no-one to administer the sacraments.[1]

In the earliest days, a saint was someone who died for his faith. The first was Stephen, a Greek-speaking Jew chosen by the apostles to care for poor widows in the church at Jerusalem. Stephen was arrested for heresy and brought before the Sanhedrin, the supreme Jewish council of the time. At the end of a brave but perhaps unwise speech in his own defence he accused the Jewish leaders of killing God's son. For this blasphemy he was stoned to death.

With Emperor Constantine's Edict of Milan (323), unrestricted Christian worship was authorized throughout the empire and the harvest of martyrs significantly decreased, and so saint-making criteria underwent a first important change. Thereafter, saints were mainly recruited from among the leading patriarchs. The first thirty-six popes were made saints, along with a number of outstanding monks and even the occasional hermit. Later, in the Middle Ages, it became fashionable to raise the founders of religious orders to sainthood. But it was only in the fourteenth century that the procedure known as 'canonization' – the inscribing of a name on

---

[1] Patrick Welsh, 'Is Sexual Dysfunction Killing the Catholic Church?' *The Washington Post*, 8 August 1993.

the canon, or list, of saints – was finally conceived. Concurrently appeared the distinction between *beati* – those venerated locally or within a religious order – and *sancti* – those canonized by the Pope as figures worthy of universal veneration.

The saint-making procedures underwent further refinement in 1588, when Sixtus V, the so-called 'Iron Pope' and architect of the modern Curia, remodelled the Roman Church's central government, creating fifteen Congregations – the Vatican's equivalent to government ministries. Each Congregation was henceforth headed by a cardinal. Six of the newly created Congregations oversaw the Church's secular administration, and the rest supervised spiritual affairs. Among them was the Congregation of Rituals, which was made responsible for canonizations. By the reign of Urban VIII (1623–44) the power of the Pope had become so strong that veneration which failed to receive his *nihil obstat* – literally, *no opposition* – was forbidden. Not until 1917, however, were the procedures for canonization formally incorporated into canon law – the law of the Church. New canonizations remained quite rare and were subject to a painstaking investigative process. For 500 years, no more than 300 new saints were placed on the canon, and the procedures changed little until 1983, when John Paul II completely overhauled them.

The person John Paul II chose to implement his reforms was Cardinal Pietro Palazzini, an ultra-conservative and staunch ally of Opus Dei. He had worked with Father Escrivá and was a frequent dinner guest of the Founder's successor. Knowing that Escrivá's cause for sainthood was high on Opus Dei's agenda, John Paul II's choice of Palazzini as Prefect of the Congregation for the Causes of Saints was therefore unusual. As a hardened professional of the Curia, Palazzini had been around the Vatican for what seemed like for ever. He had joined the Curia under Pius XII, been promoted archbishop by John XXIII, and continued to rise in the hierarchy until receiving his cardinal's hat from Paul VI. The aims of the 1983 overhaul which John Paul II asked him to implement were threefold: to make canonization less costly, more rapid and more productive for the Church.

The rules governing the saint-making process when Father Escrivá died required a five-year pause from the date of death before a candidate's cause could be introduced. Every candidate for sainthood must have a sponsor, whose first step is to petition the local bishop, referred to in ecclesiastical language as the Ordinary. If the Ordinary accepts that the cause has merit, he initiates what is known as a 'Process Ordinary'. It is designed to furnish the Congregation for the Causes of Saints with all the necessary material to make a final decision. In addition to a biography and list of witnesses, the petition has to be accompanied by a number of letters from religious and civil authorities praising the candidate's attributes. Normally, a postulator (literally, one who demands or nominates for election) is appointed for the Roman phase of the proceedings – that is, after the Ordinary has submitted his *Positio*. But Opus Dei was in a hurry.

Escrivá's remains had hardly been laid to rest in the prelatic church when Alvaro del Portillo called in one of Opus Dei's most effective media experts, Father Flavio Capucci, and asked him to become postulator general – in other words, the project co-ordinator. With its all-encompassing foresight, Opus Dei had added Capucci's name sometime before to the Congregation's list of acceptable postulators. Father Capucci had known the Founder personally and as a former editor of *Studi Cattolici*, a religious magazine published by Opus Dei in Milan, he had interviewed Karol Wojtyla when he was still Archbishop of Cracow. Portillo gave Capucci two years to prepare a postulation file that would be presented to the Ordinary once the cause was officially launched. Opus Dei hoped to have Escrivá's beatification wrapped up by 1990, and his canonization in the bag before the end of the millennium.

Shortly after Capucci's appointment, Opus Dei priests began visiting episcopal sees around the world, asking bishops and cardinals for letters supporting Escrivá's cause. While this was being done, a decision was taken on which Ordinary to petition. Normally a sponsor should petition the Ordinary of the candidate's 'home diocese', in Escrivá's case Saragossa, where he had been ordained. But, except for a few weeks, he had hardly undertaken any pastoral duties there. The first twenty years of his pastoral mission were spent in Madrid. In 1947, however, Opus Dei had moved its headquarters to Rome, so Opus Dei's hierarchy opted in favour of the Ordinary of Rome. The choice was made with good reason. The Ordinary of Rome is the Pope, and he was well disposed to Opus Dei. The

Ordinary of Rome operates in diocesan affairs through his vicar. At the time, the vicar of Rome was Cardinal Ugo Poletti, a long-time friend of Father Escrivá. And so, on 14 February 1980 – five months short of the minimal five-year waiting period – Don Alvaro del Portillo formally requested Cardinal Poletti to open the beatification proceedings. The petition was accompanied by the file compiled by Father Capucci. The file contained the seven books and collections of homilies written by the Founder during his lifetime, and 6,000 laudatory letters from religious and civil authorities throughout the world. These included 69 cardinals, 241 archbishops and 987 bishops – one-third of the world episcopacy – while among the civil authorities who praised Escrivá's saintliness was Italy's pre-eminent post-war statesman Giulio Andreotti.

Cardinal Poletti officially accepted to launch Escrivá's candidature for sainthood one year later. Since most Opus Dei members lived in Spain, the bulk of the investigative work would have to be undertaken from Madrid. The vicar of Rome, therefore, requested that the Process Ordinary be opened simultaneously in the two capitals. This was done in May 1981. Opus Dei provided a list of witnesses who had personally known the Founder and who could address the question of his saintliness 'from birth until death'. The postulator general also turned over a list of people considered 'manifestly hostile to the cause' and therefore not objective witnesses. The Rome and Madrid diocesan tribunals held a total of 980 sessions and took evidence from 92 witnesses, half of them Opus Dei members. The transcripts ran to 11,000 pages.

To be eligible for sainthood a candidate must have caused the posthumous occurrence of at least two miracles. Authentication by the Congregation of a first miracle permits the candidate to be beatified. Only after authentication of a second miracle can sainthood be accorded. In more recent years, the task of authenticating miracles has been the mandate of the Consulta Medica, a group of sixty medical experts. All men, all Italians living in Rome, half are practising specialists and half are department heads of a medical faculty. On average they examine forty cases a year. They approve less than half. They are sworn to secrecy and each of them receives a fee of $500 per expertise.

In Escrivá's case, a group of Spanish medical experts first sifted through Opus Dei's records of several thousand purported miracles kept at the regional vicariat in Madrid. One was selected. It had taken place in 1976, one year after the Founder's death. The fateful event that provided the key for the Founder's beatification was the 'sudden, perfect and permanent healing' of a Carmelite nun, Sister Concepción Boullón Rubio. The Opus Dei file related that she was on the threshold of death, afflicted by multiple, painful and spreading tumours, one of which had attained the size of an orange. Then seventy years old, the patient was resigned to death, but her fellow sisters began praying daily to Escrivá for help. Defying scientific explanation, she was cured in a single night, once again being able to lead a normal life without requiring special medical attention. She was examined by the experts in 1982. She died on 22 November 1988 at eighty-two of an unconnected cause. The Consulta Medica accepted the Madrid panel's findings without question.

The investigative phase concluded, the Congregation's scribes then had the task of drafting the *Positio super vita et virtutibus*, a 6,000-page document that took three years to complete. One-third of the document concerned the testimony of witnesses. Almost half of the evidence presented came from Portillo and Javier Echevarría, Opus Dei's vicar general who had been a member since his mid-teens. Only two pages were given to Escrivá's critics. In spite of this on 9 April 1990 the Congregation for the Causes of Saints announced its recognition of Father Escrivá's heroic virtues, an important step on the way to sainthood. The decree was signed by the Congregation's new prefect, Cardinal Angelo Felici, as Cardinal Palazzini – who was about to turn eighty – had retired. The Holy See announced that the findings of the *Positio super vita* permitted it to proceed with the beatification 'in all serenity'.

Not everyone shared this view. A few weeks later the Vatican press corps learned by an indiscretion that two of the nine judges on the Congregation's beatification panel had requested a suspension of the proceedings. This revelation was confirmed by *L'Osservatore Romano* one week before the beatification ceremony. It added, however, that when the relator general examined their reasons, and after consulting an 'ample and exhaustive' complement of information, he rejected the motions.

The leak to the press had left Father Capucci fuming. Speaking before the beatification, he emphasized that the ten-year investigation conducted by the saint-making Congregation had provided 'absolute proof of heroic exercise of virtue',[1] and dismissed allegations that the Prelature had set out to purchase Escrivá's beatification, noting that this could hardly have been the case as the cost of the proceedings had not exceeded $300,000.[2]

Capucci was above all angered by a *Newsweek* article written by Kenneth L. Woodward.[3] Woodward charged that Opus Dei had broken the rules by pushing through the Founder's cause so quickly, and inferred that the Founder himself was hardly the sort of person to whom you would entrust your soul. Questions concerning the wisdom of proceeding with such a controversial beatification were not easily brushed aside. They came from cardinals and archbishops, and respected theologians. Most significant among them was the Archbishop Emeritus of Madrid, Cardinal Vicente Enrique y Tarancón, as much of the groundwork for the *Positio ordinario* had been completed during his archiepiscopacy. But Tarancón had shown at best lukewarm enthusiasm for the cause. In 1983 John Paul II transferred his archiepiscopal functions to a newly appointed cardinal, Angel Suguia Goicoechea, an unabashed Opus Dei supporter.

Tarancón said he failed to see the need for 'such unseemly haste', particularly when the beatification of John XXIII, whom he judged a more charismatic and providential figure, was progressing nowhere near as fast. By referring to Papa Roncalli, Tarancón went straight to the heart of the matter. Regarded by many Catholics as an extremely human pope, Roncalli was the initiator of the Second Vatican Council and it was well known that Escrivá had harboured serious misgivings about the council. Escrivá's quick elevation to sainthood, therefore, would be seen as a boost for pre-Vatican II orthodoxy, at the same time heralding a further move away from the reforms of the kindly Roncalli and his successor Paul VI.

Cardinal Tarancón's remarks widened an already open wound within the Church upon which Professor Juan Martín Velasco, one of Spain's leading theologians, was quick to throw salt. The

[1] William D. Montalbano, 'Pope to Beatify Controversial Spanish Priest', *Los Angeles Times*, 16 May 1992.
[2] Patrice Favre, 'Le pape béatifie le Père de l'Opus Dei', *Le Courrier*, Geneva, 16 May 1992.
[3] The article appeared in 13 January 1992 edition of *Newsweek*. Kenneth L. Woodward has written a book, *Making Saints – How the Catholic Church Determines Who Becomes A Saint, Who Doesn't and Why*, Simon & Schuster, New York 1990.

beatification of Escrivá was a 'scandal' that would 'weaken the credibility of the Church', he warned.[1]

'We cannot portray as a model of Christian living someone who has served the power of the state and who used that power to launch his Opus, which he ran with obscure criteria – like a Mafia shrouded in white – not accepting the papal magisterium when it failed to co-incide with his way of thinking. Although Opus Dei's present leaders portray themselves as paladins of papal authority, it wasn't like that under Paul VI, at the time of the Council. Beatifying the "Father" means sanctifying the Father's Opus, including all its negative aspects: its tactics, dogmas, recruiting methods and manner of placing Christ in the midst of the political and economic arenas,' he said.

Velasco also cast doubt upon the credibility of Sister Concepción Boullón Rubio's miracle, pointing out that the Rubio family was closely linked to Opus Dei. (Sister Concepción's cousin, Mariano Navarro-Rubio, a minister of finance and governor of the Banco de España under Franco, was an Opus Dei supernumerary.) Adding more salt, Velasco disclosed that 'the team of medical experts formed to authenticate the miracle were from the University of Navarra, which belongs to Opus Dei.'[2]

Opus Dei claimed that the professor's remarks defamed not only Opus Dei but also the Pope. 'All phases foreseen under the applicable canons of law were scrupulously respected [and] anyone who wished to be heard had only to send a written application to the [beatification] tribunal,' an Opus Dei statement maintained. To suggest that the medical panel belonged to Opus Dei was going too far. 'No medical expert from the University of Navarra was a member of the authentication board, which is part of the Congregation for the Causes of Saints. Two specialists from the University of Navarra did contribute to the medical file [that was supplied to the Consulta Medica] but their work was limited to purely technical aspects and absolutely separate from the judgement as to the inexplicable nature of the cure,' the statement said.[3]

This response amounted to an artful selection of reality. It

[1] Interview in *Il Regno*.
[2] 'Béatification du fondateur de l'Opus Dei – Toujours des polémiques à propos d'Escrivá de Balaguer', APIC Bulletin No. 357, 23 December 1991.
[3] 'L'Opus Dei de Belgique réfute les "déclarations polémiques" concernant la béatification de Mgr Escrivá de Balaguer – Une réponse aux assertions critiques du Professor Velasco', APIC Bulletin No. 8, 8 January 1992.

neglected to mention, for example, that the president of the Consulta Medica was Raffaello Cortesini, a Roman member of Opus Dei. Professor of experimental surgery at the University of Rome, Dr Cortesini was, moreover, heading a project to open an Opus Dei teaching hospital in the Italian capital. In 1975 he had felt so moved by Father Escrivá's death that he had written an obituary for the Italian newspaper *Il Popolo,* describing the Founder as 'a man who loved freedom'.[1]

The revelations contained in *Newsweek* were almost too weird to be believed. Woodward had interviewed Father Vladimir Felzmann, a former Opus Dei priest. A British national of Czech origin, Felzmann had known Escrivá while studying in Rome. He had lived at the Villa Tevere and worked on the translation into Czech of *The Way,* a collection of spiritual maxims written by the Founder when a young priest. Felzmann, who had devoted twenty-two years of his life to Opus Dei, had since become director of pilgrimages and youth chaplain for the archdiocese of Westminster, in London.

Felzmann disclosed that in November 1991 he had written to the Vatican's pro-nuncio in London, Archbishop Luigi Barbarito, stating that he wished to furnish the Congregation for the Causes of Saints with information he felt might at least delay the beatification. A few days later, Barbarito informed Felzmann in writing that his letter had been forwarded to Rome. Felzmann heard nothing more from Barbarito and never received a call from the Causes of Saints.

Three of the allegations made by Felzmann were particularly fascinating for they revealed a curious twist of mind for someone portrayed as having lived heroically the virtues of faith, hope, charity, prudence, justice, temperance and fortitude. Escrivá once remarked to Felzmann that Hitler had been 'badly treated' by world opinion because 'he could never have killed 6 million Jews. It could only have been 4 million at the most'. Felzmann further noted that Escrivá had felt such deep disgust for Vatican II's liturgical changes that he considered defecting to the Orthodox Church until discovering that their churches and congregations were 'too small for us'. Felzmann's third revelation – that Escrivá had an 'idiosyncratic concept' of the truth – was so unexpected as to seem almost derisory.

[1] Salvador Bernal, *Monsignor Josemaría Escrivá de Balaguer – A Profile of the Founder of Opus Dei,* Scepter, London 1977, p. 284.

Felzmann insisted that Escrivá's ethic had left an indelible mark upon the institution. Citing an example, he said parents were systematically 'tricked' concerning the vocations of their children. He also alleged that business deals involving what the Founder called *pillería* (dirty tricks) were justified on the grounds that 'our life is a warfare of love, and for Opus Dei all is fair in love and war'.

In the matter of making saints, these were serious accusations. But Felzmann's disclosures were cast aside. Opus Dei described them as the work of a misfit attempting to justify his departure from a compassionate and caring family. The Opus Dei press office offered two reasons why Felzmann had not been called to testify. First, he did not really know Escrivá. Second, Felzmann was 'inconsistent' because 'there are documents (the latest dated 1980 when Felzmann was 41 years old) in which he testifies to the Founder's outstanding virtues: love, humility, faithfulness to the Pope, etc. In Felzmann's own words, "He is a saint for today, a saint for ever".'

Abiding by the Founder's maxim that 'all is fair in love and war', Opus Dei employed every trick in the book, including trampling over people's reputations, to steamroller the beatification through. The case of Dr John Roche, a lecturer in history of science at Oxford's Linacre College, illustrated the extremes to which it went. Roche had joined Opus Dei in Galway at 22 and remained a member from 1959 to 1973.

In September 1985, Roche wrote to Cardinal Bernadin Gantin, prefect of the Congregation of Bishops, expressing concern that 'if Monsignor Escrivá were beatified, the resultant scandal could damage the credibility of the whole process of beatification'. He proposed to submit evidence.

Gantin's reaction was to ask the Vatican's nunciature in London to find out more about Roche. On 14 October 1985, the Vatican's chargé d'affaires in London, Archbishop Rino Passigato, replied to the Congregation's secretary, explaining that Roche was 'affected by serious psychological disorders' and was most probably being exploited by 'third parties who have the perfidious intention of harming the Church and the Apostolic See by attacking Opus Dei and its Founder'. Roche had never met nor even spoken to Monsignor Passigato, and he denies having suffered from any such psychological disorders, so it is hard to imagine where the archbishop might have obtained his information.

When Roche received no reply, on 27 May 1986 he wrote to Cardinal Palazzini, who at that time was still overseeing the Causes of Saints. He told the cardinal he had a 'dossier on the life and works of the Founder of Opus Dei. It includes testimony from many former members who knew Monsignor Escrivá personally, as I did.'

Palazzini replied promptly, pointing out that Roche had sent his letter to the wrong address, as the cause had not yet reached his Congregation. He suggested the letter should be re-addressed to Monsignor Oscar Buttinelli, an official with the Regional Tribunal for Latium at the Vicariat of Rome. As it turned out, Palazzini had already written to Buttinelli, warning him to expect an approach from Roche. 'For years, Signor Roche has been engaged in a campaign of calumnies against Opus Dei; any eventual information he might send you concerning the Servant of God will have to be weighed for its reliability,' Palazzini stated.[1]

Unaware of Palazzini's correspondence with Buttinelli, Roche was more than pleased by the cardinal's apparent interest. Confidently, he enclosed in his letter to Buttinelli a brief biographical note on himself and several remarks attributed to Escrivá, intending them to be a preliminary sample of the information he could provide. Roche said Escrivá frequently commented to those close to him that he 'no longer believed in Popes or Bishops, only in the Lord Jesus Christ,' and that 'the Devil was very high up in the Church'. As an example of Escrivá's disdain for the post-Vatican II Church he cited an article appearing in *Crónica*, a confidential in-house publication, which stated: 'There is an authentic rottenness [within the Church], and at times it seems as if the mystical Body of Christ were a corpse in decomposition that stinks.'[2] Roche's letter was politely answered. He was told there was no need to send further material as the Congregation for the Causes of Saints 'knows all about you'.[3]

Of the nine judges on the beatification panel, eight were Italian, which was contrary to custom, which holds that a majority should be of the same nationality as the candidate. Monsignor Luigi de Magistris, director of the Vatican gaol, was one of the two who

[1] Letter of Cardinal Pietro Palazzini to the Rev. Mgr Oscar Buttinelli, 10 June 1986.
[2] Letter of Dr John J. Roche to Mgr Oscar Buttinelli, 28 July 1986.
[3] Peter Hebblethwaite, 'New evidence surfaces in Escrivá canonization', *National Catholic Reporter*, Kansas City, 22 May 1992.

requested a suspension of the procedure because he wanted more light shed on Escrivá's spiritual discernment. 'There were certain depositions which seemed excessive. Notably, one witness affirmed that Escrivá was frequently in a state of ecstasy, particularly when travelling on trains,' he commented. He also thought it an abuse of privilege that Alvaro del Portillo, Escrivá's confessor of thirty years, had been permitted to give evidence and asked – to no avail – that his 800 pages of testimony be excluded.

The other 'dissenting' judge was the only Spaniard on the panel, Monsignor Justo Fernández Alonso, rector of the Spanish Church in Rome. He requested a suspension because he was disturbed that 'many witnesses had not been heard'.[1] The relator general dismissed both requests. The Vatican had decided that the procedure must go forward, and so forward it went.

In spite of Opus Dei's determination, what at first glance appeared to be a simple journey of an Aragonese cult figure towards sainthood had turned into a nightmare. No other beatification in recent times had engendered such controversy. For thousands, Escrivá was an evident worker of miracles, while for others he was a charlatan. To make some sense of this contradiction and better understand the movement he founded a visit to Escrivá's birthplace offers a good beginning.

[1] 'Une béatification au forceps', *Golias* No. 30, summer 1992 (Lyons), p. 90.

BARBASTRO

To understand Opus Dei one needs to study the Founder.

Alvaro del Portillo

THE COAT OF ARMS OF BARBASTRO, WHERE ESCRIVÁ WAS BORN, represents the severed head of a bearded Moor, surrounded by five shields, under the crown of Aragon.

Barbastro is strategically near the Rio Vero's junction with the Cinca, a tributary of the Ebro, and down through the ages it has prospered as a market centre, lying amidst a broad, rolling plain of golden wheat fields and green orchards. Over the troubled centuries of Spanish nationhood, Barbastro quietly grew, so that by the time of Don José Escrivá's marriage to María de los Dolores Albás y Blanc in the summer of 1898 – the year of Spain's defeat in the Spanish–American war – the town counted 7,000 souls, all Catholic and none of them particularly poor or downtrodden.[1]

Don José's family originally came from Narbonne in France at the time of the Christian reconquest of Spain from the Moors, and settled in Balaguer, a town in Lérida province, not far from Barbastro. In

---

[1] According to *Annuario Pontifico 1992*, the diocese of Barbastro covers 4,397 square kilometres and has a population of 31,590, of whom 140 are non-Catholic.

the 1800s his grandfather, a doctor, had moved to Fonz, a hilltop village overlooking the Rio Cinca. Doña Dolores's family owned a textile shop in Barbastro. When Don José moved from Fonz to Barbastro in 1894, he became a partner in the shop. He also opened a chocolate confectionery in the basement. Chocolates, neatly done up in bright little packages, seemed to suit his nature, which was cheerful and optimistic. He was a fastidious dresser, always freshly shaven, his handlebar moustache trimmed and twisted.

The newly married couple moved into a narrow four-storey house not far from the Argensola Palace, one of the oldest buildings in town. Their first child, Carmen, was born a year later. Hardly had Doña Dolores finished nursing Carmen than she was expecting her next child, born on the feast day of St Julian, 9 January 1902. Four days later the infant was christened José María Julian Mariano in the Cathedral of Our Lady of the Assumption. His godfather was Mariano Albás, one of Doña Dolores's cousins who, like Don José's elder brother, Teodoro, was a priest.

BARBASTRO'S COAT OF ARMS

At the turn of the century Spain remained anchored in the Middle Ages, separated from the rest of Europe not only by the Pyrenees but by a gulf of economic backwardness. Fabulously rich landowners with the same rights as feudal lords lived in the midst of land-hungry peasants. Agriculture, involving more than half the population, had not been freed from its medieval fetters. The Church, too, was marked by abrupt dividing lines: parish priests who were little better than beggars lived in near-hovels, while their bishops lived in palaces. The same phenomenon occurred in the army, with 500 generals receiving imperial salaries while lower ranking officers hardly earned enough to pay for food. Medical services were primitive and limited, but the churches were full.

When in 1904 José María became ill with high fever, the local doctor and a homeopath were summoned to the house. Neither was able to diagnose the ailment or prescribe a remedy. Giving the child only hours to live, they suggested a priest would be of more use. But Doña Dolores refused to accept their verdict. With stirring faith, she beseeched Our Lady of Torreciudad, whom she held in special devotion, to intercede for the infant, promising that if her prayers were met she would dedicate the child to the Lady's work. Hours later, Escrivá's biographers tell us, the little José María was sleeping peacefully.

José María's recovery left Doña Dolores in debt to the Virgin. To make good her promise, she wrapped the child warmly and set off on horseback along the rough track to Torreciudad, in the mountains 24 kilometres away, to present him to Our Lady. Riding side-saddle, the infant in her arms, she forded the Cinca and climbed the high escarpment to a medieval beacon tower and rustic hermitage overlooking the gorge. Torreciudad had once been a Moorish outpost defending Barbastro's northern flank. Under the tower in olden times was a mosque. In 1084, when King Sancho Ramírez of Aragon recaptured Torreciudad, a wooden statue of the Madonna seated on a simple throne, the child Jesus in her lap, was placed in the mosque, henceforth transformed into a Marian shrine, and for the next 900 years Our Lady of Torreciudad continued to attract a strong local following.

Over the next five years, Doña Dolores bore three more daughters, but only María Asunción, known in the family as Chon, survived beyond the second year. With two sisters in Heaven, the young José María believed that if he prayed to the Guardian Angels his parents and two remaining sisters would be protected. But in

1913 Chon fell ill and died shortly after her eighth birthday. It made a deep impression on the 11-year-old José María. He feared that he might be the next to go. But his mother reassured him. 'Don't worry. You've been put in the care of Our Lady of Torreciudad.'[1] She often repeated how he had been saved by the Virgin. 'Our Lady must have left you in this world for some great purpose, because you were more dead than alive,' she would tell him.[2] Now when a small boy hears his mother reaffirm this proposition over and over again with all the conviction in the world, whether he lives up to the expectation or not it remains lodged in his mind for a lifetime.

The Otals of Valdeolivos, who were local landowners, lived a few houses away. Their daughter, a playmate of Chon, recalled that one afternoon she and some of José María's friends were building castles with playing cards in the Escrivá front room. Everyone was gathered around the table, holding their breath as the last cards were added to the structure, when suddenly José María toppled them with a sweep of his hand. 'That', he announced, 'is exactly what God does with people: they build a castle, and when it is nearly finished He pulls it down.'[3]

The premonition of a moody, semi-mystical child? Oddly enough, the house where the Escrivás lived was torn down in the 1960s – not by the sweep of God's hand, but to make way for a more imposing Opus Dei women's residence and cultural centre dedicated to the Founder. One of Escrivá's biographers, Peter Berglar, claimed in a revealing passage that the destruction of the house (and three adjoining houses) actually pleased the Founder, 'because he refused any idea of a cult being created around him'.[4] Nevertheless, to replace his birthplace with a much larger brickwork mansion, in the style of the Argensola Palace, might easily be interpreted as an intention of presenting a grander image of Escrivá than fitted his rather modest beginnings.

---

[1] François Gondrand, *At God's Pace*, Scepter, London 1989, p. 30; and Andrés Vázquez de Prada, *El Fundador del Opus Dei*, Ediciones Rialp, Madrid 1983, p. 51.
[2] Peter Berglar, *Opus Dei – Life and Work of its Founder Josemaría Escrivá*, Scepter, Princeton, p. 12.
[3] Bernal, *Op. cit.*, p. 24.
[4] Peter Berglar, *L'Opus Dei et Son Fondateur Josemaría Escrivá*, p. 27, MamE, Paris, 1992. This passage was not included in the English translation published by Scepter in 1994.

No-one in Barbastro today remembers the young Escrivá. The Founder's last surviving boyhood friend, Martín Sambeat, died in 1993. Therefore the most detailed image we have of him comes from the official biographies. They tell us that José María was a cheerful lad, who even had a touch of mischief in him, and that in spite of the deaths of three sisters, he continued to believe that families united in admiration of the saints enjoyed God's protection. To be sure, the family prayed the rosary together, sometimes in a private oratory belonging to the Otals. On Saturdays they would recite the *Hail Holy Queen* in the church of San Bartolomé. Afterwards they might stroll down El Coso, the broad esplanade near the Cathedral, where Barbastrians still gather on summer evenings to sip the local wines at sidewalk cafés under a canopy of plane trees.

Barbastro was known for its religious rituals. For the celebration of Corpus Christi the narrow streets, decked with flowers and red carpets, were filled with robed processions and dancing. The same cast wearing different costumes assembled again for the Holy Week processions and, during the month of June, for the fiesta of San Ramón, the town's patron saint. Escrivá's hagiographers maintain that the piety of Barbastro's citizens overflowed during these special occasions. But there were citizens of Barbastro such as the future revolutionaries Eugenio Sopena and Mariano Abad – both approximately the same age as José María – for whom these pious outpourings were odious.

It is unlikely that José María ever crossed their paths, for Sopena and Abad played in different worlds – the garbage-strewn streets of the San Hipólito quarter. They would have stolen from the alms box if they could have. In sharp contrast, José María was as pious as a church mouse. But he did not see his boyhood piety as anything out of the ordinary. His mother had explained the Sacraments to him by the age of six. His first experience with the Eucharist – the Holy Communion – was in the Cathedral. With every visit to Our Lady of the Assumption, he became immersed in the mysteries it contained. Treasures were hidden there that could make a boy's mind spin. In the apse, behind the great altarpiece, was an oval aperture. José María's mother explained that behind its tinted glass Jesus was present, perpetually waiting for the young boy's adoration.[1]

[1] Gondrand, *Op. cit.*, p. 27.

While the rhythm of secular life in Barbastro, as in every other rural Spanish town of the day, was ruled by the religious calendar, times were changing. The town acquired a Masonic lodge – the Triángulo Fermín Galán – whose members were on the whole sympathetic to the idea that Spain would be better governed as a republic. Social tension was increasing in direct ratio to the degree of economic insecurity caused by the disastrous defeat of 1898, the resulting loss of Spain's last colonial possessions and an under-employed workforce suddenly swollen by the return of disbanded units from the lost colonies.

In spite of growing tensions, the social life of Barbastro's middle class remained rooted in the engaging Spanish tradition of the *tertulia*, informal get-togethers of friends of similar standing and interests. One was organized every Wednesday evening by the Parish Friendship Circle. It was an occasion for the town's leading merchants to meet to discuss local politics. Don José always turned up for the *tertulia* smartly dressed, with bowler hat and walking stick, wearing a caped overcoat when the season turned cold. Neither he nor any other member of the friendship circle would have considered venturing into one of the narrow taverns of the San Hipólito quarter where the working class drank. San Hipólito was lost in another Spain, a world apart, and as such quite unknown to them.

3

ENEMIES OF THE CROSS

Many . . . live as enemies of the cross of Christ. Their end is destruction . . .

Philippians 3:18–19

JOSÉ MARÍA JULIAN MARIANO ESCRIVÁ Y ALBÁS MADE HIS FIRST Communion on 23 April 1912, in the tiny church of San Bartolomé. He had celebrated his tenth birthday three months before and since the age of seven had been attending the Piarist College, Barbastro's only secondary school. An old Piarist father, whom he later described as 'a good, simple and devout man', had prepared him for his Christian confirmation and taught him the formula for spiritual communion:

> I wish, Lord, to receive you with the purity, humility and devotion with which your most Holy Mother received you; with the spirit and fervour of the Saints.

The words 'spirit and fervour of the Saints' held special meaning for him, for he and the other children of his class were being filled with the fervour of the great Spanish saints like Dominic Guzmán and Ignatius of Loyola.

25

All of us in varying degrees are creatures of the cultures into which we are born. José María Escrivá particularly was marked as a son of Aragon. Raised in a deeply Catholic environment, the joys and prejudices of his traditionalist upbringing shone through in everything he did. The ancient trauma of Aragon's Moorish occupation helped shape his everyday perceptions. Moreover, the Crusading movement, so important in understanding certain of his motivations, was in a sense born at Barbastro. Aragon's early warriors were hard mountain men but their souls were softened by an intense admiration of Our Lady, whose cult was widespread on the south side of the Pyrenees. Escrivá's often brusque temperament was also moderated by the extravagant regard he paid the Virgin Mary. Above all, Renaissance Spain's concerns for purity of blood and religion were stamped upon his heart. This did not mean that he was closed to other races or religions. But he placed his faith in the Holy Trinity and he believed that there was only one key to the gates of salvation.

In exploring the world of José María Escrivá's childhood, the Piarist College where he received his early schooling deserves special attention. Staffed by a dozen priests, it was not particularly large, with less than forty students, but it enjoyed considerable prestige. José María excelled at mathematics. *Juventud*, a magazine for and about the region's youth, reported that Master Escrivá shared the first-year *Bachillerato* prize for arithmetic and geometry, and the following year he received special mention for religion and geography.[1] He developed an avid hunger for the legends of Spain's heroic past, a hunger which if anything grew stronger as he grew older.

But young Escrivá's appreciation of Spanish culture would remain selective. Though in the circumstances that might seem natural, one nevertheless is left to wonder what the Piarist Fathers taught their charges about Spain's early history. Did they explain, for example, that in 1064 Barbastro had been the site of a Muslim massacre despite a solemn papal promise of safe passage, all for the sake of greed? That would seem unlikely.

Before the Moors came to Aragon, the Visigoths had been in the

---

[1] Bernal, *Op. cit.*, pp. 21–22. Also Vázquez de Prada, *Op. cit.*, p. 55, citing *Juventud Semanario Literario (Sección de Gacetillas)*, año 1, num. 4, del 13 de marzo de 1914.

Iberian peninsula for 300 years, with their capital at Toledo. They ruled through a military aristocracy that became increasingly irrelevant as amongst themselves the Visigoth nobles could never agree about anything. To the south of the Visigoth kingdom, in North Africa, lay the westernmost outpost of the Byzantine Empire, the County of Ceuta and Tangier. In the early eighth century it was administered by Count Julian of Ceuta. He was nominally allied with Roderick, the Visigoth king of Spain. As Julian was cut off from Constantinople by the Moorish wave that spread across North Africa, he sent his daughter to be educated at Roderick's court. Roderick was struck by her beauty and attempted to court her. She rejected him. One night after a palace feast, Roderick raped her.

When informed of his daughter's deflowering, Julian went to Musa, the Emir of Qairwan, capital of the Maghreb, as the Arabs called northernmost Africa, and proposed an alliance to invade the Visigoth kingdom. Musa wanted Julian to demonstrate the enterprise's viability by leading a preliminary incursion himself, which Julian did, enlisting a small Berber force to assist him. He ferried the Berbers across the straits to Tarifa. When they returned to Tangier at the end of the summer, their galleys were loaded to the gunwales with loot.

A year later Musa followed up Julian's initial success by sending a 12,000-man expedition across the straits. The Moors landed this time farther to the east, in the lee of a rock they called Gebel Tariq – Mountain of Tariq (and later known as Gibraltar) in honour of their general. The arrival of the Moors caught Roderick off guard and he hastened south with an army said to number 100,000. In 711, Tariq's outnumbered troops defeated Roderick in a battle along the Barbate River, and the Visigoth nation departed from history's stage.

A 100,000 Moors now settled in Spain and the teaching of Islam spread. Within three years, Muslim armies had marched into France, and by 732 they had reached the banks of the Loire, where Charles Martel finally dealt them a shattering defeat. Though expelled from France, Muslim control of all but northernmost Spain remained intact. They established their capital at Cordoba. They set standards for tolerance unmatched by any society in Europe, except perhaps the eastern empire of Byzantium. Under the Emirate of Cordoba, Moorish Spain grew strong, and the cities of Cordoba,

Seville, Malaga and Toledo were said to outshine any in western Europe.

Towards the middle of the tenth century the emir of Cordoba invaded the last remaining Christian lands in northern Spain – the Marches (Catalunya), Navarra and León – and forced them to pay an annual tribute. But after his death in 961 the Christian princes stopped paying and in retaliation the emir's successor, Mohammed ibn Abi-Amir, surnamed Almanzor the Victorious, sacked the capital of León. A year later Almanzor plundered Santiago de Compostela – an unpardonable outrage as Santiago, said to be the burial place of the Apostle James, was one of Christendom's most revered sites. At that time it ranked third as a place of pilgrimage, after Jerusalem and Rome.

As communications broke down during the Dark Ages, the

IBERIAN PENINSULA IN THE TENTH CENTURY

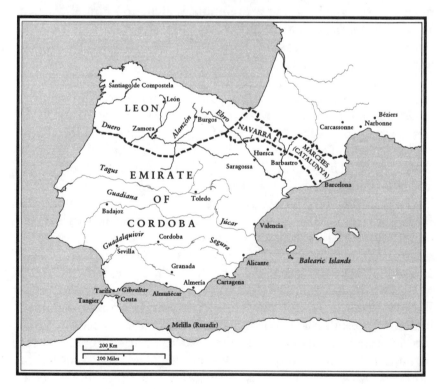

Western Church became increasingly localized. Distant dioceses, remote from papal control, led their own existence, often submerging themselves in corruption and petty politics. According to Gibbon, by the tenth century the Church of Rome had reached her lowest ebb.[1] Reform, when it came, was through the monastic movement, of which the father was St Benedict (c.480–c.550). He became the first to bring into popular use the phrase *opus Dei*.

Benedict believed that personal sanctity could only be achieved by promoting God's work – *opus Dei* – while observing the monastic vows of obedience, celibacy and poverty, which he largely defined as the complete absence of personal possessions.[2] In the Middle Ages, the Benedictine Rule transformed monasteries that had become dens of narrow-mindedness into centres of learning and hospitality. It placed heavy responsibility on the abbot. He was selected through democratic process. Once installed in office, however, he was vested with near totalitarian authority. Abbots were not elected for life but for fixed terms. The danger that they might abuse their power was guarded against by making them accountable after their retirement from office. With Benedict's reforms, the monastic movement provided the impetus for renovation within the Church.

Four hundred years after Benedict's death, the monks at Cluny, in central France, began to develop the pilgrimage as a political instrument. They noted that mass travel to the holy places – what Opus Dei today calls 'religious tourism' – could be used to reinforce Christian faith in lands threatened by Muslim domination. Thus the monks of Cluny began to promote pilgrimage as a Christianizing force. By the beginning of the eleventh century Cluny maintained the roads that led across Europe to the great Spanish shrines of Saragossa (still in Moorish hands) and Santiago de Compostela, and began to popularize organized pilgrimages to Jerusalem. Cluny now assumed a direct role in defending Spanish Christendom and preserving Christian access to the Holy Sepulchre in Jerusalem. But transforming peaceful pilgrimage into a platform for launching military expeditions against Islam presented theological problems.

Encouraging Christian princes to follow the Cross in a warlike

[1] Edward Gibbon, *Decline and Fall of the Roman Empire,* Ch. 49.
[2] Martin Scott, *Medieval Europe,* Longmans, 1964, p. 15.

enterprise infringed upon fundamental concepts of ethics and morality. But was a Christian not entitled to fight for his Creed? In 1063, Ramiro I of Aragon decided most definitely yes and began marshalling Christian forces at Graus, not far from Barbastro, for an attack on Emir Ahmed of Saragossa. Ramiro's first objective was Barbastro, held by a small garrison of Moorish troops. However, before the attack could be launched Ramiro was stabbed to death by a Muslim who had infiltrated the Christian camp. Europe was enraged. Pope Alexander II (1061–73) promised indulgence for all who fought for the Cross in Spain and set about raising an army to carry on Ramiro's work.

The campaign against the emir of Saragossa preceded the First Crusade to the East by more than thirty years. The army of Sancho Ramírez, son of the murdered Ramiro I, was joined by knights from Aquitaine, Burgundy, Lombardy, Normandy and Tuscany. The campaign began and ended in 1064 with the siege of Barbastro, which lasted forty days. It would have gone on longer but was lifted in August when Alexander II promised that everyone in the town would be spared if they laid down their arms. Upon receiving a papal guarantee of safe passage, the outnumbered garrison surrendered. The Muslims were told to assemble outside the town gates with their possessions so that they could be escorted towards Saragossa. But when the Christian troops saw the extent of the wealth passing through their hands they slaughtered every man, woman and child, and made off with the booty. The butchery committed at Barbastro moved the Muslim princes throughout the rest of Spain to take revenge. Retaliation brought counter-retaliation. Intolerance bred counter-intolerance in a spiral of fundamentalist fury.

By entrusting Aragon to Pope Alexander II's feudal care, Sancho Ramírez acquired the necessary military backing to broaden his attacks against the princes of Islam. The military expeditions of his brother, Alfonso VI of Castile, received the full-hearted approval of Pope Gregory VII, who became preoccupied with the idea of mounting a military Crusade to the East, but died before he had time to launch it.

Gregory had been edging towards a doctrine that would encourage European knights to journey to the frontiers of Christendom to fight against Islam. As reward for taking the Cross they were allowed to keep whatever lands they seized by force of arms, which became an excuse for holy larceny on a grand scale, and they were promised spiritual benefits as well. But more significant, the papacy now took over direction of the Holy Wars, launching them as an extension of Vatican foreign policy, naming their commanders and placing a papal legate at their head.

Five years after the massacre at Barbastro, almost 4,000 kilometres to the east the Seljuk Turks appeared on the fringes of Armenia and routed the Byzantine emperor Romanus IV at Manzikert. Asia Minor – Christendom's most prosperous province – fell to the invaders. The scale of the disaster at Manzikert was scarcely imaginable at the time. The Christian empire in the East was vastly more powerful than any other state. Its capital, Constantinople, sat astride the richest trade routes, making it the unrivalled financial and commercial metropolis of the world. It controlled the Mediterranean with an unmatched navy. And it possessed a dedicated and efficient civil service which administered territories from Calabria to the Caucasus.

The source of Byzantium's wealth was in Asia Minor. It was rich in natural resources and its peasants were both free and hard-working. Its cities were populated by merchants and artisans who exported their goods to Constantinople, from where they were sold to the world at large. Asia Minor was where the bulk of the empire's taxes and the largest levies for its armies were raised. Separated from its economic backbone, Byzantium was doomed. But death would be another 400 years in coming.

The Seljuks had embraced Islam before their appearance at Manzikert. They were followed by a horde of Turkoman nomads, travelling lightly armed, with their families and livestock, making for the upland prairies of which Asia Minor is well supplied. The Christians abandoned their villages and farms to be burnt by the invaders. Realizing no force opposed them, the Seljuks imposed their own laws and customs. They quickly overran the coastal cities of Smyrna and Ephesus and the more northerly centre of Nicaea. The sword of Islam severed Asia Minor from the Christian way. The change was abrupt. Only a few years before, the Christian Mediterranean had seemed a secure place, poised for years of peace. In spite of the wars against the infidel in Spain, Muslim and Christian in the eastern Mediterranean had learned to co-exist and trade with each other. At the same time the monks of Cluny had ushered in the great age of pilgrimage, sending thousands of European Christians to the Holy Land each year. But with the Seljuk eruption into Asia Minor, this religious traffic virtually dried up. More than anything else, the Seljuk victory at Manzikert hastened the coming of the Crusades.

The Cluniacs had fired a Christian longing to visit the eastern holy places, and now debated ways of re-establishing the pilgrim traffic. They finally decided that a Crusader movement would be a just and moral means for countering Islam's rise and they explained their doctrine to Pope Urban II, himself a former Grand Prior of Cluny.[1]

In 1095 Urban II was about to journey to France when he received a delegation from Alexius I, the new Byzantine emperor. Alexius was losing ground to the Seljuks and beseeched Urban to send him a force of Western knights. Urban did not reply immediately. As he travelled north to Clermont in France, where he had convened a Church council for that autumn, he struggled with the idea of calling a Holy War to open the way to Jerusalem. Finally, when the council assembled in November he proclaimed the First Crusade, which he portrayed as an armed pilgrimage to restore the Holy sites to Christendom's control.

Urban died in 1099, two weeks after the investiture of Jerusalem by the Crusaders. Almost eight centuries later, in 1881, he was beatified. But Urban might not have been pleased had he lived long enough to learn how the Christian armies had sacked the Holy City. After breaching the walls, the Crusaders rushed through the streets, into houses and mosques, killing men, women and children alike. All through the first night the massacre continued. Those who sought sanctuary in the al-Aqsa Mosque on Temple Mount were slaughtered like sheep.

When not a single Muslim or Jew was left to be slain the Crusaders offered thanks to God in the Church of the Holy Sepulchre. Some years later the Christian military orders were founded. The idea for a brotherhood that was both religious and military came from a penniless Burgundian knight who in 1118 decided to devote his life to protecting pilgrims. He and a friend took vows of celibacy and set out to win recruits. The same year that Alfonso I of Aragon reconquered Saragossa they persuaded King Baldwin of Jerusalem to

---

[1] Steven Runciman, *A History of the Crusades,* Vol. 1, p. 84.

give them a wing of the royal palace on Temple Mount as their headquarters. The Poor Knights of the Temple, as they became known, were backed by St Bernard of Clairvaux, a Cistercian who preached the Second Crusade.[1] The Templars grew into a cohesive military force and won great fame through their exploits. They had their own clergy, exempt from the jurisdiction of diocesan bishops, owing obedience only to the Templar Grand Master, who in turn reported to the Pope.

The Templars participated in most of the great Crusader battles. But their rashness led to a disastrous defeat. In 1187 a Christian army under King Guy de Lusignan and Grand Master Gerard de Ridford was trapped by the Muslim leader Salah al-Din (Saladin) in Galilee. The King and Grand Master were spared, but all Templar knights who survived the battle were beheaded. Three months later, after only eighty-eight years in Christian hands, Jerusalem fell to Saladin. Not a building was looted, not a person harmed. Upon payment of an exit tax, the city's Christian inhabitants were permitted to leave. They streamed slowly to the coast with their possessions, unmolested, in remarkable contrast to the fate of the Muslims at Barbastro.

Opus Dei historians do not tell us what the young Escrivá thought of these events. We do know, however, that he was an admirer of the Knights Templar. Several of their practices would be incorporated into Opus Dei's norms and customs when, later, they came to be set to paper. That the Templars almost took over as rulers of Aragon was undoubtedly known to him, since the Templar headquarters in Spain were situated at Monzón, a small town not far from Barbastro.

The near cession of Aragon to the Templars came about in the twelfth century when Alfonso I died without issue and bequeathed the kingdom to the Knights Templar. Rather than accept the Templars as their masters, the nobles persuaded Alfonso's brother, Ramiro the Monk, to take the crown. As Ramiro III, the new king's first duty was to marry, which he did, and within the year he sired a daughter, Petronella. Having thus performed his national service in the matrimonial bed, the pious Ramiro wanted to return to

---

[1] The Second Crusade, from 1147 to 1149, was led by King Louis VII of France and Emperor Conrad III. It was disbanded after an unsuccessful siege of Damascus.

monastic life. But the nobles insisted he wait at least until his infant daughter had reached an age when she could be respectably married. This occurred shortly after her second birthday; Petronella was given in marriage to Raymond Berengar IV of Barcelona, a warrior count in his forties. The nuptials were celebrated in Barbastro. Only then did Ramiro return to monastic life. Shortly afterwards, Catalunya was attached to the Kingdom of Aragon.

As the new king of Aragon, Raymond Berengar compensated the Knights Templar by giving them the town of Monzón. There they turned a former Moorish fort into one of the most extensive military works in Spain. Master Escrivá knew the fortifications well, having explored them on visits to his grandmother at nearby Fonz. The concept of celibate Christian warriors sworn to obedience and secrecy fired his imagination.

After the fall of Jerusalem, only seven more Crusader campaigns were dignified with a numeric prefix, signifying that they enjoyed papal approbation. The Third Crusade (1189–92) was led by Richard I of England, Philip II of France and Emperor Frederick I Barbarossa. It resulted in a military fiasco but produced a five-year truce permitting unarmed pilgrims free access to the Holy Places.

The Fourth Crusade (1202–04) was diverted to attack Byzantium for the benefit of Venice and was the most wicked. The Crusaders' looting, arson and murder that followed their capture of Constantinople horrified the world and once the rape was completed, they forgot about Jerusalem and proceeded to divide the Eastern empire among themselves.

The disaster of the Fourth Crusade weakened the defences of Christendom. The land route from Europe to the Holy Land became totally impassable and no armed expedition from the West would ever again attempt the journey across Asia Minor. Three years later King Andrew of Hungary obtained Papal approval to redress the situation by leading a Fifth Crusade. The objective was Egypt, regarded as the brawn and bowels of Muslim strength. However King Andrew achieved little and returned home with his army in 1218, transferring command of the remaining forces to Cardinal Pelagius of Spain. Pelagius took Damietta in November 1219, but after an abortive attack on Cairo he was forced to negotiate a truce and withdrew. The Sixth Crusade (1228–29), led by Emperor

Frederick II, produced the Treaty of Jaffa, which again gave the Christians access to Jerusalem. The Seventh Crusade (1248–54) resulted in Louis IX of France capturing Damietta for a second time, but another attempt to seize Cairo failed and the French monarch was taken prisoner. He was released after the French treasury paid a ransom of 800,000 gold pieces to the Sultan.

Louis IX returned to North Africa in August 1270 at the head of the Eighth Crusade. But the endeavour was cut short when he died of the plague under the walls of Tunis. The Ninth and last true Crusade was led by Prince Edward of England. He landed at Acre on the Palestinian coast in May 1271 with a mere one thousand men. While drafting plans for a march into Galilee he was stabbed by a fanatical Muslim of the sect known as the Assassins and lay ill for several months before returning to England to become king. The Crusade as a militant Christian concept was by then debased. Once reserved for the fight against Islam, it had been co-opted for other papal designs. Spiritual rewards were promised to anyone willing to fight for Rome against whomever opposed papal policy, whether Greek, Albigensian or Turk.

After the fall of Acre in 1291, the Templars moved to Cyprus. There they devoted themselves to finance, becoming the West's chief money-lenders. As bankers, the Templars were scrupulously honest. They understood the value of capital gains and were shrewd evaluators of risk. As with Opus Dei seven centuries later, they became a major financial corporation within a remarkably short time, amassing more wealth and influence than many states and any other Christian enterprise of its day. However, Philip IV of France plotted to bring the Templars under his control and to confiscate their assets. He waited until the Grand Master Jacques de Molay came to France on an official visit. During the night of 13 October 1307 he had de Molay and sixty of his knights arrested on trumped-up charges of treason, sexual perversion and devil worship. Pope Clement V acceded to French pressure and dissolved the Order. Philip had the Grand Master burnt at the stake, the traditional punishment for heretics. As the flames rose around him, de Molay damned King and Pope for betraying God's trust and he called upon them to meet him within the year before God to answer for their crime. Clement V died within the month. Philip followed seven months later. His disbanding of the Knights Templar proved another serious blow to

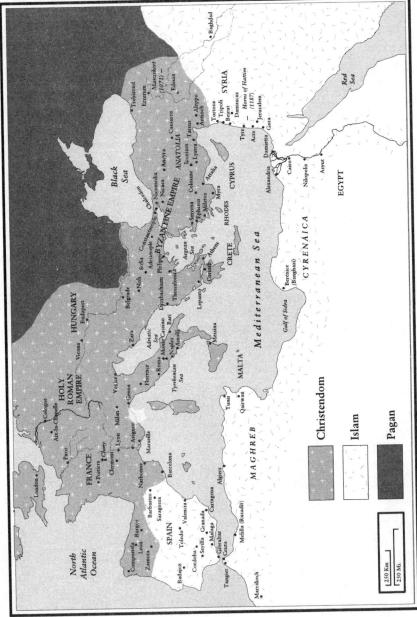

CHRISTENDOM IN THE ELEVENTH CENTURY

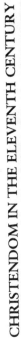

Christendom

Islam

Pagan

250 Km
250 Mi.

Christendom's defences. In little more than a decade the Turks made their first appearance in Europe, while Jerusalem became totally closed to pilgrim traffic.

After capturing Thrace and moving into the Balkans, in 1453 the Ottoman Sultan Mehmet reverted his attention to Constantinople and launched a final attack. During the night of 28 May, his Janissaries breached the Theodosian Walls and within hours the city was in Ottoman hands. After assuring that his troops committed no atrocities, nor desecrated a single monument, Mehmet converted Christendom's largest church, the Hagia Sofia, into a mosque and he changed the city's name to 'Stämbool – Istanbul.

With the disbanding of the Templars, the only Christian thorn remaining in the Ottoman flank was the Order of St John of Jerusalem, also known as the Knights Hospitaller. As a Military Order like the Templars, they were bound by vows of poverty, celibacy and obedience. The eight-pointed cross on their scarlet tunics was symbolic of the eight beatitudes. Its four arms represented the four virtues – Prudence, Temperance, Fortitude and Justice. Like the Templars, they had escaped from Acre, going first to Cyprus before establishing their headquarters on Rhodes. More than two centuries later, Sultan Suliman the Magnificent drove them from the island. As compensation, King Charles I of Spain (later Emperor Charles V) gave them the island of Malta as their ultimate retreat. But there too they would be threatened by Suliman who wanted Malta as a stepping stone for his planned attack on Rome.

Ottoman forces were by then at the gates of Vienna; the Sultan's beys ruled in Budapest and Belgrade, and in 1570 a Turkish force seized Cyprus. Pope Pius V requested Spain's help in forming a Holy League to defend Rome. The League raised a fleet under the command of Don John of Austria, illegitimate son of the Holy Roman Emperor Charles V. Don John's previous assignment for the 'vice-regent of God', as his father was sometimes called, had been eliminating the Moors from the countryside around Granada, which he carried out with a *guerra a fuego y a sangre* (war by fire and blood), a sixteenth-century euphemism for ethnic purification. Now he went on to win the famous naval victory of Lepanto over the Turks.

Had the Ottomans won the Battle of Lepanto they would have

ruled supreme in the Mediterranean. The Christian victory saved Rome.

Spain was then at the height of her power. A Spanish king was Holy Roman emperor and his armies were the Pope's enforcers. At home Spain was on the way to achieving purity of blood and faith. The process had begun well before Lepanto – about the time Christopher Columbus set sail for the New World – when Granada, Islam's last Andalusian stronghold, fell to the troops of Castile. Tomás de Torquemada, taking charge of the Inquisition, set in motion the machinery that would make Spain a uniquely Catholic country. First it was the turn of the Jews. The edict of expulsion gave them three months to convert or leave. A similar fate awaited the last of the Moors – Don John, who had killed 60,000 Spanish Muslims at a cost to the state of 3 million ducats, had not done enough – and in 1609, they too were forcibly expelled.

Spain under Charles V counted a population of no more than 6 million. Even with treasure pouring in from the New World his subjects were over-burdened and over-taxed to pay for an imperial policy that made him the Pope's protector. Arming the Holy League for the Lepanto campaign had cost the Spanish treasury over 4 million ducats. By comparison, income from the South American mines was then estimated at only 2 million ducats a year.[1] Fortunately for the West, the Ottoman Empire now faltered; slowly its armies were rolled back, thanks in part to a split between the Shiite and Sunni branches of Islam that sapped the Muslim world of cohesion and strength.

By then Spain had other enemies. Not only was she at war with France, but British freebooters were raiding her bullion fleets and disturbing overseas trade. Enforcing papal policy had exhausted the country. Charles V retired to a monastery, leaving his son, Philip II, a national debt of 20 million ducats and a war with France that was so costly it brought both countries to the edge of bankruptcy. In a final miscalculation, Philip moved the Invincible Armada against England. Its destruction raised the Spanish debt to 100 million ducats. Spain lost control of the seas and her long decline began.

By the end of the sixteenth century, Spain's chronic inability to make ends meet – servicing the national debt consumed two-thirds

[1] Paul Kennedy, *The Rise and Fall of the Great Powers*, Fontana, London 1989, p. 59.

of the gross national product – had ravaged her currency. Bullion imports from South America dried up. Deprived of fresh capital, agriculture and industry went into decline. Trade stagnated. With empty order books, shipyards closed and the merchant fleet, second to none at the time of Lepanto, shrank by three-quarters.

By the time José María Escrivá entered his final year at the Piarist College, social tensions in Spain were approaching breaking point. The origins of the unrest could be traced back to Charles V's reign. They had their roots in an imperial policy that had made the Spanish monarch God's vice-regent on earth, a policy that mortgaged the nation's wealth for generations thereafter.

BANKRUPTCY

Be patient in tribulation; constant in prayer.

Romans 12:12

IN 1902 – THE YEAR OF JOSÉ MARÍA ESCRIVÁ'S BIRTH – THE SIXTEEN-year-old Alfonso XIII ascended the Spanish throne. Brought into the world six months after his father's state funeral, the young Alfonso suffered a wholly inadequate upbringing for a future monarch. His mother, a religious hysteric, chose as his tutor an ultra-traditionalist priest, anti-Liberal to the hilt. Under Spain's existing constitution, the king, not the electorate, was the sole arbiter of governments. Alfonso made and unseated them as he pleased. In the first twenty-one years of his reign – from 1902 to 1923 – he ordered thirty-three changes of government.[1]

The Liberals' concern to free education from Church control did not make them popular with the clergy. However, when José María began his schooling something like 60 per cent of the Spanish population was illiterate. The Liberals gradually forced the introduction of universal primary education and unfettered the universities, while

---

[1] Gerald Brenan, *The Spanish Labyrinth*, Cambridge University Press, Canto edition, 1993, p. 23n.

the religious orders shifted their teaching efforts to secondary schooling. The working classes regarded this as proof that the Church was intent on educating the sons of the wealthy, while those of the poor were condemned, if they were lucky, to the drudgery of child labour.

The pope of José María Escrivá's childhood, Pius X, had been born the son of a village postman and seamstress from near Venice. He was credited with working miracles while still alive, and was made a saint forty years after his death. But because of his war against 'Modernism', he instigated an anti-Liberal reign of terror inside the Church. In 1907 he published the encyclical *Pascendi*, declaring that anyone tainted by Modernism would be excluded from holding public office or teaching. Secret informer networks were established. Anyone who opposed *Pascendi* was excommunicated.

That same year King Alfonso XIII appointed a strong Conservative, Antonio Maura, as his prime minister. Maura was described as a man of integrity, but unfortunately for Spain his home secretary Juan de La Cierva was a master of malicious, murderous Machiavellian statesmanship. Though claiming to be a devout Catholic, La Cierva believed that maiming and killing people, guilty or innocent, was a permissible political expedient.

Fed up with Madrid's incompetence, in the regional elections of 1907 the Catalan people overwhelmingly elected the Lliga Regionalista, a newly formed nationalist party. As Catalan nationalism posed a threat to Spanish federalism, this presented Madrid with a problem. La Cierva's answer was to provoke a wave of bombings in Barcelona so that the Home Office could assume direct control over the province. Within weeks some 2,000 bombs exploded in the Catalan capital. The local authorities asked an English detective to investigate; in most cases he found the bombings were the work of *agents provocateurs* in the pay of the Home Office. This did not prevent La Cierva from placing Barcelona under martial law. The Church, meanwhile, made no attempt to prevent the slide towards social upheaval and frequently hurried the process along.

Intent on countering Liberal influence at all levels of national life, a Jesuit priest, Father Angel Ayala, founded the Asociación católica nacional de propagandistas, better known as the ACNP. Ayala hoped that by infiltrating the key sectors of national life, his hand-picked ACNP militants would influence public opinion against

Liberal reform. The *Propagandistas*, as they also became known, were graduates of Jesuit colleges, laymen with an apostolic bent, but who were not required to make vows of a religious nature. Their president for the next twenty-five years was a young lawyer, Angel Herrera Oria. The *Propagandistas* never counted more than 1,000 members, but they became immensely influential behind the scenes.

The *Propagandistas* quickly mastered the techniques of news management, founding in the process a national press empire whose centrepiece was the daily newspaper *El Debate*. Herrera was a brilliant tactician who in the final analysis was probably more Liberal than Father Ayala might have liked. However the ACNP concept of deploying a secular élite to defend Church interests was something that appealed to Escrivá. When he first learned of ACNP's existence is not recorded. But the *Propagandistas* provided him with a model for the organization that he came to create twenty years later.

In the meantime, the Escrivá family business was foundering. In August 1914, Escrivá's father discovered that his partner had been embezzling funds from the partnership while trading losses went unrecorded.[1] The company went bankrupt. The event left José María – already marked by the death of three younger sisters – deeply upset.

Some Barbastrians hinted that the confectioner of *bonbons* knew all along what his partner was up to and had assisted in bleeding the business dry. José María must have heard these rumours. 'Failure is not forgiven lightly in small towns, and gossip is free,' one of his disciples later remarked.[2]

Repuatation ruined, Don José was obliged to take a job as sales clerk in a clothes shop in Logroño, 220 kilometres away. The shop was called *The Great City of London*. Logroño was reasonably wealthy for its size. It was a textile and food processing centre as well as the capital of the Rioja wine-growing region. In 1915 it was almost four times the size of Barbastro.

The next five years were unhappy ones for José María, during which he would form but one lasting friendship. The family was living in a small rented apartment in near poverty. The official

---

[1] Vázquez de Prada, *Op. cit.*, p. 56.
[2] Gondrand, *Op. cit.*, p. 31.

biographers portrayed them as following the counsel of Saint Paul, being patient in tribulation and constantly at prayer. The father was said to be nearly as saintly as the son.

'One could see he was a happy man, and extremely methodical and punctual. He dressed very smartly,' one of them quoted Manuel Ceniceros as saying. A colleague of Don José, Ceniceros remembered the dapper Escrivá with bowler hat and walking stick taking his family for Sunday strolls through the centre of town. Opus Dei numerary Salvador Bernal gives so sweet a picture of the noble shop attendant as to be almost treacly. 'He . . . learned to live with the sobriety that circumstances had imposed upon him. For his afternoon break, he had just one sweet . . . And Don José smoked little: six cigarettes a day, which he carried in a silver case . . . He rolled them himself.'[1]

José María was enrolled at the Logroño Instituto, a state secondary school, where over the next three years he completed his *Bachillerato*. The Opus Dei literature described him as an exceptional student. Others, including some classmates, claimed he was average. Exceptional or not, José María was never quite the model that his biographers made out. He was given to pouting and occasional outbursts of anger. In one incident he threw the chalk and duster at the blackboard because his maths teacher had scolded him.[2] The boy had character. Girls found him attractive. And, everyone agrees, even at the age of thirteen or fourteen he was meticulously neat. In the afternoons he received private tutoring at St Anthony's College, where he became friends with Isidoro Zorzano, who had been born in Argentina. Like José María – they were both the same age – Isidoro was concerned about his future career. Being good at maths, José María was considering architecture. But his father suggested law. Isidoro, on the other hand, would become an engineer.

Repudiation of the father, identification with his mother and a nagging uncertainty about the future became the motivating forces of José María's growing spirituality. Gradually he laid aside the objects of his childhood to experiment with those of his manhood – the *cilicio*, a barbed metal bracelet attached around the thigh,

[1] Bernal, *Op. cit.*, pp. 26, 28.
[2] Gondrand, *Op. cit.*, p. 36.

and the discipline, a braided whip-like instrument of penance. Convinced that God had chosen him for a mission, though as yet he did not know what that mission would be, shortly after his sixteenth birthday José María decided to tell his father about his vocation.

'It was the only time I saw my father cry. He had other plans in mind for me, but he didn't reject my idea. He said: "My son, think it over carefully . . . A priest has to be a saint",' Escrivá later recalled.[1]

Meanwhile the family's financial situation remained desperate. José María and Carmen spent the summers with their uncle at Fonz. In Russia, the Romanovs were murdered, causing Winston Churchill to remark that their massacre had unleashed a new kind of barbarism upon the world. It was called Communism. Countering the spread of Communism would become one of Escrivá's principal goals in life, but for the moment he focused on entering Logroño's Minor Seminary as an external student, which he did in October 1918.

A month later, the First World War ended in an armistice of relief and hope. Soon after, José María's mother announced that she was pregnant. The future cult figure had prayed so intensely for the Lord to grant his parents another son to take his place in the family that he was certain the Holy Spirit was about to unveil for him another sign. 'With this news, I had actually touched the grace of God. I saw the Lord's hand in it,' he said.[2]

José María's brother, Santiago, was born in February 1919. For the seminarian it confirmed that he was destined for a career as a servant of God. But for many, God was one of the first casualties of the changing world order. Friedrich Nietzsche had written thirty years before: 'The greatest event of recent times – that "God is Dead", that the belief in the Christian God is no longer tenable – is beginning to cast the first shadows over Europe.'[3] In fact Spain was about to begin a long journey through the Valley of the Shadow of Death when José María decided that, henceforth, he would dwell in the House of the Lord.

[1] Bernal, Op. cit., p. 62, citing RHF 20164, p. 219.
[2] Vázquez de Prada, Op. cit., p. 75.
[3] Paul Johnson, History of the Modern World, Weidenfeld & Nicolson, London 1983, p. 48.

5

'DO THAT I SEE'

The Lord God took the man and put him in the garden of Eden to till it and keep it.

Genesis 2:15

IN SEPTEMBER 1920, 'GOD'S GIFT TO THE CHURCH OF OUR TIME'[1] entered the Royal Seminary of San Carlos in Saragossa and his quest for spiritual fortune now began in an organized way. The next seven years would be a time of psychological testing, when his dreams of winning glory for God would suffer many hard knocks. To offset the hardship, he would experience his first inner locutions – which he described as encouragements from his Maker – but he kept them secret.

José María was conscious that Saragossa represented an important gateway. It was by far the largest city he had known until then. It was the capital of Aragon, and its history was of the sort he thrived upon. Founded by the Romans, it had been sacked by the Goths and taken by the Moors, who in 712 made it an independent emirate. It was reconquered for Christendom in 1118 by Alfonso I of Aragon,

---

[1] The phrase 'Gift from God to the Church of our time' was used by one of the seven judges in summing up his reasons for supporting Escrivá's beatification.

who transferred his court there from Barbastro. Saragossa possessed two cathedrals: La Seo (the See), a former mosque, was the older; but the Metropolitana del Pilar the larger and more famous. It rises from the banks of the Ebro upon the spot where, according to legend, the Virgin Mary appeared to St James the Apostle. She was said to be standing on a pillar of jasper which she left behind as testimony of her coming, and it now stands beneath the Metropolitana's eleven multicoloured domes, protected by a sheath of bronze and another of silver, and lest we forget a statue of the Virgin stands upon its summit.

To study in Saragossa, where he could follow courses in both theology and civil law, had required some extra string-pulling. An uncle, Canon Carlos Albás, lived in the city as well, but José María had little contact with him. Don Carlos did not approve of the business ethics of José María's father, blaming Don José for exposing his sister to the shame of bankruptcy.[1]

Life at the seminary took some getting used to. Many of the students arrived at San Carlos still smelling of the farmyard; some found Escrivá's manners affected. They chided him for his ostentatious piety. One remarked: 'I must say he was the only one of us who would go down to the chapel in his spare time.'[2] He spent long moments there, kneeling to one side of the altar, his gaze fixed on the tabernacle with the intensity of someone willing himself to enter the holy mysteries. It was not long before his classmates began calling him the 'Mystical Rose'.[3]

When young men share the same dormitory, few secrets remain buried for long. One of the students discovered that José María used a *cilicio*. This medieval instrument of penitence is so uncomfortable it can only be worn for an hour or two at a time. But the barbs of the bracelet were nothing compared to the barbs he received from his peers for possessing such an instrument.

What was happening outside the walls of San Carlos was largely unknown to the young seminarians. José María, for example, would have been oblivious to the fact that the world had entered a period of inflation unknown in intensity since the sixteenth century, or that

---

[1] Bernal, *Op. cit.*, p. 66; and Berglar, *Op. cit.*, p. 20.
[2] Opus Dei Newsletter No. 9, *In the Seminary at Saragossa*, p. 7.
[3] Gondrand, *Op. cit.*, p. 43; and Vázquez de Prada, *Op. cit.*, p. 88.

the Spanish army was about to be engulfed in a Moroccan catastrophe in which some 7,000 troops would be massacred by Berber guerrillas led by the legendary Abd-el-Krim. Major Francisco Franco, second in command of the Spanish Foreign Legion, got his name into the newspapers as one of the few officers to fight with distinction.

During his second year at San Carlos Escrivá attracted the attention of the archbishop, Cardinal Juan Soldevila y Romero, who recommended that he be named prefect. This required his admission to the clerical orders as a novice, which meant he had to be tonsured.[1] The Cardinal personally shaved his head in a private ceremony at the episcopal palace. He was twenty years old and henceforth was required to wear a priest's cassock. As a prefect he was responsible for maintaining discipline, which meant that his relationship with other seminarians was placed on a new footing. Also as a special privilege he received the rector's permission to enrol in the civil law faculty at the University of Saragossa.

Six months later – in March 1923 – a moderate Anarchist trade union leader, Salvador Seguí, was killed by hired *pistoleros* in the streets of Barcelona. Buenaventura Durruti, a railway worker from León, and Francisco Ascaso, a waiter, swore revenge and decided to strike at the heart of the Establishment in a manner that would provoke national outrage. On 4 June 1923 they assassinated the eighty-year-old Soldevila, riddling his body with automatics. The police never found them. They fled from Saragossa during the night and disappeared into the unknown for a decade, spent as itinerant bank robbers and booksellers, treading revolutionary paths that took them from La Paz to Paris, robbing the rich to give to the poor, and inciting workers to revolt. Unfortunately for Spain, theirs was not an isolated act, but part of a chain that was leading the country to civil war. To prevent the country from sliding deeper into chaos, in September 1923 General Miguel Primo de Rivera, the military governor of Catalonia, seized power.

José María was devastated by Soldevila's assassination. He was one year away from priesthood and he felt the loss of such a powerful sponsor even more deeply than the news received later that autumn

---

[1] This practice, begun in the fifth century, was abolished by Pope Paul VI in 1972.

that his father had suddenly died. José María admitted he had never been filled with 'filial affection'. But as head of the family, he was now required to shoulder new responsibilities for which he was hardly prepared. He found a small apartment in Saragossa into which he moved with his mother, sister and brother in time to celebrate a bleak Christmas together.

José María was ordained on 28 March 1925. Three days later the new priest received his first pastoral assignment in Perdiguera, a parish of 870 souls 30 kilometres from Saragossa. The local curate was ill and José María was named temporary regent. But he was not pleased. He feared it would cause him to miss his law exams.

José María did not remain there long. Only six weeks later his Ordinary permitted him to return to Saragossa and begin preparations for his law exams. His finals were still two years off, but once awarded his degree he immediately obtained a two-year transfer to the diocese of Madrid-Alcalá so that he could prepare for a doctorate in civil law at the Central University. He arrived in the capital in April 1927 with little else than a thick country accent and the dust of Aragon upon his cassock. He found lodgings in a residence for priests, run by the Apostolic Ladies of the Sacred Heart of Jesus, not far from the law faculty. About a dozen priests lived there and Escrivá, at twenty-five, was the youngest. He paid five pesetas a day for full room and board.

During the previous two years nothing had been heard of his longing to know God's intentions. Spain was enjoying a period of relative prosperity under the dictatorship of Primo de Rivera, who had booted out the corrupt politicians. Primo de Rivera was a prince of paradox. Never quite able to cast off his attachment for Spain's traditional past he nevertheless talked of drafting a new Constitution that would bring the country into the twentieth century. By the same measure, he proposed to overhaul the demoralized bureaucracy and restore faith in the army. His slogan was 'Fatherland, Monarchy, Religion' – all institutions that Escrivá identified with and wished to see prosper.

To end the war in Spanish Morocco, Primo de Rivera adopted a proposal put forward by the newly promoted Colonel Franco to attack Abd-el-Krim's mountain stronghold. The plan required landing a force at Alhucemas Bay. During preparations for the campaign, Franco worked with the navy, experimenting with landing craft, and one morning aboard the gunboat that was assigned to him he was served breakfast by a young naval lieutenant, Luis Carrero Blanco. The meeting was fortuitous, for in the years ahead Carrero Blanco would become Franco's closest collaborator, and by the same occasion Opus Dei's strongest supporter. But those days were still far off and no-one could have foreseen the many twists that the careers of three men – *caudillo*, priest and future prime minister – would know in the interim. Franco's battle plan met with success: Abd-el-Krim's capital of Agadir was captured and the Rif leader surrendered to the French six months later. Franco was promoted to brigadier, becoming at thirty-three the youngest general in Europe since Napoleon. As for Primo de Rivera, his standing would never be higher.

World markets were booming and Spain's raw materials were in high demand. Primo de Rivera had established good relations with the labour movement, permitting industry to improve productivity. He also introduced a public works programme that almost did away with unemployment.

But Primo de Rivera was incapable of producing any meaningful constitutional reform. As Escrivá would later point out in one of his maxims, without a plan it is impossible to achieve order. Primo de Rivera had no plan. Escrivá, on the other hand, had a plan, stimulated in part by his encounter with the Apostolic Ladies. Their headquarters – the Patronato de Enfermos, or Foundation for the Sick – had been opened on 14 July 1924 by the king, giving some indication of their social importance. As Escrivá got to know more about them, he saw an opening and offered to help. We are told that the ladies were charmed by his sweetness. In June 1927, he became their chaplain.

The Foundation provided food, medicines, clothing and spiritual help to about 5,000 ailing or infirm who were confined to the solitude of their often miserable dwellings. Through a sister organization the Apostolic Ladies also ran sixty schools in the poorer precincts of the city and operated a string of soup kitchens. Not only did Escrivá take in hand the chaplaincy but he was asked to organize catechism classes for the schools and provide spiritual care for the sick.

As soon as time permitted, he chose as his confessor a Jesuit, Father Valentín Sánchez Ruiz, who worked at one of the

Foundation's hostels. José María also registered for his first courses at the faculty of law. He proved during those first months in the capital that he was an effective organizer, ordering his life as if driven 'to cast fire upon the earth'. Most mornings he left the Larra residence before the others had come down for breakfast. He went first to the Foundation to celebrate Mass and then attended classes at the university. In the evenings he made his rounds, visiting the sick. He heard confessions and prepared children for First Communion. While fulfilling his apostolate among the poor, he celebrated private Masses for his patrons, the Apostolic Ladies.

Two years previously, Angel Herrera had told ACNP members that higher education 'was a terrain virtually abandoned by Catholics'. He described the university as the summit of society. After meeting Herrera, Escrivá saw the need for a university apostolate. He spoke of 'influencing able minds as a real source of potential good'. Intellectuals, he added, 'are like the snow-capped summits: when the snow melts, the waters pour down the valleys and make them fertile'.[1] This became his version of a holy 'trickle down' approach – that a new regard for the Church must begin on the highest summits and gradually seep down through the layers of rock and soil to the fertile valleys. If the summits are sanctified the valleys will seed themselves.

For the moment, however, while casting his regard towards the intellectual summits, Escrivá was in danger of drowning in the swamps of Madrid's slums where he administered to the sick. He found them a spiritually-inert wasteland. The ideological causes that bred this wasteland were not his concern but the weight of anti-clerical prejudices existing there did fall upon his shoulders and the burden was heavy. Moreover, the same anti-clerical prejudices he found in the slums were invading the university corridors and lecture halls. The hostility made him feel uncomfortable. Nevertheless, he sat for his first exams in September 1928. Immediately afterwards, the Vincentian Fathers held a retreat for priests. Diocesan priests were required to participate in at least one retreat a year. As it would be his last opportunity before the new term began, he decided to attend. He was given a room under the eaves where each morning after Mass he withdrew to read his diaries.

[1] Vázquez de Prada, *Op. cit.*, p. 107.

On the Feast of Guardian Angels – Tuesday, 2 October 1928 – he was in his room reflecting on the words of Bartimaeus, the blind beggar of Jericho who asked Jesus, 'Master, do that I see!'[1] when suddenly the Lord opened wide His arms and displayed before the young priest a vision of Opus Dei, 'as He wanted it, and as it would become according to His wishes down through the centuries'.[2] At least this is what the postulation for José María Escrivá's sainthood unveiled to the world more than fifty years later. In his own lifetime, however, Escrivá was reluctant to discuss what happened on that October morning. 'Please do not ask me to go into details about the beginnings of the Work . . . They are intimately connected with the history of my soul and belong to my inner life,' he told an interviewer in the late 1960s.[3]

For Escrivá, then three years into priesthood, this vision – one of several 'cornerstone' visions he would receive over the next three years – was an expression of God's will. The message was simple: 'Sanctify work, sanctify oneself through work, and sanctify others in their work.'

From his interpretation of Genesis – and particularly the fifteenth verse of the second chapter which states that God put man in the garden of Eden 'to till and keep it' – he concluded that God had created man to work. This conclusion was justified, he believed, because the Genesis reference to man's labours – i.e. 'tilling' the garden – came before his fall from grace. Therefore work was at the very heart of the human condition. It was part of God's plan. His 'Genesis 2:15 proposition' was simply reasoned. Anyone could understand and identify with it. Having set it to paper, had the young priest departed this world leaving only that proposition behind, he would have made an enduring contribution to Catholic thinking. But Escrivá did not stop there. He went on, adding over the years layer after layer of dogma to this basic affirmation, giving rise after a prolonged period of incubation to a fascinating ecclesiastical power play designed to ensure its everlasting acceptance by the Church.

Escrivá's Genesis 2:15 proposition was an important correction

---

[1] *Cf.* Mark 10:.51–52.
[2] Berglar, *Op. cit.*, p. 39, citing *Articoli del Postulatore*, section 45, Rome 1979.
[3] Pedro Rodríguez, *Palabra*, Madrid, October 1967.

of the theological principles established in the thirteenth century by Thomas Aquinas (c. 1225–74). Aquinas held that work in all its forms was a condition of man's fall from grace and therefore an impediment to sanctity. But since work was necessary, it had to be tolerated so long as goods and services were sold at a *just price*. This principle had been reaffirmed by the Council of Trent (1545–63), and declared official Catholic doctrine by Leo XIII in 1879. According to Escrivá's revelation, however, Aquinas had got it wrong.

Now Escrivá was not tackling some obscure myth. By affirming that work should be placed at the forefront of Christian living, and that a layman could attain Christian perfection through professional excellence, he was chipping away at the very foundations of the Church in order to re-orient and reinforce her theological systems. Escrivá believed that this flaw in Aquinas's philosophy was impeding the Church's ability to satisfy the spiritual requirements of a modern, industrialized society.[1]

On that October morning the Divine Sower planted a seed that in another forty years would bring about a change of Church doctrine. The seed took the longest time to sprout. It only began to show signs of life many months later, and would require a dozen years to put forth the first blossoms. Moreover, Escrivá consistently denied that Opus Dei was *his* creation. He insisted that he was only the gardener. This is important to understand. If accepted, it bestows upon Opus Dei a sort of divine licence that, in the view of its members, permits it to function in a sphere beyond the laws of man. From the very outset, then, in order to become a member one had to accept without qualification that this *Opus* was truly God's creation, and that Escrivá had only acted as proxy. If not accepted, the gates remained closed.

For Escrivá nothing that morning was without divine meaning. The birth of God's Work on the Feast of Guardian Angels meant that they had a special role to play in its development. For him, they were powerful allies and it was prudent to seek their protection. At the same moment he received the revelation, the pealing of the bells

---

[1] Thomas Aquinas (1225–74) was canonized forty-nine years after his death. This was very quick. But the canonization of the founder of the Black Friars, Dominic Guzmán (c.1170–1221), had been even swifter. He was made a saint thirteen years after his death.

from the parish church of Our Lady of the Angels, not far from the Vincentian residence, came to his ears. He took this to be another divine pointer, affirming the Marian quality of the Work.

'From that moment on, I never had any tranquillity, and I began to work – reluctantly – because I did not like the idea of being the founder of anything . . . I had my twenty-six years, God's grace and a good sense of humour, and nothing else. But just as men write with a pen, our Lord writes with the leg of a table to make it clear that it is He who is doing the writing: that is what is so incredible, so marvellous,' he explained.[1]

Marvellous perhaps, but also deceptive. Escrivá avoided defining the full range of the divine plan he received. The message as he revealed it to the world was, by his later words, not the complete message. The complete message could only be made known to initiates, according to the degree of their immersion in the Work. Thus from inception Opus Dei led a layered existence, with only the outer layer being for mass consumption; successive inner layers were reserved for higher ranks in the hierarchy.

Escrivá's principal concern was to restore the Church to a central role in society. This remains the core of the Work: 'the labour of placing Jesus [i.e., the Church] at the summit of all human activity throughout the world'. To do this requires a dedicated, disciplined militia – troops of various ranks and stations who, by sanctifying their work, sanctify (i.e., convert) others and sanctify the workplace. 'What good is it to me if so-and-so is said to be a good son of mine, a good Christian, but a bad shoemaker? If he doesn't strive to learn his trade well or doesn't give it due attention, he won't be able to sanctify it or offer it to God. Doing one's ordinary occupation as well as possible is the hinge of true spirituality,' is one Escrivá saying that Opus Dei fondly repeats.

So now we have the basics. There is a public version of the Work's founding – to promote the sanctity of work – and a hidden version that explains why a Catholic militia is needed for 'in-depth penetration' to protect and place the Church at the summit of human activity. To sum up the public version: God showed Escrivá what He

---

[1] '2 October 1928', *Opus Dei Newsletter* No. 1 (London 1989), p 9; and Amadeo de Fuenmayor et al., *L'itinéraire juridique de l'Opus Dei – Histoire et défense d'un charisme*, Desclée, Paris 1992, p. 36. Also Bernal, *Op. cit.*, pp. 109-110.

wanted – an enterprise that encouraged ordinary Christians to carry out, each in their own way and according to their own skills, a personal apostolate that would reach areas not normally accessible to priests. Very good. But there was more to come. For example, the enterprise had no name – not yet – and neither had the holder of God's proxy written down any statutes or given it a formal structure. It would grow according to no blueprint other than the memory of a vision fixed in his mind. He told nobody about it for days or even weeks.

That Tuesday was also the first day of the new university term. Was this confirmation that the Work also had a specific university apostolate? And, too, at about the same time the bells of Our Lady of the Angels began to peal, General Primo de Rivera returned to the capital from a weekend tour of the Basque provinces. As soon as the Irun Express pulled into the North Station, he was whisked off to a cabinet meeting. Did this mean that the Work had a political mission as well? Escrivá had said that nothing on that October morning was without meaning.

The first person he told about the revelation was his confessor, Father Sánchez, who encouraged him to persevere. Escrivá also spoke to a few other priests, within and outside the diocese. Then, with growing assurance, he began visiting friends and future followers, writing letters, trying to interest others in his mission. At the outset he had little success. There was no infrastructure, no tradition to build upon. Moreover, he had his duties to fulfil as chaplain of the Foundation for the Sick, lecturer in law at a private academy and post-graduate student. Gradually he dropped the latter two to concentrate more fully on God's Work.

The next cornerstone vision came on St Valentine's Day 1930. One of the founders of the Apostolic Ladies had asked Escrivá to celebrate Mass for her eighty-year-old mother, the Marchioness of Onteiro, at the family mansion. While serving Communion, Escrivá said God instructed him to create within his still unnamed work a separate section for women.

Some weeks later Escrivá had another soul-searching session with Father Sánchez. Two versions exist as to what happened. The one accepted by Opus Dei is that the Jesuit, full of enthusiasm, asked, 'And how is this *work of God* going?' Escrivá was still searching for a name for his enterprise. The one suggested by

Father Sánchez's apparently innocent question seemed providential. It fitted like a glove, a Work promoted by God – *Opus Dei*.[1] It had finally come together! But a second version of these events suggested that Escrivá lifted the name from another priest, Father Pedro Poveda Castroverde, who in 1912 had founded a similar sort of association for lay people. Poveda's Teresian Association was primarily interested in the spiritual and pastoral formation of teachers. It received diocesan approbation as a pious union in 1917 and was recognized by Rome in 1924, four years before Opus Dei was born.

Father Poveda was almost thirty years older than Escrivá and was well established in Madrid as a royal chaplain. He appeared to understand the problems and ambitions of the younger priest and tried wherever possible to help. Poveda was in the habit of referring to his Teresian Institute as the *Obra*, meaning 'Work', and Escrivá adopted it, using the Latin *Opus*, to which he added *Dei*. When he asked Father Sánchez for his opinion, the Jesuit reportedly responded that it sounded pretentious and advised him to change it. Escrivá kept the name but changed confessors.

Seven weeks after receiving the second 'cornerstone' revelation, Escrivá drafted a first pastoral letter for his handful of followers. The Work was now two years old; it apparently had a name, but little else. Escrivá himself had but one full-time disciple, Father José María Somoano Verdasco, approximately the same age.

Somoano was from Asturias. After arriving in the capital as a young priest he became chaplain at a home for young delinquents and orphans where Escrivá gave catechism classes. 'They used to come with runny noses. First you had to clean their noses, before cleaning their poor souls a little,' Escrivá would remark during public speaking tours years later. Father Somoano also played an important role in Opus Dei's earliest development and may have been running with the concept somewhat faster than Escrivá appreciated.

Escrivá's first pastoral letter was dated 24 March 1930. In the style of papal bulls, it became known as *Singuli Dies*. It set out the Work's basic programme in terms described as 'clear and limpid,

[1] Berglar, *Op. cit.*, p. 64.

like the language of the apostles'.[1] *Singuli Dies* foresaw, vaguely, the forming of a corps of Christian militants who, though they dressed the same as everyone else in their station in life, were nevertheless set apart from them. 'The supernatural mission that we have received does not lead us to distinguish or separate ourselves from others; it leads us to unite ourselves to everyone, because we are the equals of the other citizens in our country. We are, I repeat, equal to everyone else, though not *like* everyone else. We live in the same general environment, wear normal clothes, have no distinctive mannerisms. We share all the ordinary civic concerns, and those pertaining to professional work and other activities.'[2]

The letter contained twenty-two sections. From it, according to one Opus Dei specialist on canon law, the organization's first statutes were developed.[3] The text seemed to suggest that Opus Dei's mission was national and that in 1930 the Founder had not yet considered a worldwide apostolate. And yet, thirty-seven years later, Escrivá would claim, 'From the first moment, the Work was universal . . . It was born not to solve the concrete problems facing Europe in the twenties, but to tell men and women of every country and of every condition, race, language, milieu and state in life (single, married, widowed or priest) that they can love and serve God without giving up their ordinary work, their family life and their normal social relations.'[4]

Singuli Dies is viewed with suspicion by some former members who wonder whether it might not be an Opus Dei attempt to rewrite its early history. Curiously, Opus Dei refused to provide a full-text copy, claiming 'this letter and several others are being studied with the ultimate objective of publishing them with commentaries . . .'

The Founder was during this time working on bringing in disciples. Early in the summer of 1930 he had written to Isidoro Zorzano, whom he hadn't seen for many years. Then on 24 August 1930, Escrivá was on his way home, but not along his usual route, when 'by coincidence' he saw Isidoro Zorzano walking in the opposite direction.

---

[1] Taken from the French edition of Berglar's *Opus Dei* (p. 83).
[2] Berglar, *Op. cit.*, p. 66, quoting from section 5 of the letter of 24 March 1930.
[3] De Fuenmayor et al., *Op. cit.*, pp. 75–77.
[4] *Conversations with Monsignor Escrivá de Balaguer* (Peter Forbath, *Time* Magazine), Scepter, London 1993, p. 62.

'I've just been to see you, and when I found you weren't at home, I was going to look for a restaurant before catching the night train north to join my parents,' Isidoro told Escrivá. He quickly added that he was in need of spiritual advice. But there was nothing particularly spectacular about this 'coincidence', as they met literally a few paces from Escrivá's office.

'What's troubling you?' José María asked. Isidoro explained that he believed God was asking him to become more actively involved and he did not know how to respond. He enjoyed his work as an engineer with the Andalusian railways in Malaga and didn't want to give it up. Escrivá, of course, had the solution.

'The Lord has called us to the Work to be saints; but we will not be saints if we do not unite ourselves to Christ on the Cross. There is no sanctity without the Cross, without mortification,' he told Isidoro.

Zorzano had to catch his train. But before leaving Escrivá's office he asked to join Opus Dei. José María improvised an oblation ceremony, requiring Isidoro to promise before God to devote his life to apostolate while abiding by the ecclesiastic counsels of poverty, chastity and obedience.[1]

Isidoro Zorzano thus became Opus Dei's first lay member – the first to persevere – and from then onwards he called his boyhood friend *Father*.[2]

---

[1] Giancarlo Rocca, 'L'Opus Dei' – Appunti e Documenti per una Storia, Edizioni Paoline, Rome 1985, p. 20, citing the document Beatificationis et canonizationis Servi Dei Isidoro Zorzano Ledesma viri laici, signed by Cardinal Bacci in Rome, 1946.
[2] Gondrand, Op. cit., p. 80.

DIOS Y AUDACIA

Call no man your father on earth, for you have one Father, who is in heaven.

Matthew 23:9

IN JANUARY 1930, IN THE MIDST OF A WORLD ECONOMIC CRISIS AND record unemployment, with student and worker riots paralysing the capital daily, Primo de Rivera announced that Spain had become ungovernable and went into exile. Six weeks later, alone and miserable, he died in a Paris hotel.

The king took over the government, deciding one year later that the moment had come to test his popularity by calling nationwide municipal elections, and in all large towns and cities the Monarchist candidates were roundly defeated. The size of the Republican turn-out was enormous. On the following day, the nation was too stunned to react. But two days later crowds began gathering in the streets and that afternoon when the king met with his ministers they told him that if he did not leave the capital before dark 'it might be too late'.[1] The Second Republic was born during the night. Next morning – 15 April 1931 – the country learned that Niceto Alcalá

[1] Harry Gannes and Theodore Repard, *Spain in Revolt*, Victor Gollancz, London 1936, p. 47.

Zamora, a former war minister, had become provisional prime minister.

That Alcalá Zamora was a conservative landowner did little to soothe the apprehensions of the right. He appointed as his foreign minister a godless Radical, Alejandro Lerroux, whose upbringing had left him with a permanent disgust for everything connected with religion. The equally godless Manuel Azaña became minister of war. Together these three became the driving force in the Constituent Assembly that was elected two months later.

The cardinal primate, Archbishop Pedro Segura y Sáenz of Toledo, did not hesitate to draw a parallel between what was happening in Madrid and the French Revolution of 1789 – which had not only buried the monarchy but dispossessed the Church – and he delivered a violently anti-Republican pastoral that caused a national storm. Following the primate's outburst, the country's mood turned sullen. Early in May 1931, a group of right-wing officers and monarchists met at a house in the centre of Madrid to form an Independent Monarchist Club. Word soon spread that a group of conspirators were at work inside the house and the crowd that gathered in the street outside quickly degenerated into a mob setting parked cars alight and sacking the nearby offices of the right-wing *ABC* newspaper.

Next day sporadic rioting broke out. First a Jesuit residence in the centre of Madrid was gutted by fire. Then other churches and convents were set on fire throughout the city. For a moment it was feared that the mob would attack the Foundation for the Sick. José María rushed into the chapel and started swallowing handfuls of Sacred Hosts from the ciborium to prevent them from being profaned. Unable to swallow them all, with the mob drawing closer, he wrapped the ciborium in a newspaper and took it by taxi to a friend's apartment near the Cuatro Caminos Plaza, where he went into hiding. The mob left the Foundation headquarters untouched, and Escrivá returned days later, deeply upset by what had happened. Soon after, he resigned as the Foundation's chaplain.[1]

Fearing he would now be required to return to Saragossa, Escrivá discussed his problem with Father Poveda, who offered to have him appointed an honorary royal chaplain. But Escrivá turned down

---

[1] Gondrand, *Op. cit.*, p. 75.

Poveda's offer because he knew that incardination did not extend to honorific titles.[1] Incardination is like an umbilical cord that ties a priest to his diocesan Ordinary, who is responsible for him within the Church. If at this point Escrivá had been unable to remain in Madrid, Opus Dei might have shrivelled and died. But just as it seemed his academic furlough would end with no doctorate to show for his five years in the capital, providence intervened presenting him with a Palatine device.

It was Father Poveda who found the solution, suggesting to his bishop, the Palatine Ordinary, that Escrivá should be appointed to the chaplaincy of the Patronato of Santa Isabel, which consisted of a convent for Augustinian Recollect nuns, a church and women's college, located next to Madrid's General Hospital. The Patronato of Santa Isabel, because it was a royal benefice, came under the jurisdiction of the Palatine Ordinary – the bishop in charge of the royal vicariat to whom all royal chaplains were incardinated – which meant that it functioned like an independent diocese.

Santa Isabel's previous rector and chaplain had both resigned in compliance with a government decree disbanding the royal vicariat. This was later repealed, and Poveda managed to have Escrivá named Santa Isabel's new chaplain. Thus in September 1931 the Palatine Ordinary confirmed the appointment, leaving the Ordinary of Saragossa with no alternative but to acknowledge the *fait accompli*.

Even before the appointment was confirmed, Escrivá started using the church of Santa Isabel and its confessionals to administer spiritual direction to his growing circle of disciples. His only other pastoral activity at the time consisted in taking his handful of followers on weekend visits to the very sick in the city's hospitals. Understaffed and overcrowded, swarming with *staphylococci* and other lethal germs, Madrid's hospitals were said to have served as the cradle of Opus Dei.

Escrivá's closest associate at the time, Father José María Somoano, was claimed to be the first person fully to appreciate the spirit of the Work. The other disciple who accompanied Escrivá on his weekly rounds of the sickwards was Luis Gordon, a young engineer and nephew of the Marchioness of Onteiro. He became Opus Dei's second lay member, after Isidoro Zorzano, who was still

[1] Vázquez de Prada, *Op. cit.*, p. 139.

working for the Andalusian railways in Malaga. Speaking of Luis Gordon years later, Escrivá said, 'One day he collected a chamber pot from a patient with tuberculosis and it was disgusting! I told him, "That's the spirit, go and clean it!" Then I felt a bit sorry for him, because I could see that it had turned his stomach. I went after him and I saw him with a look of heavenly joy on his face, cleaning it with his bare hands.' This incident later caused Escrivá to write in one of his famous maxims, 'Isn't it true, Lord, that you were greatly consoled by the childlike remark of that man who, when he felt the disconcerting effect of obedience in something unpleasant, whispered to you, "Jesus, keep me smiling".'[1]

Somoano, on the other hand, had a gift for instilling in patients a sense of usefulness even as they were dying. In the last months of 1931, he approached one of the terminal patients at King's Hospital, a young woman whose name was María Ignacia Garcia Escobar, and confided that he needed her help. She had intestinal tuberculosis and was in constant pain after surgery had failed to stop the disease from spreading. Somoano told her, 'We must pray a lot for something that is going to help the salvation of everyone. And I don't mean just for a few days. This is a matter of great good for the whole world. It will require prayer and sacrifice today, tomorrow and always.'[2] Later he told her that the intention was Opus Dei. In April 1932, María Ignacia asked to join. She became Opus Dei's first woman member. She had but five months to live. Somoano lavished care upon her. She wrote in her diary that Opus Dei had brought to the world 'a new era of Love'.[3]

Somoano's popularity among patients overshadowed even Escrivá's charisma. Somoano wanted to bring Opus Dei to the greatest number of people, no matter if they were destitute, delinquent or at death's door. With his limitless energy he was in danger of running away with God's invention, taking it along paths not revealed to Escrivá in the 'cornerstone' visions. Escrivá had different views about Opus Dei's apostolate, based on a holy 'trickle down' approach, and – judging by his later writings – he must have resented Somoano's efforts, regarding them as an attempt to kidnap Opus

---

[1] Josemaría Escrivá, Maxim 626, *The Way*, Four Courts Press, Dublin 1985.
[2] Berglar, *Op. cit.*, p. 85.
[3] Bernal, *Op. cit.*, pp. 139–140.

Dei. 'As Jesus received his doctrine from the Father, so my doctrine is not mine but comes from God and so not a jot or tittle shall ever be changed,' Escrivá wrote almost forty years later in *Crónica*.[1] Was he jealous of Somoano? We shall never know, except that some years later Escrivá remarked to one of his earliest disciples, 'from the first day [Somoano] promised obedience, but then he began to disobey . . .'[2]

On 13 July 1932, Somoano suddenly fell ill. Four days later he died in terrible agony. Though not present at the moment of his death, Escrivá had spent hours at his bedside, praying. The young priest was thought to have been poisoned by 'anticlerical elements' in one of the hospitals, but apparently no autopsy was undertaken and no charges were ever pressed.

María Ignacia Garcia died in September 1932, and two months later, Luis Gordon also fell ill and died. Said Escrivá: 'Now we have two saints in heaven. A priest and a layman.'[3] This remark suggests that the Founder never really considered María Ignacia a member. As for Luis Gordon, it seems that nobody questioned whether encouraging a civil engineer to spend his Sunday afternoons tending patients with contagious diseases in Madrid's hospitals – without any training on how to avoid the risk of contamination – had contributed to his premature death. In any event, soon afterwards Escrivá abandoned the hospital apostolate.

With only his duties as chaplain at Santa Isabel to occupy him, Escrivá was now able to devote more time to recruiting. His family had moved to Madrid by then and he found them an apartment in a narrow five-storey building at 4 Paseo del General Martínez Campos. The apartment was reasonably close to the main university faculties, and large enough to invite ten or twelve people at a time for a *tertulia*. Doña Dolores and sister Carmen helped prepare food for these gatherings. Young Santiago was said to be dismayed by the student appetites. Escrivá contended, however, that it was important for his disciples to develop a sense of belonging to a family. Isidoro Zorzano, his first apostle, was hoping to be transferred to Madrid to help the Father expand the Work's apostolate.

[1] *Crónica* I, the internal publication for Opus Dei numeraries, Rome, 1971.
[2] Miguel Fisac, Notes, 8 June 1994.
[3] Berglar, *Op. cit.*, p. 84.

Juan Jiménez Vargas, a medical student who came to the Martínez Campos *tertulias*, asked to join in January 1933, becoming the second apostle. José María González Barredo, a research chemist and third apostle, joined a few weeks later. He was a valuable addition because, like Zorzano, he was earning a salary, which he contributed to the general funds of the Work. Ricardo Fernández Vallespín, an architecture student, joined in June 1933, becoming the fourth apostle.

In spite of these first successes Escrivá found that the Martínez Campos apartment, though cosy and clean, lacked sufficient class to provide his recruits with a feeling of belonging to a select, close-knit family. The building was quite shabby and its ground floor was let out as a shop and a working man's wine bar which Escrivá thought detracted from the general salubrity of the location. And so after months of hesitation he finally moved his family into the rectory of Santa Isabel.

The customs and norms destined to transform Opus Dei into a strong sect-like organization were slowly evolving. Novices were put through an initiation rite. Even in those early days, according to one of its first members, Opus Dei possessed a strong Crusader element, which for some heightened its mystery and appeal. Opus Dei was to have three main apostolates, each placed under the protection of an Archangel. The Work of Archangel Raphael was to oversee the recruiting of new members into the Work, and quickly it became the focus of Opus Dei's existence, initially targeting university students before they embarked upon professional careers. At this stage, Opus Dei only had celibate members, known as numeraries. Once brought into the movement, their ongoing care and guidance was entrusted to Archangel Michael, the Guardian of God's Chosen People. This meant that while one arm of Opus Dei worked at recruiting, another laboured at maintaining the motivation of those already inducted into the organization.

The work of Archangel Gabriel, God's Special Messenger, came later. It was to look after the spiritual well-being of married members and co-operators – the future bread and butter of the organization. In the 1930s, however, celibacy remained a prerequisite for membership. Supernumeraries – noncelibate members – would only be admitted in the 1950s, after the development of the Women's Section.

By December 1933, Escrivá was ready to launch Opus Dei's first corporate work. He had Zorzano rent a first-floor apartment at 33 Calle Luchana not far from the city centre. They transformed the apartment into a private institute offering supplementary courses for university students and called it the DYA Academy, claiming the three letters stood for *Derecho y Arquitectura* – Law and Architecture. Only secretly were some students – those viewed as likely recruits – told that DYA really stood for *Dios y Audacia* – 'God and Audacity'.

Ricardo Fernández, the fourth apostle, became the DYA's director. The Luchana premises had a visitors' room, two small classrooms, a study room, small living room and an office for the Founder that contained a bare wooden cross. Escrivá heard confessions in the kitchen, which also served as José María González's chemistry lab. The furniture was borrowed from Doña Dolores or came from the *Rastro*, Madrid's flea market.

The Republican party of Manuel Azaña, then the serving prime minister, was almost annihilated in the November 1933 elections that followed the adoption of a new constitution. A right-wing coalition came to power in which the dominant figure was José María Gil Robles, Angel Herrera's successor as head of the Propagandistas. Herrera had resigned to become national chairman of the Catholic Action movement, but still exerted strong influence over his successor at the ACNP.

Gil Robles had distinguished himself as a leader writer for the ACNP's *El Debate* newspaper. He had married the daughter of one of Spain's richest grandees, and took her on a honeymoon to Germany, where they attended Hitler's first Nuremberg Rally, bringing back to Spain many of the Nazi propaganda techniques. He demonstrated his organizational ability by forming a nationwide federation of right-wing Catholic parties – the CEDA. He claimed that CEDA had more than 700,000 members, making it the largest political grouping in Spain. But Gil Robles lacked Herrera's tactical brilliance and self-restraint, and this would lead him into a particularly acrimonious confrontation with his Republican 'Popular Front' opponents.

In the meantime, however, the Gil Robles alliance set for its objective the revocation of Azaña's restrictive legislation against the Church. At first he was content to stand aside from a cabinet posting, satisfied that if the Radical party kept its part of the bargain the Church could 'live in the Spanish Republic with dignity, respected in her rights and the exercise of her divine mission'.[1] This, of course, interested Escrivá as in April 1933 the Azaña government had abolished the Palatine jurisdiction, leaving the recently appointed chaplain of Santa Isabel without an Ordinary, an ecclesiastical oversight that lasted for the next eight years. An unusual situation, it nevertheless permitted Escrivá full freedom to concentrate on Opus Dei's development. Nor did it stop him from requesting that the new government appoint him to the vacant post of Santa Isabel's rector. As required by the Law of Congregations, his appointment was confirmed by the President of the Republic in December 1934, by which time he had already moved his family into the rector's house.

Within months of the DYA's opening, Escrivá decided to transform it into a student residence since he believed this would provide a better atmosphere for recruiting. Three larger apartments were found at 50 Calle Ferraz and turned into accommodation for twenty students. Escrivá also kept an office there – known as the 'Father's room' – with a bathroom whose walls were frequently flecked with blood from the 'pious flagellation' he inflicted upon himself. In March 1935 he requested permission from the diocese of Madrid to install a chapel, which was granted.

Within weeks of the first Mass being celebrated in the new chapel, a student from the School of Civil Engineering by the name of Alvaro del Portillo came to see Escrivá. Portillo's aunt, one of the Apostolic Ladies, had told him about the Father's work with students. Portillo met Escrivá several times over the next few months but seemed unable to make up his mind about joining. Escrivá therefore asked another DYA resident, Francisco Pons, to befriend Portillo and help draw him closer to the Work. Pons told Portillo that becoming a member was like being a 'Crusader with cape and sword'.[2]

In July 1935, Portillo became the fifth apostle. The sixth apostle, José María Hernández de Garnica, another engineering student, joined two weeks later. After him came Pedro Casciaro and

---

[1] Gannes and Repard, *Op. cit.*, p. 71, citing *El Debate*.
[2] Fisac Notes, 8 June 1994.

Francisco Botella, both architecture students. They drew in fellow classmate Miguel Fisac.

It took quite a while to get the twenty-one-year-old Fisac to 'whistle' – the term used by Opus Dei when a recruit decides to join. He was pressed to attend the weekly sessions at which Escrivá would comment upon readings from the Gospel, and talk of the necessity of observing certain Christian norms, such as making offerings to a good cause, reciting set prayers, going to confession once a week and examining one's conscience – all of which Fisac later learned were obligatory norms for Opus Dei members.

In no case during these sessions was reference made to Opus Dei. The introduction was done privately, on a one-to-one basis. An early paradox that Fisac noted was that Escrivá insisted there was no need for secrecy, only discretion, for exactly the same reasons that people did not broadcast to the world their most intimate thoughts. Then pretending he wanted to know more about his students, the Father asked those who interested him to fill in a form, giving full biographic information about themselves, down to their preferred hobbies and sports.

When Fisac was asked to join he was caught off balance. 'I did not dare refuse, and it was a weakness that I began to regret the same day,' he later wrote to a friend.[1]

In spite of his reservations, Fisac became the ninth apostle. He was required to write a letter requesting admission – still a standard procedure for new recruits – and then Escrivá sent him on a three-day retreat. For the next twenty years he remained a close observer of Opus Dei's inner workings. He remembered on one occasion Escrivá telling Casciaro and Juan Jiménez Vargas that for certain inner-circle ceremonies he was thinking of having them wear white capes emblazoned with a red cross whose four extremities would be shaped like arrowheads.[2]

Fisac was followed in 1936 by a philosophy student, Rafael Calvo Serer, who became the tenth apostle, a history student, Vicente Rodríguez Casado, the eleventh apostle, and an internationally known research chemist, José María Albareda Herrera, the twelfth apostle. Like Zorzano, Albareda was the same age as Escrivá.

Fisac said that when he joined Opus Dei the mood of religious

[1] Miguel Fisac letter to Luis Borobio, 18 February 1995.
[2] Fisac Notes, 8 June 1994.

persecution in Madrid created a reaction of 'genuine exaltation' among staunch Catholics that strengthened their faith. In Angel Herrera's case, he resigned from Catholic Action to enter the priesthood. Then early in 1936 new elections were called. Gil Robles and José Antonio Primo de Rivera, son of the ex-dictator and founder of the Falange Movement, banded together to form a National Front in opposition to the left's Popular Front. Spain was now completely polarized. The Popular Front received 34.5 per cent of the vote and the National Front 33.2 per cent. Bitterly, Gil Robles assailed the results as a 'revolution against law and order, respect for religion, property, the family, and national unity'.[1]

By May 1936 the situation had become so tense under the Popular Front that Escrivá, never knowing when he might be attacked in the street, was in a state of nervous exhaustion. A few weeks before, a fellow priest had almost been lynched because it was rumoured he had distributed poisoned sweets to the children of factory workers. More religious houses and churches were sacked, and Escrivá felt that the Patronato of Santa Isabel was no longer safe. He found another apartment for his mother, sister and brother across town, closer to Calle Ferraz.

DYA quickly outgrew its premises and a vacant building was found down the street at 16 Ferraz. After the death of Uncle Teodoro earlier that year, Escrivá persuaded his mother to sell the family property at Fonz so that the proceeds might be used to purchase the 16 Ferraz building. It was well situated, directly opposite the Montaña Army Barracks. The building was owned by the Conde de Real who had fled to France. Doña Dolores could refuse her son nothing and 16 Ferraz was purchased by a company called Fomento de Estudios Superiores. Isidoro Zorzano was its president. Escrivá immediately addressed a letter to the diocese of Madrid asking for permission to transfer the 'semi-public' DYA chapel to the new address. As in previous letters, no mention was made of Opus Dei, only the DYA residence. Officially Opus Dei did not exist. It was registered neither with the diocese nor with the state.

At the beginning of July, with tension stretched at the breaking point, a depressive Father Escrivá informed his 'children' that he

---

[1] Gannes and Repard, *Op. cit.*, p. 117.

intended to expand Opus Dei's mission by opening an office in Paris.[1] This was said to have 'greatly surprised' them. He had already begun to make travel arrangements, but political events moved faster than anticipated.[2]

On 12 July 1936, Lieutenant José del Castillo of the Republican Assault Guards was gunned down by Falangists. Retaliation was immediate. That same night a prominent right-wing politcian was shot and the outrage that followed spurred the Nationalist generals, who were already plotting rebellion, to move against the Republic. But even for them the Spanish Civil War began one day earlier than planned. Fearing they were about to be arrested, a handful of conspirators at Melilla, the easternmost city of Spanish Morocco, jumped the gun in the early evening of Friday, 17 July 1936, and shot their commanding officer. The garrisons of Tetuán and Ceuta rose hours later. After receiving news of the uprising, Franco flew from the Canary Islands, where he had been appointed military governor, to take command of the Army in Africa and immediately appealed to Hitler and Mussolini for military aid.

One of Franco's closest friends, Colonel Juan de Yagüe, then in command of the Spanish Foreign Legion, was probably the first to use the word 'Crusade' to describe the Nationalist uprising. Whether Yagüe's or someone else's innovation, crusade perfectly suited the motivation of the conspirators and it quickly became conventional usage in Nationalist propaganda. The re-invention of holy war in Spain was accompanied by the same propensity for atrocity as during the Crusades of old.

All Opus Dei members supported the Nationalist cause. Some, however, because they resided in areas that remained faithful to the Republic at the outset of the rebellion, were conscripted into the Republican army. The rising was immediately successful in the north and north-west of Spain, and in isolated pockets in the south. Elsewhere, the Republicans maintained control, though in Madrid they barely had the situation in hand.

At sunrise on Monday, 20 July, a crowd gathered in the Plaza de España and began chanting 'Arms for the People' and 'Death to the Fascists'. Then one of the agitators perceived that the gauntlet of Don Quixote, whose statue stands in the centre of the plaza, was

[1] Gondrand, *Op. cit.*, pp. 127 and 128.
[2] *Ibid.*, p. 128.

pointing towards the Montaña Barracks. The crowd took this as a sign to storm the barracks. Two brightly coloured beer trucks commandeered by the Anarchists wheeled into place three antiquated artillery pieces that had been discovered in a nearby depot.

From the DYA building across the street, Escrivá watched the attack on the fortress-like barracks. The three field pieces opened fire at virtually point-blank range. They were more than a match for the trench mortars inside the barracks. After several hours of pounding, the troops inside the barracks turned on their officers and drove them into the central courtyard, where scores were despatched by machine gun. The frenzied mob stormed through the breached walls and applauded as a giant loyalist soldier threw the remaining officers to their deaths from the highest parapet.

When the smoke cleared, the Father changed into worker's overalls and slipped out of the building. Accompanied by Zorzano and González, he hurried to his mother's apartment, close by. As the *milicianos* were summarily shooting priests like game in the streets, he remained at the apartment while Juan Jiménez Vargas met in the afternoon with Alvaro del Portillo to exchange information about what was happening in the rest of Spain. News bulletins mentioned a limited rebellion which the government said would soon be crushed. According to these reports, loyalist troops had already recaptured Seville and loyalist warships were shelling the North African garrisons. None of this was true.

In Barcelona, on the other hand, the uprising had failed miserably, not because of decisive government intervention but because Durruti and Ascaso – by then under sentence of death in four countries but national heroes in Republican Spain – had taken over the city arsenal and with arms seized there mounted a successful assault on the Atarazanas Barracks in which Ascaso was killed. The military governor, General Manuel Goded, was captured and executed, and the city reorganized under a revolutionary committee. Durruti formed the 'Ascaso Column' consisting of six thousand Anarchist 'minutemen' and marched out of Barcelona to liberate Saragossa, which had gone over to the Nationalists. His second in command was Domingo Ascaso, brother of the fallen Francisco.

Inside Saragossa, the Virgen del Pilar was named supreme commander of the city. Whereas the Fourth Division in Barcelona had collapsed, the Fifth Division in Saragossa under its new commander remained a viable fighting force. Moreover, the city's population became enraged when a lone Republican aircraft dropped a bomb on the Basilica del Pilar. The bomb actually dislodged Our Lady from her column, but – miracle of miracles – it failed to explode.

After receiving Axis air transport, on 5 August 1936 Franco began airlifting troops from Ceuta to Salamanca and started advancing northwards. Nine days later, in retaliation for the wholesale executions that followed the fall of Badajoz to the Spanish Foreign Legion, guards at the Model Prison in Madrid butchered the inmates, among them Fernando Primo de Rivera, brother of the Falange leader. Days later militiamen looking for spies searched the building in the Calle de Sagasta where Escrivá had gone into hiding. They found no-one, but that night he and Jiménez Vargas moved to the apartment of José María González's father, where they remained for the next few weeks.

On 28 September 1936, the Nationalist junta met at Salamanca and accepted Franco as *generalísimo*. They had little choice. Franco held all the cards. His German and Italian allies made it clear they would deal only with him. Three days later, Franco moved his headquarters to Burgos in northwest Spain. His arrival was celebrated by the ringing of church bells throughout the city. He formed a military government which was sworn in with medieval pomp and a special Mass at the ancient Abbey of Las Huelgas.

PART TWO

ADVERSITY

SPAIN AFTER THE OUTBREAK OF CIVIL WAR
JULY 1936

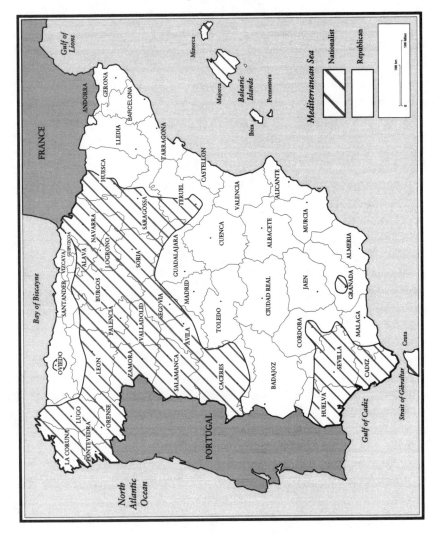

7

SABRES AND CHASUBLES

Our war is not a civil war . . . but a Crusade . . . Yes, our war is a religious war. We who fight, whether Christians or Muslims, are soldiers of God and we are not fighting against men but against atheism and materialism.

Generalísimo Francisco Franco

However many Fascists there may be in Spain, there will not be a Fascist regime. Should force triumph against the Republic we will return to a military and ecclesiastical dictatorship of the type that is traditionally Spanish . . . There will be sabres and chasubles, military parades and processions honouring the Virgen del Pilar. On that score the country is not capable of anything else.

Manuel Azaña

WITH THE OUTBREAK OF THE CIVIL WAR, FATHER ESCRIVÁ REMOVED his cassock and did not wear one again in Spain under the Republic. He also let his tonsure grow out and took to wearing his mother's wedding ring. He told his disciples that even though he was prepared to become a martyr, he had been entrusted with a divine mission and therefore it was his duty to do everything possible to remain alive.

No place in Spain suffered more during the Civil War than Escrivá's birthplace of Barbastro, known at the time as a town of soldiers and priests. It boasted a Benedictine monastery, missionary college, Piarist school, seminary and a strong Cathedral chapter, all of which became a butt of leftist anger, led by the Anarchist agitator Eugenio Sopena. The seminary was demolished, and next Sopena ordered all priests arrested. 'Death to the blackbirds' became the cry. But Sopena was heard to mutter: 'We can't allow any carnage around here.' Among those rounded up by Sopena's leftist vigilantes were the bishop, Don Florentino Asensio Barroso, and the Cathedral canon, Mariano Albás, José María Escrivá's godfather.

From Barcelona the 6,000-strong 'Ascaso Column' divided into two pincers. The southern wing, commanded by Durruti, continued up the Ebro valley towards Saragossa. The northern section, under Domingo Ascaso, arrived in Barbastro on the afternoon of 25 July, having gutted the thirteenth-century Lérida cathedral the day before. The first men, dressed like Jacobins with bandannas tied around their heads, reached the town by train. They were accompanied by prostitutes from Barcelona in workmen's coveralls and the riffraff freed from prisons along the way. They were followed towards dusk by a convoy of trucks with machine guns and field pieces. That afternoon the first executions began.

The commander of the local barracks, Colonel José Villalba Rubio, embraced the leaders of the Ascaso Column and paraded his troops through the streets with them. The next day he sent out a joint patrol towards Huesca, but this was ambushed by a rebel Civil Guard detachment and took heavy losses. That night Barbastro was overcome by an orgy of violence. Churches were emptied of their statuary and other religious objects, which were burned in the streets. In the Cathedral the rioters dismantled the main altarpiece, stole all the silver, and the baptismal font was thrown into the Rio Vero. The churches of San Bartolomé and San Hipólito were reduced to rubble.

When Durruti learned that five hardened Anarchists who were conveying precious booty to Barcelona had been shot as looters, he came personally to Barbastro to exact vengeance. He had his twelve heavily armed bodyguards convene the Anti-Fascist Committee and in a violent harangue he accused its members of executing five true and loyal Anarchists while Barbastro's prison overflowed with blackbirds and Blue Shirts. Alarmed, the committee quickened the pace of executions.

That evening Mariano Abad, an Anarchist agitator whose sobriquet was 'the Undertaker', went to the prison and handed the guards a signed and stamped piece of paper marked, 'Good for 20'. His instructions were to collect any twenty from among the 400 or so prisoners and execute them. In the middle of the night they were taken to the cemetery, where they were joined by another group from the town hall. The staff at the hospital watched as they were lined up against the exterior wall of the cemetery and shot.

After being locked up for seventeen days, Bishop Asensio was brought before the committee, meeting that night in the town hall. The first thing the Bishop was told was, 'Don't be afraid. If you've prayed well you'll go to heaven.' The hearing lasted a few minutes. Satisfied he was a Nationalist collaborator, they tied his hands behind his back and returned him to the holding cell while other prisoners were heard. Once the night's quota was filled, bishop Asensio was brought back into the room. When he refused to answer further questions he was kicked in the groin, then castrated, after which he was taken to the cemetery. One of his torturers shouted: 'Hurry up, pigs.' The bishop replied: 'Do what you like . . . I will pray for you in heaven.' Another guard said, 'Here, take Communion,' and hit him in the mouth with a brick.

But his agony was not over. At the cemetery he survived the firing squad's volley of shots and was heaped upon a pile of corpses where he lay for more than an hour before receiving the coup de grâce. Next morning the head doctor at the hospital complained to the committee that the executions were disturbing his patients, making it impossible for them to sleep. In deference to the doctor the remaining priests, including Canon Albás, were shot at night-time at kilometre three on the road to Berbegal, a village to the south of Barbastro.[1] By the end of the month more than 800 Barbastrians had been executed – including 200 priests – some 10 per cent of the local population. In Madrid, three out of every ten priests were killed during the reign of terror. In Barbastro, nine out of every ten lost their lives.

Mariano Albás, though martyred while administering the last rites

---

[1] Gabriel Campo Villegas, *Esta es Nuestra Sangre*, Publicaciones Claretianas, Madrid 1992. Details of Bishop Florentino Asensio's martyrdom were taken from this book and the author's interview with Father Campo in Barbastro on 22 June 1994. Don Florentino's beatification is being considered by the Congregation for the Causes of Saints in Rome.

to a group of seminarians executed with him, has not been beatified, and no mention of his fate is found in the 'official' Escrivá biographies. In stark contrast to the Calvary suffered by Barbastro's priests, Escrivá found asylum in a psychiatric clinic on the outskirts of Madrid, where he learned to simulate the behaviour of the mentally ill. He spent five months doing his best to feign insanity. But one day the *milicianos* came to search the building. When the pseudo-madman was about to be questioned, one of the *bona fide* patients went up to the officer, pointed at his gun and asked, 'Is that a string instrument or a wind instrument?' The officer considered the question for a moment and then turned to Escrivá and asked, 'Who are you?'

'I am Dr Marañón,' he replied, pretending he was one of Spain's best-known personalites.

That was quite enough for the officer and abruptly he called off the search.

In early October 1936 the Nationalist forces resumed their advance and Madrid was about to fall when the first units of the Communist International Brigades arrived, followed by Durruti with 4,000 Anarchists. In the counter-attack the Anarchists came face to face with Hitler's élite Condor Legion and fled into the Parque del Oeste, pursued by a *bandera* of the Spanish Foreign Legion. Durruti was wounded, perhaps shot by one of his own men, and died five days later. In reprisal, the Popular Front executed José Antonio Primo de Rivera, who had been in a Republican jail since March 1936 on a charge of disturbing the peace. Their advance stopped, the Nationalists dug in on the western outskirts of Madrid for the remainder of the war. Afflicted by food shortages and frequent power cuts, the mood in the capital became sombre and street-corner executions were common. The staff at the asylum grew suspicious of 'Dr Marañón' and three months later Escrivá was asked to leave.

He found refuge at the legation of the republic of Honduras, along with his brother Santiago, Juan Jiménez Vargas, Eduardo Alastrué and José María Albareda. Until then Albareda had been hiding in the Chilean embassy, but it had become unsafe. Alvaro del Portillo, who had been arrested inside the Finnish embassy and detained for three months, also joined them. The six shared a room that was two and a half metres by three, with a narrow window opening onto an interior courtyard. They called it the 'Honduran cage'. For the next five months it served as their home, office and chapel. They had little to eat; lunch and supper (no breakfast) usually consisted of stale carob beans, mixed with 'proteins', which meant the insects that came with the beans. To keep their sanity, the Father established a programme of prayers, work and meditation.

During those next five months, Albareda became very close to the Father. He told Escrivá about José Ibáñez Martín, a secondary school teacher whom he had met while hiding in the Chilean embassy. Like Escrivá and Albareda, Ibáñez was a son of Aragon. He was also one of Angel Herrera's *Propagandistas* and a former CEDA deputy. José Ibáñez and Albareda were compatible souls and their talks during the long hours with nothing else to occupy them focused on the New Spain that would rise after the Civil War.

News that the Vatican had recognized the Burgos authorities as the official government of Spain stirred Escrivá to attempt a crossing to the Blue Zone. By then Albareda had received word that his brother had successfully fled the Republic on an underground 'railroad' that smuggled people over the Pyrenees to Andorra. To arrange passage, travellers had to contact a conductor in Barcelona known as the 'Milkman'.

Escrivá convinced the consul general to furnish him with a letter stating that he was the general manager of the Honduran legation. At the beginning of October 1937, he, Albareda, Tomás Alvira and Manuel Sainz de los Terreros, a road engineer in whose apartment he had found refuge the year before, obtained travel permits for Valencia. Juan Jiménez went ahead to make contact with Miguel Fisac and Francisco Botella. The others left by overnight coach. Isidoro Zorzano, Vicente Rodríguez, José María González and Alvaro del Portillo were unable to obtain the necessary papers and remained in Madrid.

In Valencia, the travellers gathered at the home of 'Paco' Botella. He and Pedro Casciaro had been pressed into the Republican army but upon seeing the Father again they decided to leave with him that same evening by train for Barcelona, 350 kilometres north along the Mediterranean coast. According to Albareda, Escrivá prayed during most of the journey, which took twelve hours. They spent the next six weeks waiting for additional papers, during which time they made contact with the 'Milkman'. He demanded payment in banknotes issued by the Bank of Spain before 18 July 1936. Between them they had just enough. They split into two groups, leaving behind Alvira and Sainz to wait for Portillo, who was still attempting to raise enough money to join them.

In mid-November 1937, Escrivá, Albareda, Juan Jiménez, Botella, Casciaro and Fisac boarded a bus for Seo de Urgel, nine kilometres south of the frontier. The police checkpoints became more frequent as they approached the mountains. Their instructions were to leave the bus at a crossroads near Peramola, a small village off the main road south of Seo de Urgel. Waiting there was the first of their guides. They slowly progressed towards the border, sleeping in a hayloft and even a large outdoor oven where, in the damp and cold, there was barely enough room to accommodate them. Escrivá wanted to turn back. He felt guilty about leaving Portillo behind in Madrid. Over supper he had an argument with Juan Jiménez, who told him, 'We're going to get you to the other zone, even if I have to drag you there by your hair.'[1] The Father sobbed and throughout the rest of the night he cried and prayed to the Virgin for a sign confirming that he was following God's wishes. The sign he suggested was that, in the late autumn of the high Pyrenees, a rose might bloom.

At dawn, Escrivá climbed out of the oven and went into the ruins of the nearby church to pray. The altarpiece had been destroyed but he found among the debris a carved wooden rose that apparently had broken off a statue of the Virgin. He took it as the sign he had requested and, showing it to his followers, called upon them to prepare for Mass.

During the next four nights they continued their journey, Alvira and Sainz having caught up with them, crossing four high mountain passes. Their new guide, Antonio, had a robust constitution and a concrete mixer for a digestive tract. He farted with great gusto, emitting foul odours that caused Fisac to turn and remark to the Father, 'If he keeps on like that he'll asphyxiate me.'[2]

On the last night a drizzle turned to snow. Several times they had to cross the Arabell River and Fisac carried Escrivá on his back. They

[1] Miguel Fisac Notes, 8 June 1994.
[2] Reflections by Miguel Fisac on Pedro Casciaro's book, *Soñad y os quedaréis cortos* (Dream and you will not believe what happens), November 1994.

were soaked. The ground was freezing. Finally Escrivá's strength gave out. He complained that his limbs were numb; his teeth chattered uncontrollably and he could hardly walk. During breaks, Juan massaged his legs. But Antonio was in a hurry. Border patrols had orders to shoot on sight and he said one was close by. They crossed another torrent, and saw the lights of a house. Dogs started barking. They descended into a valley and after entering the woods on the opposite slope Antonio told them they were in Andorra. He then disappeared.

A few days later they reached San Sebastian in Nationalist Spain. Escrivá's 'sons' reported for military service. The Father, still in possession of the carved rose, which later became the symbol of the Women's Section, spent Christmas with the Bishop of Pamplona. On 8 January 1938 – the day before his thirty-sixth birthday – he arrived in the Nationalist capital of Burgos, and moved into a modest hotel with Albareda, Casciaro and Botella. Albareda had again met up with José Ibáñez Martín. The Aragonese chemistry teacher was now deputy minister of education in the new Franco cabinet. He found Albereda a job with the National Secretariat of Culture. By pulling strings, Escrivá was able to have Casciaro and Botella posted to desk jobs at the military headquarters in Burgos while Fisac and the others were sent to the Front.

Escrivá's first concern in Burgos was to re-establish the Work. He immediately travelled south to Salamanca and tried to interest the principal benefactor of the Teresian Institute, María Josefa Segovia, to back him, as Father Poveda, the Teresian founder, had been shot during the first days of the Red terror in Madrid.

'I am again with Don José María,' María Josefa wrote in her diary. 'He fills me with such emotion. He looks like a ghost, and he cries . . . He spoke of his last conversation with Father Poveda a few days before our Founder was martyred. With his words, we relived all the horror of the persecution. Apart from that, he comes full of projects.'[1]

In this encounter Escrivá appears to have taken considerable liberty with the truth while playing upon the wealthy aristocrat's sentiments. We know from his biographers that once the Civil War

---

[1] Diary of María Josefa Segovia for 21 January 1938, as cited by Flavia-Paz Velázquez in *Vida de María Josefa Segovia*, Publicaciones de la Institución Teresiana, Madrid 1964, p. 205.

broke out he never saw Father Poveda again and did not learn of the elder priest's martyrdom until some three months after the event. Poveda was killed by the *milicianos* on 27 July 1936.[1]

It is not known whether María Josefa Segovia contributed to the Work's empty coffers. But after returning from Salamanca, Escrivá began anew his doctoral thesis, transforming it into a study of the Abbess of Las Huelgas. The seed for the change had been planted more than a year before, when he had remarked to Pedro Casciaro that the future juridical solution for the Work lay under two tomb-stones set in the floor of the Santa Isabel church in Madrid. Both were for Palatine Ordinaries, who under canon law held the status of Prelates *nullius* – that is, an Ordinary without a diocese but with his own congregation and clergy.[2]

What interested Escrivá about the medieval Abbey of Las Huelgas, just a twenty minute walk from his hotel, was its unique-ness in the annals of the Church, having been chartered as *prelatura nullius*. The abbey was founded in 1187 by Alfonso VIII at the behest of his wife Eleanor, daughter of England's Henry II. It was dedicated to promoting the monastic life of women, possessing its own lands and congregation, and therefore not attached to an episcopal see but coming under its own prelate, the Abbess of Las Huelgas. Her status was similar to a *prelate nullius*, making her the highest-ranking woman in the Church, and that intrigued Escrivá. Las Huelgas remained a *prelatura nullius* until the mid-nineteenth century, when its status was finally changed.

While Escrivá developed his thesis, the Work's very existence became threatened. A Nationalist finance ministry official, Don Jorge Bermúdez, originally from Albacete, where the Casciaro family also lived, accused Pedro Casciaro's father, a Freemason and serving Republican officer, of being responsible for the deaths of many National Front supporters in Albacete. He also affirmed that the son shared the father's political convictions, having personally seen Pedro distributing Marxist tracts at Albacete before the February 1936 elections. Bermúdez further claimed that Pedro was

[1] Father Poveda was beatified by John Paul II in October 1993.
[2] The prelates were Antonio de Sentmanat, Patriarch of the Indies, Chaplain of King Charles IV of Spain, Vicar General of the Royal Armies on Land and at Sea (1743–1806), and Jacobo Cardona y Tur, Patriarch of the West Indies, Titular Archbishop of Zion, Major Chaplain of the Royal Household and Vicar General of the Army (1838–1923).

a Republican spy. He had no proof, but that did not bother him, even though the consequence of such an accusation would have been an investigation of Escrivá's activities and, because suspected spies were offered little legal protection, Casciaro's likely execution before a firing squad.

Escrivá and Albareda went to see Bermúdez at the finance department and appealed to the man's Christian conscience. But Bermúdez turned a deaf ear. Even if the son was innocent, which he doubted, Bermúdez insisted that Pedro had to answer for his father's crimes. When finally they left Bermúdez's office, Escrivá was overcome by a premonition of death. Descending the stairs, he turned to Albareda and, eyes almost closed, predicted, 'Tomorrow, or the day after, there'll be a funeral in that family.'[1]

They returned to the hotel and Escrivá explained to the others what had happened. Fisac was in Burgos on leave at the time. He now picks up the story: 'We went downstairs for lunch and afterwards everyone left on their own business, with the Father and me remaining alone in the room. We were leaning on the railing of the porch watching the river when he told me in a hushed voice, "Tomorrow, a burial in that house." I was afraid and we remained silent,' he recalled.

'A short while later, the Father proposed that we go to the Cathedral and visit the Holy Ghost. We passed under the Arch of Our Lady and entered the Cathedral, leaving it after long meditation by the side door. We descended the steps, but before arriving in the plaza we stopped at a public notice board. One of the notices, bordered in black, was very recent. The Father read it and became quite agitated. "What's happened?" I asked. He replied, "The gentleman I saw this morning is dead."

'I was deeply struck by this news. We walked on for a few more metres and entered a bistro where we ordered a fruit juice. It was then that the Father told me not to make any judgements on the departed soul. I remember that we probably said a prayer for him. Afterwards, the Father told me that it would be prudent if Pedro and I left Burgos for a few days, and he suggested we go the same evening to Vitoria with José María Albareda. We went directly from the

---

[1] Pedro Casciaro, *Soñad y os quedaréis cortos*, Ediciones Rialp, Madrid 1994, p. 162.

bistro to the General Headquarters. I entered the building and asked Pedro and Paco to come out for a moment; in the street we explained what had happened. The Father said it would be better if Pedro left for two days until after the funeral. So Pedro requested a furlough for Vitoria, as that weekend it was the Festival of La Blanca.'[1]

When Fisac returned to Burgos three days later he was asked by the others to sign a statement describing what had happened in words dictated by the Father. He said he was convinced that when the Father said, 'Tomorrow, a burial,' he was referring to the Bermúdez son who was at the Front. After hesitating, he finally signed the text and the matter was never discussed again.

Pope Pius XI died on 10 February 1939 and was succeeded by Cardinal Eugenio Pacelli, who took the name of Pius XII. Four weeks after Pacelli's election the Civil War ended. The new pope immediately despatched a telegram congratulating Franco on his 'Catholic' victory.[2] Escrivá's return to Madrid with the first Nationalist columns on 28 March 1939 marked the close of Opus Dei's embryonic period.

One of Franco's first measures as the new master of Spain was to launch a campaign of repression against anyone suspected of Republican sympathies. To facilitate the arrest of state enemies, Franco's police issued special blue forms for denunciations, which citizens were invited to fill out if they suspected their neighbours or possessed information that might assist in uncovering Popular Front collaborators.[3] The 'cleansing' of Spanish society that followed the Nationalist victory added another 200,000 victims to the more than 500,000 who lost their lives during the Civil War.[4]

Escrivá immediately began stitching the Work back together, making it the standard bearer of a concept known as 'authoritarian clericalism'. With his brother Santiago, Ricardo Fernández Vallespín and Juan Jiménez Vargas he inspected the DYA Residence. The building had been shelled during the 1937 battle for Madrid and had

---

[1] Miguel Fisac, Notes, 11 November 1994.
[2] Paul Preston, *Franco*, HarperCollins, London 1993, p. 322.
[3] *The Times*, London, 21 April 1939.
[4] Brian Crozier, 'Spain under its little dictator,' *The Times* (London) 18 October 1993. Also Gabriel Campo Villegas, the Civil War historian of Barbastro, in an interview with the author in June 1994, placed the number of victims during the war and subsequent years of repression at around 750,000.

to be written off. As the Fomento de Estudios Superiores had made no further payment, the owner repossessed the property. Escrivá, however, was determined to open a new student residence before the beginning of the academic year that October.

As the rest of Europe prepared for world war, during April and May 1939 Spain was treated to a series of victory celebrations that culminated with Franco's entry into Madrid on Thursday, 18 May. The capital was ablaze with the red and gold colours of the new Spain. Some 200,000 troops had been brought into the city to take part in a grand victory parade. Parks were transformed into military cantonments and the streets jammed with tanks, armoured vehicles, artillery pieces and both mechanized and muledrawn transport. Madrid was said to be overawed by Franco's military *hubris*. The parade was 30 kilometre long and lasted five hours. It included élite Italian and German units, and line after line of regular Spanish troops sometimes twenty abreast, among them Falangist Blue Shirts, Carlist *Requetés* carrying huge crucifixes, the battle-scarred Army Corps of Navarra, Moorish regulars in baggy trousers and the dreaded Spanish Foreign Legion.

That Sunday Franco attended a solemn *Te Deum* Mass at the royal basilica of Santa Bárbara. The approach to the basilica was lined with young Falangists waving palms of peace. The choir of the Monastery of Saint Dominic of Silos greeted him with a tenth-century Mozarabic chant written for the reception of princes. Surrounded by military relics of Spain's crusading past, including Don John of Austria's Lepanto battle standard, Franco presented his 'sword of victory' to the Primate of all Spain, Cardinal Isidro Gomá, who laid it on the high altar before the great crucifix of the Christ of Lepanto from the Cathedral of Barcelona. Franco then requested divine help in leading the Spanish people 'to the full liberty of the empire of Your glory and that of Your Church'.[1]

At the end of September 1939, Father Escrivá published *The Way*, a collection of 999 religious maxims offering spiritual advice which he promoted as a guide to salvation. 'If these maxims change your own life,' the introduction read, 'you will be a perfect imitator of Jesus Christ, and a knight without a spot. And with Christs such as you, Spain will return to the ancient grandeur of its saints, its sages

[1] Tom G. Burns, 'Fresh Thoughts on Franco', *The Tablet*, 21 November 1992.

and its heroes.' Escrivá's followers described it as 'a classic of spiritual literature, an à Kempis for modern times.'[1]

Some critics, however, claimed the work was 'superficial', which may be so, but as a criticism it missed the point. *The Way* was more accurately a handbook of authoritarian clericalism. Professor José María Castillo went even further. He claimed it lacked discernment, a serious charge, for in theological terms discernment is a loaded word. 'Discernment is the expression of the true cult of Christians; it puts into practice our living as "children of the light" rather than "children of darkness",' explained Castillo, a Jesuit professor of theology at the University of Granada.

'If a book which claims to be a programme of spiritual life says nothing about Christian discernment, one can say quite surely that it has only a superficial veneer of Evangelical spirit. One can, in fact, say that, deep down, the book is not Christian,' Castillo wrote in an article that engendered Opus Dei's wrath. Shortly after, Castillo's licence to teach theology was revoked.

But what exactly is discernment? It has to do with determining the authenticity of mystical experiences – whether they result from God's influence on the soul or are humanly induced. Ignatius of Loyola's concern for discernment constitutes an essential aspect of his *Spiritual Exercises*. Ignatius was so absorbed by the problem that he conceived a set of rules for the discernment of spirits that he applied to his own spiritual life. Perhaps because of his concern for discernment, Ignatius never claimed that God created the Society of Jesus. The same concern for discernment, Castillo claimed, was not reflected in *The Way*. In fact, *The Way* tolerates neither doubt nor criticism. It affirmed that true Christians must be disciplined and obedient to a spiritual director. To this extent, maintained Father Castillo, the roots of Opus Dei's fanaticism are contained in the maxims of *The Way*.

Written in simple, rough language, Escrivá's maxims engender a spirit of superiority in anyone who identifies with them. The reader is told that he cannot be 'one of the crowd. You were born to be a leader! There is no room among us for the lukewarm. Humble yourself and Christ will set you aflame again with the fire of Love' (Maxim 16). Maxim 387 states: 'The standard of holiness that

---

[1] Preface to the Four Courts edition of *The Way*, Scriptor 1985.

God asks of us is determined by these three points: holy intransigence, holy coercion and holy shamelessness.' Convinced he possessed the undeniable truth, Escrivá wrote in Maxim 394 that 'to compromise is a sure sign of not possessing the truth. When a man gives way in matters of ideals, of honour or of Faith, that man is a man without . . . honour and without Faith'.

Discernment denied, Escrivá's lay children would be unlikely to attain spiritual maturity. They are told that if they wish to achieve Christian perfection they must give up their inner self to a superior. Maxim 377 states this clearly: 'And how shall I acquire "our formation", how shall I keep "our spirit"? By being faithful to the specific norms your Director gave you and explained to you, and made you love: be faithful to them and you will be an apostle.' The special formation is 'ours' and none other. 'Our spirit' consists of fulfilling the specific norms dictated by 'your Director'. In other words, there is no recourse to one's spiritual discernment, only to one's Spiritual Director.

What Escrivá seemed to be saying is that obedience to the Father, through each member's spiritual director, offers the key to the gates of Heaven. Consider Maxim 941: 'Obedience, the sure way. Unreserved obedience to whoever is in charge, the way of sanctity. Obedience in your apostolate, the only way: for in a work of God, the spirit must be to obey or to leave.' According to Maxim 623 one must obey in every 'little detail', even if it seems 'useless and difficult. Do it!' Maxim 59 tells us that everyone needs guidance. 'Here is a safe doctrine that I want you to know: one's own mind is a bad adviser, a poor pilot to steer the soul through the storms and tempests and among the reefs of interior life. That is why it is the will of God that [your soul] be entrusted to a Master who, with his light and his knowledge, can guide us to a safe harbour.' But this guidance is not attributable to the Holy Spirit. It is attributable to a man, the Father, the only person who can insure that one's sanctity will be achieved. 'Follow my word, and I promise you heaven.'

With the elimination of discernment, the Gospel is empty, faith alienated and the individual demeaned. Paul told the people of Corinth, 'For anyone who eats and drinks without discerning the body eats and drinks judgement upon himself.'[1] Once alienation has

---

[1] 1 Corinthians 11:29.

been achieved, the foundations of a cult have been established. Father Castillo concluded: 'The Way leads inevitably to the alienation of the individual, and to an ill-conceived complicity with "the world" which Jesus rejected, and by which He was rejected, unto death.'[1]

[1] José María Castillo, La Anulación del Discernimiento (The Elimination of Discernment). Father Castillo is also the author of El discernimiento cristiano segun San Pablo (Granada, 1975).

8

PIOUS UNION

Whatever is written about us, let us never forget that just as our enemies are wont to exaggerate our defects, so our friends are wont to magnify us in their praise; and in the end we are no other than what we are in the sight of God.

St Francis, *Mission*

TO CLAIM ESCRIVÁ WAS ONLY INTERESTED IN THE SPIRITUAL well-being of his disciples and the manner in which they carried out their apostolate – openly and without guile, bringing the Good News to family, friends and workmates – was nonsense. Escrivá was interested in power. He was a schemer. God's schemer. And he wanted to control higher education, and later government ministries, to assure that there would be no return to Anarchism, Liberalism and Marxism. Defeating this constellation of evil – the ALMs complex – was central to Opus Dei's mission. It was the key, as he might have expressed it, 'to looking God in the eye'.

To maintain that Opus Dei had no political mission was, consequently, being less than forthright. It did have one, and Escrivá himself explained why: 'It seems substantially better to me that there be many highly qualified Catholics who, while not posing as "official" Catholics, work within the political structure from positions of responsibility to create a true Catholic presence, sustained by an upright love for their co-workers.'[1]

What could be clearer? Opus Dei's mission had little to do with saving individual souls. It had to do with saving Father Escrivá's employer, the Roman Catholic Church. That was Opus Dei's principal Crusade. But it was not a message that Opus Dei broadcast openly. It went only to the officers. To the world at large, Opus Dei's mission was to spread the word that holiness can be achieved through work, and that work was an essential part of the human condition and therefore it needed to be sanctified.

'What does it matter to me if a member be a cabinet minister or a street sweeper? What I care about is that he grows in love for God and all men in and through his work,' Father Escrivá replied when, in 1957, he was congratulated by a cardinal because two of his 'sons' had been appointed government ministers. The remark was cited by Cardinal Albino Luciani a month before becoming Pope. 'This reply tells us everything about Escrivá and the spirit of Opus Dei.'[2] But really it told us more about Luciani's innate goodness and naivety. This story, often repeated by Opus Dei, was devious, for it gave a misleading impression of Opus Dei's mission. Of course Escrivá was convinced that members who followed his spiritual guidance grew 'in love for God and all men'. For him it was perfectly evident. If members carried out to perfection their apostolate – keeping the Church pure while recruiting new members into the militia – then Escrivá would tell them, 'I promise you heaven.'[3] But to gain access to heaven, they had to *do battle for the Church*. That was the other half of the story. The guarded half. As a natural consequence of doing battle for the Church, souls were saved. Church first, souls second. And to protect the Church, Opus Dei sought to create 'a true Catholic presence' in the Secular City by occupying 'positions of responsibility'. That was the essential character of Opus Dei from 1939 onwards.

Opus Dei might claim this to be the diatribe of an outsider who

[1] Berglar, *Op. cit.*, p. 119, citing Escrivá's letter of 16 June 1960, sections 41 and 42.
[2] Cardinal Albino Luciani, article reprinted in *The Universe*, 29 September 1978.
[3] *Crónica* I/71: 'When the years pass you will not believe what you have lived. It will seem that you have been dreaming. How many good and great and wonderful things you are going to see . . . I can assure you that you will be faithful, even though at times you will have to suffer. Besides, I promise you heaven.'

has misunderstood the inner workings of a divinely inspired organization. Its directors would surely point out that Escrivá himself told the world: 'There is no soul whom we do not love.' Did he not also explain: 'Whoever does not thirst for all souls does not have a vocation to Opus Dei. As children of God . . . you and I must think of souls when we see people'?[1]

Of course the Founder said those things. But one of the troubles about citing anything by Escrivá is that he was a master of double talk and dual standards. He said one thing for the outside world and another for his children. Even more telling, he said one thing for some of his children, while maintaining something else for his staff officers, the inscribed numeraries. He also had two layers of publications: one for the general public, *The Way* for example, and another reserved for elect numeraries. Strict orders were issued that copies of *Crónica*, the monthly review for staff officers, be kept under lock and key in each centre.[2]

So, yes, the Founder did say, 'Whoever does not thirst for souls does not have a vocation to Opus Dei.' But he also said: 'We do not go to the apostolate to receive applause, but to defend the Church in the front line when it is hard going to be a Catholic, and to pass unnoticed when Catholicism is in fashion.'[3]

Because Opus Dei had no more than a handful of members in 1939, no money, no headquarters and not even legal status, its agenda over the next few years might have seemed outrageously ambitious. But it was an agenda known only to the Founder and a few of his apostles. It was also an agenda that needed a plan. Escrivá, the master strategist, was by definition a master planner. He gathered his strategies into a portfolio which he called his Plan of Life. 'Without a plan of life you will never have order,' he claimed in Maxim 76. After 1,000 days of Civil War Escrivá arrived back in Madrid with a small copy-book in which 'point by point he had

---

[1] Both quotes are from Escrivá's letter to his children of 6 May 1945, section 42, as cited by Bernal, *Op. cit.*, p. 159.

[2] Opus Dei claims that *Crónica*, which commenced publication in 1954, is 'a journal written by members of Opus Dei, with articles from different parts of the world about their work, activities, anecdotes, memories, etc.' But this simplistic description omits to mention that *Crónica*'s essential role is to explain and comment upon Opus Dei's interpretation of key doctrinal issues; its distribution is limited to numeraries. Opus Dei refused to provide the author with copies of *Crónica*.

[3] Escrivá's letter to his children of 9 January 1932, as cited by Gondrand, *Op. cit.*, p. 170.

made a note of his projects of reconstruction and apostolic expansion, identifying the steps to be taken and the goals to be achieved'.[1] This was his outline for Plan 'A'.[2] The war clouds hanging over Europe at that time required it to remain national in scope. In any case, God's proxy needed to establish a secure home base before exporting Opus Dei's apostolate to the rest of the world.

Plan 'A' was many times modified as events progressed towards Opus Dei's registration as a secular organization belonging to the Church. But essentially it had four basic components. It was built around a political focalizer: constructing an ALMs bulwark. To do this Opus Dei needed a general staff, national headquarters and structure. But in addition, it needed troops – the work of Archangel Raphael. This meant opening new Opus Dei centres in Madrid and the provinces. The strategic objective was to control higher education.

Unbelievable? Megalomania? Here was this provincial priest without means, a nobody thinking he could take over Spain's universities. But the country bumpkin with the dust of Aragon upon his cassock had come a long way since arriving in the capital from the provinces. He had survived Communist persecution. He had escaped from the control of his Ordinary. He had, in a sense, broken the mould. He had a firm hand on the infallible means mentioned in Maxim 474 – Love, Faith, the Cross – but now he had other means, provided by José Ibáñez Martín, providential man of the moment.

Love and Faith, his followers would agree, were commodities that Father Escrivá possessed in supernatural abundance. His Cross was the ideology of authoritarian clericalism. But there was nothing original in all this. It was pure ACNP dogma. The root of modern Spanish evil for Escrivá, as for Angel Herrera and Ibáñez Martín, was the ALMs syndrome; it had taken hold with such tenacity in the 1920s and 1930s that the Liberals assumed control over national education. To erase Liberal influence, national education had to be sanitized. Franco shared this conviction and the man he chose to carry out the cleansing was the owlish Ibáñez Martín, naming him

---

[1] Vázquez de Prada, *Op. cit.*, p. 200.
[2] Plan 'A' is not Opus Dei terminology; it is used by the author as a label for Opus Dei's development strategy in the immediate post-Civil War years.

as his education minister in April 1939. With the help of José María Albareda, Ibáñez Martín developed a national education strategy that fitted Opus Dei's intentions perfectly.

Ibáñez Martín's most urgent task was to create new professors to fill the empty chairs and to check the credentials of those who remained after the Civil War to determine whether they were 'politically reliable'. One hundred and fifty new professors had to be appointed within the next three years. Ibáñez Martín turned the selection process upside down, removing any autonomy from the universities. The five-member selection juries were henceforth named by him and served at his discretion. Two Opus Dei members were immediately given a chair: José María Albareda (agronomy) and DYA alumnus Angel Santos Ruiz (physics). Scores more would follow during the next few years.

Another of Ibáñez Martín's earliest initiatives was the Law of 24 November 1939 which created the Consejo Superior de Investigaciones Científicas, or National Scientific Research Council (NSRC), which became the principal cover for Opus Dei's assault on higher education and also helped finance its expansion abroad. Ibáñez Martín named himself chairman. As vice-chairman he appointed an Augustinian priest, Father José López Ortiz, who was one of Escrivá's closest confidants, having first met him at the University of Saragossa in 1924. But the person Ibáñez Martín chose to run the Council was Escrivá's twelfth apostle. Known for his research in soil chemistry, Albareda was well suited for the job. He became the high priest of Spanish science, a position he maintained until his death in March 1966.

Under the broad definition Ibáñez Martín and Albareda gave to science, the Council's prerogatives extended from theology to economics. To carry out his mandate, Albareda surrounded himself with Opus Dei recruits. The NSRC was described as the matrix of Opus Dei.[1] It determined who would obtain scholarships for post-graduate and doctoral studies abroad. It disbursed the grants and travel allowances. Anyone wishing to study in a foreign land could only do so with the NSRC's approval and, because of

---

[1] Ynfante, *La Prodigiosa Aventura del Opus Dei – Génesis y desarrollo de la Santa Mafia*, Editions Ruedo ibérico, Paris 1970, p. 37; Artigues, *Op. cit.*, p. 37, citing *Notas sobre la investigación científica en España*, Mañana, November 1965.

stringent foreign exchange controls, their foreign stipends were paid by the NSRC through official banking channels.

The NSRC had a strong state-funded budget and it received private donations as well, the dispensing of which Opus Dei was able to influence. It hired its own auditors and was not subject to the Intendant General of Finance. Its resources were truly enormous for Spain at the time. Between 1945 and 1950, the NSRC received 259 million pesetas in public funding, while only 84 million pesetas went to the construction of sorely needed primary schools.[1]

Ibáñez Martín opened many doors and provided access to academic trappings that matched Escrivá's growing status as the Founder of a politico-religious movement. He told Father López Ortiz that Escrivá was preparing a doctoral thesis. López Ortiz visited Escrivá and enquired how the thesis was progressing. 'It was practically finished,' the Augustinian recalled. 'The date for its defence could therefore be fixed for the end of December . . . I was on the tribunal . . . It was a work of juridical investigation carried out with an ability and style which were truly extraordinary. All of us who were part of the tribunal were impressed and the thesis was given the best mark.'[2]

What could have been more expedient? An aura of mystery, nevertheless, surrounded Escrivá's civil law doctorate. The thesis dealt with the canonical framework constructed in the Middle Ages for the *prelatura nullius* of Las Huelgas. Therefore it was not about civil law at all. To clarify this anomaly, an editor of the Madrid newspaper *Cambio 16* reported that he had initiated a search for Father Escrivá's academic file. In vain. 'At the Ministry of Education and Science we were told that "since 1930 until today there has never been a university student registered under this name". At Saragossa our search was also without results.'[3] Was Father Escrivá's first

---

[1] Ynfante, *Op. cit.*, pp. 40 and 44.
[2] Bishop José López Ortiz in *Testimonies to a man of God*, Volume 2, p. 5-08, Scepter 1992. The other members of the tribunal were Inocencio Jiménez, professor of criminal and procedural law, Alfonso García Valdecasas, professor of civil law, and Mariano Puigdollers, professor of natural law and the philosophy of law. The president was a Professor Magariños.
[3] 'The Insignificant Saint,' *Cambio 16*, 16 March 1992. The article stated in part: Josemaría Escrivá 'claimed he was a graduate in law. But did he finish his degree? The authorized biographers leave no doubt: he finished it in Madrid with a doctoral thesis, which was read on 18 December 1939 and received the highest note possible, *cum laude*. The sceptics ask: "But where is his diploma?"'

doctorate – years later he was awarded a second from the Lateran Pontifical University in Rome[1] – a gift from Ibáñez Martín?

To attract a young élite, Opus Dei needed to open student residences, and it needed to open them quickly. Ibáñez Martín was preparing a new law governing universities. The new law would require students, as a condition of enrolment, to belong to a *Colegio Mayor* or hall of residence. Halls of residence could be either state or privately run. The law would be introduced in 1943, but Opus Dei wanted to have several residences operating before then.

The Jenner Residence became the first of these. In July 1939, Zorzano took a three-year lease on three apartments in a building on Calle Jenner, off the Castellana. The building was pleasant; the apartments large. Escrivá had them joined together: one was equipped with an oratory, refectory, common room, study hall and catering facilities, the others converted into accommodation. The Father moved into the Jenner Residence with his family in August 1939. When the Residence opened two months later, Doña Dolores – now called 'Grandmother' – and sister Carmen – whom members addressed as 'Auntie' – took in hand the domestic duties of caring for up to forty male students. The Father had his own suite consisting of bedroom, office and bathroom where he punished himself with the discipline, which he made more biting by attaching pieces of razor blades to its braided hemp tails. He practised self-mortification with such ferocity that it caused his children to wince. One numerary who worked as a surgeon in a Madrid clinic became concerned when he found the Father covered in blood. Next morning, while Escrivá was absent, he threw the discipline on to the roof of a neighbouring building.[2]

By the end of 1939, with centres in Barcelona, Valencia and Valladolid, Escrivá was the spiritual overseer of one hundred souls. He went on prospecting trips to provincial universities often accompanied by the NSRC's deputy chairman José López Ortiz. Until named Bishop of Tuy-Vigo in July 1944, Father López was so close to Escrivá that he was considered a member. By his own account, he met Escrivá every day and he knew personally most of the other members, being in the case of Isidoro Zorzano his

---

[1] According to Opus Dei, it was awarded on 20 December 1955.
[2] Ynfante, *Op. cit.*, p. 16.

confessor. Escrivá had by then put together a general staff. In addition to Zorzano, his administrator general, it included another six of the twelve apostles: Paco Botella served as Secretary General; Alvaro del Portillo was procurator general; and José María Albareda was the prefect of education. José María Hernández de Garnica, Ricardo Fernández Vallespín and Pedro Casciaro were consultors.

Incorporated into Plan 'A' was a project to provide the Founder with an enhanced pedigree, as if at last he felt a need to shake the dust of Aragon off his cassock. He consulted his sister and brother. Evidently his mother did not go along with the idea as she was not a co-signatory of the petition sent to the Ministry of Justice. The application 'to change our family name to Escrivá de Balaguer, in order to distinguish us from other Escrivás by adopting the ancestral form of address', was heard that spring in the Madrid Civil Court. José María, Carmen and Santiago justified their request by stating: 'Escrivá is an extremely common name in the regions of Levante and Catalonia, which can cause prejudicial and annoying confusion. It is therefore desirable to add to our surname the family's town of origin.'

The family had never resided in Catalonia or Levante where they alleged that being called Escrivá without any qualifier was such a vulgar burden. No matter. The court approved the name change. Henceforth the Founder of Opus Dei was to be addressed as Dr José María Escrivá de Balaguer.

By then acquiring a suitable headquarters had become urgent. The Jenner Residence proved so successful that it soon had a waiting list. A private mansion with small garden was found in Calle Diego de León. According to Opus Dei, the three-storey mansion was rented by the Fomento de Estudios Superiores, represented by Ricardo Fernández Vallespín, for 13,000 pesetas a month, then equivalent to about $300. According to an Opus Dei budget director, the property was finally purchased at the end of the 1940s for 6 million pesetas ($140,000) from the Marquesa de Rafal. At first it was claimed that insufficient funds were available to repair the heating system or even to buy coal. If this was the case, it was because money was lavished on other interior modifications, such as transforming an oval sitting room into an elaborately decorated oratory. Escrivá moved in with his family in December 1940. He had a small room on the third floor and an office on the second beside the oratory. His mother, brother and sister shared an apartment on the main floor. Even before the transformations were completed, the building was too small and in the 1960s four new floors were added.

Nothing on the outside of the building indicated that it was the headquarters of Opus Dei. Maintaining a headquarters, however, required an administrative staff and bookkeeping. This was entrusted to Isidoro Zorzano. The first apostle was suffering from an undiagnosed ailment that over the next two years left him increasingly weak. The strain of so many years in the wilderness had also left its mark on the Founder; in May 1944 he was diagnosed as having diabetes and thereafter required daily insulin injections.[1]

Dr Escrivá de Balaguer was now operating across diocesan boundaries and this was causing problems. We are told that a whisper campaign started against him. One of the rumours was that he and his disciples were practising Masonic rites. Two young men, professing an interest in joining Opus Dei, took part in a benediction service at the Jenner Residence and reported that the oratory contained cabalistic symbols. The Diego de León oratory was likewise denounced to the Holy Office in Rome because it was elliptically shaped. The Dominicans were asked to investigate. They found no pagan symbols in the Jenner oratory, and the Diego de León chapel was elliptical because that happened to be the shape of the room. The source of the rumours was never determined. Some believed the Jesuits were responsible, and indeed at this time the Father definitively broke with his Jesuit confessor. The reason given was that Escrivá de Balaguer found him less than enthusiastic about Opus Dei's chances of receiving formal approbation from the Church, something that until then had been neglected.[2]

López Ortiz was also subject to criticism for his pro-Opus Dei bias in the university. He had nominated his assistant, the 24-year-old Opus Dei numerary José Orlandis, for the post of professor of

---

[1] De Fuenmayor et al., *Op. cit.*, p. 185.
[2] In 1952 Bishop Eijo y Garay told Cardinal Joseph Frings of Cologne that a Jesuit had come to him and said, 'Do you know that a new heresy has started: Opus Dei?'

history of law at Saragossa University. Orlandis received the post, but never took it up. In November 1942 he and fellow numerary Salvador Canals made a wartime journey to Rome to continue their studies in canon law at the Vatican. Did they benefit from NSRC grants? Opus Dei answered that they received grants from the Ministry of National Education, which amounts to the same thing. In reality, both were instructed by Escrivá de Balaguer to make friends among the Roman Curia and inform them about Opus Dei. By their presence in Rome they established the first unofficial Opus Dei centre abroad.

Well after midnight one night the telephone rang in the Diego de León headquarters. When the Father answered, a voice addressed him by his Christian name and pronounced in Latin the words of Jesus to Simon Peter: 'Simon, Simon, behold, Satan demanded to have you, that he might sift you like wheat, but I have prayed for you that your faith may not fail; and when you have turned again, strengthen your brethren.'[1] Only the caller used the Latin word for 'sons' rather than 'brethren'.

Escrivá de Balaguer had recognized the voice of Leopoldo Eijo y Garay, Bishop of Madrid-Alcalá. He took the call as a warning that more persecution was on its way. He claimed he had always kept Don Leopoldo informed of Opus Dei's development and insisted that because Eijo y Garay had bestowed his 'oral approval' upon Opus Dei no approval *in scriptus* was needed. But months before, Don Leopoldo had in fact told Escrivá de Balaguer to register Opus Dei *in scriptus* with the diocese. Escrivá refused. He felt to register Opus Dei as a 'pious union' was too narrow. A pious union is defined as 'an association of faithful with a broad mandate for exercising works of piety or charity, capable of receiving spiritual graces and especially indulgences'. It is the simplest form of ecclesiastical institution, requiring nothing more than the approval of the local bishop. Instead he replied to Don Leopoldo that no provision existed under canon law that suited Opus Dei. The sense of his response was that Opus Dei should not be required to bend its structures to comply with canon law, but that canon law should be made to accommodate Opus Dei. He must have received a 'rocket', because on 14 February 1941 he wrote a letter requesting after all

[1] Luke 22:31–32.

the status of a pious union. As a concession, Don Leopoldo agreed to keep Opus Dei's rules, regulations, customs and ceremonies in the episcopacy's secret archives.

Escrivá de Balaguer's letter was noteworthy for several reasons. It marked the first time that the name 'Opus Dei' appeared in an official document. Thirteen years after its founding, God's Work could be said to have emerged from its hidden existence. It was also one of the earliest documents on record in which the Founder joined together his first two Christian names, signing his request as *Josemaría Escrivá de Balaguer*. Opus Dei claims that in fact the Founder had begun using 'Josemaría' as early as 1936, but some former members dispute this, stating that throughout the 1940s he signed internal documents as 'Mariano', a middle name that he started using as a cover during the Civil War. They claim that 'Josemaría' only came into general use after the Founder moved to Rome and began thinking about posterity. It has been pointed out that the Vatican's index of saints contains many San Josés but no San Josemaría.

A month after Opus Dei's registration as a pious union, the 'Grandmother' came down with pneumonia and died. Escrivá ordered a Gothic crypt to be built in the basement of the Diego de León residence and obtained municipal permission to bury his mother there. He then arranged for the remains of his father to be reinterred alongside her, recreating in dynastic solemnity the family union.

While Opus Dei was now registered with the Church, Escrivá de Balaguer momentarily was not. Though still officially the rector of Santa Isabel, he had become a priest without an Ordinary. This over-sight was only rectified in February 1942 when he was incardinated in the diocese of Madrid. So once again Escrivá de Balaguer found himself, and Opus Dei as well, under diocesan control.

On Saint Valentine's Day 1943, while celebrating Mass in the first Women's Residence in Madrid, Escrivá de Balaguer saw a new light. It told him that Opus Dei must obtain 'title' to ordain priests. This addition, it was said, would complete the divine organization of Opus Dei, providing it with a clergy formed from among its own members.

But Vatican approval was needed to found a priestly society. Accordingly, with the Bishop of Madrid's consent, in May 1943

Escrivá de Balaguer sent Don Alvaro del Portillo to Rome to negotiate the new status. In the middle of the Second World War, a flight from Madrid to Rome was not without adventure. Don Alvaro was able to observe from the window of the aircraft an attack on an Allied convoy headed for Malta. Salvador Canals and José Orlandis were waiting for him when he landed. They introduced him to Archbishop Arcadio Larraona, a Spanish Claretian and friend of Generalísimo Franco. Larraona was a canon lawyer who served as pro-secretary of the Congregation of Religious, the Vatican ministry responsible for relations with the nearly 1 million nuns and 150,000 priests belonging to religious orders (i.e., as distinct from secular or diocesan priests).

In Spain the tradition of guilds – medieval associations that regulate a trade or profession – remained strong. During the Middle Ages, guild members wore uniforms that indicated the rank and experience they had achieved within their trade. These uniforms were *de rigueur* on all formal occasions such as court appearances or state banquets. The custom was abolished by the Republic, but under Franco guilds returned to favour for certain professions. They were, moreover, a notion that suited Opus Dei's doctrine of pride of profession and sanctity of work. On 6 June 1943 Don Alvaro was accorded his first audience with Pope Pius XII. He arrived wearing the guild uniform of a Spanish civil engineer. The appearance of this regal-looking emissary from an unknown Spanish order caused considerable excitement in the papal antechambers.

Don Alvaro handed the Pope Opus Dei's request to found a clerical association. Don Giovanni Battista Montini, the assistant secretary of state, and Archbishop Larraona had already laid the groundwork with the Holy Father so that when Don Alvaro returned to Madrid a month later he was able to announce that pontifical approval would be forthcoming within weeks.

Winning papal approval for a priestly society marked an important step in the development of Opus Dei. But the Father's joy was short-lived. A few days after Don Alvaro's return, Isidoro Zorzano died of Hodgkin's Disease. He had been hospitalized since January. His confessor, Father López Ortiz, said, 'he died a holy death'. Preparations began for declaring the departed Zorzano apt for sainthood. The process was officially inaugurated in 1948 when Cardinal

FATHER ESCRIVÁ'S TWELVE APOSTLES

		Joined	
1.	Isidoro Zorzano	1930	(died 1943)
2.	Juan Jiménez Vargas	1933	
3.	José María González Barredo	1933	(died 1993)
4.	Ricardo Fernández Vallespín	1933	(died 1988)
5.	Alvaro del Portillo	1935	(died 1994)
6.	José María Hernández de Garnica	1935	(died 1972)
7.	Pedro Casciaro	1935	(died 1995)
8.	Francisco Botella Raduan	1935	(died 1987)
9.	Miguel Fisac	1935	
10.	Rafael Calvo Serer	1936	(died 1988)
11.	Vicente Rodríguez Casado	1936	(died 1990)
12.	José María Albareda Herrera	1937	(died 1966)

Compiled from information provided by Opus Dei, except
for Miguel Fisac, who is considered a non-person
as he left the Work in 1955.

Antonio Bacci was charged with presenting Zorzano's case for beatification.[1]

The day after Zorzano's death, Archbishop Larraona drafted a report for the pope describing Opus Dei as 'a new and modern type of institution perfectly suited to the requirements of modern society'. He concluded: 'It is most opportune – I would say almost necessary – to confer as quickly as possible the juridical status of [clerical]

[1] Peter Hebblethwaite, *Paul VI – The First Modern Pope*, HarperCollins 1993, p. 321. Also Rocca, *Op. cit.*, p. 20n.

society upon Opus Dei, which already counts so many fine initiatives on its balance sheet.'[1] In his report, Larraona defended Opus Dei's right to secrecy 'to better penetrate the world.'[2]

After being notified of the Vatican's approval, on 8 December 1943 – the feast of the Immaculate Conception – Bishop Eijo y Garay issued a decree constituting the Priestly Society of the Holy Cross as a corporate subsidiary of Opus Dei. The pious union continued to function as before, but now a clerical association existed alongside it. In June of the following year, Bishop Eijo personally ordained the first three Opus Dei priests – Alvaro del Portillo, José María Hernández de Garnica and José Luis Múzquiz. All were civil engineers. Opus Dei had now completed the second phase of its development and Escrivá de Balaguer with the help of his newly ordained priests was already planning the next phase – the extension of Opus Dei's presence to more than eighty countries on five continents.

---

[1] De Fuenmayor et al., *Op. cit.*, pp. 144 and 161.
[2] Rocca, *Op. cit.*, p. 31.

VILLA TEVERE

Christ demands humility.

Josemaría Escrivá de Balaguer

AT THE END OF THE SECOND WORLD WAR, OPUS DEI OPENED ITS FIRST
student residence outside Spain, in the Portuguese university town
of Coimbra, Portugal being the only European country that looked
kindly upon General Franco.

For having supported Hitler and the now defunct Axis, Franco's
Spain found herself in the doghouse of nations. She was blacklisted
by the Allied powers, excluded from the United Nations, her
frontier with France sealed and her aircraft banned from Allied
airspace.

Escrivá de Balaguer nevertheless confidently placed Britain,
France and Ireland on Opus Dei's post-war expansion list. But it
was perfectly evident that if the Work went into those countries as
a Spanish institution, it risked not being well received. He decided,
therefore, that Opus Dei must become an institution of pontifical
right.

Opus Dei was already represented in Rome by Salvador Canals
and José Orlandis. Their work with Archbishop Larraona now
turned to crafting a new apostolic constitution that would

transform the pious union into an institute subject to the Holy See's jurisdiction and none other. This was an important step, and one that some might have imagined unwarranted for an association with so few members.

The Father again despatched Alvaro del Portillo to Rome, this time as a priest of the Holy Cross. He carried with him a file detailing the expansion of Opus Dei beyond the borders of a single diocese, indeed beyond those of a single state, supported by letters from eight cardinals and sixty bishops praising Opus Dei for its apostolate. His mission was not a success, and in order to get around the Curial roadblock, Escrivá de Balaguer decided to go to Rome himself.

He was briefed about what to expect. Half a million Italians were homeless. In the province of Reggio Emilia roving Marxist bands had murdered fifty-two priests since the Liberation, while in Rome every evening the Communists took over the square in front of the Lateran Palace, and wooed thousands of Romans with music, speeches, banners and grub. The Italian Communist newspaper, L'Unità, was hammering at the Church, and accused its favourite target, Giovanni Battista Montini, of being a 'meddler in politics'.

On his way to Rome, the Father stopped at Saragossa to beseech the Virgin of Pilar to intercede in Heaven and Rome, at Montserrat to pray before the Black Madonna, and in Barcelona to pray before Our Lady of Ransom. Once in Rome he waited five days before obtaining a meeting with Montini, who presented him with an autographed photograph of Pope Pius XII and recommended patience.

Dealing with the Roman Curia, no matter how you looked at it, cost money. By then Opus Dei maintained four persons in Rome, soon to become six or seven. This required cash – not pesetas, but lire. With exchange controls, however, lire were not easy for Spaniards to come by. While the Rome delegation was by no means wallowing in funds, it had sufficient resources – Ministry of National Education resources – to enable its staff to concentrate on assisting Larraona in his work of rearranging canon law better to accommodate Opus Dei, turning it into a new type of association that would be known as a Secular Institute.

Before returning to Madrid, Escrivá de Balaguer obtained papal recognition for his endeavours in the form of two documents: an

Apostolic *Cum Societatis*, signed by Pius XII, conceding a number of papal indulgences to Opus Dei members. These included 500 days of remission every time a member kissed 'with devotion' the plain wooden cross placed at the entrance of all Opus Dei oratories. The other, a *Brevis sane*, signed on 13 August 1946 by Cardinal Lavitrano, amounted to the Holy See's 'approval of Opus Dei's aims', not only in Spain 'but also in other regions, carrying the light and truth of Christ especially to the minds of intellectuals'.

Once back in Madrid Escrivá de Balaguer told his children that his first contact with the Roman Curia had robbed him of his innocence. It also taught him that when it came to promoting God's work some holy hi-jinx might be needed. He had decided by then to return to Rome in November and take charge of the final stages of Opus Dei's incorporation as a universal institution. He was not particularly well; in spite of daily insulin injections, his diabetes made him tired, often cranky and he was gaining weight.

Montini, who Escrivá de Balaguer claimed was the only friendly soul he met in the Curia under Pius XII, counselled him on how to proceed. The Vatican was transfixed by events in eastern Europe. Very quickly the Soviets had let it be known that the Church would not be spared the Cold War's chill by sentencing Joseph Schlypi, the Major Archbishop of the Ukrainians, to life at hard labour for collaboration with the Nazis. At the same time the Uniate Church, of which Schlypi had been patriarch (and which owed its allegiance to Rome), was forcibly incorporated into the Russian Orthodox Church. This meant that in one swoop Rome lost 8 million souls. Later there would be persecution of the Church in Yugoslavia, Czechoslovakia, Hungary and Poland.

Escrivá de Balaguer was able to convince Montini that Opus Dei's 'apostolate of penetration' could be useful in combating the spread of Marxism, and Montini used this argument to persuade Pius XII to make provision in canon law for a type of association whose features were purpose-built for Opus Dei. In February 1947, Papa Pacelli issued a decree known by its opening words as *Provida Mater Ecclesia*. It established the *Secular Institute* as a juridical structure under pontifical law and provided an Apostolic Constitution that associations accorded this status were henceforth required to adopt. *Provida Mater* acknowledged that through the medium of a secular institute lay Catholics could seek to attain a 'state of perfection' while living an everyday existence in the secular world. In its canonical sense, 'state of perfection' had over the centuries come to mean living within a religious community according to the three monastic vows of poverty, chastity and obedience. Members of secular institutes did not have to wear distinctive habits or live a cloistered existence. Members of secular institutes, on the other hand, were required to take private vows. And they could continue to practise their trade or profession while striving for Christian perfection. Secular institutes nevertheless had certain points in common with religious orders. Responsibility for their oversight, therefore, was assigned to the Congregation of Religious in Rome.

Escrivá de Balaguer and Don Alvaro del Portillo pressed the Congregation of Religious to make Opus Dei the Church's first secular institute. As a matter of prestige, Opus Dei had to be a paragon, because as God's creation it was inimitable. Three weeks after publication of the Papal bull, the Congregation of Religious issued a decree entitled *Primum Institutum seculare*, transforming Opus Dei into the premier institute of the genre, a singular honour for a body that had less than 300 members, including all of nine priests.

Opus Dei now needed to move its headquarters to Rome. But Escrivá de Balaguer wanted them to be grand. Montini took the matter in hand. Through his aristocratic connections, a villa was found in Rome's fashionable Parioli district. The villa's owner, known only as *Il Nobile Mario* (the nobleman Mario), wanted a quick sale, and in Swiss francs. As Escrivá de Balaguer did not have enough money even to pay the deposit, he entrusted to the nobleman Mario some gold coins. Supposedly he had intended to melt down the coins and make sacred vessels out of them. Once Mario received the Swiss francs he promised to return the doubloons. In this way the Father secured the title deeds and was able to obtain a mortgage with which he made good the commitment to pay the nobleman within two months.[1]

Not only does this explanation provided by Opus Dei smack of sharp practices, it tries the writer's credulity. No Italian bank in 1947 would have provided a mortgage in Swiss francs – it was

---

[1] Opus Dei UK Information Office, 30 October 1994.

against the law. Nor would any Swiss bank have accepted at that time a mortgage in Italy. Moreover, Opus Dei claimed not to know the full name of the owner.

The owner was Count Mario Mazzoleni. Opus Dei closed the deal with him in July 1947. Escrivá de Balaguer at last had his grand headquarters, which he named Villa Tevere. And even though he professed not to have money, he immediately planned to build a new wing for his growing court of ministers. Its construction was placed under the supervision of Miguel Fisac, whose architecture studio in Madrid was at the time Opus Dei's biggest money spinner. Fisac donated his skills, but the works themselves were financed through donations from contributors in several countries. 'The construction of the central offices was considered the work of everybody,' Opus Dei explained.

Spain maintained exchange controls well into the 1980s, and Italy kept them until the beginning of the 1990s. That Opus Dei had access to large quantities of Swiss francs in 1947 was an indication of its growing resources. The situation may have been influenced by the fact that in 1947 the NSRC opened a Rome office with the aim of 'continuing the progress of Spanish science and research in the Eternal City, and of developing and co-ordinating the work of Spanish researchers in Italy'.[1]

At the time at least six Spanish researchers were in Rome, all members of Opus Dei. The material needs of Escrivá de Balaguer and his disciples in the Italian capital were becoming increasingly extravagant. Construction work at Villa Tevere commenced immediately and continued for the next twelve years. No figures were ever published, but the final cost has been estimated at more than $10 million.

It was now that Opus Dei obtained permission to alter its internal rules to allow married, noncelibate persons to join the Work as 'supernumeraries'. True to Opus Dei's 'strategy of discretion', Alvaro del Portillo also obtained extraordinary authorization to have the complete text of Opus Dei's Constitutions placed under seal in the secret archives of the Congregation of Religious. This remained the case until the 1980s, even though a purloined copy was published in 1970 by the Spanish author Jesús Ynfante in his

---

[1] Ynfante, *Op. cit.*, p. 44.

exposé of the Spanish phenomenon. But Opus Dei's insistence on secrecy had served its purpose, preventing other Church groups from modelling their statutes along similar lines.

The spiritual life of Opus Dei members was likewise given a secretive norm, as the institute's Constitution shows:

189 – To attain its goals in the most effective manner, the Institute as such must live an occult existence . . .

190 – Because of [our] collective humility, which is proper to our Institute, whatever is undertaken by members must not be attributed to it, but to God only. Consequently, even the fact of being a member of the Institute should not be disclosed externally; the number of members should remain secret; and more expressly, our members must not discuss these matters with anyone outside the Institute.

191 – . . . Numerary and supernumerary members must always observe a prudent silence regarding the names of other members; and never reveal to anyone the fact that they belong to Opus Dei . . . unless expressly authorized to do so by their local director . . . [1]

Shortly after the Villa Tevere acquisition, Escrivá de Balaguer was made a domestic prelate of the papal household, which gave him the right to be called Monsignor, add a touch of purple to his robes and wear buckled shoes. One of his biographers tells us that the Father, who found his own name so common that he ennobled it by adding 'de Balaguer', was reluctant to accept this honour.[2]

Escrivá de Balaguer's promotion in clerical rank was organized by Montini, who by then had introduced him to a rising young politician and future stalwart in the battle against Communism, Giulio Andreotti. Montini knew the twenty-nine-year-old Andreotti from before the war when he had been chaplain to the Italian federation of Catholic student unions, of which Andreotti had been a president. Pius XII had given Montini the task of putting some political backbone into Catholic Action in Italy, which had significantly more members than the Italian Communist party, and Montini asked Andreotti to handle liaison between it and the Christian Democrat

---

[1] The 1950 Constitutions, articles 189–91.
[2] Vázquez de Prada, *Op. cit.*, p. 249.

party during the 1948 election campaign. Two factors marked the campaign: first, the enormous resources poured into the fray by Washington through the newly created Central Intelligence Agency; and, second, the Vatican's own covert activities, coordinated by Montini.

Both were decisive in defeating the Communists. CIA funds on deposit with the Vatican bank, the IOR (Istituto per le Opere di Religione), were used to stage popular rallies throughout the country. Catholic Action also organized a Youth Congress whose theme was 'Christ has overcome Marx', and its members plastered campaign posters over the entire peninsula at a rate of 1,000 a day. In the end, the Christian Democrats triumphed with 48.5 per cent of the vote against 31 per cent for the Communists.

From the Christian Democrat victory emerged a Vatican strategy to counter Communism in which Opus Dei, with its growing financial resources, would play a role. The strategy was defined by Montini with help from Andreotti and it revolved around developing a secular network to alert public opinion to the Marxist threat. It enjoyed CIA backing and marked the beginning of a working relationship between Opus Dei and the CIA. As the strategy took shape, Montini told the French ambassador that the Vatican hoped to see Europe's three leading Catholic powers – Italy, France and Spain – come together in an anti-Communist union. He castigated the French for keeping their border with Spain closed.

Escrivá de Balaguer meanwhile reported that Opus Dei had 3,000 members, including twenty-three priests, and more than 100 centres in a dozen countries. But as the organization continued to grow he became disenchanted with the status of secular institute and began working on a 'final solution' that he anticipated would make him a prelate *nullius* – in other words, a bishop without a diocese. He was disenchanted, he said, because Archbishop Larraona had cheapened the secular institute concept by raising seventy other church groups to the same status. He never forgave Larraona for this. Seventy institutions in the world like Opus Dei did not exist. The Work was unique. Moreover, he claimed in *Crónica* that the concept was supposed to have been reserved for Opus Dei, and Opus Dei alone.

COLD WARRIORS

The reality of Communism means the persecution of the Church and continued assaults upon the elementary rights of the person. Some, it is true, make declarations against violence. But deeds do not follow these words; and as anyone can see, the Church is as mistreated by one group as by another.

Josemaría Escrivá de Balaguer, Letter of 24 October 1965

ESCRIVÁ DE BALAGUER, WHOSE ASSESSORS AT THE CAUSES OF SAINTS would claim 'stood out in the history of spirituality on a level with the traditional greats', proposed to provide Pius XII with a corps of Cold Warriors capable of exercising a discreet Catholic influence in key economic sectors and ministries throughout the free world. This represented a new phase in Opus Dei's development, requiring a change in the type of persons recruited into the Work. The archetypal prospect thus shifted from university scholar to banker, company director and public administrator, reflecting the institute's need for greater resources not only to guarantee its survival but to extend its apostolate to all of Christendom.

Escrivá de Balaguer was perfectly aware that no institution with a bunch of street sweepers as members could influence key public sectors, nor pull in the kind of income needed to achieve all that he had in mind. Opus Dei, therefore, was not interested in street sweepers and to suggest otherwise was hypocritical. Angel Herrera – a political strategist *par excellence*, who would later become a cardinal – had always stressed that the only way to make a mark on society, state or institution was by dominating its summit, advice that Escrivá de Balaguer assiduously followed. But Escrivá de Balaguer went further than Herrera, subordinating his political agenda to a cult of discretion.

'Remain silent, and you will never regret it; speak, and you often will,' was his advice in Maxim 639. Discretion can be an admirable attribute, but when developed into a cult it usually covers an aspiration for power. After moving to Rome, Escrivá de Balaguer had his eyes opened and thereafter he viewed the world differently. In Rome he saw how the Church was really run and, according to his closest collaborators, it shocked him. He realized that power came from conquering positions of influence. For Opus Dei, the source of its growing power was the access of its members to important positions, whether in education, finance or politics. Juan Bautista Torello, a leading Opus Dei ideologist, argued that the conquest of important positions was a 'typically Christian calling'.[1]

Escrivá de Balaguer, his followers would assert, lived the cardinal virtues of prudence, justice, temperance and fortitude with heroic devotion. But he also taught them that wielding influence was a more legitimate objective than adopting a policy of abstentionism, which allowed key posts to fall to people who were indifferent or even hostile to the Church.

To better fulfil its apostolate, Opus Dei's reach for influence had to be discreet so that its 'enemies' – and already it had a fair number – were kept in the dark as to its real intentions. To protect the Church, Opus Dei had to wield ecclesiastical power. For this, Escrivá de Balaguer anticipated being made a bishop. But for public consumption, his cult of discretion required an opposite expression of humility. You tell the enemy one thing, and do another. With clear conscience, the Father could therefore declare: 'I never talk politics. I do not approve of committed Christians in the world forming a political-religious movement. That would be madness, even if it were

[1] Juan Bautista Torello, *La Espiritualidad de los laicos*, Rialp, Madrid 1965, p. 35.

motivated by the desire to spread the spirit of Christ in all the activities of men'.[1]

However, Opus Dei manifestly was a politico-religious movement and Article 202 of the 1950 Constitutions proved it: 'Public office . . . constitutes a privileged means for exercising the Institute's apostolate.' In line with Article 202, some of Escrivá de Balaguer's Spanish sons were hard at work plotting the formation of a political 'Third Force' that would stand apart from Franco's Falange and the newly emerging Christian Democrats.

The Third Force was conceived by a core of Opus Dei intellectuals who were running the NSRC. More precisely, three of the Father's more agile disciples had put forward an idea for a cultural magazine that would serve not only as the mouthpiece for the NSRC's good intentions in culture and science, but also as a platform for Opus Dei's political designs. Rafael Calvo Serer, Raimundo Panikkar and Florentino Pérez-Embid brought out the first issue of *Arbor* in March 1943. As the NSRC's monthly review, *Arbor* was funded lavishly from the Council treasury and soon it became one of Spain's most prestigious publications.

Of *Arbor*'s three co-founders, Calvo Serer was the most outspoken. He had joined Opus Dei at nineteen, becoming the tenth apostle. At twenty-six he was appointed professor of history in Valencia, and later worked as director of the Spanish Institute in London. The trio's most colourful figure was Raimundo Panikkar, technically a British subject, his father being Indian and his mother Catalan. He had spent the Civil War in Germany, where his father ran an import-export business. Raimundo passed his baccalaureate in Germany and returned to Barcelona in 1940. He was then fluent in half a dozen languages and by the late 1940s he held doctorates in chemistry, philosophy and theology. This made him a valuable asset for Opus Dei. He was ordained in 1946 at the age of twenty-eight. During the 1950s he was considered Opus Dei's most provocative theologian.

In Opus Dei's structure the Archangels were made the guardians of recruiting, numeraries and supernumeraries. Each Archangel was given an intercessor, called a 'vocal', at headquarters and on regional levels. The vocal oversees the work entrusted to the Archangel he

[1] Escrivá de Balaguer, *Christ is passing by*, from the homily 'Christ the King', given on 22 November 1970, Four Courts Press, Dublin 1985, p. 245.

represents. A key person in the work of the Archangel Raphael was the eleventh apostle, Vicente Rodríguez Casado, appointed professor of modern history at Seville University in 1942. He brought into the Work more than a score of exceptionally gifted young men, among them Florentino Pérez-Embid.

Pérez-Embid had joined the Falange and saw Civil War action on the Cordoba front, being cited for bravery. In 1946 he shifted his activities to Madrid and fell under the spell of Calvo Serer, taking over as *Arbor*'s chief editor when Calvo Serer went to London. In 1949 he was given the chair of history of discovery at the University of Madrid. With Calvo Serer he co-founded Ediciones Rialp in Madrid, which became the cornerstone of Opus Dei's publishing empire.

Calvo Serer's book *España sin problema*, published by Rialp in 1949, won the first Francisco Franco National Literary Award. It and a second work, *Teoria de la Restauracion*, published by Rialp in 1952, defined an ideological platform for Opus Dei's progressive wing. Both books maintained that the basis for Spain's value system was the Catholic Church. The history of the Church and the history of Spain were interlocked. Consequently, the national tradition was a religious tradition. While Europe was faced with the dilemma of choosing between the American Dream or Sovietization, Calvo Serer and Pérez-Embid both believed that the Old Continent would be better served by a combination of German efficiency and Spanish spirituality.[1]

Calvo Serer and Pérez-Embid agreed that post-Civil War Spain presented a God-given opportunity to recreate a militant Catholicism that in the sixteenth century had brought the Spanish empire to the height of her creative success. They reasoned that with the modern world committed to godless materialism, whether Capitalist or Communist, the only way to head off catastrophe was to resume Charles V's crusade, not this time with the resources of a single nation, but through a powerful and vital transnational Catholic movement. Escrivá de Balaguer encouraged them: in his view Opus Dei had been divinely conceived as a Catholic Regenerator with worldwide reach.[2]

[1] Artigues, *L'Opus Dei en Espagne*, Editions Ruedo-ibérico, Paris 1968, p. 136.
[2] *Ibid.*, p. 140.

The development of an ideological front within Opus Dei had two consequences. First, it led to a rift among members. The progressive wing wanted Opus Dei to assume a direct political role, while the traditionalists wanted to concentrate uniquely on the spiritual lives of its members. Escrivá de Balaguer became a prisoner of his own double-speak and sat on the fence throughout most of the disruption.

Holding the wrong political view was sufficient cause for exclusion from Opus Dei. Just as obviously, the institute also held that only certain political criteria were acceptable for the divine plan. This soon became evident from the second consequence of the Third Force platform, which brought Opus Dei in Spain into direct conflict with the Falange.

The Falange was the only political party officially tolerated by Franco, but as the fuzzy tenets of its doctrine called National Syndicalism were gradually set aside other political tendencies became accepted as long as they did not seek to create a party organization. This applied mainly to the Christian Democrats and Monarchists. Until the rise of the Opus Dei technocrats, all Franco governments were delicately balanced mosaics, the main colour being Falangist blue, offset by the pale white of Franco's apolitical cronies whose loyalty went unquestioned, together with a smattering of Monarchist gold and Christian Democrat green.

The Falangists jealously guarded their position as the only legal party and regarded Opus Dei's growing political influence unfavourably. The Falangist youth movement operated a residence for students in Madrid called the Colegio César Carlos. Its lieges, all young militants, protested against the selection process for professors, claiming it favoured Opus Dei candidates. The César Carlos students took to the streets, and to make their demonstrations more biting, they composed some amusing but less than complimentary couplets or *letrillas* about Escrivá de Balaguer which immediately soared to the top of the student hit parade. In a classic rebuttal Escrivá de Balaguer called the criticism garbage and denied that his gifted sons 'would preoccupy themselves with chasing after professorships at obscure provincial universities and risk compromising their eternal salvation for a ridiculously small salary.'[1]

---

[1] Artigues, *Op. cit.*, p. 145.

The Cold War was in full gale by the late 1940s. Each new gust reconfirmed for the Father that Communism remained more than ever the Church's most serious enemy. After Cardinal Mindszenty's three-day show trial in Budapest, Pope Pius XII told the French Minister in Rome: 'The Church is now engaged in a life-and-death struggle with the Soviet Union, in which the stake is the fate of 65 million Catholics – a sixth of the world's Catholic population – living in the Soviet satellite states.'[1] Not long afterwards, the primate of Poland, Cardinal Stefan Wyszynski, was arrested.

Escrivá de Balaguer was determined to expand Opus Dei's apostolate in the fight against Marxism. But, he told his faithful, 'I don't want to make martyrs of my sons. I can't do anything with martyrs.' The missionaries he selected were ascetic young professionals trained in spiritual fortitude by himself and his apostles. He sent them into the world to work for God, or rather to do God's work, but not as ordinary missionaries. Proselytizing as practised by the Jesuits was, in his view, a concept of the past. God's work needed to be done in the boardrooms, banking halls and ministerial chambers of the secular state.

At first the numeraries and a few wealthy co-operators were alone in underwriting these efforts. Numeraries were required to hand over their salaries to the Work's general funds and they received back a small allowance. But it was always a strain to balance the books as Escrivá de Balaguer had grand tastes. Then married persons – the supernumeraries – were admitted into the Work. Their presence greatly enhanced the financial situation. The secular institute was not required to look after their physical well-being, something it was obliged to do for numeraries. Supernumeraries, on the other hand, could not be required to hand over their full salaries, as they had family obligations, and so were asked to make 'voluntary' contributions, at 10 per cent of their annual income, paid in monthly instalments. The result was not inconsequential. Due to the work of the Archangel Gabriel, capital flowed into Opus Dei's treasury like never before. That capital had to be managed. Opus Dei needed its own banks and, in a time of stringent exchange controls, a parallel financial network that permitted it to circumnavigate capital transfer restrictions.

[1] Anthony Rhodes, *The Vatican in the Age of the Cold War*, Michael Russell, 1992, p. 50.

PART THREE

PILLERIA

SPANISH ENGINEERING

If Opus Dei had ever played politics – even for a minute – I would have left the Work at that very moment of error.
Josemaría Escrivá de Balaguer, *Noticias* 1970

WITH THE VATICAN'S STAMP OF APPROVAL IN HIS PASSPORT, ESCRIVÁ de Balaguer at last felt equipped to launch Opus Dei on the most active expansion drive in its history. He expected his soldiers – his *milites Christi* – to be as catholic as the Church herself in terms of geographical reach and racial diversity, placing his *Obra* at least on an equal footing with the Jesuits and the other great religious orders, though in his heart he knew that in the long run Opus Dei, being divinely inspired, was destined to surpass them all.

In establishing a strong Catholic – i.e., Opus Dei – presence at the summit of society, Escrivá de Balaguer believed that the use of *pillería* – dirty tricks – was permissible and, indeed, frequently necessary. 'Our life is a warfare of love and in love and war all is fair.' The theory behind this reasoning was that in politics and big business the most successful practitioners resorted to devilish tactics and therefore their use should not be denied to those whose sole intention was to further the work of God.

In the next five chapters several cases of holy *pillería* will be analysed as examples of Opus Dei's evolving *modus operandi*. But first, after considering its international expansion we will examine how Opus Dei came to dominate the Spanish political establishment during Franco's last decades. Because of the strange status it had fashioned for itself – neither religious nor secular, but nevertheless God-inspired – Opus Dei was prepared to operate in spheres that no other organization of the Church would dare imagine.

As in Europe, the Founder wanted a strong Opus Dei presence in Latin America. In January 1949, the seventh apostle, Pedro Casciaro, architect and theologian, left for Mexico City with hardly any money, a ceramic portrait of Nuestra Señora del Rocío and a list of wealthy contacts. Within the next few years he built such an efficient network that Mexico became Opus Dei's third strongest power in terms of membership, after Spain and Italy.

The United States came next, although Father José Luis Múzquiz and his colleagues, Salvador Martínez Ferigle and José María González Barredo, found proselytizing in the US hard-going, the spiritual soil being relatively barren, with the result that by 1995 Opus Dei had no more than 5,000 members in the US.[1] Father Múzquiz, however, did have an introduction to the Shriver family which he put to good use. Yale graduate R. Sargent Shriver, Jr., would marry Eunice Mary Kennedy, a member of America's leading Catholic family, and would play a leading role in John Kennedy's presidential campaign, subsequently becoming the first director of the US Peace Corps. Both Eunice and her husband became active Opus Dei co-operators.

The terrain in Italy was infinitely more fertile. In one month – August 1949 – thirty Italian students asked to join and began their intensive training at a villa belonging to the Holy See near the Pope's summer residence at Castelgandolfo. Opus Dei later replaced this rather run-down building with the more opulent Villa delle Rose, a women's residence attached to the Roman College of Saint Mary.

In March 1950 it opened centres in Argentina and Chile followed in 1951 with an official presence in Venezuela and Colombia. In 1952 it opened residences in Germany, Brazil, Ecuador, Guatemala, Peru and Uruguay.

---

[1] Originally from Badajoz, Spain, Múzquiz adopted American citizenship and twice served as Opus Dei's regional vicar in the US. He died in Plymouth, Massachusetts, in 1983 at the age of 70.

International expansion generated a need for increased staff at the Opus Central headquarters in Rome. Escrivá de Balaguer had transferred from Madrid a beautiful dark-haired NSRC research assistant, María del Carmen Tapia, to become his private secretary. María del Carmen had been recruited four years before by Raimundo Panikkar and to her parents' dismay she abandoned fiancé, marriage plans and a newly purchased post-nuptial home to devote her life to Opus Dei.

When she arrived in Rome she found that not only was she required to run the Founder's secretariat but also to surpervize between eighty and ninety assistant numeraries who worked as domestics, looking after the housekeeping of the 300 to 400 male numeraries employed at the Villa Tevere. The domestic staff, living under the same vows of celibacy, poverty and obedience as other numeraries, were often required to work twelve or more hours a day without time off and no place to go as they were not allowed out on their own.

Perhaps as a result of his Civil War experiences, Escrivá de Balaguer had a fear of police, and civil authority in general. Everyone who worked at Villa Tevere had to surrender their passports to María del Carmen, and they were kept under lock and key in the Father's office, partly because they were needed in support of requests for Italian residence papers. In post-war Rome, residence permits were not easy to obtain as the number of foreigners any enterprise might employ was restricted. Opus Dei never had enough permits to go around, even though it obtained extra ones through the Congregation of Religious. The permits were issued by the police. The Father realized that María del Carmen's sparkling, slate-green eyes rendered her almost irresistible to young Italian police officers and he made her responsible for obtaining and renewing residence permits. Moreover, he insisted that on her visits to the local commissarist she take Pilar Navarro-Rubio, then head of the kitchen staff, with her – Pilar was so elegant that the tradespeople called her 'Princess' – and a couple of bottles of cognac as an innocent favour.

The Father was not only concerned about the caprices of the civil authorities. During the summer of 1951, he began to fear a plot was afoot to remove him from control of Opus Dei. As the weeks passed, his foreboding became more acute and he decided to visit the Marian shrine of Loreto, south of Ancona, to seek the Virgin's protection.

When he returned he gave orders to the kitchen staff that henceforth all his food had to be tasted in his presence before being placed on the table, a practice reminiscent of the Borgias and one he retained for the rest of his life.

In 1957, Escrivá de Balaguer was informed that the Pope wanted Opus Dei to run a newly created *prelatura nullius* in Peru so that it might test the Founder's authoritarian clerical ideas for countering the spread of Marxism in Third World countries. The Prelature of Yauyos, with its seat at Cañete, 150 kilometres south of Lima, covered a vast mountain region one-third the size of Switzerland with a population of around 300,000. The operation was supported by Adveniat, which in turn was funded by a religious tax in Germany as well as voluntary offerings from Germany's 28 million Catholics. Adveniat concentrated on aiding traditional Church work in Latin America, such as the training of priests, and became one of the biggest supporters of Opus Dei's apostolate in Latin America, providing millions of dollars each year. Politically speaking, the fund's guardian, Bishop Franz Hengsbach of Essen, was somewhere to the right of General Franco and there is no doubt that he admired Escrivá de Balaguer.

With Adveniat funds, an FM radio transmitter – Radio Estrella del Sur – was installed in Cañete to broadcast religious programmes and diocesan news. In September 1964 a second station, Radio ERPA – Escuelas Radiofónicas Populares Andinas – started broadcasting educational programmes to 300 district schools. All twenty-five of the prelature's parishes, some not served by hard-surfaced roads, became radio-linked, enabling them to exchange information and report social unrest.

Opus Dei's methodology in Yauyos was to organize secular life around the Church, which provided opportunity and employment, and put in place an educational system where previously none existed. The Church controlled the media, oversaw the enforcing of civil order and in some cases directed local investment. Above all, Opus Dei rarely employed its own funds in carrying out these works, but used whatever private or public monies that were available to it, such as grants from private foundations or institutions like Adveniat and US AID.

In October 1963, Paul VI rewarded Don Ignacio de Orbegozo – the first prelate of Yauyos – by elevating him to titular bishop of

Ariasso. By the time of his consecration, he could report to Rome that the prelature of Yauyos had thirty seminarians studying in Cañete – when there had been none before his arrival – and more than 1,000 students attending the prelature's agricultural and trade colleges. But Opus Dei's ultimate success in Peru was due to the influence that its regional vicar Manuel Botas came to exert over the papal nuncio, convincing him that the best way to counter a liberalizing Jesuit influence in the country was to entrust the most tainted dioceses to Opus Dei's care. Within a short time, another five Opus Dei priests in Peru received bishop's mitres.

Spain during these years had not been of much help in financing Opus Dei's overseas expansion as the country's economy was in crisis, and despite a ministerial reshuffle in 1951 the situation continued to deteriorate. Education, on the other hand, changed radically under its new minister, Joaquín Ruiz Giménez, a former ambassador to the Holy See. And whereas Ibáñez Martín's disappearance from the political scene – he was named ambassador to Portugal – might have seemed an insurmountable blow for Opus Dei, a new man of providence rose from Franco's *Presidencia* to replace him, giving Escrivá de Balaguer's militia even broader access to the country's highest councils. No one was closer to Franco than Admiral Carrero Blanco.

In the autumn of 1950, however, Carrero Blanco's marital problems became the talk of Franco's entourage. His wife had gone off with an American aviator, bringing the couple into disfavour with Franco's wife, Carmen, who was prudish about such things and wanted him replaced.

A thirty-year-old Opus Dei numerary, Laureano López Rodó, was helping at the time to draft Spain's Concordat with the Vatican. These delicate negotiations were overseen for Franco by Carrero Blanco. Inevitably López Rodó met Carrero Blanco and they became friends in spite of a seventeen-year age difference. They frequently dined together at Madrid's finest restaurants and one day Carrero Blanco mentioned his marital problems. López Rodó introduced Carrero Blanco to Amadeo de Fuenmayor, a law professor recently ordained an Opus Dei priest. With tact and good sense, Fuenmayor, who became Carrero Blanco's confessor, was able to restore unity to the admiral's broken marriage. Franco's wife assuaged, Carrero Blanco was promoted secretary general of the *Presidencia*. After the

Caudillo, he became the strongest man in the cabinet and remained grateful to the two Opus Dei numeraries for saving his career.

At the time a handful of senior Opus Dei members were actively conspiring to insure that post-Franco Spain would revert to a monarchy. In spite of Escrivá de Balaguer's contention that the Work would never become involved in politics the country's future political system began to take shape at a secluded Opus Dei estate in the hills of Segovia. Escrivá de Balaguer followed all aspects of the plan and he even met with the various claimants to the throne to harvest their reactions.

Opus Dei's political energies were channelled into two separate streams. The most visible, and undoubtedly the pump-primer for the constitutional changes that followed, was the so-called 'Third Force', led by the tenth apostle, Calvo Serer. But the deeper and more enduring stream began with López Rodó. A successful lawyer and law professor who practised with fervour the Opus Dei ethic of professional virtuosity, he viewed the success of whatever department he headed as a sign of his Christian perfection.

Calvo Serer and López Rodó were opposites, not only in temperament but although guided by similar goals they employed different means. Calvo Serer burned himself out relatively quickly. A dedicated technocrat, López Rodó went on to dizzying heights, leaving a lasting impact on the institutions that govern Spain. He represented everything that was noble, though elitist, in the Opus Dei ethic.

The tenth apostle launched his Third Force with the intention of promoting closer links between the monarchists and Franco; he favoured a restoration of the monarchy under Don Juan, Alfonso XIII's son who lived in exile in Portugal. López Rodó, on the other hand, preferred Don Juan's eldest son, Juan Carlos, a choice that was more palatable to Franco. In either case, a climate of confidence had to be created between the Caudillo and the official Pretender, Don Juan.

In September 1953, Calvo Serer, at some personal risk, published in Paris an article criticizing the Falange, which opposed the restoration of the monarchy, particularly under Don Juan, because his mother was English and he had sided with the Allies during the Second World War. The article called the Falange administratively incompetent, economically inefficient and totally misguided in its autarkistic beliefs. By the same measure, he branded the Christian Democrats as wishy-washy and claimed that the educational policies of Ruiz Giménez lacked cohesion. He set forth a Third Force platform based on tighter controls over public spending, decentralized government, a more liberal economy and 'representative' monarchy. The article caused a furore.[1]

For the first time a public figure known to belong to Opus Dei had adopted a political stance. Inside the secular institute there was criticism of Calvo Serer's intentions. Some feared they might compromise the Work's canonical status.

Clearly Opus Dei was not interested in traditional power politics – i.e., the political system *per se*, with its party structure, special interests and alliances. But it was interested in the politics of its own apostolate – *that Christ may reign in every aspect of human endeavour*. This, of course, was coloured by its vision of how Christ should reign, which was not necessarily the same as everyone else's vision, nor even the vision of every other Catholic.

In the end, Franco ignored the Third Force, and Calvo Serer passed into political limbo. Franco's confidence went instead to López Rodó.

The Concordat with the Vatican was signed in August 1953. It ended Spain's diplomatic isolation. But Franco had to pay a price. The Church was exempted from taxation and given grants with which to construct new churches. Her bishops acquired the right to demand that publications found offensive be withdrawn from sale, while diocesan publications were freed from state censorship. The Concordat also gave the Church the right to found universities and for this reason it was as important to Opus Dei as it was to Franco.

As education minister, Ruiz Giménez blocked Opus Dei from acquiring further influence over higher education – by the early 1950s one-third of all university departments in Spain were headed by Opus Dei members. Escrivá de Balaguer, therefore, decided to found Opus Dei's own university: the Estudio General de Navarra in Pamplona. To begin with it only had a law faculty and, under a 1949 law governing independent institutions of higher learning, was

---

[1] Calvo Serer's article, *La Politique Intérieure de l'Espagne de Franco*, appeared in the September 1953 issue of the right-wing *Ecrits de Paris*.

not entitled to issue degrees. This problem was solved by attaching it to the University of Saragossa. It soon opened a medical school, followed by arts and science and journalism faculties.

As soon as Franco signed the Concordat, Opus Dei moved to transform the Estudio General into a pontifical university. But 'insurmountable difficulties' were raised to bar its way to a papal charter and the project was only saved by the new nuncio, Monsignor Ildebrando Antoniutti. He was so pro-Opus that he could have been a member. His entire staff, from chauffeur to cleaning ladies, was reported to be Opus Dei and the joke circulated in Madrid that he was not the apostolic nuncio but the *opustolic nuncio*.[1] Escrivá de Balaguer took it for granted that, with Antoniutti in charge, the Holy See's approval would be forthcoming and he began referring to Estudio General as the University of Navarra shortly after the new nuncio's arrival in Madrid.

During the lobbying for Navarra's pontifical charter a miracle occurred at the Villa Tevere for which the medical fraternity had no explanation. The Founder's diabetes had become progressively worse in spite of the daily insulin injections. Some days he would be unable to stand up. Sight in his right eye was failing. He was forbidden the use of the discipline and cilice because they provoked skin irritations that easily became infected. He had a bell installed by his bedside so that he could call for the last sacraments during the night.

On Tuesday, 27 April 1954 – the feast day of Our Lady of Montserrat – the Father was seated at the dinner table in his private dining room when he passed out. 'Something very peculiar happened,' explained Don Alvaro. 'He changed colour instantly: first a deep red, then a purplish colour, and finally a kind of tawny yellow. Above all, he seemed to dwindle and shrink, slumping over to the side.'[2]

Don Alvaro gave him absolution and then called for the doctor. To counterbalance the effect of the insulin, he put some sugar in the Father's mouth. By the time the doctor arrived, the Father had regained consciousness. He was unable to see for several hours. But with the return of his sight, he was no longer diabetic. He had been cured of the illness that had accompanied him for more than ten

[1] Yvon Le Vaillant, *Sainte Maffia – Le Dossier de l'Opus Dei*, Mercure de France, Paris 1971, p. 181.
[2] Vázquez de Prada, *Op. cit.*, p. 278.

years. Soon after his cure, people started calling him the 'Miracle Priest'. As Don Alvaro remarked, a reason exists for everything. 'Nothing falls outside divine Providence.'[1]

What finally propelled the Opus Dei technocrats into power in Spain were the January 1957 worker riots in Barcelona. They highlighted the worsening economic situation. Inflation was out of control and Spain's balance of payments was disastrous. The country was a victim of chronic overspending, encouraged by a lack of ministerial controls, and no coherent monetary or fiscal policy. In an effort to head off a moratorium on foreign payments and a massive devaluation, Franco ordered a cabinet restructuring that marked one of the great watersheds of Opus Dei's development.

The architect of the restructuring was López Rodó. His recommendations sounded the death knell of the Falange. After the July 1957 changes, the Falange retained but three minor ministries – labour, housing and the portfolio of the Falange Movement itself – while three anti-Falangists were placed in the key portfolios of interior, foreign affairs and army. And then came the Opus Dei technocrats, interested not in playing politics at all but in integrating Spain into the European economy. Thanks to Opus Dei – or at least to López Rodó – Spain found herself, without realizing it, in the process of leaving the ranks of world dictatorships.

López Rodó announced that the new government's first objective was a minimum annual wage of $1,000 for every working citizen. 'If we are able to achieve this, the rest – social and political – will follow quite naturally,' he predicted.[2]

Who were the Opus Dei technocrats preparing to modernize Spain? Mariano Navarro-Rubio became finance minister. A 43-year-old Aragonese lawyer from Teruel, he had fought with distinction on the Nationalist side during the Civil War, and was three times wounded. Competent, hard-working, he was also on the board of Banco Popular Español and was one of the architects of that bank's spectacular growth. He would be credited with giving Spain a stable monetary policy.

The new Minister of Commerce was numerary Alberto Ullastres, also forty-three, professor of political economy and deputy governor

---

[1] *Ibid.*, p. 278.
[2] Ernest Milcent, 'Ainsi Naquit Opus Dei,' *Notre Histoire* No. 46, Paris 1988.

of the Spanish Mortgage Bank. He had studied in France and Germany, and fought with the Nationalist forces on the Asturian front. López Rodó, Navarro-Rubio and Ullastres worked together as a team and they brought other Opus Dei technocrats into key government positions.

Soon after the new cabinet was announced, Opus Dei's Spanish headquarters issued a statement denying the institute's involvement in politics. 'Its activities are directly and exclusively apostolic and because of its dedicated spirituality it is not involved in the politics of any country.'[1] Strictly speaking, that was true. Opus Dei was not a political party and had no pretensions of becoming one. Nevertheless it did have political goals – however well hidden – that were consistent with its spiritual beliefs and role as Catholic Regenerator. And its members, whether government ministers or company directors, were subjected to a degree of spiritual guidance far more encompassing than required of any other Catholic lay person – extending, as will be shown in Chapter 16, to 'all professional, social and other questions'.[2]

Political considerations aside, the Opus Dei ethic was soon to pay real dividends for the Spanish people. During the fifteen years from 1960 to 1975, a period referred to as the *años de desarrollo* – the years of development – Spain's economy grew faster than any other, except Japan. Average annual income would attain López Rodó's magic benchmark of $1,000 annually by 1968. When Spain's first economic miracle ended in the mid-1970s, due to a world economic slump rather than her own economic shortcomings, she was ranked as the world's ninth industrial power. In 1957, one in every hundred Spaniards owned a car. By the end of the 1960s, the figure was one in ten. Almost every home had a telephone and more than half had washing machines and refrigerators. By the mid-1970s, illiteracy had dropped to under 10 per cent, and the student population had doubled. The important change, however, was in expectations. Surveys showed that workers could expect much better jobs, in terms of pay and prestige, in the 1970s than their fathers had known. And so it could be said that, largely thanks to Opus Dei, by the early 1970s Spain had become part of the modern European economy. With wealth came corruption.

[1] *El Correo Catalan*, Barcelona, 13 July 1957.
[2] Reference to Article 58 of the 1950 Constitutions.

THE MATESA SCANDAL

Don't be afraid of the truth, even though the truth may mean your death.

Maxim 34, *The Way*

OPUS DEI'S FIRST REPORTED USE OF *PILLERÍA* IN FINANCIAL MATTERS involved the Matesa scandal. As a result of fraud a large sum of money disappeared, never to be traced, and two bankers directly or indirectly involved in Matesa's operations lost their lives. Publicly, Opus Dei denied it was involved with Matesa, but privately members were reported to have joked about the operation, inferring that the movement's coffers were enriched by the misdealings. Two things can be said for certain: Spanish ratepayers were ultimately handed the bill; and the person who took the blame for the scandal eventually received a royal pardon. His name was Juan Vilá Reyes. He was one of the first graduates of IESE (the Instituto de Estudios Superiores de la Empresa), Opus Dei's prestigious business administration school in Barcelona.

In July 1956, Vilá Reyes founded a technical support company for the textile industry. He called it Maquinaria Textil del Norte de España Sociedad Anónima, which he shortened to Matesa. During the late 1950s, 'technology' and 'technocracy' had become buzz words in Spain. Vilá Reyes was quick to see that a corporation dealing in 'hi-tech' and directed by outward-looking 'technocrats' offered high potential in a country that was hungry for export successes. He doted Matesa with a capital of $80,000, only a small portion of which was paid in, against the issue of 200,000 shares, held in majority by himself as managing director. His brother Fernando, their sister Blanca, and brother-in-law Manuel Salvat Dalmau were the other shareholders. The next step was to learn how to become a technocrat. And so in October 1958 he signed up for IESE's top management programme. At this point he was not even a co-operator of Opus Dei, although his brother-in-law and sister were supernumeraries.

A slight digression is necessary to understand what follows. Opus Dei's success was and remains dependent upon its ability to recruit new members. Recruitment, however, is not a word that Opus Dei likes. It maintains that people are not recruited into the Work at all. Rather, they *ask* to join in recognition of a God-given vocation that guides them to dedicate their lives to the apostolate. Nevertheless, in spite of efforts to keep the troops fully committed, a constant erosion of members due to natural causes or disillusionment requires expansion-minded Opus Dei actively to seek new members. It has over the decades developed a recruiting structure which is surprisingly efficient. Not just anyone is targeted, nor accepted. Rather like a tennis club, 'new members might ask to join. But they have to be compatible with the club's aims. If they're only interested in chess or learning to rumba, they would be out of place and therefore there is no sense in accepting them,' a member commented.

A dossier prepared by former numerary John Roche examines Opus Dei's recruiting procedures in some detail. A certain awareness of Opus Dei vocabulary, however, is necessary. 'Proselytism' is synonymous with 'recruiting', even if the targets are fellow Catholics. 'Winning vocations', means 'bringing in new members'. In his analysis, Roche states:

The single most important activity in the life of a member of Opus Dei is recruitment or 'proselytism'. The Founder, Monsignor Escrivá, emphasized this repeatedly:

We do not have any other aim than the corporate one: prose-lytism, winning vocations . . . Proselytism in the Work is precisely the road, the way to reach sanctity. When a person does not have zeal to win others . . . he is dead . . . I bury cadavers. [*Crónica* V, 1963]

[G]o out to the highways and byways and push those whom you find to come and fill my house, force them to come in; push them . . . we must be a little crazy . . . You must kill yourselves for proselytism . . . [*Crónica* IV, 1971]

None of my children can rest satisfied if he doesn't win four or five faithful vocations each year. [*Crónica* VII, 1968]

. . . Every member is supposed to have at least fifteen 'friends', five of whom at any moment are being 'worked on' actively to 'whistle'. Effort and success in proselytism is tied so closely to sanctification that it often becomes the single most important source of spiritual anxiety for the less successful. The obligation to win recruits is stern and unrelenting.

. . . Opus Dei's publicly known corporate enterprises are dedicated to proselytism. According to the Founder, 'University residences, universities, publishing houses . . . are these ends? No, and what of the end? Well, it is two-fold. On the one hand, personal sanctity. And on the other, to promote in the world the greatest possible number of souls dedicated to God in Opus Dei . . .' [*Crónica* V, 1963]

The primary purpose, therefore, of all of Opus Dei's schools, hostels, clubs, cultural centres, catering colleges, pre-university courses, summer schools and international gatherings is the recruitment into Opus Dei of those who attend. Members are frequently reminded privately of this priority, but publicly the Founder insisted that its corporate activities are primarily 'a disinterested service to humanity'. Because of this, these activities are frequently supported by public money.[1]

The IESE to which Vilá Reyes was admitted in 1958 had been founded that same year by two numeraries as an extension of their apostolate. They obtained a grant of $50,000 from the Banco

---

[1] John J. Roche, 'Winning Recruits in Opus Dei: A Personal Experience', *The Clergy Review* No. 10, London, October 1985.

Popular Español. IESE was attached to the University of Navarra and later aligned its syllabus with the Harvard Business School, with which it became associated. Some of Opus Dei's best cadres have over the years been formed at IESE, but also many of Spain's top business executives. But it had a hidden objective. Upon graduation, students became tracked in their professional careers – and assisted if deemed appropriate – so that directly or indirectly they became associated with the Work. Some slipped away, of course, but most willingly and even enthusiastically participated in the process without thought as to whether they were being used. It was all very convivial, with nothing so crude as pressure ever being applied; after all, they were encouraged to believe that they belonged to an élite executive club. One early graduate, for example, was Spain's future ambassador to Moscow, Juan Antonio Samaranch, who, when he became head of the international Olympic movement in the 1980s, transformed it into a vast money-spinning enterprise, according to the 'Christian and scientific principles' he learned at the IESE. And then there were the ambitious few, aware of what Opus Dei expected of them, who played the game to the hilt, exploiting the contacts it gave them. Vilá Reyes was one of these.

The contacts acquired by Vilá Reyes during his year at the IESE enabled him to accelerate Matesa's development. After graduation, he retained as legal counsel José Luis Villar Palasí, a multilingual attorney with offices in Madrid. Villar Palasí was closely linked to Opus Dei, though the Work asserts that he was never a member nor even a co-operator.[1] In 1962, the Minister of Commerce, Opus Dei numerary Alberto Ullastres, appointed Villar Palasí as his under-secretary. This meant that for the next six years Vilá Reyes never looked back. A multitude of doors opened for his 'hi-tech' company whose only sophisticated technology was its telex machine and an electric typewriter.

Matesa acquired – one is not quite sure how – a French patent for an industrial loom. The patent cost all of $12,000.[2] The loom was known as the Iwer, no doubt after its inventor. Vilá Reyes hyped its technical novelties. He said it was revolutionary because, shuttleless, it could weave virtually any type of material from silk to fibreglass.

[1] Opus Dei UK Information Office, 30 October 1994.
[2] Le Vaillant, *Op. cit.*, p. 345 (The sum mentioned is 500,000 pesetas), converted at 42 pesetas to the dollar.

A prototype was shown at the 1959 Milan Industrial Fair, where it aroused modest interest.

Villar Palasí introduced his client to Laureano López Rodó. They became friends. López Rodó introduced him to the Opusian banker Juan José Espinosa San Martín, who in July 1965 took over from Mariano Navarro-Rubio as Minister of Finance. Navarro-Rubio was named Governor of the Bank of Spain.

With the Iwer patent and an IESE diploma, Vilá Reyes was able to obtain sufficient credit to build an assembly plant in Pamplona. In Barcelona, Matesa installed a research department that employed several hundred technicians. Then began the search for export markets. While the fabulous Iwer was being presented to potential buyers in the US, Latin America and Europe, López Rodó introduced Spain's first Five-Year Economic Development Plan. An important aspect of the plan was the stimulus it gave exporters by introducing a mix of fiscal enticements and state subsidies.

Matesa was said to have an 'export vocation'. Juan Vilá Reyes went to the state trough and came back with warehousing loans, discounting for its bills of exchange, and a revolving credit to help finance its export orders. It was a game. Against the outlay of state funds, Vilá Reyes sent donations to IESE, the University of Navarra, and some of the Work's educational projects abroad. But Spain was still in the grips of foreign exchange controls.

Rather than exporting the fabulous Iwer, a subsequent public enquiry revealed that Matesa apparently exported much of its state funding. Vilá Reyes set up a maze of foreign convenience companies, many of them in the Swiss canton of Fribourg, lenient in its taxation of locally domiciled holding companies. Finance minister Espinosa San Martín had excellent contacts with the Giscard d'Estaing family in Paris, and with Prince Jean de Broglie, a co-founder of the Giscardian Independent Republican party. Valéry Giscard d'Estaing was elected to the French National Assembly in 1956, the year that Matesa was founded. In January 1962, General de Gaulle appointed Giscard as his minister of finance. Though replaced in 1966, he remained in the wings of the Elysée Palace, waiting to serve as a future president of the Fifth Republic.

Prince Jean de Broglie was the man who kept Giscard's political agenda up to date. Senator and member of the National Assembly's foreign affairs committee, he was a successful financier, with extensive contacts in the right-wing pan-European movement. In 1967, Giscard d'Estaing sent Jean de Broglie on a mission to Madrid. The exact nature of the mission is not known. But during de Broglie's stay in the Spanish capital, he was introduced to Juan Vilá Reyes.

Whatever the reason for the Madrid meeting, when de Broglie returned to Paris he gave instructions to an assistant, Raoul de Léon, to create for Matesa a holding company in Luxemburg, Sodetex S.A., with a paid-in capital of 1 million French francs ($170,000). The capital was transferred to a Sodetex account in Luxemburg by Brélic S.A., Fribourg, a Matesa subsidiary. Chairman of Sodetex was Prince Jean de Broglie, and Robert Leclerc, the head and principal shareholder of Banque de l'Harpe (which became Banque Leclerc) in Geneva, was one of the board members.

By June 1968, Matesa's capital had increased to $2.4 million. Now a multinational enterprise, it was touted as a showcase of the new Spain's entrepreneurial spirit. But sales of the Iwer loom were never what they were purported to be. It was a delicate machine, over-priced and, plagued by production problems, delivery was uncertain. In Spain, purchasers of the loom could be counted on the fingers of one hand. Sales abroad were overstated. A consignment of Iwer looms, supposedly destined for New York, was found abandoned on the docks of Barcelona. The head of customs who uncovered the fraud, Victor Castro Sanmartín, was an Opus Dei member.[1] He probably did not realize the significance of Matesa for the financial arm of Opus Dei, given the institute's penchant for internal secrecy that was every bit as strong as its external secrecy, and he filed a detailed report with his superior, the Minister of Finance. A copy of that report landed on the desk of Manuel Fraga Iribarne, the Minister of Information. Fraga was the senior Falange member in the cabinet, opposed to the influence wielded by the Opus Dei technocrats.

The Falange had been watching Matesa's growth and wanted revenge after its humiliation by the Opus Dei technocrats in the 1957 cabinet reshuffle. The surviving Falange ministers saw in Castro Sanmartín's report an opportunity to break Opus Dei's hold over key government portfolios. In the summer of 1969 the Falange unleashed a press campaign that hinted Matesa's

[1] Santiago Aroca, 'Opus IV – The Occult Children – Politicians, Military, Secret Agents', *Tiempo* No. 219, Madrid, 21 July 1986.

foreign orders were a ruse to qualify for export credits.

Matesa's Luxemburg subsidiary, Sodetex, was planning to launch a 15 million Swiss franc ($3.6 million) debenture issue through Banque Leclerc in Geneva. But the anti-Matesa press campaign finally spread to the foreign media and in August 1969 the debenture offering was cancelled. The negative publicity also killed, according to Vilá Reyes, outstanding orders for the Iwer loom.

Until then Franco ignored the scandal. When the Falange Movement minister José Solís Ruiz personally complained to him that the Opus Dei ministers were not 'perfect gentlemen', the Caudillo remarked curtly: 'What have you got against the Opus? Because while they work you just fuck about.'[1]

By September 1969 the brouhaha over Matesa had become too much for even Franco. He was particularly infuriated by the foreign publicity. Vilá Reyes and his brother were arrested. Investigators quickly found the company insolvent. But Matesa had acquired $180 million in government export financing. Where had the money gone? Espinosa San Martín and Fausto García Moncó, another Opus Dei banker who replaced Alberto Ullastres in 1965 as minister of commerce, did not have an answer. They resigned. Nevertheless Franco was not appeased, though ironically he did not direct his anger against Opus Dei. He was upset with the two Falange ministers Fraga and Solís as they had permitted the media to reflect the reality of Spain in the 1960s – a country that was 'politically stagnant, economically monopolistic and socially unjust.'[2]

Rumours abounded of a ministerial bloodletting. It was widely believed that Opus Dei's influence in government was on the wane and that Franco, fed up with the intrigues, would remove the technocrats altogether. But Franco had grown tired of the Falange and instead it was the technocrats who triumphed.

Madrid was stunned when state television interrupted its evening programme on 29 October 1969 to announce the new cabinet. Of the nineteen ministers, ten were Opus Dei members or co-operators. They were led by López Rodó (Economic Development), Gregorio López Bravo (Foreign Affairs), Enrique Fontana Codina (Commerce) and Alfredo Sánchez Bella (Information and Tourism).

Of the remainder, five were said to be close to Opus, among them

[1] Preston, *Op. cit.*, p. 745n.
[2] *Ibid.*, p. 745.

José Luis Villar Palasí (Education and Science) and Alberto Monreal Luque (Finance). Three others were known to work with Opus Dei. That left only the Prime Minister, Luis Carrero Blanco, and everyone knew where his sympathies lay. López Rodó was portrayed as the architect of this velvet 'coup d'état'. Although Carrero Blanco was prime minister, it was really López Rodó's government. But others said that the new king maker was Luis Valls Taberner, a monk-like and enigmatic Opus Dei numerary who was Banco Popular Español's deputy chairman. Valls Taberner and López Rodó lived in the same Opus Dei residence in Madrid.

The new government named a commission of enquiry. It found that most of the missing loot had been transferred abroad. It also disclosed that Matesa's network of foreign companies had made some grants to the University of Navarra, and one relatively small contribution to President Nixon's re-election campaign. Other monies were paid to Vilá Reyes's alma mater in Barcelona, the IESE. Not mentioned in the commission's report, and vehemently denied by an Opusian vocal, were rumours that substantial indirect payments had been made to Opus Dei through its 'auxiliary societies'.

A spokesman stated: 'Opus Dei received no donations whatever from Matesa. Vilá Reyes did make some *personal* donations over several years to the IESE business school. These totalled 2 million pesetas (£12,000) and were well documented. The charge that he gave 2,400 million pesetas (£14 million) to various Opus Dei institutions in Spain, Peru and the United States is absolutely false.'[1]

The denial is an interesting example of Opus Dei's bending the truth. It began with, 'It is important to note that Juan Vilá Reyes . . . and his legal adviser, José Luis Villar Palasí, were not members of Opus Dei . . .' This may have been true, but Juan Vilá's sister and brother-in-law were both members of Opus Dei and shareholders of Matesa. Moreover the Opus Dei denial neglected to mention that another Opus Dei supernumerary, Angel de las Cuevas, undersecretary of industry in the Finance Ministry and deputy chairman of the Banco de Crédito Industrial, the state bank that accorded the export financing to Matesa, was charged with complicity in the fraudulent scheme.

Perhaps more telling, a former Opus Dei budget director

[1] William O'Connor, *Opus Dei – An Open Book*, Mercier Press, Dublin 1991, p. 139.

confirmed privately that 'my office only received *minor* contributions from Matesa'.[1] Needless to say, there is a difference between a categorical 'no contributions' and 'minor contributions'. But even this does not represent the full story because the budget director was the first to point out that international transfers did not pass through his office. They were handled by Dr Rafael Termes Carrero, at the time regional director of Banco Popular Español in Barcelona. Rafael Termes was very close to Luis Valls, and it was Termes who set up the Andorra by-pass, engineering the acquisition of Credit Andorra, on whose board of directors he sat. Credit Andorra was the principality's largest and most active commercial bank. It was acquired in 1955 with Banco Popular's assistance by an Opus Dei auxiliary company called Esfina.[2]

By the late 1950s, with an economic upswing underway, Spain was financing almost half of Opus Dei's world-wide operations, and Andorra – which had no exchange controls – acted as one of the staging centres for the exported funds. They were collected there and redirected to the money-market centres where funds were most needed – in general, Frankfurt, London or Zurich. If money was going to Rome, the Villa Tevere was informed by Madrid in a coded message that, for example, 'fifteen collections left today'. A 'collection' equalled $1,000, so that fifteen collections meant that $15,000 was en route from Credit Andorra to Opus Dei's account with the IOR (the Vatican bank).

Opus Dei never disclosed whether it received, directly or indirectly, any payments from Matesa's Luxemburg subsidiary, Sodetex, or from any of Matesa's other foreign affiliates. Sodetex went into liquidation soon after the scandal erupted. Sodetex's role in the disappearance of the $180 million was never investigated. The Spanish receivers claimed that Sodetex owed Matesa only $1 million, a rather paltry sum compared to the $179 million that still remained unaccounted for.

The state prosecutors found tracks that led to Andorra for a small amount of the missing money. In October 1967, a special court for exchange control violations found Juan Vilá Reyes and one of his employees guilty of illegally exporting $2.5 million through the principality. The money, in bundles of 1,000 peseta notes, was taken

[1] Francisco José de Saralegui, Madrid, 24 February 1995.
[2] Ynfante, *Op. cit.*, p. 249.

by car from Madrid or Barcelona to Andorra where it was deposited with the Credit Andorra. The court concluded that the money went from Andorra to Switzerland.[1]

Vilá Reyes's recompense was a few months in prison, many more months under house arrest and millions of pesetas in legal fees. He was financially ruined. In May 1975, he was sentenced to three years in prison. But six months later, Franco passed away and Prince Juan Carlos became head of state. One of the future king's first acts was to pardon the champion exporter.

For Prince Jean de Broglie the recompense was the Lord's vengeance. In 1974, after long negotiations, he agreed to repay the $1 million which the Spanish liquidators claimed Sodetex owed Matesa. The terms of the agreement stated that the money with interest would be returned in two annual instalments, beginning on 15 November 1975. But when the first instalment fell due, Prince de Broglie reneged. Forty-four days after the due date for the second instalment, Jean de Broglie was gunned down in a Paris street by a professional hitman.

In May 1977, Banque Leclerc in Geneva was ordered into liquidation. Days later, the bank's general manager, Frenchman Charles Bouchard, fell into Lake Geneva, not far from his front door, and drowned. According to his widow, he was an excellent swimmer and in good health. Twenty years later, she still maintains that her husband was murdered.

One of the lawyers in what became known as *l'Affaire de Broglie* was Roland Dumas, who served as a foreign minister during François Mitterand's presidency. Dumas asked the investigating magistrate handling the de Broglie case to look into the connections between Sodetex and Matesa, which until then had been covered up. Dumas focused on whether the French police report on de Broglie's murder had purposely glossed over the links between the prince and Matesa.

'A more probing investigation would have shown that Matesa was an instrument of Opus Dei, whose tentacles stretch everywhere in western Europe. No investigation of this connection was undertaken in the criminal information [against Matesa's management] opened in Madrid or Luxembourg. The reason no doubt resides in the evident links that exist between Opus Dei and the political

[1] *Ibid.*, p. 250.

party of the Independent Republicans whose principal leaders were the friends of Prince de Broglie,' Dumas told a French journalist.[1]

Robert Leclerc was charged in Geneva with fraud in connection with the collapse of his bank. At trial, his attorneys claimed that a stroke had deprived Leclerc of his ability to speak. In spite of remaining mute, he was convicted and served a light sentence in a prison hospital. Released, he miraculously recovered his voice, but never disclosed what had gone wrong inside Banque Leclerc. He died of old age in 1993.

In spite of the Matesa setback, Opus Dei continued to develop its financial network outside Spain. The Matesa affair had provided an important lesson. Opus Dei theologians view the world through the tinted spectacles of Christian fundamentalists. They believe that Christ was crucified and rose again to break the stranglehold of evil so that the world might be fashioned anew, according to God's design. For Opus Dei, God's design extends to all mankind.

Bearing this in mind, Opus Dei members believe strongly that God spoke to Moses, and also to Escrivá de Balaguer, but that money speaks to the world. Opus Dei was out to build an earthly empire to the glory of God. Opus Dei's strategists realized this required a vast amount of capital – more than any Church body, royal house or banking empire had ever assembled. Just as important, Opus Dei's strategists are not stupid people, enclosed in a world of incense and icons. The Father and his apostles had recruited into the Work some of Spain's brightest lights. By the 1960s, they were doing the same throughout Europe and farther afield, the Work by then being present in almost thirty countries.

For the first time, a handful of dedicated people, most of them Spaniards, began to chart how to harness the financial establishment and the monetary system to spread the Good News. They were fashioning a holy conspiracy. Opus Dei has no financial apostolate? Opus Dei undermines its credibility by maintaining that it lives from Divine Providence, as if it received financial manna from Heaven. In this respect a professor at the University of Madrid made me aware of something I have called the 'Law of Financial Hegemony'.

'Opus Dei's hierarchy knows very well that money rules the world and that religious hegemony in a country or a continent is dependent

---

[1] Thierry Oberlé, *L'Opus Dei – Dieu ou César*, J-C. Lattès, Paris 1993, p. 220.

upon obtaining financial hegemony,' affirmed Javier Sainz Moreno.

If this is accepted, then much of what transpired on the economic and financial fronts during the next twenty-five years – from the demise of Matesa to the forced winding up of an Opus Dei auxiliary operation known as the Fundación General Mediterránea – can be explained by this 'law' when applied to the Work's main apostolate, which, according to *Crónica*, is to 'fulfil a command of Christ, who tells us, "Go forth into all the world and preach the gospel to all creatures" . . . the marvellous seeding of sanctity *in all the environments of the world.*'[1]

Opus Dei's corporate aims, according to Professor Sainz Moreno, were, first, to control the Vatican finances in order to control the Vatican itself, and, second, to achieve the largest degree of financial hegemony wherever possible. But for God's Work to succeed on the scale that Escrivá de Balaguer's lieutenants envisaged, a way of generating and deploying stateless capital had to be developed.

The most fruitful field for generating odourless capital is international trade. Hidden profits can be easily created through the transfer of goods and services between countries with different fiscal and legal systems. Matesa's foreign transfers had shown that. Physical transfer across frontiers of suitcases stuffed with banknotes was outmoded. New methods were devised through the drafting of international contracts that transferred profits, commissions or brokerage to distant jurisdictions for warehousing. From these warehouses the monies could then be shunted about, putting resources to work where they were most needed. About this time, Opus Dei was becoming one of the largest players in the Eurodollar market – a market that experienced exponential growth in the 1960s and 1970s.

When it moves into a new country, Opus Dei's secular arm concentrates on developing foreign trade outlets – especially between states where Escrivá de Balaguer's children are already well placed in government. Thus when Opus Dei opened a new centre in India in 1993, a Spanish wool merchant was one of the numeraries sent to Delhi with the intention of establishing a trading company for operations between India and Europe. In this light, one understands how important the Matesa experiment was. In a sense, Matesa's demise marked the beginning of a new era of growth.

[1] 'Freedom and Proselytism', *Crónica* VIII, 1959 (emphasis added).

VATICAN II

In my life I have known several popes, many cardinals, a multitude of bishops. But on the other hand, Founders of Opus Dei, there is only one!

Josemaría Escrivá de Balaguer, *Crónica* I, 1971

DURING HIS YEARS IN ROME, ESCRIVÁ DE BALAGUER DEVELOPED A highly idiosyncratic view of the papacy. He held Pius X, the Pope of his childhood, in high esteem, considering him the fairest Pontiff of modern times. He never forgave Pius XII for three times refusing him a bishop's mitre, and intensely disliked him because of it.

When Angelo Roncalli, Patriarch of Venice, was elected the new Pope in October 1958, he surprised everyone by taking the name of John, which no Pope had used in more than 600 years. His next surprise followed almost immediately when he removed his biretta, the red skull cap of a cardinal, and placed it upon the head of Alberto Di Jorio, who had been secretary of the Conclave but also was head of the Vatican bank. This act instantly raised Di Jorio to the cardinalate.

The world knew relatively little about the 76-year-old Roncalli. He was the third of thirteen children from a frugal Bergamo farming family. Most of his ecclesiastic career had been spent in the Vatican

139

diplomatic service in places like Romania and Turkey, and as nuncio in Paris. Only Opus Dei remembered that in July 1954, the year after becoming Patriarch of Venice, Roncalli had made a pilgrimage to Saragossa and Santiago de Compostela. In both cities he stayed in Opus Dei residences. This indicated that the kindly patriarch was certainly familiar with some of the more open aspects of the secular institute.

Opus Dei, however, was far from John XXIII's concerns. His first priority was to rejuvenate the College of Cardinals. Within days of his coronation he distributed another twenty-three red hats. His list included the first cardinals ever for the Philippines, Japan, Mexico and Africa. At the top of the list were Giovanni Battista Montini, by then Archbishop of Milan, and Domenico Tardini, whom John asked to become his secretary of state. A year later, he added to the list Opus Dei's former friend, the 72-year-old Arcadio Larraona.

In January 1959, John XXIII announced that he would convene the first Ecumenical Council in ninety years. Within weeks, a committee was formed under Cardinal Tardini, Opus Dei's protector in the Curia. He named Opus Dei's secretary general, Alvaro del Portillo, chairman of one of the sub-commissions. Nevertheless Escrivá de Balaguer had to wait almost eighteen months for his first audience with the new Pope. The audience lasted less than thirty minutes. The Father, accompanied by Don Alvaro, wished to explain to John that Opus Dei no longer felt at ease in the clothing of a secular institute. In ten years it had grown from 3,000 to 30,000 members, including 307 priests. The Spanish prelates proposed that Opus Dei should be transformed into a prelature nullius. This would have given Escrivá de Balaguer the mitre he so cherished.

Pope John was puzzled by Opus Dei. He did not reply to the request for almost two years – another snub of major proportions. In May 1962, he finally had Cardinal Amleto Cicognani, who had taken over as secretary of state after Tardini's unexpected death, inform Opus Dei's founder that transforming the institute into a prelature nullius would present 'almost insurmountable juridical and practical difficulties' and therefore the request was denied.[1]

Within three weeks, Escrivá de Balaguer was inside the papal apartments, making known his 'profound disappointment'. Since the

---

[1] De Fuenmayor *et al.*, *Op. cit.*, p. 422.

previous year one of his leading experts in canon law, Professor Pedro Lombardía Díaz of the University of Navarra, had been working on defining a 'floating diocese' that possessed most of the characteristics of what later became known as a personal prelature. Papa Roncalli counselled patience as the Second Vatican Council would begin its work that autumn, and one of the items on the agenda was the creation of a new legal structure for mixed lay and religious organizations like Opus Dei. Escrivá de Balaguer was not pleased and came away from the meeting with what some former children have described as 'a profound dislike' of Pope John. Thereafter in moments of anger he referred to Roncalli as 'a peasant with body odour'.[1]

One of Escrivá de Balaguer's closest collaborators at this time[2] reported that the Founder was obsessed by the notion that popes could be chosen from outside the College of Cardinals and raised to Peter's throne by acclamation. His seventh apostle, Pedro Casciaro, was convinced that this could occur and confided to a member of the Spanish hierarchy that the next Conclave might produce a major surprise. Because of his age, Roncalli was regarded as a transitionary pope whose reign would be short.

Three years into John XXIII's pontificate, Escrivá de Balaguer sought to establish closer contact with the outspoken Cardinal Giuseppe Siri of Genoa. He knew that Siri, one of the electors of John XXIII, regretted that he had helped place the rotund Roncalli on the papal throne. Escrivá de Balaguer wanted Siri to know that they shared similar concerns. He was convinced that, in the name of reform, evil forces were eroding the Church from within and he saw in Siri a potential ally in stopping the decay.

Siri's archdiocese of Genoa, with one million Catholics, was one of the richest in Christendom. He had established an administrative section to manage its finances, placing the archiepiscopal treasury under the direction of a young mutual fund salesman, Orazio Bagnasco, who was later adopted as one of Giulio Andreotti's protégés. Andreotti, Siri and the two Spanish prelates considered John XXIII's diplomatic opening to the Communist world as dangerous. Siri began describing Pope John's pontificate as 'the greatest disaster

---

[1] Interview with Peter Hebblethwaite, Oxford, 5 October 1993.
[2] Antonio Pérez Hernández.

in recent ecclesiastical history'. By 'recent', Peter Hebblethwaite claimed, Siri meant the last 500 years.[1] Siri and Escrivá de Balaguer were said to view the Second Vatican Council as an unnecessary sideshow destined to complicate the work of the Pope's successor.

Getting Vatican II under way was no easy task. Papa Roncalli made it clear that he intended to open its doors to all religions – a revolutionary step. Pope John would also turn the procedural rules upside down.

Pope John's opening address to the Council explained Vatican II's purpose: to ensure that 'the sacred deposit of Christian doctrine – the common patrimony of all mankind – be preserved and taught in a more effective way . . .' But Roncalli had no plan. It was Montini who offered a plan. He proposed that the Council focus on one theme: the nature of the Church and her *aggiornamento* (renovation) in preparation for the third millennium. The Council fathers were called upon to consider the roles of the Church's constituents: bishops, priests, religious and lay people. Montini also reasoned that the council should consider the mission of the Church at the end of the second millennium, and he proposed a discussion on the Church's relationships with other religions, including her traditional 'enemies'.

Vatican II took place in the public eye. This also went against Opus Dei's principles. Moreover the Father feared that the large number of experts whom Pope John allowed to take part would overwhelm the less sophisticated bishops. A bishop needed strength of mind to remember that his authority came from his mystical consecration as Christ's apostle and not from the divergent opinions of counsellors, no matter how learned. Because of this, the Father believed that 'the potential expansion of the Devil's field of action' which Vatican II provided was 'beyond the Council fathers' imagination'.[2]

Escrivá de Balaguer refused to participate in the work of Vatican II. It is said that Pope John wanted to appoint him a consultor, but he would have nothing of it. Pope John, therefore, made Don Alvaro del Portillo the secretary of the Commission on Discipline of the Faith. Throughout the three years that the Council sat, Escrivá de

[1] Peter Hebblethwaite, *John XXIII – Pope of the Council*, Geoffrey Chapman, London 1985, p. 368. Hebblethwaite added, 'In his evidence to the beatification process of Pope John, Siri withdrew this judgement and said that he had been wrong.'
[2] Berglar, *Op. cit.*, p. 246.

Balaguer brooded in the Villa Tevere, dubbing it the 'Council of the Devil'.

Pope John did not live to see the work of his great enterprise completed. He died on 3 June 1963. Escrivá de Balaguer believed that the 'peasant Pope' had embarked upon a destructive exercise. Cardinal Larraona commented more charitably: 'John's goodness and simple-mindedness had led him astray.'[1] Siri, more direct, remarked, 'It will take the Church four centuries to recover from John's pontificate.'[2]

Montini became the next pope. Although the Father had not forgotten Montini's help in transforming Opus Dei from diocesan association to an institute of pontifical right, he considered the Archbishop of Milan, now Paul VI, weak on important doctrinal issues. Montini was also strongly anti-Franco.

Rather than rejoicing over Paul's election, Escrivá de Balaguer was indignant, especially as Paul VI made it clear that he was committed to completing the work of the Council. The second session closed in December 1963, with Paul promulgating a new Constitution on Liturgy, which was said to have made Escrivá de Balaguer tremble with rage. Paul opened the third session in September 1964, for the first time admitting women – religious and lay – as auditors, and closed it in November 1964.

At Escrivá de Balaguer's first meeting with Pope Paul he pressed for a revision of Opus Dei's status. Paul counselled him to wait until the close of Vatican II, still almost two years away. The Founder fretted, but Pope Paul remained firm, and when *Gaudium et Spes* was finally published in December 1965 it offered Opus Dei a few pearls. For example the Church accepted for the first time that work was part of the divine plan: 'We hold that through labour offered to God man is associated with the redemptive work of Jesus Christ.'[3] While Escrivá de Balaguer might have privately cursed the Council, Opus Dei publicly claimed that *Lumen Gentium*, the Decree on the Apostolate of the Laity and *Gaudium et Spes* all drew their inspiration from his teachings.

The Council now over, Pope Paul began implementing its decisions, steering the Church through a period of difficult change.

[1] Hebblethwaite, *Paul VI (Op. cit.)*, p. 320.
[2] *Ibid.*, p. 321.
[3] *Gaudium et Spes*, paragraph 67.

He substituted the vernacular in the liturgy, and in pursuit of ecumenism he held meetings with the Archbishop of Canterbury and the Patriarch Athenagorus I. Then in July 1968 he issued *Humanae Vitae*, condemning artificial methods of birth control. But it disappointed many, not least because a majority of the pontifical commission appointed to examine the subject had been in favour of contraception under certain conditions. Pope Paul had ignored the majority view. He was said to have been profoundly shaken by the critical international reaction this harvested. A horrified Escrivá de Balaguer had actually worked to oppose *Humanae Vitae*, because he felt it was not strong enough in its rejection of contraception. He was, on the other hand, encouraged by the role that Cardinal Karol Wojtyla had played in turning Paul's hand. It was said that Wojtyla had convinced Pope Paul to pull back from changing Church doctrine in favour of artificial birth control.

Escrivá de Balaguer was convinced that he was living in a time of heresies. He increasingly viewed Opus Dei as the core of the real Church, a lean and sleek Church. His sons were her guardians, the Catholic counterpart of Islam's *Mutawah,* a religious police sworn to maintain discipline and silence dangerous revisionists. 'God', he believed, 'has chosen Opus Dei to save His Church.'[1] Inside the Work, his word was law. He established Opus Dei's own Index of Prohibited Books, similar in intent to the one established by Paul IV in 1557 and renewed by Leo XIII in 1900. He bombarded his regional vicars with written directives that were filed in each centre's praxis manual. The subjects varied from Note S-4 of 30 August 1952, which in one curt sentence warned against talking about internal matters to persons outside the Work, to the latest additions to the Index.[2]

One theme that recurred over and over again was the vigilance needed to prevent 'philo-Marxism' from corrupting the doctrines of the Church. He instructed Opus Dei's sons and daughters 'in positions of government or teaching' (contrary to its public statements that it never interfered in the professional lives of members) to root out and report on Marxist infiltration. Six months later he issued another directive forbidding members to

[1] *Golias* No. 30, *Op. cit.,* p. 65.
[2] Note S-4 stated: 'Tell them that we abominate secrecy, but that they must shut up: the things of the family are for the family.'

read certain Catholic publications he deemed contaminated by Marxist philosophy.

For several years numeraries had been reading in *Crónica* such affirmations as, 'the heritage of heaven comes to us through the Father',[1] or were informed by their spiritual directors that, ' . . . the will of the Father is the will of God.'[2] Escrivá de Balaguer believed he was in possession of divine confidences. These confidences told him that *Humanae Vitae*, because it was too weak, had thrown the Church into disorder.

John Roche said, 'The Opus Dei hierarchy in Rome was starting to prepare us for schism. They said, "Saints have been in schism before." They were preparing us for the possibility of leaving the Catholic Church and becoming a separate church. This was an indication of the paranoia that spread through Opus Dei in the early 1970s. I remember asking one of our Irish priests who he would choose if it came to schism, the Pope or the Father? "The Father, of course," he replied.'[3]

In the early 1970s, Escrivá de Balaguer pulled back from schism. According to former insiders, Alvaro del Portillo counselled a more subtle approach to solving the Church's problems. Portillo pointed out that, like Opus Dei, many cardinals were convinced that Paul VI's pontificate was a disaster. He proposed that Opus Dei should attempt to form a common front with the more conservative members of the cardinalate. Few cardinals knew very much about Opus Dei. If the secular institute was to make itself heard, it had to open its apostolate to the hierarchy of the Church. Portillo proposed the creation of a Roman centre for priestly gatherings – the Centro Romano di Incontri Sacerdotali (CRIS) – and to use it as a forum for putting across to the hierarchy with as much tact as possible Escrivá de Balaguer's fears for the Church. Before agreeing to this proposal, the Father wanted guidance from the Virgin Mary and he embarked on a pilgrimage to four Marian shrines in Spain, Portugal and Mexico. One of these was at Torreciudad, where he had commissioned an imposing basilica, which he termed 'my last folly'.

---

[1] *Crónica* I, 1961.
[2] María Angustias Moreno, *El Opus Dei – Anexo a una historia*, Editorial Planeta, Barcelona 1976, p. 228.
[3] Dr John Roche, 8 October 1994.

Construction began shortly before his April 1970 visit and required five years to complete.

The fact that the Father had chosen another member, Heliodoro Dols, and not Miguel Fisac, to design the basilica was because the ninth apostle had turned his back on Opus Dei. After nineteen years in the Work, during which he had paid over all his earnings – a separate revenue account in the Spanish ledgers carried the label 'Estudio Fisac' – he was surprised by how little baggage he had to take with him.

'I remember that, when I left the Diego de León residence with a very small suitcase, I told myself all the way to my parents' home, "Now, Miguel, you will always tell the truth and you will try to be a good person, and nothing more." This thought underscored the moral anxiety in which I found myself, with so many secrets, so many lies, and also this indignation for rules and prayers that corseted the lives of Opus Dei's numerary members.'[1]

Fisac, by then one of Spain's most famous architects, described his relationship with Escrivá de Balaguer as that of the servant to a grand dame of the stage. The servant knows all the grand dame's foibles and secrets. 'She tells me in confidence about her agent, her lovers, her fellow actors on the stage and her fans. Well, with Escrivá it was very similar; he told me everything . . . I could recite for you in the smallest detail what he said about the people he liked a lot and who held him in great respect – people like José Ibáñez Martín or Ricardo Fernández Vallespín. In the final analysis, however, I do not want to nauseate you . . . With the exception of Alvaro del Portillo, he never had a good word to say about anybody,' Fisac wrote to a fellow architect many years later.[2]

Three months after leaving Opus Dei, Fisac married an architecture student who knew nothing about secret societies. His sister, Lola, who had joined the Work soon after the Civil War, was not permitted to attend the wedding. But Antonio Pérez Hernández, Opus Dei's secretary general in Rome at the time, sent a telegram with the Pope's benediction.

The Fisacs had three children, the third of whom died, aged six. On the day of the funeral, Fisac and his wife were visited by Francisco

[1] Fisac Notes, 8 June 1994.
[2] Fisac letter to Luis Borobio, 18 February 1995.

Botella, who had been his confessor, and Antonio Pérez Hernández, then back in Madrid as rector of Saint Michael's church. According to Fisac, in offering their condolences 'they made gestures of horror and let it be understood that what happened was God's punishment for having left Opus Dei.'[1] Fisac showed them the door.

Fisac revealed that a vain and often choleric Founder actively prepared for sainthood during his lifetime. 'Escrivá told us about a discussion he had with several Jesuits who complained that the original companions of St Ignatius did not consider it important to conserve the objects, buildings and sites which were important in Loyola's career. He added that it would be stupid if we did the same thing... Then one day, a long time after I left Opus Dei, Juan Jiménez Vargas came to my office with a collection of photos of the region of our flight across the Pyrenees: the outdoor oven and chapel [where Escrivá found the rose], and other places where we stopped along the way. He told me that Opus Dei was in the process of buying these sites in order to conserve them as relics. The question he wanted to ask me was whether the ladder used to climb into the oven shown in the photo was the original one ... And at the time Escrivá was still alive!'

Torreciudad was designed as yet another stage in Escrivá de Balaguer's journey towards sainthood. While dedicated to the Virgin of Torreciudad, it was in reality a shrine to the greater glory of the Founder of Opus Dei. With proper humility, Escrivá de Balaguer affirmed that the sanctuary was conceived purely and simply to promote Marian devotion and therefore he insisted that it was to be a place of conversion and reconfirmation. Consequently, the specially cast water fountains throughout the sanctuary were clearly marked 'Natural Drinking Water' so there could be no suggestion that it was holy water. He would not allow shops or souvenir stalls inside the sanctuary, not even a restaurant. 'People will come here to pray, to honour Our Lady and to seek God's way, not to buy baubles. I dislike the idea of God's house being turned into a bazaar,' he said.

Heliodoro Dols had not fully understood the message. On that April 1970 pilgrimage, the architect was on hand to explain for the Father the plans, including where in the basement level he intended to place a self-service cafeteria. The Father would not hear of it. He

---

[1] Fisac Notes, 8 June 1994; also his letter to the *Scottish Catholic Observer,* 26 March 1993.

ordered that a display of ceramic murals depicting the Mysteries of St Joseph take its place. 'That will prepare pilgrims for confession,' he said. Dols took note and suggested that ten confessionals would be sufficient. The Father insisted on forty. 'Everybody told him it was too many,' Torreciudad spokesman Manuel Garrido recalled.

'It may seem like too many now, but the time will come when it will seem too few,' he replied with assurance.

Escrivá de Balaguer returned to Rome feeling relieved and began making plans for the inauguration of the CRIS premises at Opus Dei's Residenza Universitaria Internazionale in the EUR surburb of the city. As a think-tank for Catholic orthodoxy it served Opus Dei better than even Portillo had imagined. CRIS's inauguration marked the beginning of Opus Dei's real power within the Church hierarchy.

Opus Dei's vitality could not help but stir the cardinals who attended the CRIS meetings. The meetings were held behind closed doors and participants could speak their mind without fearing indiscreet leaks. The cardinals were able to meet the young priests of Opus Dei who had rallied to Catholic orthodoxy with such evident enthusiasm that it was difficult not to be impressed. Opus Dei appeared to have an inner cohesion which the rest of the Church lacked. The concept worked brilliantly because CRIS was a two-way forum where cardinals gave their views but also received those of Opus Dei. Nobody who attended a CRIS meeting left with any doubt that a crisis of faith, moral confusion and indifference to society's permissiveness was undermining the Occident.

Opus Dei was particularly partial to the German bishops since they received $2,500 million annually in tax money to distribute among Catholic charities and aid organizations. One of the German treasure-chest guardians, Cardinal Höffner of Cologne, made his first appearance at CRIS in 1971. He was followed in 1972 by Franz Hengsbach, Bishop of Essen, a ferocious opponent of Marxism. Cardinal Casariego of Guatemala also made a notable appearance to speak out against the dangers of Liberation Theology and praised the Founder for being 'the only priest who during his lifetime has brought to the priesthood some one thousand men – professionals from five continents, engaged in different sectors of science and the liberal professions'.

Of the eastern cardinals, Karol Wojtyla was considered the most receptive to Opus Dei's ideas. When in January 1964 Paul VI named Wojtyla Archbishop of Cracow, he was already considered Poland's most outstanding bishop. Wojtyla's orthodoxy appealed to the Father. Before becoming Poland's second cardinal, it was rumoured inside Opus Dei that Wojtyla had been inducted as an associate into the Priestly Society of the Holy Cross, which ran CRIS. He made three CRIS appearances and his talks were bound into a book under the title of *La fede della Chiesa*.

Escrivá de Balaguer was unable to break down Paul VI's resistance to transforming Opus Dei into a floating diocese. Paul's appreciation of Opus Dei was said to have been influenced by the views of his most trusted assistant, Archbishop Giovanni Benelli. The son of a bakery worker from Pistoia, Benelli had served under Montini at the Secretariat of State; in 1962 he was sent to the nunciature in Madrid. Benelli's posting to Spain brought him into contact with Opus Dei. Not only did he deplore its secrecy, but he suspected that Escrivá de Balaguer wanted to create a church within the Church.[1]

In 1969, Paul replaced the ageing Cardinal Cicognani, his secretary of state, with the chain-smoking French cardinal, Jean Villot. At the same time, he named Benelli as Villot's under-secretary. Back in Rome, Benelli became Opus Dei's most outspoken Curial critic. Forceful, direct and not concerned about walking on the toes of others earned Benelli the sobriquet of 'Gauleiter' or 'Berlin Wall'. He overshadowed Villot, who couldn't stand him. Villot and Opus Dei therefore became natural allies.

If Opus Dei remained indefinitely blocked by Benelli's intransigence, its influence inside the Curia would decline, and gradually it risked being marginalized, proving it was an invention of man and not the divine creation that the Founder claimed. In order for Opus Dei to remain an ascending movement, it became imperative to find a way around Benelli's opposition.

---

[1] Hebblethwaite, *Paul VI (Op. cit.)*, p. 563.

PUFFS OF PRIDE

Honours, distinctions, titles: things of air, puffs of pride, lies, noth-ingness.

Maxim 677, *The Way*

IN JANUARY 1968, THE *BOLETÍN OFICIAL DEL ESTADO* IN MADRID published the following Ministry of Justice notification:

> Don José María Escrivá de Balaguer y Albás has requested the re-habilitation of the title of Marquis, granted on 12 February 1718 by the Archduke Charles of Austria to Don Tomás de Peralta, the inter-ested party having chosen in grace the distinction of Marquis of Peralta. The provisions of Article 4 of the Decree of 4 June 1948 for granting the request having been satisfied, a delay of three months from the publication of this edict exists for any persons wishing to make known their opposition. Madrid, 24 January 1968.

The notice was signed by the Ministry's under-secretary, Alfredo López, an Opus Dei supernumerary. A few paragraphs below in the same issue, Don Santiago Escrivá de Balaguer y Albás requested the rehabilitation of the barony of San Felipe. To many outsiders, the fact that Escrivá de Balaguer wished to dust off an old title seemed untypical for someone whose profound humility would be mentioned twenty years later as one of his cardinal virtues. But in the eyes of his children the Father's behaviour was at all times irreproachable.

The Opus Dei faithful quickly assimilated the anomaly of their Founder's seeking a 'puff of pride' with the exercising of a fundamental right. Escrivá de Balaguer, moreover, was insistent that he had not made the request for his own benefit. He maintained that the title was for his nephews, the children of his younger brother, Santiago. It was said that he wished to compensate his parents [already long dead] his sister [also dead] and his brother, for the sacrifices they had made in order to permit him to carry out the Work. Thus the Father portrayed his act as 'a matter of filial piety and justice.'[1]

According to research carried out by genealogists at the University of Navarra, the Marquisate of Peralta was bestowed upon one of Escrivá de Balaguer's more distant ancestors who had been minister for war and justice in Naples following the Treaty of Utrecht in 1713. The Father's claim to the lapsed title was thus given a mantle of legitimacy. The fact that so much effort and resources were invested in producing a pedigree of nobility indicated that, however much he might protest, the Father enjoyed collecting social distinctions. He had in recent years been awarded the Spanish Grand Cross of St Raymond of Penafort, the Grand Cross of Alfonso X the Wise, the Grand Cross of Isabel the Catholic, and the Cross of Charles III. But to show his modesty, we are assured that he never wore them. When an army officer congratulated him for having been honoured with a coveted distinction, he replied: 'My son, it is very important for you military fellows to be awarded one of these medals. For me it isn't. The only important Cross for me – and I know you feel the same at heart – is the Cross of Christ.'[2] This remark gives us the very essence of Escrivá de Balaguer as he laboured in the 1960s to cut a new suit of juridical clothing for Opus Dei. The deal that he was seeking from the Holy See's highest authority was the Work's 'final approbation' as a prelature of the Church. It became his window on immortality, and it was a fixation from which, in the last decades of his life, he could not be weaned.

---

[1] Vázquez de Prada, *Op. cit.*, p. 348.
[2] *Ibid.*, p. 319.

The fixation was like a beacon that guided his manoeuvrings with the Curia. Nothing was left to chance. There was a reason – divinely inspired, his children believed – for everything. Only when the outsider realizes the depth of adoration paid to him by his more dedicated followers do their seemingly incongruous excuses for his outrageous inconsistencies become more comprehensible: 'The Father sought nothing for himself. He simply was fulfilling a strict family duty.'[1] To the outsider it may seem a transparent lie, but for members living in an enclosed and carefully controlled climate of a religious sect, it was not only evident but part of the divine plan whose mysteries were not always explainable.

The comments which the notice in the *Boletín Oficial* provoked in the salons and bars of Madrid were pungent. One wag suggested that *The Way* by Josemaría Escrivá would soon be re-issued under a new title: *The Super Highway* by the Marquis de Peralta.

But the question remained: why did Escrivá de Balaguer leave himself open to such derision? Some, of course, saw in it the act of a penitent son paying off the social debt of his father, the bankrupt shopkeeper from Barbastro. But at least two other theories were put forward. By late 1966, Escrivá de Balaguer would have known from his sons in government – particularly Laureano López Rodó – that Franco was about to designate the twenty-eight-year-old Prince Juan Carlos as his successor and future King of Spain.[2]

According to one theory, the Founder rehabilitated the Peralta title because he expected, or hoped, to be named Regent in the transitionary period between the designation by Franco of his royal successor and the actual coronation. It was said that with the title of marquis Escrivá de Balaguer believed he possessed the three prerequisites which he considered necessary for the job: public stature, priesthood and nobility.[3] He was in direct contact with the prime minister, Luis Carrero Blanco. Moreover, in preparation for the restoration, he had met with Don Juan de Borbón, Juan Carlos's father, then living in exile at Estoril, in Portugal.[4]

Another hypothesis that tickled the imaginations of some was that

[1] *Ibid.*, p. 348.
[2] This occurred on 22 July 1969, when Franco announced that he had chosen Juan Carlos, grandson of Alfonso XIII (who died in February 1941), to succeed him.
[3] 'The Double Life of Saint Escrivá – Names, Titles and Ambitions', *Cambio 16*, Madrid, 30 March 1992.
[4] *Arriba*, Madrid, 13 May 1967, and *El Pensamiento Navarro*, Pamplona, 17 May 1967.

Opus Dei's directorate in Rome had considered attempting a takeover of the Sovereign Military Order of the Knights Hospitaller of Saint John of Jerusalem, called of Rhodes, called of Malta, as it was the only Church institution to hold the status of an independent state. Some titled Opusian gentlemen were already members of the Order and its sovereign council in Rome feared a *coup d'état*. As Marquis of Peralta, Escrivá de Balaguer might have thought he was eligible for the highest rank of the Maltese Cross as the Order's regulations permit only celibate knights of noblesse to become Grand Master. In addition to being recognized as a sovereign head of state, the Grand Master holds a rank in the Church that is equivalent to a cardinal and this, too, would have appealed to the newly titled prelate. But when it was learned that the Grand Master had to be a secular person, this plan was dropped.

By the early 1960s some of Escrivá de Balaguer's children were moving in rather rarefied spheres. Alfredo Sánchez Bella was one. He had broken with Opus Dei in the early 1940s but returned to Escrivá de Balaguer's fold in the 1950s.[1] In 1949, the year after the Communist takeover of Czechoslovakia, he co-founded with Archduke Otto von Habsburg the European Centre of Documentation and Information (CEDI), whose objective was to construct around the Spanish Borbóns a federation of European states united in Christianity and anti-Communism. This sounded very much like a modern resurrection of the Holy Roman Empire over which Charles V had reigned. Like the Spanish empire of old, the envisaged Catholic federation was intended to have large-spectrum antennae in Latin America and the United States.

CEDI was believed to be an auxiliary operation of Opus Dei.[2]

---

[1] Ynfante, *Op. cit.*, p. 353; also Artigues, *Op. cit.*, pp. 38 and 149. In a lawsuit brought by the German branch of Opus Dei in 1985 against Rowohlt Taschenbuch Verlag, publishers of the *Aktuell Rororo Yearbook*, lawyers for the Prelature claimed *inter alia* that 'Alfredo Sánchez Bella is not a member of Opus Dei and was not a member when he supposedly occupied [public office].' A decision against Welt Aktuell required that the 1986 edition of the yearbook be withdrawn from sale. However, Opus Dei admitted to the author on 30 October 1994 that Alfredo Sánchez Bella had indeed been a member, though he 'disconnected himself from Opus Dei before holding a fixed political system [sic] or a position in Spanish public life.' According to María del Carmen Tapia, he rejoined the Work as a supernumerary after marrying in London. The Barcelona newspaper *La Vanguardia* in its 28 June 1995 edition claimed Alfredo Sánchez Bella was still a member.

[2] Jean-Pie Lapierre, 'Puissance et rayonnement de l'Opus Dei', *Revue politique et parlementaire*, Paris, September 1965. The article claimed that CEDI was an instrument of Opus Dei. This was repeated by Le Vaillant, *Op. cit.*, p. 151.

Although headquartered in Munich, it held its annual general meetings at the Monastery of El Escorial, near Madrid, and it continued functioning throughout the Cold War. Its tentacles spread among Catholic Monarchist circles throughout western Europe. Archduke Otto, who was educated in Spain and completed his studies at the Catholic University of Louvain, reportedly became one of Opus Dei's most treasured Old Guard supernumeraries.[1] Like Opus Dei, CEDI published no membership lists, but the president of its Belgian chapter, Chevalier Marcel de Roover, was known to have close ties with the Belgian royal family. Indeed, Archduke Otto's nephew, Lorenz von Habsburg, son of international banker Karel von Habsburg, married Princess Astrid of Belgium, daughter of King Albert II. Astrid's aunt, the former Queen Fabiola, was related through the House of Aragon to the Spanish Borbón family. Professor Luc de Heusch of the Free University of Brussels, an expert on Sacred Kingship, maintained that Queen Fabiola, a disciple of Escrivá de Balaguer, 'introduced Opus Dei to the Catholic aristocracy of Europe.'[2]

An idea of the company CEDI kept can be gathered from the membership of a sister organization, the Pan-European Union, headquartered in Zurich. Also headed by Archduke Otto, among its members were two Belgian prime ministers, an Italian industrialist close to the Vatican, a former French prime minister, his legal counsellor, an aide to Valéry Giscard d'Estaing, the secretary of Giscard's Independent Republican party, a professor of theology at the Grand Seminary of Fribourg who was a Secret Chamberlain to the Pontifical Household, the deputy head of NATO's intelligence division, a director of West German intelligence, the Spanish ambassador to the European Community and Alfredo Sánchez Bella, who had served as Spanish ambassador to Colombia, the Dominican Republic, and, in the 1960s, Italy. While in Rome, he headed the Office of Diplomatic Information, Spain's exterior secret service for Europe.[3] Franco named him Minister of Tourism and Information in 1969.

Many Pan-European members belonged to a right-wing associ-

[1] 'La Maffia blanche', *Golias* No. 30, Lyon, Summer 1992, p. 168.
[2] Professor Luc de Heusch discussion with the author at University of London lecture on 'Monarchy, Spiritual and Temporal', 14 October 1993.
[3] Ynfante, *Op. cit.*, p. 353.

ation that had little formal structure but became known as the 'Pinay Group', after Antoine Pinay, a former French prime minister. In a sense it was broader than the Union because its participants were not exclusively Catholic and its meetings were regularly attended by right-wing Americans. These included former CIA director William Colby, banker David Rockefeller and public relations pioneer Crosby M. Kelly. But the Pinay Group was essentially a European Community lobby established to counter Marxism. It was plugged into virtually every west European intelligence service. Although it met under the auspices of Pinay, the co-ordinator for the Group was Jean Violet, a right-wing Gaullist and friend of Giulio Andreotti.[1] The Pinay Group was said to be another Opus Dei auxiliary operation, and its principal protagonists, Pinay and Violet, were variously reported to be connected with the Work.

Rumours of Nazi collaboration led to Violet's arrest following the war, but he was quickly released 'on orders from above'.[2] Shortly afterwards, he offered his services to SDECE, the French counter-espionage establishment referred to in the trade as *La Piscine* (the Swimming Pool). He joined Antoine Pinay's entourage in 1955. By this time Violet had become close to several Opusian personalities, among them Alfredo Sánchez Bella and Otto von Habsburg.

In his journeys, Violet came to know Father Yves-Marc Dubois, a French Dominican who was in charge of international relations for his Order. But Dubois represented more than the foreign policy interests of the black friars of Faubourg Saint Honoré. He was described as a 'member of the Vatican's intelligence network, if not its head'.[3] He popped up from time to time as an unofficial member of the Holy See's delegation to the United Nations. When in Paris, he stayed in the Dominican chapter house at 222 rue Faubourg Saint Honoré, in the Eighth Arrondissement, within walking distance of Jean Violet's apartment at 46 rue de Provence, in the Ninth Arrondissement.

[1] Antoine Pinay was a member of Marshal Pétain's wartime National Council until the closing days of the Second World War when he helped General de Gaulle to power. He served as prime minister in 1952, under the Fourth Republic. He died on 13 December 1994, aged 102. Various sources claim that Pinay was an Opus Dei supernumerary, most recently Nicolas Dehan in 'Un étrange phénomène pastoral: l'Opus Dei', *Le Sel de la Terre* No. 11, Paris, Winter 1994–95, p. 139.
[2] Pierre Péan, V, Fayard, Paris 1984, p. 41
[3] *Ibid.*, p. 49

Dubois introduced Violet to his 'Swiss correspondent', Father Henri Marmier, the 'official' of the diocese of Fribourg and editor-in-chief of APIC, the Catholic International Press Agency based in Fribourg. Father Marmier and a Polish Dominican, Father Josef-Marie Bochenski, founded under the auspices of the University of Fribourg the Institute of Sovietology. The Institute's extra-curricular activities included the running of a clandestine network that provided aid to Catholic groups behind the Iron Curtain, par-ticularly Poland. The Institute was in part funded by what officials in Fribourg euphemistically called 'the American grant'. According to the registrar's office at the University of Fribourg, Opus Dei sent several of its members to the Institute.

Another of the Institute's supporters was Violet's boss, General Paul Grossin, chief lifeguard at the Swimming Pool from 1957 to 1962. Grossin was said by some to have transferred fees owing to Violet directly to Father Marmier's 'charities' in Poland.[1] (Violet was made a Chevalier de Légion d'Honneur by General de Gaulle. He claimed to British author Godfrey Hodgson that he was in charge of covert political operations for SDECE until he retired as an active spy in 1970.[2] According to Count Alexandre de Marenches, the chief lifeguard from 1970 to 1981, Violet was 'given the heave' because he cost the French government more than any other spy on SDECE's long list of secret agents. De Marenches further claimed that Violet had been a triple agent working in addition for the Vatican and the West German BND. Other sources said that he was in fact fired because he knew too much about the sexual follies of one of France's leading ladies.)

Others who attended Pinay Group meetings included Franz-Josef Strauss, head of the Christian Socialist Party in Bavaria and for a time West German Defence Minister, Dr Alois Mertes, another West German minister, and Prince Turki bin-Faisal, a Deputy Minister of Defence and director of Saudi intelligence. Both Strauss and Mertes were said to be linked to Opus Dei, though Mertes later denied it. Prince Turki's elder brothers were King Faisal and Prince Sultan ibn Abdul Aziz, the Saudi Minister of Defence.

Sánchez Bella, von Habsburg and Violet were convinced that a

---

[1] *Ibid.*, p. 50.
[2] Interview with Godfrey Hodgson at Oxford, 11 September 1993.

Europe united against Communism required a strong figurehead – e.g., King Juan Carlos of Spain – who could act as the torchbearer of Catholic morality, and around whom the Occident could rally as a figure of wholesome fortitude. However a figurehead with all the moral fortitude in the world would be hamstrung if he lacked sufficient resources to act on the same plane as popularly elected governments. They also realized that to achieve this would require some financial cobbling of heroic proportions. A plan began to take shape at a luncheon at the Hotel Westburg in Brussels in the autumn of 1969 that was attended by Alain de Villegas, his brother-in-law Florimond Damman, a devotee of the archduke, and Jean Violet. Whether the plan was another example of *pillería* by the sons of Escrivá de Balaguer is open to interpretation. Although ultimately uncovered as a racket, it proved relatively profitable. Some of the funds that subsequently went missing were traced to religious works in Spain.

Alain de Villegas had studied engineering at Louvain. He was an ecologist, antinuclear to the core, and believed in flying saucers. He was above all a staunch European and ferociously anti-Communist.

Convinced that the world was running out of water, Villegas used to say, 'We can live without oil, but not without water.' He disclosed to alleged triple agent Violet that he had invented a machine capable of detecting ground water. Violet did not need to be told that such a machine, if it performed as claimed, could be immensely valuable to a country like Spain, whose tourist industry was hobbled by lack of water, or to Middle Eastern countries.

Villegas explained that he and his associate, Professor Aldo Bonassoli, had developed a low-energy desalination process capable of transforming seawater into fresh water, and as a result of this they were developing a 'water-sniffing' machine. They claimed that their invention could determine underground structures up to depths of six kilometres. Villegas showed Violet a small-scale prototype and convinced the lawyer of its potential. As financing was needed for a full-scale prototype, Violet agreed to speak to his friend and client Carlo Pesenti, an Italian industrialist close to the Vatican, and to Crosby Kelly in New York.

Crosby Kelly made no bones about his political leanings. 'I am a Rightist, Conservative and anti-Communist,' he told Hodgson. He was said to be a sometime CIA operative. He had designed and launched the sales campaign for the first Ford motorcar produced after the Second World War, and was among Robert McNamara's original 'whiz kids' at Ford. For thirteen years he had been on the board of Litton Industries. Kelly told Violet he would not invest a penny until satisfied that the invention was capable of finding water. Pesenti, on the other hand, put up some capital. Spain's new tourist minister, Sánchez Bella, placed several test sites at the team's disposal. Kelly monitored Villegas's progress. He told Hodgson that the Spanish government paid the drilling costs.[1]

The search for water went on with slight success for two years until interrupted by the Yom Kippur War of 1973, which brought about an Islamic oil boycott and subsequent quadrupling of world oil prices. Villegas kept his project alive by announcing that his 'sniffer machines' could also detect oil. Pesenti was persuaded to invest additional funds.

As the world geo-political equation had suddenly changed, the project was transformed into a crusade to liberate Christian Europe from dependence upon Islamic oil. Pesenti's engineers equipped a DC-3 with one of the 'sniffing' machines. Using contacts provided by Antoine Pinay, they flew to South Africa and were given government authorization to conduct tests over Zululand. A promising site was identified and drilling began, but by the end of 1975 the costs had become so heavy that Pesenti again opted out. The Zululand borehole eventually bottomed out at 6,000 metres, having broken the drill stem, with nothing more than traces of Karoo basalt to show for the millions spent in drilling expenses.

By this time Violet's Spanish associates lost interest. In fact, with the assassination of Carrero Blanco in December 1973, Opus Dei's political fortunes had changed and the new prime minister swept the Opusian technocrats from government. But they had done their job well, preparing the way for a restoration of the monarchy under Prince Juan Carlos, which occurred upon Franco's death two years later. Meanwhile, thanks in part to Prince Turki, southern Spain had become a playground for Saudi royals. Madrid and Riyadh enjoyed such friendly relations that even the State Department in Washington was envious. Spain was given long-term access to Saudi oil on preferential terms.

---

[1] Sniffer article (unpublished) by Godfrey Hodgson, p. 24.

A known technique for transferring profits in international transactions is to use 'sandwich companies' domiciled in offshore jurisdictions whose laws insure strict secrecy. As the name implies, a sandwich company inserts itself between the parties to a transaction in the guise of providing a service, such as facilitating a contract for, say, 100 million tons of Saudi crude. As the crude passes from wellhead to market, the sandwich company collects a commission or passes on the merchandise to the purchaser at a marginally increased price through back-to-back contracts. The real principals of the sandwich companies are rarely known and it is virtually impossible to pierce their veil of corporate secrecy. There is nothing illegal about these operations, provided they do not infringe the laws of disclosure in the jurisdictions concerned, and vast sums can thus be accumulated without anyone outside the inner circle being any the wiser.

With the Spaniards no longer interested in the Villegas invention, and Carlo Pesenti's pockets empty, Jean Violet used his counter-espionage contacts to interest the French petroleum company ELF in the 'sniffing' machines. In May 1976 at the headquarters of Union Bank of Switzerland (UBS) in Zurich, ELF's chairman entered into a contract with a Panamanian sandwich company called FISALMA, supposedly representing Villegas. The FISALMA contract gave ELF the exclusive use of two electronic 'sniffers' – Delta and Omega – for one year against payment of $50 million.

ELF's chairman was no fool. He was credited with creating both France's nuclear power industry, one of the most advanced in the world, and the French nuclear *force de frappe*. UBS is Switzerland's largest commercial bank. Its chairman at the time was Philippe de Weck, and one of its board members was the Panamanian consul in Zurich, Dr Arthur Wiederkehr. The de Wecks are a well known patrician family from Fribourg. Although FISALMA – a company that issued from the law offices of Dr Wiederkehr – was controlled by Villegas, de Weck acted as its president.

Tests started in June 1976. Delta came up with nothing and so Villegas proposed mounting the more powerful Omega in the aircraft. Omega found what was described as a large deposit at Montégut in the Languedoc, nine kilometres long and a kilometre wide, 3.9 kilometres below the earth's surface. Excitement was intense. Drilling began in January 1977. By April no oil had been hit, but in June 1977 ELF nevertheless renewed the FISALMA contract for another year. The Montégut borehole was halted at a depth of 4,485 metres, still bone dry. By then drilling had begun at a new site where Omega was said to have uncovered a more promising formation.

ELF was persuaded in a 1978 meeting at UBS's main conference centre near Zurich to extend the FISALMA contract a second time and triple its investment. The company received authorization from the French Treasury to keep the transaction hidden from government auditors. The new payments, bringing the total French investment to 450 million Swiss francs ($150 million), was to be advanced to FISALMA by UBS in four instalments of 50 million Swiss francs each. UBS charged the French government 6 per cent interest, holding state-guaranteed ELF debentures worth 500 million Swiss francs as collateral.

Present at the meeting were three members of ELF's senior management, the two inventors, Antoine Pinay, Jean Violet, Philippe de Weck and the two priests, Dubois and Marmier. De Weck introduced Marmier as a diocesan judge from Fribourg who specialized in marriage annulment cases. De Weck said he had specifically requested Marmier's presence. What role Marmier really played was not known, but divorce between ELF and FISALMA was avoided and the new contract signed.

Valéry Giscard d'Estaing was then in the sixth year of his presidency. He had been discreetly following the project and was alarmed to learn that ELF had committed, drilling costs included, more than $200 million to the sniffers. He now became directly involved. The 88-year-old Pinay convinced him to attend a demonstration arranged for early April 1979. Philippe de Weck was present. The test was so negative that Giscard requested an immediate investigation and suspended further government financing.

The President of the Republic was thus able in a few minutes to see through a fiasco that the managing directors of France's largest company had been unable to detect in three years of dealings with Villegas and Bonassoli. Once Giscard gave his instructions, the machines were sequestered and found to be fakes (their 'decoders' turned out to be two video cameras linked to a special-effects generator).

Threatened with legal action, UBS returned 250 million Swiss francs and all of the debentures. Liquidators seized Villegas's fleet of 'sniffing aircraft' parked in a top-security hangar at Brussels International Airport. By then the fleet included a Boeing 707, a Fokker 27 and a Mystère 20 executive jet for transporting personnel. Together with the sale of other assets and the attaching of bank accounts, ELF recouped another 41 million Swiss francs. Villegas and Bonassoli, whose only degree was a diploma qualifying him as a television repair man, were never prosecuted.

Albin Chalandon, the new chairman of ELF, told a parliamentary commission: 'We were dealing with madmen rather than crooks. They faked their machines, but they believed in their invention. Villegas was a mystic on the outer edge of normality, and Bonassoli lived in an unreal universe that made him believe in his own make-believe.' They had, in other words, struck a gusher of intellectual *pillería*. As for the Pinay Group, it continued to meet and produce confidential reports that were circulated to selected government ministries and intelligence services in several countries.

Enquiries have shown that no detailed accounting for the ELF moneys paid to FISALMA was ever rendered. About $2.8 million was known to have been used by Villegas to finance the construction of a new church for an organization called Foyer de Charité in the south of France. Dedicated to Holy Mary Mother of God, the church was inaugurated in June 1979. Villegas also donated $52,000 to build a Catholic workshop for Indians in the Chocó region of northern Colombia. Through a foundation created in Liechtenstein he helped finance Catholic aid projects in Niger, Rwanda, Upper Volta and Spain totalling another $7 million. The aid projects in Africa included the drilling of water wells and purchase of a small fleet of ambulances, leaving one to conclude that the bulk of the Liechtenstein trust money went to Spain. FISALMA also maintained an account at the IOR (the Vatican bank) which allegedly was used 'for investing in secret political schemes.'[1]

ELF got back $100 million. But what happened to the remaining $50 million? As with Matesa's $180 million it had gone astray through the use of cleverly drafted contracts and fast-service sandwich companies, the junk food of transnational finance. These two ventures alone – Matesa and FISALMA – meant that more than $200

---

[1] Péan, *Op. cit.*, p. 212.

million in Spanish and French ratepayers' money could be sloshing about in the international monetary system, free of controls and ready for use in any number of causes, as for example defeating Communist insurgency in Latin America or taking control of a strategic European bank.

OCTOPUS DEI

Members of Opus Dei act either individually or by means of associations which may be cultural, artistic, financial, etc., and which are called 'Auxiliary Societies'. These societies and their activities are also placed under the obedience of the hierarchical authority of the Institute.

Article 9 of the 1950 Constitutions

WHILE ESCRIVÁ DE BALAGUER WAS COLLECTING 'PUFFS OF PRIDE', OPUS Dei was building corporate pyramids and developing the praxis of profit-transfer accounting. Using *anstalts*, *stiftungs* and offshore shell companies, it created veils of corporate secrecy to hide its many tentacles. A *stiftung* (foundation) is a form of corporate trust developed by the Swiss and often used for intricate financial dealings. *Anstalt* (establishment) is a Liechtenstein speciality, modelled on an Austrian forerunner, the *Privatanstalt*. It has a fixed capital but issues no shares. Both are so shrouded in confidentiality that their 'founder-in-fact' or 'founder-in-due-course' – i.e., the real owners – are absolutely unidentifiable to the outside world.

Opus Dei's reliance on these devices came about in stages as it grew in size and sophistication. A first stage was its use of ordinary onshore trusts to disguise the ownership of property, but new layers were added in the mid-1950s. One of the most important of these was created by lawyer Alberto Ullastres, before he became minister of commerce. Known as Esfina, its initial capital was not quite $1 million. Esfina promoted a new Opusian invention, the so-called 'common works'. These were quite different from 'corporate works', which were concentrated in the educational field and openly linked to Opus Dei, the University of Navarra being a prime example.

Common works, on the other hand, although part of the apostolate, were considered as commercial vehicles, financed whenever possible with other people's money but run by Opus Dei personnel. Many of the Esfina holdings were in the 'AOP' (Apostolate of Public Opinion) sector, established to influence public opinion, under the guidance of an oversight committee. In Spain, the first AOP overseers were Laureano López Rodó, Alberto Ullastres and Professor Jesús Arellano.

AOP was a cover for *pillería* of a different nature. Opus Dei was, and remains, a privileged institution of the Church that claims – indeed insists with all the piety it can muster – that its only interest is the spiritual well-being of members and that it never interferes in their daily lives. It doesn't own anything, certainly not a bank, and it never plays politics. But now, with its AOP ministry, Opus Dei wanted to covertly influence public opinion, having first conditioned its members to adopt a set of moral values that set them apart from the rest of society.

In a first phase, the Apostolate of Public Opinion concentrated on founding or taking over public companies involved in broadcast and print media, publishing and communications. A majority of the share capital in each company was held in trust by Opus Dei numeraries, supernumeraries or tested co-operators. In all cases, the trustees were required to execute undated contracts of sale for the shares they held which were kept in a safe at the regional headquarters.

In Spain, the common works were funded through Esfina, which raised its capital from the families of members and friends. In each case the capital so raised was treated like a savings account at a private bank, receiving interest at rates moderately above commercial bank rates and every account being individually managed with full diligence and discretion. In addition to tax advantages, Esfina's depositors had the satisfaction of believing their money was financing 'God's work'.

Esfina's first chairman was Pablo Bofill de Quadras, an Opus Dei numerary who also served on the board of the Spanish subsidiary of a Vatican-controlled company, Condotte Española. His deputy chairman was José Ferrer Bonsoms, a young banker and supernumerary whose family owned extensive holdings in Argentina. Esfina acquired or founded with the monies of others Ediciones Rialp, Opus Dei's flagship publisher, Editorial Magistero Español, publisher of secondary-level school books, and SARPE, which in turn owned *Alcázar*, a conservative newspaper, *Actualidad Español*, a news magazine, *Actualidad Economica*, a business weekly, *Telva*, a popular women's magazine, and *Mundo Cristiano*, a religious magazine.

These publications, managed and predominantly staffed by members, in turn needed a press agency, and so Europa Press was born. Their advertising and sales promotion was handled by an Esfina-owned agency, and they used printing presses belonging to Rotopress S.A., also a child of Esfina. All were dependent upon the financial backing of Opus Dei as frequently, serving AOP needs rather than purely commercial pursuits, they ran at a deficit.

In 1958, Esfina branched into banking, acquiring a small private bank in Barcelona, which it renamed Banco Latino. Months later it added Credit Andorra, the largest bank in Andorra. In 1959, Esfina formed Universal de Inversiones S.A. to manage its more speculative investments. Universal's president was Francisco Planell Fontrodona, until ordained in 1964. He was assisted by Alfonso López Rodó, brother of Laureano López Rodó, until Alfonso also was ordained.

The Falange regarded SARPE's activity with hostility. Strict censorship still reigned in 1962, as rivalry between Opus Dei and the Falange was moving towards a final showdown, and the Falangist minister of information wanted to close SARPE on grounds that it was the propaganda arm of an unauthorized political movement. Opus Dei denied its involvement with SARPE, which was manifestly untrue. When threatened with an expropriation order, Opus Dei's regional administrator telephoned Navarro-Rubio and Calvo Serer to inform them that overnight they had become SARPE's controlling shareholders. The Falange backed down and SARPE was saved by a sleight of hand that would not have been necessary had Opus Dei been what it claimed to be: a spiritual organization that did not engage in politics.

A major Opus Dei benefactor immediately following the Civil War was the Catalan industrialist Ferran (Fernando) Valls Taberner, who had financed the opening of a NSRC commission in Barcelona and insured that it was staffed by Opus Dei numeraries and who had founded Banco Popular de los Previsores del Porvenir (the Popular Bank for Future Needs) which after some major face-lifting in the 1950s became the cornerstone of Opus Dei's financial edifice in Spain.

With Valls's sudden death in 1942, Felix Millet Maristany, an ultra-religious Catalan financier, became the bank's chairman. In 1947 he changed the name to Banco Popular Español and listed it on the Madrid Stock Exchange. His right-hand man was Juan Manuel Fanjul Sedeño, an Opus Dei supernumerary who, like Millet, had been close to Ferran Valls. Fanjul was proxy-holder for an important block of the bank's shares belonging to the Valls family.[1] Through Fanjul, Opus Dei began its penetration of the bank's directorate.

Ferran's eldest son, Luis, became an Opus Dei numerary. At 24 he was an assistant professor of law, first at Barcelona and then at Madrid. In 1950, his Opus Dei superiors decided he should become the Vocal of St Gabriel, looking after the spiritual requirements of supernumeraries and their families. But after two years of struggling with the Archangel's duties, he told his spiritual director that he was not cut out to be a counsellor of souls and wanted to become a banker. In the world of banking Luis Valls became for Opus Dei what López Rodó represented in the world of government.

In 1953, he entered the family bank and was taken in hand by Mariano Navarro-Rubio. Banco Popular Español had by then moved its main offices to Madrid. A restructuring of the Valls holdings concentrated the banking interests with Luis and his brothers Javier and Felix. Manufacturas Valls, the family textile combine, was left in the hands of their uncles. In any event, Luis and Felix, also a numerary, continued to hold shares in Manufacturas Valls, which soon branched into nuclear engineering. As Opus Dei was more interested in banking than textiles, Banco Popular was brought solidly under its domination. Opus Dei has never owned the bank, not legally at least, because control was ultimately run through a series of offshore trusts.

[1] Ynfante, *Op. cit.*, p. 233.

The joke around Opus Dei was that Esfina really was a coded abbreviation for 'we take money from unholy souls to finance holy works'. The cynical would say that this notion fitted the Opus Dei ethic perfectly, in that as the end-product (money) was destined for holy works, the source from which it came was of no account. Escrivá de Balaguer often said this and believed it was morally upright. But Esfina also brought headaches. Using the common works to promote Opus Dei's political agenda, namely the liberalization of the economy and a modernizing of Spain's political structures, involved a degree of risk. The common works also constituted a financial burden. These factors provoked an unexpected reaction from Opus Central. One day in 1963, the regional administrator was informed that the Father in Rome had decreed: 'No more common works!'

Buyers were found for a few of the more viable concerns, and in one or two cases – *Telva*, for example – friendly banks financed a staff buy-out. But overall the experience of arbitrarily being required to liquidate the common works was traumatic for most concerned. Many members had put their hearts and sometimes their family's savings into these enterprises, believing they were doing God's work, only to be told that God wasn't interested any more.

The liquidation of the common works did not mean that Opus Dei abandoned the AOP concept. It was continued under another form. A few of the common works, moreover, were sacred. These included the Rialp publishing house and Talleres d'Arte Grande, which supplied religious art for Opus Dei centres around the world.

After winding down the common works, Esfina's newly freed capital was invested in the banking sector. The first target was Banco Atlántico, a small regional bank whose major shareholder had been killed in a train crash. Negotiations were entrusted to Barcelona industrialist Casimiro Molins Robit, an Opus Dei supernumerary, who led the sellers and public to believe that he was acting on behalf of Banco Popular Español. The deal successfully concluded, Molins became Atlántico's new chairman, while management was taken over by the Bofill-Ferrer tandem. They built the bank into one of Spain's top dozen, modifying its statutes along the way to permit 15 per cent of the profits to be donated to social causes. As Bofill and Ferrer were informed that their brother in the faith, finance minister Mariano Navarro-Rubio, was drafting new legislation that would permit commercial banks to branch into merchant banking, they planned to launch Atlántico's own merchant bank, baptized Bankunión. But they wanted to bring international partners into the new unit. The managing director of the Vatican-controlled Condotte d'Acqua S.p.A., Loris Corbi, introduced Bofill to John McCaffery, the Rome representative of Hambros Bank.[1] Bofill offered McCaffery a participation. But Hambros was already committed to form a merchant bank with Banco Popular Español. McCaffery therefore suggested that Bofill and Ferrer contact the up-and-coming Milan financier Michele Sindona.

Bankunión was registered in October 1963 with a share capital of $24 million. Banco Atlántico directly held only 10 per cent of the capital. It is uncertain whether Sindona ever joined the consortium. If he did, he participated through one of the anonymous foreign investment companies that became Bankunión's majority share-holders. Other investors included Esfina and Condotte Española.[2] Like Banco Atlántico, Bankunión's statutes required that 15 per cent of its profits be donated to social causes.[3]

Sindona, in the meantime, succeeded in selling a 24 per cent interest in his Banca Privata Finanziaria of Milan to Continental Illinois Bank & Trust of Chicago. Continental Illinois was at the time the seventh largest bank in the United States. The move proved astute as Continental's chairman, a Mormon bishop by the name of David M. Kennedy, became Richard Nixon's Secretary of the Treasury. Sindona was introduced to him by Paul Marcinkus, a priest from Chicago turned Vatican diplomat who became Pope Paul VI's travel director. Sindona in turn introduced Bofill and Ferrer to David Kennedy. They interested the Mormon bishop in acquiring for Continental Illinois an 18 per cent interest in Banco Atlántico. The transaction was run through a Swiss company, Greyhound Finance AG. Greyhound was domiciled in the Zurich offices of one of Europe's leading confidential money experts, Dr Arthur Wiederkehr.

---

[1] Condotte d'Acqua provided the City of Rome with its water supply. Condotte was also a major Italian construction company. It built *autostradas* (motorways) and had completed the Italian side of the Mont Blanc Tunnel under the Alps. Condotte was at that time owned by APSA, the Administration of the Patrimony of the Apostolic See. Condotte d'Acqua would later be sold to Italian financier Michele Sindona in a complicated operation involving the IOR and Sindona's Banca Privata Finanziaria, Milan.

[2] Ynfante, *Op. cit.*, p. 251.

[3] Ernesto Ekaizer, *José María Ruiz Mateos – el Ultimo Magnate*, Plaza & Janes, Barcelona 1985, p. 167.

During the negotiations, Bofill and Ferrer met Wiederkehr, whose talents were much in demand by international capital movers. Sindona used Wiederkehr, and he also told fellow Milan banker Roberto Calvi about the Zurich lawyer's services. Almost as an aside, Sindona introduced Calvi to the Madrid crowd.

Opus Dei at the time was re-organizing its corporate holdings worldwide along the guidelines established in Spain. Ownership and management of assets were generally split between two separate corporate entities which in turn were owned by one or more private trusts or holding companies. This gave Opus Dei an almost invisible corporate profile but also theoretically gave it access to a percentage of the funds received as grants by certain of its auxiliary societies.

In Ireland, for example, the Work had been present since July 1947. Its property investments there were placed under the umbrella of University Hostels Limited. But the properties themselves were managed by another company, Hostels Management Limited. Sixty-two per cent of University Hostels' shares held in the name of Father Patrick Cormac Burke were transferred to Lismullin Scientific Trust. University Hostels' remaining shares went to Tara Trust. While it is unclear who were the owners of these trusts, both listed their address as Knapton House, which was an Opus Dei residence in Dun Laoghaire, County Dublin.

In 1977 the Reverend Doctor Frank Planell was named Opus Dei's regional vicar for Ireland. As Francisco Planell Fontrodona, 'Frank' had already served Opus Dei as chairman of Esfina's Universal de Inversiones S.A. One of the most gifted Irish numeraries under Planell was Seamus Timoney, a professor of mechanical engineering at University College, Dublin. When not lecturing, Timoney tinkered with advanced weapons systems, designing and patenting a sturdy armoured personnel carrier known as the Timoney APC. Timoney, however, was no marketing expert. Was it too much to assume that Father Frank referred the matter to Opus Central, which happened to be aware that the Argentine Army needed this type of equipment? It is known that the Timoney APC went into production in 1978 and that an undisclosed number were sold to the Argentine Armed Forces.[1] If normal prescriptions were followed, 10 per cent of the proceeds of the Argentine sale would have been paid to Opus Central.

[1] Maurice Roche, 'The Secrets of Opus Dei', *Magill Magazine*, Dublin, May 1983.

Professor Timoney was an interesting case. Associated with Opus Dei since the 1950s, he was internationally known for his weaponry inventions. In 1957, he incorporated Industrial Engineering Designers Limited, which became an Opus Dei auxiliary society. Five of the six founding directors of Engineering Designers were Opus Dei numeraries. Netherhall Educational Trust, the principal Opus Dei charitable trust in the UK, received a 'gift share'. Several prominent Opus Dei members in Ireland and the UK also put up capital, and yet Opus Dei claimed, 'No funds of Opus Dei were ever sought by Professor Timoney, nor given to him.'[1] Technically, that may have been correct, but it did not prevent Timoney in his various ventures from calling upon the resources of the Opus Dei network, bringing to Ireland associated engineers from Britain, Spain and the US. Industrial Engineering Designers Limited's manufacturing facility, Advanced Technology Limited – one supposes another auxiliary society – was set up in 1975. Ad Tec, as it became known, built and tested prototypes of the Timoney APC. One of the largest orders for the vehicle came from the Belgian Army. It was also produced under licence in General Pinochet's Chile.

If not disturbed by the fact that an Opus Dei numerary, supposedly dedicated to achieving Christian perfection, spent his spare time designing armoured personnel carriers and other military machines, then one will not be bothered by the fact that numerary Michael Adams supported the throwing of bombs by IRA terrorists. Adams was managing director of Four Courts Press, publishers of *The Way* in Ireland, and he lived at Opus Dei's national headquarters, Harvieston, in Dublin. What he really went on the record to state was that throwing bombs in Northern Ireland was defensible if it brought the British to the negotiating table. This is what he wrote: 'None – let's hope – of the guerrillas in the North [i.e., Ulster] enjoys killing English soldiers, yet they will celebrate in a kind of poignant exhilaration the death of each soldier because each death builds up the only language which the British seem to understand . . . It is pathetic that the sorrow of bereaved English families should need to be compounded . . . but somebody has to die, somebody has to get hurt. If the "hurt" can be achieved through civil disobedience that certainly is preferable and more "Christian"; but it is difficult to

[1] O'Connor, *Op. cit.*, p. 152.

believe that anything less than violence can at this stage keep the pot boiling and so lead to fruitful negotiations . . . Bombs seem to work.'[1]

One of the uglier rumours that surfaced concerning the Vatican bank's hidden activities was the unproven allegation that it provided funding for the IRA. The first mention of this was made by a former Italian Secret Service agent and since then it has resurfaced from time to time, but never substantiated. What is known, however, is that in May 1981 John Paul II sent one of his personal secretaries, Father John Magee (now bishop of Cloyne), on a secret mission to Ireland, during which Magee met the IRA's Bobby Sands, then on a fast to death in an Ulster prison. Also a Panamanian company, Erin S.A., of uncertain origin but later linked to the Vatican bank, received almost $40 million in loans that were transferred to it through a Peruvian bank. Nothing connects Erin to the IRA, or to Ad Tec for that matter, but the name was certainly suggestive. Nor is it known what actually happened to Erin's $40 million, other than it was added to the pool of stateless capital in the international monetary system.

Opus Dei's ownership of French assets was even more complex. Although Father Fernando Maicas and Alvaro Calleja had arrived in Paris in October 1947, Opus Dei was not registered under French law until May 1966. Both came with NSRC grants and a piece of Isidoro Zorzano's death shroud to hang in the oratory of the residence they opened in boulevard Saint Germain in the Latin Quarter.

A first corporate holding was established in 1955 under the name of Association de Culture Universitaire et Technique (ACUT). It was registered as a charitable trust and was placed under the patronage of three illustrious Sorbonne professors, the vice-president of the French Senate, a former Gaullist minister and a senior Quai d'Orsay diplomat.

One wonders whether the patrons realized what they were patronizing, because Opus Dei, not yet registered in France, was nowhere mentioned in ACUT's statutes. ACUT acquired a seventeenth-century château near Soissons, north-east of Paris, which became an Opus Dei conference centre. The managing director of ACUT was a 21-year-old student at the Institute of Political Studies in Paris, Augustin Romero.

After completing his studies Romero went to work for the Banque

---

[1] Michael Adams, Letter to the Editor, *The Irish Press*, 14 September 1971.

de l'Union Européenne, one of Banco Popular Español's correspondent banks.[1] This little-known institution was also partly owned by Banco Ambrosiano of Milan. Opus Dei used it to transfer money into France. In the meantime, a series of covert holding companies with strange acronymic names like SEPAL, SAIDEC, SOCOFINA, SOFICO and TRIFEP began to mushroom throughout the country.

SAIDEC (Société Anonyme d'investissement pour le développement culturel) was founded in 1962 with a minimum capital of $2,000. Nicolas Macarez, a Spanish national, was listed as its managing director. Initially the largest individual shareholder was Romero, but with successive capital increases 90 per cent of its shares were taken up by TRIFEP.[2] This seemingly straightforward detail was confused by the fact that SAIDEC owned 90 per cent of TRIFEP and the two companies had interlocking boards of directors.[3]

SAIDEC's capital rose to $3 million over the next dozen years. In 1976, one of the contributors to a major capital increase was the Société Anonyme de Financement pour les investissements culturels, a totally anonymous company headquartered in Liechtenstein. SAIDEC became the owner-of-record of the château and a Paris building in rue Ventadour, which housed its registered offices. The rue Ventadour was on the opposite side of the Avenue de l'Opera from the Banque de l'Union Européenne. This proved convenient because the Banque de l'Union Européenne was banker to SAIDEC.

Also in 1962, Banco Popular Español acquired 34,900 shares of Banque des Intérêts Français, representing 35 per cent of the Paris bank's share capital. The Banque des Intérêts Français belonged to the Giscard d'Estaing family and its chairman was father of the future French president. Rafael Termes Carrero, at the time one of Banco Popular's managing directors, became a Banque des Intérêts Français director, seconded by numerary Andrés Rueda Salaberry, head of Banco Popular's European Department, who was described as the 'invisible overseer of Opus Dei's financial interests in France'.[4]

Opus Dei's corporate presence in the United Kingdom was no less

---

[1] Dr Filippo Leoni, Banco Ambrosiano's general manager for international business, in testimony before the Italian P2 Parliamentary Commission, Vol. CLIV, Doc. XXIII, No. 2, Ter 7, p. 228.
[2] Romero was later ordained and became Opus Dei's regional vicar for France.
[3] Oberlé, *Op. cit.*, pp. 86–87.
[4] *Ibid.*, p. 88; Ynfante, *Op. cit.*, p. 239; and Ekaizer, *Op. cit.*, p. 276.

confusing. In the autumn of 1946, Juan Antonio Galarraga, a chemist, arrived from Madrid on a NSRC research grant. By 1950, Galarraga had only been able to recruit one Briton. He was Michael Richards, a former army officer involved in debriefing prisoners after D-Day but who in Opus Dei legend quickly became a war hero. Escrivá de Balaguer referred to him as his 'English rascal'.[1] He was sent to Kenya to reconnoitre the terrain for an Opus Dei presence in East Africa, after which the Father discovered his late vocation and had him ordained.

With monies transferred from abroad Opus Dei acquired a small hotel in Hampstead, which opened as a student residence in April 1952 as Netherhall House. A group of assistant women numeraries were sent from Spain to look after housekeeping and catering, and suddenly Opus Dei was in business in the United Kingdom, though still not registered.

Registration only occurred in April 1954 when John Galarraga and Michael Richards formed the Sacerdotal Society of the Holy Cross and Opus Dei Charitable Trust. The deed of incorporation indicated that the purpose of the trust was 'the advancement of the Roman Catholic religion'. Its real aim, however, was to spread the apostolates proper to Opus Dei. The deed gave the trustees absolute discretion over the buying and selling of property and all forms of securities; for reasons unknown, it did not officially apply for the tax-exempt status until 1965. At that time it listed three properties as assets: Grandpont House in Oxford, which had been acquired in 1959, the new national headquarters in Orme Court, Bayswater, and a residence in Manchester. By then, most of Opus Dei's other UK properties had been transferred to the Netherhall Educational Association (NEA), founded in 1964 with an input of funds from abroad.

Three Opus Dei numeraries arrived in Switzerland in October 1956 and opened the first centre in Zurich's well-to-do residential district of Fluntern. Two of them were Catalan. Their leader was Father Juan Bautista Torello. He was accompanied by Pedro Turull, an architecture student, and Hans Rudi Freitag, a Swiss economics graduate who had worked in Valencia. In 1961 they founded Kulturgemeinschaft Arbor as the owner of record of the Work's

---

[1] Vázquez de Prada, *Op. cit.*, p. 302.

corporate undertakings in Switzerland. Zurich became a key money centre for Opus Dei after the formation of Fundación General Mediterránea (FGM), a 'charitable' trust that received a percentage of Banco Atlántico's profits. FGM had two known subsidiaries – Fundación General Latinoamericana (Fundamerica), based in Caracas, and the FGM Foundation in Zurich.[1] But it also appeared to have a third off-shoot in Argentina that helped finance the forming of neo-Perónista cadres under Carlos Menen. FGM spawned Limmat-Stiftung, a Zurich trust that initially had a capital of $42,000. Limmat-Stiftung's corporate envelope came out of the offices of Dr Arthur Wiederkehr. Its undertakings were 'exclusively within the public-interest domain, particularly in the field of education, both in Switzerland and abroad', which assured it of tax-exempt status. Limmat-Stiftung received donations from Banco Atlántico while at the same time it was listed as a Bankunión shareholder. Wiederkehr served on Limmat-Stiftung's board.

Dr Wiederkehr is also said to have sold the Zurich-based Nordfinanz Bank to Opus Dei. This institution was founded a year before the outbreak of the Second World War, when the Zurich attorney was starting out in the legal profession. It had led a sleepy existence under the name of Verwaltungs Bank until 1964, when Wiederkehr sold 80 per cent of its capital to a Nordic finance group. According to Spanish sherry magnate José María Ruiz-Mateos, Opus Dei controlled Nordfinanz, though he did not explain how. On the other hand, Wiederkehr remained the bank's chairman for many years, finally resigning in favour of his son, Dr Alfred Julius Wiederkehr.

When still a young man, Arthur Wiederkehr's talents had come to the attention of Lord Selborne, the UK minister of economic warfare. In 1942 Lord Selborne placed the Zurich lawyer on a wartime Statutory List of persons suspected of trading with the enemy or acting as Nazi agents. The *Daily Mail* of 25 November 1942 carried this report of proceedings in the House of Lords:

Relatives and friends of people in Occupied Territories are being blackmailed into parting with thousands of pounds as payment for exit permits for people under German domination. If the money is not

[1] *Golias* 30, pp. 40 and 133. Arthur Wiederkehr was a founding director of FGM Foundation, Zurich.

*forthcoming the victims, and sometimes their families, too, are . . .
sent to concentration camps.*

*First news of this 'racket in freedom' was given yesterday in the
House of Lords by Lord Selborne, minister of economic warfare . . .
Two principal agents – Dr Arthur Wiederkehr, a Swiss lawyer, and
Anna Hochberg, a Dutch Jewess – operate the racket. Both live in
Zurich . . .* [1]

After the war, Wiederkehr appeared before a disciplinary commission of the Zurich Bar Association, which absolved him of any
misconduct. He served on the board of Union Bank of Switzerland
from 1975 to 1981, during the period when Philippe de Weck was
UBS chairman. Opus Dei certainly appreciated his services. He set
up for the institute or its associates untold numbers of convenience
companies, including Supo Holding S.A., Zurich, with a capital of
1,000,000 Swiss francs. Spelt backwards, Supo becomes Opus.

The most striking feature of Opus Dei's financial operations was,
and remains, the element of secrecy. 'Opus Dei is poor. We have no
money,' claimed Andrew Soane, the UK spokesman. Soane is a chartered accountant, an unusual qualification for a media spokesman,
and in an interview with him I tried to find out about Escrivá de
Balaguer's wishes to open an Opus Dei college at Oxford. This was
not something to be entertained by a poor organization. But the
Father had designed a coat of arms and drafted plans for the college.
He wanted it to have a clock tower crowned by a statue of the Virgin
Mary, which at night would be floodlit.[2] To concretize the Father's
intentions, Opus Dei submitted a report to the diocesan authorities
claiming that its members were helping combat the spread of
Communism in Africa by indoctrinating African students with
Western ideologies, which seemed a political undertaking of serious
proportions. But Opus Dei is a spiritual organization. That pre-
sumably is why the headmaster of its Strathmore College in Kenya,
Yale graduate David Sperling, a friend of US Peace Corps president
Sargent Shriver, allowed the US Embassy in Nairobi to use the
college, which was partly funded by the UK government, as an

---

[1] Reginald Eason, *Daily Mail* (London), 25 November 1942. Another article under the heading of 'Allies Stop Nazi Traffic in Exit Permits', appeared in *The Daily Telegraph* (of the same
date). At 1994 exchange rates, 100,000 Swiss francs was worth about £50,000.
[2] Vázquez de Prada, *Op. cit.*, p. 303.

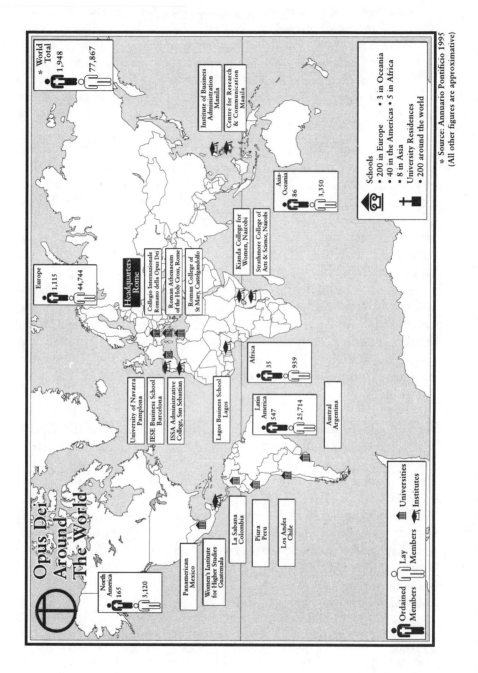

Opus Dei Around The World

* World Total 1,948 • 77,867

Europe 1,115 • 44,744

Headquarters Rome

Collegio Internazionale Romano della Opus Dei
Roman Athenaeum of the Holy Cross, Rome
Roman College of St Mary, Castelgandolfo

University of Navarra Pamplona
IESE Business School Barcelona
ISSA Administrative College, San Sebastian

Lagos Business School Lagos

Kianda College for Women, Nairobi
Strathmore College of Arts & Science, Nairobi

Institute of Business Administration Manila
Centre for Research & Communication Manila

Asia-Oceania 86 • 3,350

Africa 35 • 939

Latin America 547 • 25,714

Austral Argentina

La Sabana Colombia
Piura Peru
Los Andes Chile

Panamerican Mexico
Women's Institute for Higher Studies Guatemala

North America 165 • 3,120

Schools
• 200 in Europe   • 3 in Oceania
• 40 in the Americas • 5 in Africa
• 8 in Asia
University Residences
• 200 around the world

Ordained Members • | Lay Members | Universities | Institutes

* Source: Annuario Pontificio 1995
(All other figures are approximative)

'orientation centre' for African students seeking scholarships in the United States. 'Orientation centre' was a CIA euphemism meaning recruitment base.

Pending a reaction from the Oxford authorities, Opus Dei's UK charitable trust acquired Grandpont House, a listed eighteenth-century mansion on the Thames. Escrivá de Balaguer's proposal for an Oxford college was rejected, causing him 'great distress'. He said it was the Catholics who torpedoed him and he designed another coat of arms for Grandpont House that reflected his sorrow – the Virgin Mary with the words *ipsa duce* above a bridge with white and blue waves underneath it.

One of the points of this story – other than the Work's apparent willingness to allow its Nairobi installations to be used as a CIA 'orientation centre' – is that 'poor' Opus Dei was able to call upon important sums of money, even then, to finance its undertakings. A more grandiose example was the Sanctuary of Torreciudad, which opened in 1975. It was said to have as much construction below ground as above it. Certainly the above-the-ground structure rivals Saint Peter's in volume and the total was reported to have cost in the neighbourhood of $30 million.

As we have seen, physical ownership of Opus Dei's world-wide patchwork of assets can rarely be traced. This is intentional. The financial operations must remain confidential to give its *Corps Mobile* the greatest chance of success. Therefore, in addition to the praxis of profit-transfer accounting, Opus Dei's strategists developed a system of spiritual rather than physical control for its network of interests. But the system is by no means infallible. In fact it had to be significantly overhauled after a trusted son, Gregorio Ortega Pardo, momentarily disappeared in the mid-1960s.

The regional administrator in Portugal, Ortega was a collector of 'puffs of pride' – including Spain's Grand Cross of Civil Merit, which was awarded to him while Ibáñez Martín was ambassador to Lisbon – and he possessed a devilish love for luxury. He acquired for Opus Dei control of the Banco de Agricultura in Lisbon, an interest in the Banco Comercial de Angola, and in 1963 he founded Lusofin, a finance company enjoying governmental support. In the autumn of 1965, Ortega Pardo was arrested in a five-star Caracas hotel with two suitcases containing $225,000 in cash and $40,000 worth of jewellery, having been reported to the authorities by a prostitute.

Ibáñez Martín suggested he had gone to Venezuela to purchase a new residence for the local Opus Dei chapter. In any event, he was extradited to Spain. Waiting journalists were disappointed not to be able to interview him, for he was whisked away to a psychiatric clinic run by an Opus Dei doctor. The charges against him were eventually dropped and two years later he was expelled from the Work with a one-way ticket to Argentina.

The Ortega affair presented a number of puzzling contradictions. The organization insists it is poor when quite obviously it controls, through a complicated network of trusts and other devices, a large assortment of assets for which no public accounting exists. Outwardly it attempts to create a placid, pious image when in reality it is driven by a strong inner sense of mission. It denies interfering with the private lives and careers of members when manifestly the opposite is true, down to determining the choice of books they read. In a more general context, it appears to pursue opponents or those imagined to have done it harm with all available means, including *pillería* and the use of physical muscle. On top of all this, it portrays itself as just another branch of the Catholic Church when it has developed a strong sectarian approach, with oblates becoming bogged down in fundamentalist doctrines that demand their submission to a lifetime of servitude not to the Church but to the Father.

Impossible, you say? The Church would never allow such a thing. I thought so, too. But perhaps the single most telling fact is that when the Church had a perfect opportunity to investigate, during the beatification hearings for Escrivá de Balaguer, no-one so much as thought to ask such a basic question as why God's Servant, who was said to have lived the seven Christian virtues so heroically, needed to adopt the lapsed title of a Spanish grandee.

When former members wanted to put their doubts, fears or observations before the beatification tribunals, they were systematically excluded from doing so because they were portrayed as being mentally unbalanced or sex fiends. And yet no independent verification of the claims was ever made. As for an institution of the Church imprisoning members or making them accomplices in their own loss of freedom? The next chapters will examine Opus Dei's system of governance to determine the manner in which the Church's most powerful secular organization regulates its existence.

PART FOUR

GOVERNANCE

THE STRUCTURE OF OPUS DEI

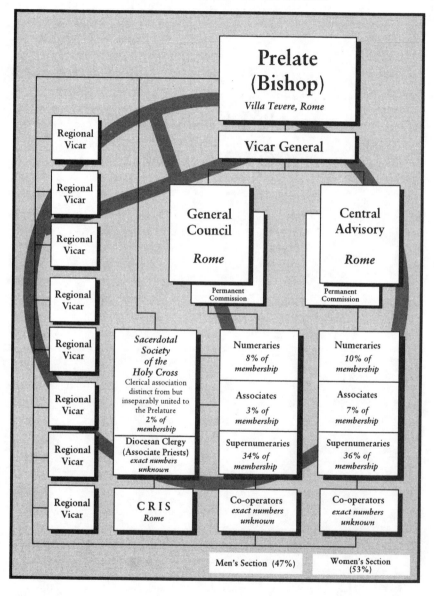

Prelate (Bishop)
Villa Tevere, Rome

Vicar General

Regional Vicar

Regional Vicar

Regional Vicar

Regional Vicar

Regional Vicar

Regional Vicar

Regional Vicar

Regional Vicar

General Council
Rome

Central Advisory
Rome

Permanent Commission

Permanent Commission

Sacerdotal Society of the Holy Cross
Clerical association distinct from but inseparably united to the Prelature
2% of membership

Diocesan Clergy (Associate Priests)
exact numbers unknown

CRIS
Rome

Numeraries
8% of membership

Associates
3% of membership

Supernumeraries
34% of membership

Co-operators
exact numbers unknown

Numeraries
10% of membership

Associates
7% of membership

Supernumeraries
36% of membership

Co-operators
exact numbers unknown

Men's Section (47%)

Women's Section (53%)

16

THE INNER WORLD OF OPUS DEI

*We must always be ready to spend our life for what God asks of us.
And He has asked us to leave our entire life for Opus Dei. That is why
we must live very close to God, to Our Lady and to the Work which
so needs our help.*

Josemaría Escrivá de Balaguer, *Crónica* I, 1971

MOST PEOPLE JOIN OPUS DEI OUT OF LOVE FOR GOD. BY THE SAME
measure, most who leave do so for the same reason. Once inside the
organization they may find that love of God comes second to love of
the Father, who is perfect because he is the son of God. Not prepared
to serve God through the Father, they opt out. Vladimir Felzmann,
who left Opus Dei after twenty-three years to become a priest of the
Westminster diocese in London, explained his departure in this way:
'As God brought me into Opus Dei, it was His love that let me out.
Once I could see that I could leave without breaking my word to God,
I left. But it took me many, many hours of prayer until . . . I saw that
the Work of God is not identical with God.'[1]

Felzmann believes that people who live inside Opus Dei for any
period of time become so conditioned by 'mortification of intellect'
that they become emotionally dependent and totally bind themselves

[1] Vladimir Felzmann, 'Why I left Opus Dei', *The Tablet*, 26 March 1983.

over to the organization. It starts from the moment of their oblation and is strengthened by the 'means of formation' to which thereafter they must submit. These factors combine to form a powerful mind control system, making a mockery out of Opus Dei's claim that it never, repeat never interferes in the private or professional lives of members. Through this system highly intelligent people are induced to surrender their capacity for ethical reasoning to a superior authority, in some cases abdicating all moral responsibility for their conduct in the secular world. Never before published, Opus Dei's 'means of formation' are worth considering in some depth as they represent the conduit by which its recruits are transformed into Christian fundamentalists.

THE OPUS DEI OATH OF FIDELITY

The Oblate declares:

> In the full exercise of my freedom, I ...... declare my firm intention to strive with all my ability to attain a state of sanctity and to exercise the apostolate, according to the spirit and customs of Opus Dei. From this date until renewing my oath on 19 March next, I pledge:

1. To remain obedient to the Prelate and other authorised persons of the Prelature, and apply myself in all things that pertain to the specific undertakings of the Prelature; and

2. To fulfil all duties that pertain to being a numerary of Opus Dei and to observe the Norms by which the Prelature is governed, and also to observe all legal prescriptions of the Prelate and other authorised persons of authority belonging to the Prelature – in accordance with its Codex Iuris, spirit and apostolate.

A Regional Vicar of the Prelature declares in the presence of the Oblate and two witnesses, members of the Prelature, at least one of whom must be a numerary:

> As a Regional Vicar of the Prelature, I ...... solemnly declare that beginning from the moment you join the Prelature as a numerary member, and for as long as you remain a numerary member, Opus Dei assumes the following responsibilities:

1. To give you a continuous formation - doctrinal, spiritual, ascetic and apostolic – and also to provide you, through the priests of the Prelature, with personal pastoral guidance; and

2. To undertake such other responsibilities which, in relation to Prelature's faithful, are set out in the Codex Iuris proper to the Prelature

After serving five years as a novice, in order to be accepted as a numerary the oblate must swear an Oath of Fidelity in the presence of the regional vicar and two witnesses, one of them the oblate's spiritual director and immediate superior. The oath is administered before a plain wooden Cross without its crucified in the darkened chapel of an Opus Dei centre. A ring is then slipped upon the oblate's finger, for as a full numerary member he or she is now married – not to the Church, but to Opus Dei. To consolidate the marriage the oblate is required to read aloud a passage from the Work's catechism, affirming his or her responsibilities to the organization and its hierarchy.

As in everything pertaining to Opus Dei, a reason exists for the oblation rite. Not only is it one of the distinguishing features of a religious sect but, according to sociologist Alberto Moncada, the symbolism of the empty Cross is important because it is intended to reinforce one's feeling of inadequacy and guilt. This is clearly set forth in Maxim 178 of The Way: 'When you see a poor wooden Cross, alone, uncared for, and of no value . . . and without its Crucified, don't forget that that Cross is your Cross . . . the Cross which is waiting for the Crucified it lacks; and that Crucified must be you.'

Opus Dei denies that members must submit to an oblation rite or that they are required to take vows of any kind. Just as 'recruiting' is not a word used by Opus Dei, also 'oblation' and 'vows' are not part of its lexicon. But on 5 June 1946 Don Alvaro wrote to the Sacra Penitenzieria Apostolica in Rome explaining *inter alia* that Opus Dei members do emit vows, to the Virgin Mary, St Joseph, the three Archangels and the Apostles Peter, Paul and John.[1] Moreover, every 19 March – the feast day of St Joseph – Opus Dei numeraries are required to renew their vows of chastity, poverty and obedience in a partial repetition of the oblation rite. This practice still continues.

Just as important as the oblation and renewal of vows in cultivating Opus Dei's sectarianism are the six 'means of formation' – known as the Confidence, Brief Circle, Examination of Conscience, Confession, Fraternal Correction and Weekly Meditation – as they set the Work apart from all other organizations of the Catholic Church. 'The idea of the formative norms is to keep you humble and in a constant state of unworthiness. The norms have both a positive

---

[1] Rocca, *Op. cit.*, document 22, pp. 154–155.

OPUS DEI MEMBERSHIP CATEGORIES

Opus Dei's membership is characterised by four types, depending upon each individual's availability for the works carried out by the Prelature:

Numeraries – lay people who dedicate themselves to celibacy and full availability for the needs of the Prelature. They usually live in an Opus Dei residence. Among the women numeraries are **assistant numeraries**, who dedicate themselves to the material administration of the centres of Opus Dei, such as maintenance, cleaning, laundry and catering. A few of the male numeraries are ordained to the priesthood and incardinated in the Prelature.

Associates – lay men or women who dedicate themselves to celibacy, but generally do not live in an Opus Dei residence. Male associates may also become priests of the Prelature.

Supernumeraries – lay men and women, either single or married, who live their vocation to Opus Dei in the setting of their families.

Members of the Priestly Society of the Holy Cross – includes the Prelature's own priests as well as diocesan priests incardinated in their own diocese (called associate or supernumerary priests) who wish to receive spiritual formation from Opus Dei and who participate in Opus Dei's apostolate. The Priestly Society spreads the spirit of Opus Dei among the clergy not otherwise linked with the Prelature.

An association of **co-operators** exists for persons who are not members, but who help with their 'prayers, donations, gifts and other forms of assistance'. In an unusual twist for a Catholic organization, Opus Dei's co-operators can be of any religion.

and a negative side. They act as a check on self-satisfaction. Anybody who is self-satisfied is a dangerous animal. But also it tends to worsen one's feelings of inadequacy and guilt,' explained Felzmann.

Whatever one's rank inside the Work one must submit to the formative norms. Conditioning begins while still a novice. Every novice is placed under the supervision of a local director who observes and tests his or her reaction to spiritual suggestion. Novices are also assigned an Opus Dei priest through whom they must practise the sacrament of penitence at least once a week. The obligations become more embracing once one takes the oath of fidelity. Members are required to participate fully in the life of the local centre to which they are assigned. If a husband and wife are both members, they are never assigned to the same centre, nor attend the same Brief Circle, as the separation of sexes is strictly adhered to throughout the Opus Dei structure. Each centre also serves as a house of residence for a certain number of numeraries, insuring a constant mix between celibate and noncelibate members.

Each member's first obligation is the weekly Confidence. This is a one-on-one session with the spiritual director who is always a lay numerary. Set topics are discussed, the recruiting of new members being the most important. Also reviewed is one's personal and professional conduct. Faults in attitude or personal behaviour, whether self-confessed or reported by others, are remedied by what is known as 'fraternal correction' – an act of contrition, or punishment, required by the spiritual director.

Members are encouraged to place full 'confidence' in their spiritual director. Several former members believe – and on occasion have affirmed it publicly – that collusion exists between the spiritual director (a layman, not covered by the seal of the confessional) and the confessor (who must be an Opus Dei priest). This is a serious charge. But it is one that is almost impossible to prove. Opus Dei knows this and denies it vigorously. Still, the potential for manipulating minds and emotions is evident. Consequently, Opus Dei insists that once members receive the spiritual help they require (everybody needs spiritual help, according to Maxim 59), its job is finished. But one's professional career is the central pillar of each member's personal apostolate. Therefore it is of direct interest to the Work. This filters through in the Brief Circle, a formative norm that, like the Confidence, is held weekly.

The Brief Circle is described as the ground-floor mechanism through which Opus Dei gains the greatest degree of leverage over its members. It is a group function that includes never more than twenty participants, all of them socially, intellectually and professionally matched to form a homogenous cell-like nucleus. Each Brief Circle is chaired by the local director. He opens it with a short talk, supposedly on the Gospel but invariably on some aspect of Opus Dei or the Father's teaching. Participants then recite aloud the 'Plan of Life', which provides discipline and structure to their existence. The full programme is as follows:

I.   Invocation, in Latin, of the Holy Spirit and the Virgin Mary, source of Hope and seat of Wisdom.

II.   The Director's Commentary on the Gospel.

III.   Reading aloud the Plan of Life – everyone must stand while it is read – followed by a commentary on some point of the Plan, Norms or Customs.

Plan of Life

Daily: Morning offering. Mental prayer (half an hour in the morning and evening). Holy Mass. Communion. Visit to the Blessed Sacrament. Reading of the Holy Gospel and of some spiritual book. Holy Rosary. Examination of conscience. Recital of the *Angelus* or *Regina Coeli*.

Weekly: Sacramental Confession. Corporal mortification (for numeraries) and recital of the *Hail Holy Queen*, or *Regina Coeli*, on Saturdays. Weekly meditation service.

Monthly: One day of recollection.

Yearly: Spiritual Retreat.

IV.   Examination of Conscience. Each member is required to ask:

1. Have I omitted the meditation or shortened it, except in the case of illness?
2. Have I practised presence of God and considered my divine filiation frequently each day?
3. Have I sought to give my first and last thought each day to God?
4. Have I omitted a particular examination of conscience, or hurried over the general examination?
5. In the Holy Mass each day, have I remembered the Work of God, my brothers, and especially my Directors?
6. Have I borne the annoying things of each day well?
7. Have I omitted the customary mortifications?
8. Do I endeavour to acquire a spirit of penance?
9. Have I sought a right intention, anxious only for the glory of God in everything?
10. Have I said the *Preces* of the Work and the other vocal prayers calmly and with attention?
11. Have I lived a spirit of sacrifice in the apostolates entrusted to me by my Directors?
12. Have I been docile to my Directors in those things that refer to my spiritual life and apostolate?

13. Have I fulfilled with due diligence the apostolic tasks entrusted to me by the Work?

14. Have I taken special care to practise charity in my relations with my brothers?

15. Am I especially mindful of the Norms of charity and prudence whenever it is necessary to make or accept fraternal correction?

16. Is my spirit of proselytism borne out by my deeds?

17. Am I conscious of having caused Opus Dei any definite harm through my apathy, imprudence, tepidity, or coldness in attending to my religious, social or professional duties?

18. What efforts have I made in my intellectual development which is essential to my purpose, in my study and in making the best use of my time?

19. Have I spent money unnecessarily, out of extravagance, capriciousness, vanity, laziness, etc.?

20. Have I always been deeply sincere with my Directors, combining the capacity for initiative and personal responsibility with the virtue of humility in order to identify myself with the indications I have received for my spiritual and apostolic work?

21. Have I despised sacrifice in the little things of each day?

22. Do I try to live order in my work so as to make it more effective and to give greater glory to God?

23. Do I do my work when I ought (today, now), or do I deceive myself by leaving it for later, which is the same as not doing it at all?

24. Am I careful to see that there is nothing odd or annoying in my outward appearance that might not be in keeping with my duties and position?

25. Do I allow myself to be dominated by gloominess, without realizing that it is an ally of the enemy?

26. Do I always work with the happiness of one who knows he is a son of God?

V. Help us in the name of God.

Confiteor Deo . . . May the Almighty and Merciful God release us from the chains of our sins.

After which, those who have obtained previous permission go

by turns on their knees and accuse themselves of their faults [not of their sins or any matter of conscience, which must be confessed to a priest, in confidence], saying at the beginning, 'In the presence of God, Our Lord, I accuse myself of . . .' and at the end, ' . . . for these faults I beg pardon and penance.'

The Director imposes penance on each, according to Custom.

VI. Reading and commentary on some spiritual book, or talk.

VII. Conversation about affairs of the Work.

VIII. *Preces* (Prayer).

The Brief Circle establishes each member's spiritual menu. It has all the necessary minerals and vitamins for a healthy diet. Members are told that anyone who follows it religiously can become a saint. The eighth item of the Plan of Life, after reading from the Gospel or the works of the Father and reciting the Rosary, requires members to perform the third formative norm, the Examination of Conscience, or simply the Conscience. It is a private exercise that numeraries accomplish in the oratory of their residence, usually prior to the major silence, and others in the evenings before retiring. It requires ten or fifteen minutes to ask oneself the twenty-six questions of the Conscience, during which notes of weak points should be made so that they can be discussed at the weekly Confidence or raised in Confession. Four of these questions concern professional attitudes. Another three evoke the mind-conditioning character of Opus Dei's inner world: members are expected to be 'docile' with their superiors; they are required to practise due diligence in fulfilling special apostolates – i.e., missions; and finally they are reminded of the omnipresent 'enemy'.

The last of the means of formation is the least intensive, consisting of the Weekly Meditation: a meditation service in the chapel directed by the resident chaplain. Its purpose is to explain some activity of the Work, for example one of the norms or perhaps a new order from Opus Central, always placing it in a spiritual context as serving the wishes of the Father.

The lifestyles of numeraries and supernumeraries are by necessity quite different. A supernumerary is expected to live a pious, disciplined existence within the context of his or her family. Lay numeraries are the second-level élite (priests being the first). A numerary's day is crowded with spiritual and other obligations that leave no time for idleness and little for leisure. Custom requires numeraries to rise in silence and kiss the floor, after which they are accorded a half-hour to wash and dress. This is followed by another half-hour of silent prayer before attending Mass in the residence chapel. After morning Mass the 'Major Silence' is broken and breakfast is served in the refectory, following which those who work outside leave for their place of employment. During the day they are required to read from the Gospel as well as some other spiritual book, and pray the Rosary. At midday they should recite the *Angelus*.

Returning to the residence after work, the numerary completes his spiritual reading and spends another half-hour in silent prayer. Each member has some apostolic responsibility and usually this is the time to fulfil it. The apostolic duties might be presiding over a circle – there are three types of circles: St Raphael for persons under recruitment; St Michael for numeraries; and St Gabriel for supernumeraries – or meeting the local director.

The numerary's day ends in the chapel for the Conscience. Afterwards, residents gather for a reading from the Gospel. The reading and commentary on it is assigned to a different numerary each evening. The commentary has to be reviewed by the director beforehand to make sure it hits the right spiritual note and that there are no out-of-place remarks. One passage that frequently gives rise to light-heartedness is a commentary on the Five Foolish Virgins. A remark at the end of the commentary such as, 'And don't you be like the foolish virgins and forget your lamp', can cause a bout of giggles that destroys the desired atmosphere of devotion. After the reading the Major Silence begins.

Requiring male numeraries to sleep on the floor once a week is a custom. Women numeraries sleep on boards covered by a blanket. When an Opus Dei member greets a fellow member he must say, *Pax*. The automatic response is *In aeternum*. Another custom that started in the late 1960s is called 'Spoliation'. It applies only to numeraries and takes place on the Feast of St Francis of Assisi. On that day the director can come into a numerary's room and remove any object to which the numerary is thought to have become over-attached. 'This could be a teddy bear or a pair of gold cufflinks, but if it happens to be a watch given to you by your mother it hurts,' one former numerary explained.

As the membership profile changed in the 1960s, becoming more professionally oriented, Opus Dei was accused of possessing a rakishly Capitalist image. Because of the bad press this generated, Opus Dei's hierarchy began to fear for its canonical status. Accordingly, the institute re-oriented its main apostolate towards primary and secondary schools, youth clubs and inner-city social centres, thereby moving the Work into areas that previously had been Jesuit preserves.

As Opus Dei remains élitist, the preferred clientele for its grammar schools and youth clubs are middle-class children whose families can afford the relatively high tuition fees which go with the privilege of having their sons and daughters become targets for recruitment. From registration to graduation, the spiritual development of its academic wards is followed and encouraged. At the same time a selection process singles out the more apt pupils, and little by little those selected are prepared for their formal incorporation into Opus Dei, preferably as celibate members.

This new phase started in the 1970s. 'It focuses on guaranteeing the institution's survival by recruiting young adolescents at a primary level while the higher aim is controlling power in the Vatican,' Moncada, a former numerary, wrote in a controversial treatise on Opus Dei's sectarianism. But recruiting children under eighteen years of age is against the canons of the Church, and Opus Dei is unlikely to scoff openly at the legal prescriptions of the Church.

'To be sure, general principles of canon and civil law forbid incorporation before the age of eighteen. However, in this as in other aspects of its activity, Opus Dei has discovered how to combine external respect for the law with functional pragmatism which allows it, for instance, to snare youngsters with emotional complicity in their own loss of independence, all the while proclaiming neutrality and concern for the freedom of the affected children to parents worried about premature decisions,' Moncada explained.[1]

Opus Dei denies that it recruits adolescents, but one only need consult the relevant source material on the subject (not, however, available to the general public – nor even to all Opus Dei members) to understand the importance it attaches to the young mind:

[1] Alberto Moncada, 'Catholic Sects: Opus Dei', *Revista Internacional de Sociología*, Madrid, December 1992.

... Youth is the time of formation. It is a time in which ... the direction and the meaning of one's entire life is fixed. It is a time of ideals and of love, a time when the soul opens – is vigorously receptive – to the light of doctrine ... It is a more opportune time for an effective sowing ... [1]

With the extension of its school network during the 1980s, Opus Dei began attracting more reliable, dedicated members, trained from childhood to devote themselves to a lifetime of promoting the Prelature's worldwide strategies and interests.

The Father, in the person of the prelate general, is the primary bond that encourages members to transfer their capacity for rational analysis to a superior authority. This authority conditions them to abide by internal covenants that would not be tolerated in an external society. Commented Moncada: 'Since one must be submissive to the Father and those who stand in his stead, and even "sacrifice one's judgement", the negation of individual rights is plain.' Such obedience frowns upon internal criticism and stifles all personal opinions concerning the apostolate. Under these conditions, one's brothers in the faith turn into secret informers.

'From the time of entering the Work, a member is forbidden to go to confession with any priest who does not belong to the institution. An ample literature on the theme of the "good shepherd" and the maxim of "washing dirty linen at home" legitimizes the sealing off of members' consciences from the outside and makes mental control by superiors more simple. Opus Dei priests, furthermore, employ information received in the confessional to design the strategy to be followed with candidates for membership. To tighten the circle of mental dependence and group loyalty further, all members must make a weekly "confidence", similar in nature to confession, with the director of their house or centre in which the most explicit sincerity is encouraged towards a person with no sacerdotal qualifications,' he added in his treatise.

The absolute surrender of one's judgement to a superior, it has been suggested, breeds a form of ethical childishness. Another consequence is that it provokes abnormally high stress levels among younger members. 'Stress is a consequence of the constant

[1] 'The Seed Bed of the Work', editorial in *Crónica* VII, 1962.

dissimulating towards the outside . . . Aspiring numeraries, for example, are advised to tell their parents that they have made no commitment to the Work. From the outset, one's sense of honesty is distorted, Moncada continued.

Opus Dei rejects the suggestion that its means of formation result in a collective distortion of moral standards. 'Opus Dei does not get involved, indeed cannot get involved . . . in the professional, family, social, political and cultural matters of its members,' it repeats. But Opus Dei remains keenly interested in influencing public opinion by placing certain of its members in key media positions. This obviously has advantages, but it also makes a lie out of the affirmation that it does not involve itself in the professional, social or economic affairs of its members. Opus Dei, nevertheless, remains firm in dismissing any such intention. Opus Dei controls the lives of its numeraries by a subtle combination of suggestion and 'holy coercion'. One example illustrating how the Prelature works in this domain, and the psychological damage it can produce, is told by a former British numerary:

'From the day I wrote my letter to the Father requesting admission, I handed over my [university] grant and all other income (e.g., allowance from my family) . . . I was attracted to Country Dancing and Gilbert and Sullivan societies, but both of these were no-go areas for a numerary, who cannot attend theatres or mix with the opposite sex unless professional life demands it . . . During my first year as a numerary, my Directress was a young Portuguese. She persistently told me that I had a flair, an asset for the apostolate. She heard my "Confidences". Opus Dei members have a weekly talk with their Director or Directress. This is called the "Confidence", and supplements the weekly confession with an Opus Dei priest. The Confidence, combined with a fortnightly talk with the priest (not limited by the seal of confession), is perhaps the most effective means of control within Opus Dei. Members are required to give a detailed account of every aspect of their lives: prayer, reading, apostolate, money, mortification, plan of life, etc.

'My Directress suggested that with my distinction in English 'A' level, and command of the language, I might think of becoming a journalist. (Internal documents, as I later discovered, encouraged superiors to watch out for potential media professionals . . .)'[1]

[1] Eileen Clark, *Opus Dei – An 11-Year Experience of the Women's Section*, February 1995 (unpublished), pp. 4–5.

After some years this UK numerary began suffering depressions, and one day collapsed from nervous exhaustion. She was put in the care of an Opus Dei doctor, who prescribed Librium and Tofranil, which she took 'out of obedience'. She was eventually enrolled in the University of Navarra's Institute of Journalism.

When she returned to London she took a job on the foreign news desk of the *Guardian*. She never personally sought to be a journalist; in her own words she 'was not cut out to be one'. The depressions kept recurring, and she was finally admitted as an out-patient to a psychiatric hospital, where she was treated by a psychiatrist who was also an Opus Dei numerary. She finally left Opus Dei in 1971, after four years on medication and psychiatry administered by Opus Dei members. She had £100 to her name, and had to give up her job for health reasons. Her family doctor, who treated her for the next two years, compared her condition to that of a former prisoner of war. Her freedom restored, she reverted to her original career preferences – dance and languages.

Another example was given by a top Milan corporate lawyer who was attracted to Opus Dei by its work ethic. Then he found out, in his words, that 'complicity exists between the director and chaplain. They combine to interfere in your personal affairs and pressure you to make decisions that affect your private and professional life . . . Every effort is made to make you spiritually dependent upon the organization. You must open your soul, be trusting and slowly they work upon you to empty yourself and acknowledge that in spiritual matters you are like a child, unknowledgeable and in need of help. Once you begin to accept the notion that you are a child in spiritual matters, then the next step is to get you to obey. "Obey intelligently but blindly," the local director would repeat.'

Humble yourself before your superior. That is the sure way to sanctity. Accept that and you have become a member of Christ's militia. 'It is surprising the number of strong-minded people who will give in to this concept of spiritual immaturity and the need to entrust your soul like a child to the Father,' he added. 'You see others do it – your peers, whom you respect – and you start saying, "OK, why not me?" And soon you're hooked.' In his circle were one of Italy's leading investment bankers, the managing director of the second largest privately held financial and industrial conglomerate, and a retired Fiat director.

Elizabeth Demichel was 'hooked' while a high school student in the Swiss city of Fribourg. Opus Dei has been active in Fribourg, a Catholic university centre of 40,000 inhabitants, since the 1960s. In her after-school hours Elizabeth frequented a youth club run by Opus Dei. She wanted to become a simultaneous translator and the club director suggested she take a four-year language course in Vienna. She was eighteen and it was her first time away from home. Her parents were only too happy when she announced that she had found lodging in a student hostel run by Opus Dei.

The atmosphere at the Vienna centre was warm. Other young women there, most more advanced in their careers than her, helped her and smothered her with friendship. When she announced to the directress that she would like to become a supernumerary, the directress replied that a 'state of grace' enabled her to detect vocations and she recognized in Elizabeth the vocation of a numerary. The directress explained that even though numeraries took a promise of celibacy, they enjoyed the same liberty as other lay people. Surprised by the revelation that she had a vocation, Elizabeth became confused. The directress suggested she should talk about it to her confessor, the house chaplain, which she did. He was understanding and proposed that she go on a three-day retreat to reflect and question her soul. She didn't really want to go on a retreat, but agreed anyway.

During confession towards the end of the retreat, the priest suddenly affirmed, 'Well, you've decided, no?' Not expecting such a direct approach, Elizabeth replied, 'Yes'. And so she came to 'whistle' inside the confessional. Collusion? Of course not. Nevertheless she learned afterwards that the house numeraries held a celebration when told she had written her letter to the Father.

After 'whistling', Elizabeth was more fully indoctrinated into the ways of Opus Dei. She was given the internal Catechism, a booklet with 500 questions and answers which novices must learn by heart. As it had to be returned to the directress's office each evening, she was only allowed to study it for two or three hours at a time – in addition to her language courses. She was also required to study the Ceremonial Book – the *Vademecum de ceremonias liturgicas*. Another secret document, it too was kept in the house safe, along with the Opus Dei song book which contains the internal hymns and songs that women numeraries sing at *tertulias* and other gatherings. The song titles included *Going Fishing* and *I Whistle So You'll*

Whistle Too. 'Fishing' is Opus-speak for recruiting and 'whistling' is when a recruit decides to join. The women numeraries sing these songs in front of prospective recruits who are unaware of their meaning.

When Elizabeth informed her parents that she had signed a 'contract' to become an Opus Dei numerary, she explained that it was not definitive because of a five-year acceptance period. Then towards the end of Elizabeth's final year of studies her parents suggested she should come home and think of looking for a job. They had spoken by then to the directress of the Opus Dei centre in Fribourg about the obligations of a numerary and were assured:

(1) A numerary lived in the same manner as any other lay person, with freedom to choose her employment and work as she pleased, where she pleased; (2) no vows or promises were required, but only a 'contract simple' by which the Work undertook to give numeraries the spiritual help they required, doctrinal formation, and guidance by the Work's priests in carrying out their apostolate, against which numeraries undertake to remain celibate, live in an Opus Dei residence if their work permits, and donate free time to the Work's collective apostolate; (3) if at any time a numerary discovered that she was not adapted to the Work's mission, she was free to leave; (4) numeraries retained full control over their personal possessions and inheritance, and contributed from their income as they saw fit.

Not long afterwards, Elizabeth wrote to her parents: 'To travel to another country can only be approved by the Father, while travel to another city or even another centre must be approved by the local directress. Therefore if I should return to Switzerland, it is because the Father wishes it and I will accept that as the will of God . . .'

Concerned, the parents contacted the Opus Dei vicar delegate for Switzerland who assured them that he understood their concern and promised to do everything in his power to find a solution that would be in the family's best interests. Shortly afterwards, Elizabeth wrote to her parents: 'Daddy always wanted me to take a doctorate. That is exactly what I am now going to do! You also want me to leave Austria. That, too, I am going to do (after obtaining my degree)! In fact Monsignor Alvaro wants me to go to Sweden to enrol at the university there (it is important that it be re-Christianized) . . . I have already enquired about the conditions of enrolment at the University of Stockholm.' After asking her parents to continue paying for her tuition, she added, 'Personally, I see in this request of the Father the will of God, Who always arranges everything for our greatest well-being.'

A psychologist had advised the parents that any show of opposition to their daughter's intentions would be exploited to turn her against them. Elizabeth now told her mother that she was going to make a will in favour of the Work. 'Don't worry, it's only for the little things that we have in our room,' Elizabeth said.

Her mother had read the Constitutions by then – which the directress had never shown Elizabeth – and knew that it was more serious. But it made her think. Whenever money is mentioned, Opus Dei becomes most attentive. She told her daughter that she was going to have a serious operation and wanted to bring her will up to date. She said Elizabeth was needed to co-sign the various papers with her brothers and sisters before going to Stockholm. Elizabeth talked to her directress, who agreed that she should go through Fribourg on her way to Stockholm. Permission for her to stay at home was denied. But her mother said that before the operation she wanted to take Elizabeth on a three-day retreat at a convent near Fribourg. The local directress agreed. During the retreat the mother mentioned the unethical practices of a sect she had read about. Elizabeth agreed that she could never belong to such an organization. At that point the mother showed Elizabeth a file on Opus Dei detailing everything she had mentioned. Elizabeth was shocked because the experiences related in the file so resembled what had happened to her and therefore it had to be accurate. As if an enormous weight was lifted from her conscience, she fell into her mother's arms. 'I can't belong to an organization like that, can I?' she cried.

To extract Elizabeth from Opus Dei was not easy. She had to write to the Father in Rome asking for permission to leave. In the meantime she kept out of sight as numeraries who knew her waited on the commuter station platform near her home on the outskirts of Fribourg to intercept her. Finally the vicar delegate called and accused the Demichels of 'kidnapping' their own daughter.

Opus Dei's first vocation in Britain, Father Michael Richards, also became disenchanted with the Work and in 1973 decided to leave. Tormented and by then a hypochondriac, he took a position as chaplain at the University of Bangor in Wales. He withdrew into himself and stopped taking medication, until he died of a cerebral haemorrhage in August 1977. When Vladimir Felzmann asked to leave the Work, the regional vicar took him to Michael Richards' graveside and said, 'You see, Vlad, what happens to people who leave the Work.'

Raimundo Panikkar, one of the Father's most gifted sons of the 1940s and 1950s, was sent to India to open an Opus Dei presence there with funding provided by the NSRC. A few years later Escrivá de Balaguer called him to Rome to become chaplain at Opus Dei's Residenza Universitaria Internazionale. But it was not long before Panikkar decided that Opus Dei was suffocating him and in 1966 he prepared to leave. In the midst of these preparations he accepted to give a lecture at the Sacred Heart Convent in Bonn, where his sister had been a student. When he arrived at Bonn railway station, two former university friends – both lapsed women numeraries – were waiting to accompany him to the lecture. However, before they could greet him, Panikkar was intercepted by the regional vicar, Rev. Dr Alfonso Par, and another Opus Dei priest. They whisked him away to the regional vicariat in Cologne. Concerned, his friends informed the Archbishop of Cologne, then Cardinal Josef Frings, of Panikkar's apparent sequestration. Cardinal Frings immediately had his secretary call the Opus Dei centre and ask to speak with Panikkar as the cardinal wanted to invite the celebrated theologian to lunch. He was told that Panikkar had changed plans and was leaving instantly for Rome.

Panikkar was escorted to Rome and then held at an Opus Dei residence for priests for the next ten days. Escrivá de Balaguer was said to be furious over his suspected defection and asked that the Vatican secularize him. Paul VI, meanwhile, had been informed by a mutual friend of Panikkar's rough handling and replied that rather than the Church lose a priest, Panikkar should be released from Opus Dei. Panikkar in fact was expelled and, handed a one-way ticket back to India but no money, he was put on a flight to Delhi.

These recitals of loss of personal freedom, in which the members themselves are often willing accomplices, were related by people who left the organization. What about the views of those who remain inside? The 'extraordinary freedom' that an Opus Dei member enjoys was explained by Manuel Garrido, the information officer at the Sanctuary of Torreciudad. When asked where, for a numerary, the division lies between the spiritual and secular world, he avoided giving a direct answer by insisting that individual members enjoy total 'freedom'. He was clearly intelligent, extremely engaging and no reason existed to doubt his sincerity. But one wondered what would happen if he wished to expand his professional horizons by undertaking additional studies in London. Would he be free to do so?

'Of course,' he answered. But the 'of course' was tempered by an important proviso. He would be required to submit a detailed proposal and reasons for soliciting the move to his superiors. And what would happen if his superiors said no? He replied that it would be his 'joy' to continue the work he had been doing for close to twenty years. He wasn't forced to, he insisted, but he did it because of his 'love' for God, the Father and Opus Dei.[1]

That Opus Dei had developed a strong sect-like character did not seem to concern the Vatican unduly. The Work had amassed significant resources and was sworn to protect the Church from her enemies, which any pope could not fail to appreciate. Opus Dei's success was a reflection of the wisdom and foresight of its central directors. To understand the workings of Opus Central better a peek behind the massive black doors at 73 viale Bruno Buozzi in Rome is necessary.

[1] Manuel Garrido, interviewed at Torreciudad, 21 June 1994.

17

KREMLIN ON THE TIBER

The Work is a family and a militia at the same time.

Crónica VII, 1964

OPUS DEI'S HIGHEST AUTHORITY IS THE PRESIDENT (NOW PRELATE) general. Internally, he is addressed as the Father. The symbol of his succession is a piece of the 'True Cross' that he wears like an amulet around his neck. His authority is absolute. His term of office is indefinite. He is assisted in carrying out God's wishes by a vicar general. The statutes stipulate that both the Father and his vicar general must be priests, each with at least five years of sacerdotal experience, and not younger than forty. Their place of residence is the Villa Tevere, which is also the seat of Opus Dei's central government.

The Father rules through two administrative councils – a General Council for the Men's Section and a Central Advisory for the Women's Section. Each sits at the Father's pleasure, meeting to no fixed schedule. The General Council corresponds to a presidential cabinet of ministers. Its sessions are held in secret, around a council table polished to an immaculate sheen by an army of assistant women numeraries, under the gaze of the Virgin Mary whose portrait dominates the council chamber. In addition to the vicar general, the council consists of a procurator general, who as well as handling relations with the Roman Curia serves as Opus Dei's secretary of state, three deputy secretaries, each a vocal for one of the Archangels, a prefect of studies and a general administrator, who acts as the minister of finance. He is assisted by a *Consulta Técnica General* staffed only by inscribed numeraries. The cabinet is completed by the priest secretary, who handles relations with the Women's Section, a central spiritual director, who watches over the common spiritual direction of all members, and a number of regional delegates representing the various regional vicariats around the world.

The women's Central Advisory, as the name suggests, is purely advisory. The Women's Section, for example, may express an opinion on who, in its view, should be the Father's successor, but women have no elective role and in general little impact on forming the Work's overall policies. Presided over by the Father, assisted by his vicar general and central priest secretary, the Central Advisory has a composition that mirrors the General Council.

Members of the central government are appointed for eight-year terms. The Council and Advisory each have a Permanent Commission, which in the case of the men corresponds to a standing inner cabinet. Appointments to and movements within the Council and Advisory are reported in a semi-annual bulletin, *Romana*, which is available upon subscription to the general public.

Authority over the fifty or so regions is vested with the Father. He is represented within the boundaries of each region by a regional vicar. The regional vicars serve at the Father's discretion. They must supply him with reports about all developments of importance in their jurisdictions. Each regional vicar is assisted by a Regional Council and a Regional Advisory. A Regional Council usually consists of ten members:

- **Secretary** – a layman, he co-ordinates the work of the Regional Council;
- **Priest secretary** – the regional vicar's assistant, he handles liaison between the Regional Council and the Women's Section;
- **The defender** – always a layman, insures that the statutes are properly implemented and maintained;
- **Regional administrator** – equivalent to the minister of finance;

- **Vocal of St Raphael** – oversees the recruiting and formation of new members;
- **Vocal of St Gabriel** – oversees the spiritual well-being of the supernumeraries;
- **Vocal of St Michael** – looks after the spiritual, physical and material well-being of the numeraries;
- **Studies delegate** – primarily concerned with the Work's theology and philosophy programmes;
- **Regional delegate** – he also sits on the General Council in Rome and is Opus Central's official liaison with the region;
- **Regional spiritual director** – a priest, he is a non-voting member of both regional councils for men and women.

In some respects the regional delegate acts as a countercheck to the regional vicar, as both report directly to Rome. The regional spiritual director, although he has no vote, may also act as Opus Central's coadjutor, reporting directly to the Father or his vicar general if required.

Some regions – e.g., Spain, Italy, Mexico and the United States (except California and Texas) – are so large or important in terms of membership that they are divided into delegations, equivalent to sub-regions. Each sub-region is governed by a vicar delegate, assisted by delegation councils which are structured like regional councils. California and Texas are both constituted as separate regional vicariats.

Opus Dei's third level of government is the local management committee that runs each centre or residence. A management committee usually consists of a director, assistant director, secretary and chaplain. The director and his two assistants are always lay persons and the only priest – the chaplain – is non-voting. But because lay members are subject to an authoritarian form of clericalism, they are expected to follow suggestions of the non-voting priest.

In any event, regional vicariats and local centres enjoy little autonomy because they must abide by a 'Praxis' which interprets all policy handed down by the General Council in Rome. Described as 'an operating manual that tells Opus Dei members how absolutely everything must be done', it is regularly updated and kept in a series of loose-leaf binders. It used to be available for consultation in every centre but was withdrawn after some parts were photocopied by persons leaving Opus Dei to be used against it. Together with copies of *Crónica* and other sensitive documents, it must now be kept in each centre's safe, and may only be consulted with the specific permission of the local director.

Opus Dei denies the existence of a Praxis manual and when I mentioned it to Andrew Soane, the UK information officer, he replied: 'Perhaps you could send me your copy, as we do not have one.' The problem may have been that Soane truly did not recognize the manual under that name. Its proper title is the *Vademecum* and it comes in seven colour-coded volumes, covering internal publications (red), local councils (navy blue), apostolate of public opinion (orange), liturgy (burgundy), priests (purple), management of local centres (green), and ceremonies (grey).

It is available in Spanish only. And it describes in encyclopaedic detail everything a member needs to know about the spirit, life and customs of the institution – from how the Founder's birthday must be celebrated to a correct specimen for a will which new numeraries are required to draft in their own hand, leaving blank the date, names of heirs, legatees, executors and the fees to be paid to the executors. Nothing is left to individual judgement; everything is regimented so that numerary members are fully programmed. More leeway is permitted married members, but they too must follow a code of behaviour established by Opus Central in Rome.

Villa Tevere is more than the seat of Opus Dei's central government; it is the nerve centre of an empire that receives information from around the world through an efficient intelligence gathering network. The intelligence is sifted by an army of analysts who prepare reports for the permanent commissions or in some instances directly for the vicar general. Just as directives from Rome never go through the mails but are hand-carried by special couriers, the most confidential incoming reports are likewise not entrusted to public-access communications systems.

It took twenty-five years to complete the remodelling of Villa Tevere. The facade of what originally had been the Hungarian embassy to the Holy See remained mostly intact, although raised to six stories. But the rest when viewed from the exterior has an austere fortress-like aspect, though from inside the whimsical jumble of architectural styles resembles a Disneyland for clerics.

The gardens of the original villa have disappeared under a mass of concrete and brick. The inner courtyard has a classic Florentine touch to it. Two new wings were added: the Casa del Uffici, which houses the men's central government; and the equally Florentine Villa Sacchetti, headquarters of the women's section, with a separate entrance in the side-street of the same name. While the entire complex retains the Villa Tevere name, the original building is now called the Villa Vecchia. Its courtyard entrance is guarded by two imperial eagles perched on stone columns. A monumental reception hall with stained glass windows has a ceremonial staircase in stone leading to the Father's office and living quarters. An eighteenth-century tapestry depicting a biblical scene that was donated by a wealthy family in Rio de Janeiro hangs in the stairwell. The furniture throughout is in dark, massive wood, the chairs covered in red velvet. In addition to the main library and treasure vault, the Villa Vecchia contains an important juridical section and the apartments of the Vicar General and Procurator General.

Semi-attached to the Villa Vecchia is a high tower called the Casa del Vicolo. On a different level behind the Villa Sacchetti is La Montagnola, a six-storey building given over to the Central Advisory and the apartment of the central directress. The women's compound also includes the Casetta, Il Ridotto and Il Fabbricato Piccolo. All street-level windows are barred, which in Rome only seems prudent, but also the higher windows of the Casa del Vicolo and some other upper-storey windows as well.

The complex contains no less than a dozen chapels, among them one dedicated to the Holy Family of Nazareth and another to the Sacred Heart of Jesus. Two of the more distinctive are the Chapel of Relics and Chapel of Chalices. What became the Prelatic Church of Our Lady of Peace is entirely finished in bluish marble. The high altar is austerely set with six tall candlesticks. At the back of the apse is a throne-like armchair for the Father, surrounded on either side by six chairs for his principal ministers. Fisac designed the prelatic church to accommodate two hundred worshippers. At the Father's request, the gallery for women numeraries was angled in such a way that the congregation below cannot see the women in the blue sky above them.

After ten years as head of the Venezuelan women's section, María del Carmen Tapia was summoned back to Opus Central to appear before the Father. By her own account, Opus Dei had transformed her into a religious fanatic. She was totally dedicated to the cause. During her years in Caracas she had religiously transmitted the required tithe – 10 per cent of the revenues from the Venezuelan women's section – to an Opus Dei account at the IOR, representing a considerable fortune for the young women, admittedly all from wealthy families. She thought the money went towards training priests at the Roman College of the Holy Cross. When she arrived back in Rome she was placed under house arrest in the Villa Sacchetti, cut off from the outside world. The charges against her were never specified, yet she was repeatedly pressed to confess her guilt. Callers were told she was absent or unwell. She felt like her world had caved in. The directress was coldly distant. For weeks she was permitted no other human contact. At forty-five her hair turned white. Finally, word came from the Father that, having refused to repent, she must resign. He said her management of the women's section in Venezuela had damaged the Work's unity. As far as she could tell, this referred to her insistence that women numeraries in Venezuela be allowed to confess to the Opus Dei priest of their choice. After devoting twenty years to the Work, María del Carmen suddenly found herself standing on the doorstep of 36 via di Villa Sacchetti with only her passport and little more than the clothes on her back, without ever understanding why.

That she was abandoned, Opus Dei told the relator general of the Causes of Saints, was a perfect lie. María del Carmen Tapia was expelled, the postulator affirmed, because she had perverted a group of women numeraries by practising upon them 'the worst sort of sexual aberrations'. Moreover she had caused the Father such grief that he subjected himself to extra flagellation for her salvation. And, after all the harm she had done, he helped her find a job when she left, the postulator maintained.

María del Carmen Tapia was not alone in receiving this kind of charity. Staying in the room next to her at the Villa Sacchetti was Aurora Sánchez Bella, sister of Alfredo. She wanted to leave the Work and return to Spain. But this was refused. She was a nervous wreck and paced the floor night after night. Another numerary who passed through Rome on her way from Mexico to London was Rosario 'Piquiqui' Morán. She also was unhappy and wanted to leave. After arriving in London she jumped out of a top-floor window at the Rosecroft House residence and broke her pelvis.

According to Eileen Clark, who lived in the same Rosecroft residence but was absent that day, another resident gave this description of the incident:

> During the morning meditation, we heard almighty screaming. I can still see the person who continued to read aloud from *The Way* as if she was a puppet. There was general chaos. Afterwards, as we had an aperitif to celebrate something or other, one of the Directresses announced that if members of the Work had been *privileged* to bear witness to something (she never named that 'something', nor did the priest, who also talked about it in a meditation), we had a duty to live 'holy discretion'. When I was eventually allowed to see her, she was in a public ward in the Royal Free. I remember protesting and pleading for a private room for her. I can clearly remember her first words were 'you were a long time coming', but needless to say I was never allowed to be alone with her again.[1]

Piquiqui Morán was left a permanent invalid. After months on traction at the Royal Free, she was transported back to Spain, where she died of cancer after receiving treatment at the University of Navarra hospital.

Except for the difference in size – the Kremlin being somewhat larger – the physical similarity between the two seats of government was striking. Both are a maze of towers, chapels and secular buildings linked by courtyards, interior patios, covered passageways and underground tunnels crammed within the narrow confines of a walled city state. 'Behind the entrance to [the Villa Tevere] in Rome is a gigantic machine by which the superiors of Opus Dei manipulate their members, men and women, like puppets throughout the world,' María del Carmen said.[2]

Opus Dei's secretariat of state at the Casa del Uffici is the guardian of the organization's Strategic Plan. The Plan's existence is unknown to the ordinary run of members, but it shapes the Work's apostolate of penetration. It is administered by a small corps of priestly technocrats hand-picked by the Vicar General for their devotion and

---

[1] Eileen Clark , *Op. cit.*, p. 12.
[2] María del Carmen Tapia, *Hinter der Schwelle – Ein Leben im Opus Dei*, Benziger Verlag, Zurich 1993, p. 23.

discipline, and they function behind closed doors without any manner of public oversight.

Opus Dei has been accused of playing a behind-the-scenes role in unlikely situations ranging from Latin American coups d'état to international weapons deals. Needless to say, Opus Dei denies such involvements. Nevertheless one of its senior members in Ireland designed an armoured personnel carrier that entered the weapons inventories of at least three armies. The vehicle was manufactured under licence in Chile by Explosivos Industriales Cardoen, a firm that also manufactured 500-lb cluster bombs. During the first Gulf War Cardoen sold planeloads of cluster bombs to Iraq.

Towards the end of Paul VI's reign a battle erupted in the Roman Curia between Progressive and Conservative factions. The Progressive faction, which wanted tighter financial controls and opposed greater influence for Opus Dei, was led by Paul's closest aide, Archbishop Benelli. He was credited with resolving one of the most serious crises of the post-Conciliar Church – the break-up of the Company of Jesus, a project that allegedly had its roots inside the Villa Tevere. Benelli's efforts insured that the 26,000 Jesuits remained under the command of one general superior, who at the time was Don Pedro Arrupe.

Benelli was said to have wanted to keep the Company of Jesus intact because it represented the only effective counter-balance to Opus Dei. Moreover, Benelli also made known his distaste for the mercantile morals of Bishop Paul Marcinkus, the head of the Vatican bank whom he regarded as an Opus Dei sycophant. One would have thought that Benelli, as Paul's under-secretary of state, was in a good position to make his concerns heard. But when a showdown finally occurred, Benelli lost out.

In June 1977, Paul gave Benelli a red hat and sent him to Florence. The Pontiff had little more than a year of life left in him. It was almost as if by separating himself from Benelli the fire in his heart was extinguished. Their collaboration had spanned more than thirty years. But by making Benelli a cardinal and sending him into the field to gain pastoral experience, Paul must have realized he was placing his favourite son among the front-runners for his succession.

18

DICTATORS AND JESUITS

If one of my children abandons the fight and leaves the war, or turns
his back, let him know that he betrays us all, Jesus Christ, the Church,
his brothers and sisters in the Work; it would be treason to consent to
the tiniest act of unfaithfulness.

Josemaría Escrivá de Balaguer, *Crónica* 1972

DURING THE LAST YEARS OF FRANCO, WITH GOVERNMENT IN THE
hands of the Opus Dei technocrats, Madrid became an important
hub for European investment and political interest in Latin America.
This development was encouraged by the Vatican, and supported by
the right-wing Christian Democrats in Italy and Spain.

The Occident's regard towards Latin America, and particularly
Argentina, reflected the interests of the anti-Communist lobby,
whether led by the Church or purely secular, to stop the spread of
Marxist subversion. To strengthen these forces, partly due to a strategy directed from Rome but also because of the affinity of a common
cause, the Masonic movement in Europe became seeded with
Conservative Catholics. The principal strategists behind this evolution were Italy's Giulio Andreotti and Spain's foreign minister
Gregorio López Bravo. They were supported by the great Vatican
door-opener, Umberto Ortolani, his general dogsbody, Licio Gelli,

and a Masonic notable, Pio Cabanillas, who was one of the founders of Spain's Alianza Popular.

Of the five, Andreotti took precedence in matters of policy, being nearest to the power structures of the Church and the Free World's political systems. Andreotti was the closest layman to Paul VI and he had his admirers in every capital of the Western Alliance. In European councils he befriended López Bravo, with whom he shared – so he said – the same religious values. Andreotti had been on an Opus Dei retreat at the Castle of Urio on Lake Como, in northern Italy, and was received at the Villa Tevere by Escrivá de Balaguer.

Umberto Ortolani, a Roman lawyer, was a secret chamberlain of the Papal Household and a member of the inner council of the Knights of Malta. He was the senior member of the group, and, according to some sources, the illegitimate son of Cardinal Giacomo Lercaro. Andreotti and Gelli were the same age, being born in 1919. López Bravo was their junior by six years.

The subversive forces in Argentina had understood the importance of severing the investment pipeline from Europe. They mounted a series of daring attacks against foreign interests, bringing their underground war to the business and financial districts of Buenos Aires. Two of their most chilling successes were the assassinations in broad daylight of financier Francisco Soldatti, dean of the Swiss community and patriarch of the country's richest family, and businessman Giuseppe Valori, through whom most of Italy's heavy investment in Argentina was channelled.

Madrid during these years had become a haven for Latin American political refugees. The most prominent was the former Argentine strongman, Juan Domingo Perón, who had invested $250,000 of the loot he had stolen from the Argentine treasury in a luxury villa on the city's northern outskirts which he named the Puerta de Hierro (the Gate of Iron). The larger part of his fortune, including an immense hoard of gold, had been placed under the tutelage of the Spanish government as an unstated condition for his asylum in Spain.

Although no greater rogue had appeared on the political scene since his exile in the mid-1950s, Perón's charm and personal prestige paradoxically attracted a certain nostalgia for the 'good times' when Argentine meat and cereals sold well in world markets and the country enjoyed relative stability. The Crusading forces began to view the ageing caudillo of the 'shirtless ones' – the Argentine workers – as the key to defeating the leftist guerrillas and restoring political equilibrium to a country that otherwise faced civil war.

Opus Dei was active in Argentina during these unstable times. Its first emissaries had arrived in 1950 and by the mid-1960s the institute had recruited 1,000 members throughout the country. General Juan Carlos Onganía was one of them. Onganía's coup in June 1966 was welcomed by the middle-class entrepreneurs, by Perón, and by the trade unions. Perón told journalists who visited him in Madrid, 'I regard this [development] with sympathy, because . . . Onganía has ended a period of complete corruption. If the new government acts well it will succeed. It is the last opportunity for Argentina to avoid a situation where civil war is the only way out.'[1]

Onganía's four-year dictatorship was described by the American writer Penny Lernoux as 'the forerunner of Argentina's virulently right-wing regimes in the late seventies'. Onganía felt himself 'personally called' to shape the country's destiny during a religious retreat at an Opus Dei centre shortly before his 1966 coup, and many of the generals and industrialists appointed to his cabinet shared his belief that the 'Christian and military virtues of Spanish knighthood' – a mix of authoritarian clericalism and enlightened dictatorship – would restore mental, cultural, social, and political discipline to Argentina.[2]

Onganía's belief in an élite corps of lay people – professional and military – called by God to serve the nation was pure Opus Dei dogma. He abolished political parties and purged the universities. Popular discontent with his Conservative ideals began to crystallize towards the end of 1969 with a wave of guerrilla attacks on police stations, army outposts and banks. Onganía's growing inability to cope marked a first failure for authoritarian clericalism in Argentina.

In June 1970 General Alejandro Lanusse took power and opened negotiations with Perón's chef de cabinet, José López Rega. Known as the Rasputin of the Pampas, or *El Brujo* (the Wizard), López Rega belonged to a right-wing Christian sect of which relatively little is known. He had made a fortune selling a youth tonic formula in Brazil, and joined Perón's staff in 1966, soon casting a spell over the leader and by the same token charming his wife, Isabelita. She and

[1] *Primera Plana*, Buenos Aires, 30 June 1966.
[2] Penny Lernoux, *Cry of the People*, Penguin, New York 1991, p. 160. On p. 305 Lernoux states that Opus Dei organized the retreat.

López Rega began to promote Perón as the only person capable of restoring civil order to Argentina.

One of the most dedicated supporters of Perón's return was Giancarlo Elia Valori, younger brother of the assassinated Giuseppe Valori. In 1960, when twenty-three, he had been named a secret chamberlain of the Papal Household, becoming one of Umberto Ortolani's protégés. In the mid-1960s, he was named secretary of the newly formed Institute for International Relations, a more formalized version of the Pinay Group. As such he knew just about every prominent anti-Marxist on three continents. When Perón came to Rome, he stayed at Valori's villa, while conducting his business during the day from the Hotel Excelsior in the Via Veneto. If Perón wanted an introduction to the head of Banco Ambrosiano, Valori arranged it. If he wanted a meeting with the Vatican's secretary of state, Valori saw that it was done. One day Ortolani called Valori to his office and introduced him to Licio Gelli who suggested that Valori should join the P2 Masonic Lodge. Valori did not reply immediately. But when in April 1973 he gave a lecture at the University of Madrid on *The Concept of the Christian State*, he sent a warmly worded letter to Gelli inviting him to attend.

On Perón's next visit to Rome, Valori was not surprised to find Gelli cruising the lobby of the Excelsior. Gelli rushed over and asked to be introduced to the General's personal secretary, López Rega. 'Your excellency,' the suave Gelli said in perfect Spanish, 'they say you are a man of God.' Indeed López Rega believed he spoke directly with the Archangel Gabriel. Gelli charmed López Rega, who he soon initiated into the P2 Lodge. Gelli described Perón as a 'misunderstood genius'.

By the early 1970s it was apparent that if the military remained in power, the Argentine state would collapse. Lanusse wanted to hand over to a legally elected president but an existing law prevented Perón from again holding public office. López Rega and Isabelita counselled Perón to nominate one of his more pliant followers, Dr Héctor J. Cámpora, to run for president in his stead, knowing that if Cámpora won he could change the law and call new elections.

Lanusse announced new presidential elections for May 1973 which Cámpora won easily. Following the script written in Madrid, he repealed the ban against Perón, called new elections for the autumn and resigned. López Rega is said to have requested the support of the Opus Dei technocrats in organizing the strong-man's return. Perón was in need of a mountain of cash to bribe the Montoneros guerrillas into acquiescence and cover the costs of the Cámpora as well as his own presidential campaigns.

With Opus Dei's Luis Coronel de Palma as governor of the Banco de España, the Villa Tevere strategists would have known that the Spanish government was tutor for the 400 tons of gold that belonged to the Argentine bully boy of the 1950s. The Conservative Right bargained that Perón still retained sufficient charisma to restore order to a country which since his departure had known eleven governments and spiralling inflation. However, the Spanish government's approval was needed for Perón's gold to be placed on the market. According to intelligence sources an arrangement was concluded that required the proceeds of a bullion sale to be placed in a foundation for furthering social causes (such as forming Perónista ministers) in Argentina.

Perón's 400 tons of bullion came very close to equalling the Bank of England's bullion reserves. At then current market rates, it was worth in the neighbourhood of £700 million. In early 1973 it was put on sale in an off-market operation code-named BOR 1345. The seller was not disclosed, but an account used for the transaction was opened at the Swiss Credit Bank branch in Chiasso, on the border with Italy, under the name of VITALITA. The seller's agent, a Chilean businessman living in Madrid, was offering a commission of 10 US cents per ounce to go-betweens. The transfer agent was Professor Vincenzo de Nardo, an Inspector-General of the Italian Finance Ministry.

When contacted, De Nardo confirmed that he was connected with the transaction. But he quickly added: 'This operation has nothing to do with my official functions at the Italian Ministry of Finance. It is a private operation and the Italian government is not involved.' He stressed that the origin of the gold was 'quite normal'. It came with a certificate of authenticity. The origin of the certificate, he said (note the certificate, not the gold), was European.

When asked whether the merchandise was of South American origin he answered evasively: 'The merchandise is being held by a government. The government did not sequester it. This government will certify to its legality. But this is not a commercial operation of the government concerned; it is of a political nature. A sale on the bullion market did not suit the government in question . . . Officially, the seller of the merchandise will be me. When I get a letter of credit from a prime Swiss bank I will send confirmation of the gold's existence. The merchandise will be delivered to a Swiss bank . . . I was asked to handle the operation because the government in question did not want to be mentioned in the contract of sale.'

Interested parties were requested to address a letter from a top-rated bank to the seller's agent or Professor de Nardo at the Italian Ministry of Finance confirming their intention to close the sale.

I have no idea what ultimately happened to the gold. Later that autumn bullion prices shot up, as if an unseen but deeply felt market constraint had been removed. And though nothing more was heard of the BOR 1345 transaction, one of the passengers on the plane that carried Juan Perón, Isabelita and López Rega back to Argentina was Licio Gelli. After Perón's triumph in the September 1973 election, the Venerable Master of the P2 Lodge was appointed the honorary Argentine consul in Florence and became one of the government's economic advisers.

In June 1974, Escrivá de Balaguer flew to Buenos Aires on the second leg of a grand Latin American tour. He stayed at an Opus Dei retreat and made a pilgrimage to the shrine of Our Lady of Lujan, the patroness of Argentina. People came from as far away as Uruguay and Paraguay to see him. For two of his public appearances his sons rented the Coliseo Theatre in the centre of Buenos Aires, and on each occasion more than 5,000 people crowded through the doors.

Escrivá de Balaguer stayed a month in Buenos Aires, then flew to Chile. Two days later General Perón died. Isabelita became president and López Rega her chief minister.

Since the opening of its first centre in 1950, middle-class Chileans had taken to Opus Dei like lemmings in search of spiritual nourishment. Within no time at all, the Work claimed to have 2,000 members and 15,000 co-operators. Chile was reported to be one of Opus Dei's best financed operations in Latin America.

One of the first persons sent from Spain was José Miguel Ibáñez Langlois, a young priest who became Opus Dei's leading Latin American ideologist. Two of his earliest recruits were right-wing activists Jaime Guzmán and Alvaro Puga. In the 1960s both Guzmán and Puga became editors of *El Mercurio*, Chile's oldest newspaper. Ibáñez Langlois moonlighted as *El Mercurio*'s literary critic.

The Vatican had initially supported the Christian Democrat leader, Eduardo Frei, but became uneasy about reports from Ibáñez Langlois that Frei was building bridges to the radical trade union movement. Until then, the Vatican had regarded Chile as a possible model for social change in Latin America. While Vatican doubts set in, the Jesuits continued to insist that Frei was the only person capable of stopping Marxism in Chile.

This view was not shared by Ibáñez Langlois or his politically active recruits. With a Chicago-trained economist Pablo Baraona, they formed a Conservative think tank, the Institute for General Studies, which attracted a following of free-market economists, lawyers, publicists and technocrats.

Frei's social programme made US president Richard Nixon see red, and at his insistence the CIA began financing the Institute for General Studies in the hope that it could form a counter-élite to the Christian Democrat party. Even when Frei's government had almost mastered Chile's runaway inflation, Nixon still wanted Frei 'hammered' should he be returned to the presidency in the next elections. The right-wing extremists led by Guzmán and Puga fractured the Conservative vote, with the result that Salvador Allende won instead by a narrow margin.

The Madrid technocrats were opposed to Allende. The Spanish ambassador in Santiago contacted his American counterpart to see what could be done about the 'smiling doctor', as Allende was sometimes known. A broad section of Chileans regarded Allende's election success as a promise of national renewal, but his radical left wing did not wait to consolidate their position constitutionally. They launched 'People's Power', consisting of Peasant Councils that took over the larger farms and Workers' Assemblies that occupied the factories.

Under such conditions, the extreme right was not long in making itself felt. The 'spoiling operation' ordered by the CIA was planned inside the Institute for General Studies and resulted in the September 1973 coup by General Augusto Pinochet. His spokesman was the Institute's co-founder Alvaro Puga. Another Institute director, Herman Cubillos, became Pinochet's foreign minister, and the Institute's co-founder, Pablo Baraona, was minister of the economy.

The third Institute co-founder, Jaime Guzmán, drafted the new constitution. At least two members of the military junta, Admiral José Merino and General Jaime Estrada Leigh, were said to be 'sons' of Escrivá de Balaguer. Estrada, who previously headed the Nuclear Energy Commission, became housing minister.

Guzmán wrote Pinochet's Declaration of Principles which promised to 'cleanse our democratic system of the vices that had facilitated its destruction'. The nation's educational system was taken in hand by three successive Opus Dei ministers, an Opus Dei superintendent of education and an Opus Dei dean of the Catholic University. The Opus Dei technocrats who surrounded Pinochet administered the country very much as their counterparts had done in Spain. Before long, however, a power struggle developed between the technocrats and the military over the activities of Pinochet's secret police, the DINA. Having learned from earlier experiences in Spain and Argentina, the Institute strategists wanted gently to shift Pinochet aside, as the Spanish technocrats had done with Franco. Pinochet became suspicious and fired foreign minister Cubillos.

Escrivá de Balaguer stayed in Santiago for ten days, visiting the shrine of the Virgin Mary at Lo Vasquez, 100 kilometres from the capital, and then left for Lima. The mayor of Las Condes, a well-to-do suburb of Santiago, had been so enthusiastic about his meeting with the Spanish prelate that he named a street after him. Not long afterwards, Alvaro Puga wrote a book about his campaign to bring down Allende. Titled *Dario De Vida de Ud*, it was published with a CIA grant[1] and reprinted a collection of Puga's most biting *El Mercurio* columns during the Allende years. In the foreword, fellow Opusian Enrique Campos Menendez, an *El Mercurio* editor, pointed out that Puga had accurately predicted key political assassinations, Allende's death, and the date of the military coup. Campos concluded: 'Nobody could have known of these future events, except through magic parapsychology or divine premonition.'[2] Divine premonition was something that the Father had claimed almost forty years before when he foretold the death of the Nationalist bureaucrat who threatened to denounce one of his apostles for treason. As for Puga's brother in the faith, Jaime Guzmán, he was convicted but

---

[1] Fred Landis, 'Opus Dei: Secret Order Vies for Power', *Covert Action*, Washington, Winter 1983.
[2] *Idem*.

never sentenced for the machine-gun slaying of a former military chief of staff judged too soft on Allende. After his election as senator Guzmán was assassinated by Marxist terrorists and was also honoured with a street named after him.

Under John Paul II, Chile's episcopacy was purged of its 'soft' bishops and replaced by Opus Dei prelates. Opus Dei also opened the University of Los Andes in Santiago. Liberation Theology – a theology that promoted 'a more viable option for the poor of Latin America' – was not on the syllabus.

Liberation Theology had been the brainchild of Gustavo Gutiérrez, a Peruvian priest who had become disillusioned by the insensitivity and corruption of the so-called Christian Democrats in Latin America who were doing everything possible to enrich themselves with what Gutiérrez regarded as the complicity of the Church. To better understand the causes of social oppression, Gutiérrez turned towards Marxism, using Marxist analysis while rejecting its ideology to assess the problems of the poor. In 1968 he published his thesis on a new pastoral approach that encouraged 'the efforts of the people to develop their own grass-roots organizations for the ... consolidation of their rights and the search for true justice'.[1] Liberation Theology upheld the right of the poor to think out their own faith and social development. As such, it stood in direct opposition to authoritarian clericalism. Escrivá de Balaguer rejected Liberation Theology and his campaign to suppress it became the first major battleground between the Jesuits and Opus Dei.

Given his roots, it is hardly any wonder that Escrivá de Balaguer believed Liberation Theology was dangerous. In Opus Dei it was taught that the poor must work to improve their earthly lot within existing social structures while preparing through devotion and obedience for eternal salvation. This meant that they should remain meek and hard toiling throughout their lives on earth in order to enjoy the majesty of after-life in Christ's kingdom.

Gutiérrez described the world of Latin American poor as a universe ruled by injustice to which the 'Church of the Rich' contributed. Nine out of ten Latin Americans were baptized Catholics, but four out of every five were born to die poor. Not only

---

[1] Gustavo Gutiérrez, *A Theology of Liberation*, SCM Press, London, revised version, 1988, p. 68.

were they deprived of the liberation promised by Christ, they were not even aware of his promise. 'In the final analysis, poverty means lack of food and housing, the inability to attend properly to health and education needs, exploitation of workers, permanent unemployment, lack of respect for human dignity, and unjust limitations placed on personal freedom in the areas of self-expression, politics and religion. Poverty is a situation that destroys people, families, and individuals... Misery and oppression lead to a cruel, inhuman death, and are therefore contrary to the will of the God,' he wrote.[1]

The Jesuit General Pedro Arrupe urged his troops to become more involved with social justice and did not rule out 'a critical collaboration with Marxist-inspired groups and movements'.[2] This placed Arrupe on a direct confrontation course with Opus Dei, whose members were very much part of the 'Church of the Rich'. The first battle was for control of the Catholic universities in Latin America. The flash point was Piura, a rapidly developing industrial city 1,000 kilometres north of Lima. The well-to-do bourgeoisie of Piura wanted a conservative university for their sons and daughters. They claimed the Jesuit-run university in Lima was too far to the left. That the university in Lima had become a hotbed of Liberation Theology could not be denied. The wealthy families around Piura told the papal nuncio that they were willing to finance the kind of university they wanted. Opus Dei backed them and offered to take charge of the project. In the summer of 1966, sociologist Alberto Moncada and another numerary were sent from the University of Navarra to take the project in hand.

In Peru, Moncada came face to face with what he described as the 'enormous rift between the teachings of Escrivá de Balaguer and the stark realities facing Third World Catholics'. After three years in Piura he quit the Work. 'In addition to controlling universities, what Opus Dei wanted,' Moncada contended, 'was to enter the economic and political superstructure in Latin American countries. In this they were successful in Argentina, Chile and Uruguay, while in Peru, where they were trying to organize a coalition of entrepreneurs and high-ranking bureaucrats, it was much harder [because the ruling

[1] Gutiérrez, Op. cit., pp. xxi–xxii.
[2] Eric O. Hanson, The Catholic Church in World Politics, Princeton University Press, Princeton 1990, pp. 88–89.

junta was leftist-oriented] until they persuaded the nuncio to appoint six Opus Dei bishops,' he explained.[1]

That Opus Dei was hostile to Liberation Theology and attempted to prevent Catholic progressives from operating in Latin America was first brought to my attention by Father Giuliano Ferrari. In the late 1950s he became a lay assistant to Cardinal Eugène Tisserant until discovering he had a late vocation. He was ordained in 1962, after completing a degree in theology at Tübingen University, where he decided to found an ecclesiastical services organization to assist under-manned dioceses in Latin America. Tisserant encouraged Ferrari and enrolled him in the Pontifical Academy for Ecclesiastics, the Vatican's diplomacy school. At that time the Academy only accepted fifteen candidates a year. Each was given 'a suite with bathroom and a bar stocked with the best duty-free champagnes . . . At the Academy it is difficult to accept that Jesus Christ in his original incarnation was merely a carpenter.'[2] Academy graduates are accorded the right to call themselves monsignors.

John XXIII's call for priests to go to Latin America gave Father Ferrari the idea of founding the Society of God for Humanity. His plan was to recruit volunteers in the Philippines, which he regarded as a crossroads between east and west. In Manila he ran into his first opposition, coming from an Irish priest, Father Eamon Byrne, who raised so many obstacles that the nuncio told him to return to Rome and report to Archbishop Antonio Samoré at the Secretariat of State. The conservative Samoré, Ferrari said, virtually controlled the Church in Latin America, and was very close to Opus Dei. He had been nuncio in Bogotá before John XXIII brought him back to Rome. But John soon accused him of 'unspeakable manoeuvrings' and would have nothing more to do with him.[3] 'I give the orders around here,' Samoré warned Ferrari. 'If you don't obey me, I'll have the Pope excommunicate you!'[4]

Ferrari spoke five languages and had a quick mind. He understood the workings of the secular world better than most clerics, having been in business for his own account before going to work for Tisserant. He was full of passion for the Church, and his creative

[1] Interview with Alberto Moncada, Madrid, 1 March 1995.
[2] Giuliano F.G. Ferrari, *Vaticanisme*, Perret-Gentil, Geneva 1976, p. 22.
[3] Hebblethwaite, *John XXIII (Op. cit.)*, p. 483.
[4] Ferrari, *Op. cit.*, p. 89.

exuberance somehow seemed suited to his scuffed shoes and ruffled cassock. Ferrari's free spirit was certainly the antithesis of Opus Dei's neatly regimented world. As with Samoré, Ferrari was not destined to hit it off with the priestly sons of Escrivá de Balaguer.

After setting up an office in Guayaquil, Ecuador's main port and largest city, to conduct a diocesan census, he flew to Germany to ask Bishop Hengsbach, overseer of Adveniat, for funding. He had been asked to conduct similar surveys in San Salvador and Guatemala City, but neither archiepiscopacy had the money to pay for them.

Hengsbach told Ferrari that he would need favourable opinions from two prelates who vetted projects for Adveniat in Latin America. One was a professor at Louvain and the other a doctor of theology in Madrid. He spoke to both but never received a reply. Ferrari concluded that Opus Dei had acquired veto power over Adveniat's disbursements in Latin America.

Still hounded by Samoré, in January 1969 he moved to San Salvador to begin the census there. He rented a house and hired a servant recommended by the archdiocese. Soon afterwards he started having headaches and his blood pressure rose dangerously. He consulted a doctor who prescribed medicine to stop the headaches, but his blood pressure remained abnormally high. His fingers and ankles swelled and, getting up from table one evening, he was overcome by dizziness and collapsed. He remained partially paralysed for three days.

Father Ferrari noticed that each time he left San Salvador on business the symptoms subsided. In June 1969, his house was broken into. The police arrested his servant as an accomplice and held her for three days. She was released for lack of proof, but in any event Ferrari dispensed with her services. Almost immediately his health improved. Two doctors examined him and concluded that he had been ingesting an unknown, odourless, colourless drug – possibly digitalis, a potent cardiac glycoside: the intention could only have been to provoke heart failure. Ferrari said he suspected the attempted poisoning was the work of Samoré's agents,[1] although he had no proof.

In December 1969, Father Ferrari moved to Guatemala, a country where, in the 1940s, roughly 98 per cent of the cultivated land had

[1] *Ibid.*, p. 241.

been owned by a mere 140 families and one or two corporations. It was a desperate situation that needed social change. After Jacobo Arbenz Guzmán was elected president in 1950 he introduced sweeping land reform, expropriating 400,000 acres of idle banana plantations belonging to the United Fruit Company, and was over-thrown by a CIA-sponsored *coup d'état*, thereby saving Guatemala from 'falling into the lap of international Communism'.

When Father Ferrari arrived in Guatemala City he found the arch-diocese in the hands of smartly starched Opus Dei priests. They had literally taken over the local curia and were running it for Cardinal Mario Casariego. The Cardinal was inflexible in his dislike of 'Marxist-tainted' peasants. He preferred the company of the country's strongman, Colonel Carlos Arana, a former military attaché in Washington who slaughtered thousands of 'subversive' Guatemalan peasants.[1] Casariego had become Archbishop of Guatemala City in December 1964. By the late 1960s he was so detested that several hundred priests and laymen petitioned the Guatemalan Congress to have him expelled.[2] But he enjoyed Colonel Arana's protection.

When Paul VI made Samoré a cardinal and placed him in charge of the first section of the Secretariat of State, it became impossible for Ferrari to continue running the Society of God for Humanity in Latin America. The last of his funds were cut off, and so he decided to cancel the society's charter and return to Rome. And when Cardinal Tisserant died, Ferrari found himself without a protector. He eventually returned to pastoral work in the slums of Guatemala City, but not for long. One day he was summoned to the archdio-cese, still in the hands of Opus Dei priests, and told that his work in the *favellas* was more political than pastoral and therefore he was no longer welcome in Guatemala. He was given a one-way air ticket to Switzerland for the next day. To insure that he didn't miss the flight, two Opus Dei priests picked him up at his lodgings and drove him to the airport. In the car they told him that should he return to Latin America they would learn about it and his life would be in jeopardy.

When I met Ferrari for the last time in 1978, he gave me a copy of the book he had written about his Latin American experience and

[1] Lernoux, *Op. cit.*, pp. 186–187.
[2] *Ibid.*, p. 43.

another not authored by him on the Vatican's finances. He wanted me to write about his having been hunted and finally hounded out of Latin America because he supported the Church of the Poor. He said that what he knew about the misuse of Vatican funds in Rome and Latin America would cause a major scandal. I proposed that he gather together some documentation so that we could discuss the project further at our next meeting. But I never heard from him again. Some weeks later, I asked the friend who first brought us together, 'Where's Giuliano?'

'Haven't you heard?' he replied. 'He was found dead in a train between Geneva and Paris.'

Father Ferrari, forty-eight, was reported to have died of a massive heart attack. But as far as could be determined, no autopsy was performed – at least not by the Department of Legal Medicine in Geneva – and sixteen years later a copy of his death certificate was no longer to be found in the archives of the city and canton of Geneva.

Ferrari's death came weeks before the first of the 1978 conclaves. He had been devoted to the Church and deeply concerned by the problems of moral permissiveness, poverty and drug addiction. But also he was aware that in a quarter of a century the population of Latin America had more than doubled from 164 million to 342 million. From what he had seen in San Salvador and Guatemala he was convinced that Capitalism was not going to look after these souls. Who, then, was going to feed them?

Opus Dei could only have agreed that moral permissiveness and drug abuse were agents of the Devil. But as far as the sons and daughters of Escrivá de Balaguer were concerned, Capitalism remained preferable to Marxism, and Liberation Theology was the invention of Lucifer, who after all was the first revolutionary. Opus Dei's opinions about how to bring social justice to the world had placed it in direct opposition to the Company of Jesus. Over the next few years Jesuit influence would come under increasing attack, undermined in part by an anonymous campaign of *pillería*. The battle lines for the next conclaves had already been drawn. The doctrinal Conservatives were aligned against the Progressives, supported by the New Theologians who had found expression in the Church as a result of Vatican II.

19

DEATH OF THE FOUNDER

If it should happen that anyone should teach you something different from what I have taught you, whether it be ourselves or an Angel from Heaven, let him be anathema.

St Paul [Galatians 1:8]

ESCRIVÁ DE BALAGUER WAS UNABLE TO HIDE HIS ILL HUMOUR OVER Archbishop Giovanni Benelli's efforts to block Opus Dei's transformation into a Personal Prelature. He and Alvaro del Portillo were determined to force the issue. They went ahead with convening an Extraordinary General Congress of Opus Dei members to align the Work's statutes with the new decrees relating to Personal Prelatures following the Second Vatican Council. The Congress had adjourned in September 1970 and a staff of rapporteurs at Opus Central spent the next two years analysing the results. Once set to paper, Escrivá de Balaguer asked the secretary of state, Cardinal Villot, to arrange a new audience with the Pope. It took place on 25 June 1973. Paul VI was said on this occasion to have been more receptive. What, then, lay behind this apparent softening of attitudes?

The only threatening cloud on the Vatican's horizon at the time was its finances. The costs of running the Curia and maintaining St Peter's in a state of perpetual splendour were escalating. As a result, the Vatican City State began reporting a long series of financial deficits that in the years ahead would bring it to the brink of bankruptcy. There is little doubt, though no actual proof, that at the June 1973 audience Opus Dei's two senior prelates tabled a proposition, which I call the Portillo Option, to assist the Vatican with its financial problems. After first falling upon deaf ears, the Option began to find favour in the papal chambers. According to some sources, a deal was finally struck whereby Opus Dei would be elevated to a personal prelature in return for taking in hand the Vatican finances.

A preliminary protocol was said to have been signed, setting out the modalities of the Portillo Option. A copy of it turned up among the papers of an Italian Parliamentary Commission investigating the P2 affair (see Chapter 23), but subsequently disappeared. However the Milan banker Roberto Calvi told his family that he assisted Opus Dei in elaborating such a plan, which included Opus Dei's assuming control of the IOR, the Vatican bank. Indeed it was said that the head of the Vatican bank, Bishop Paul Marcinkus, went to Madrid to discuss aspects of the plan with senior Opus Dei bankers there. Opus Dei denies that any such deal was cut – i.e., that the Portillo Option never existed.

'The Holy Father was pleased and encouraged our Father to continue with the work of the General Congress,' was all that Don Alvaro reported about the June 1973 audience.[1] For the moment, then, the question 'remained open'. But one thing is certain. Portillo used the interval to move closer to Cardinal Villot. Paul, increasingly ill, deferred more to Villot. Marcinkus also realized he had an ally in Opus Dei and in Cardinal Villot. They all feared Benelli; he overshadowed Villot, wanted Marcinkus sent back to Chicago and his feelings for Opus Dei were well known.

Opus Dei's discussions on how to cure the Vatican's financial problems only really began in September 1974, after Escrivá de Balaguer and Portillo completed the last leg of their triumphant journey to South America. The timing was significant. Unfortunately for the Vatican, its most trusted financial partner at the time, Michele Sindona, was a major currency speculator. Prior to the Yom Kippur War of October 1973 Sindona had speculated the wrong way on the

---

[1] Alvaro del Portillo, 'Transformation of Opus Dei into a Personal Prelature', Memo, 23 April 1979, paragraph 10.

dollar and when the forward contracts began to unwind, his empire – wired together by an uncommon system of back-to-back deposits – collapsed.

In September 1974, a ministerial decree placed Sindona's Milan bank in liquidation. The losses were more than $386 million. A month later in New York, Sindona's Franklin National Bank went to the wall, becoming the largest banking failure in US history up to that time. In January 1975, the Swiss authorities closed Finabank in Geneva, in which the Vatican held a 20 per cent interest. Sindona was by then a fugitive from Italian justice.

According to Prince Massimo Spada, a former IOR general manager, the Vatican lost $55 million in the crash of Sindona's empire. But Charles de Trenck, the general manager of Finabank, estimated that 'the Vatican's overall loss on investments in the Sindona group ran as high as $240 million.' Whatever the final sum, Paul VI was said to have been devastated.

Reticence to accept the Portillo Option began to fade. But the papal advisers insisted on conditions. They wanted the amount of Opus Dei's contribution to be fixed in advance. Any protocol between Opus Dei and the Holy See would remain domiciled in the Vatican's secret archives. According to the missing parliamentary commission document, the Pope – or was it really Opus Dei? – insisted on protecting the privileged arrangement between the IOR and Banco Ambrosiano.[1]

While negotiations continued, in February 1975, Escrivá de Balaguer returned to Venezuela. His visit was another immense success. According to Opus Central, his four public appearances were attended by sixteen thousand people. They came from as far afield as Colombia, Ecuador and Peru, and the questions they put to him steamed up 'like bubbles racing to the surface in a boiling kettle'.[2]

A different description was given by Caracas lawyer Alberto Jaimes Berti. With a friend, Pedro José Lara della Pegna, he went to hear the Founder talk about his career in the service of the Church. Berti said that at the end of an unexceptional speech the audience was invited to ask questions. A long silence followed. Finally Lara

[1] José María Bernaldez, 'The Rumasa Affair Soils the Vatican and Opus', *Tiempo*, Madrid, 1 August 1983.
[2] Vázquez de Prada, *Op. cit.*, p. 472.

della Pegna, the uncle of Cardinal José Rosalio Castillo Lara, asked rather innocently whether Opus Dei was really a secret organization as people often claimed. Escrivá de Balaguer stared coldly at Lara della Pegna. 'What is your profession?' he asked.

'I am a lawyer,' Lara della Pegna replied.

'Well you must be a third- or fourth-rate lawyer to ask such a silly question,' the Father observed curtly. He then moved into a stinging harangue of Lara della Pegna. His sudden rage created a shock and people started to leave. Seated close by was the rector of the Catholic University of Caracas, José Luiz Aguilar Gorrondona. Berti noticed that Aguilar had recorded the speech on a cassette recorder. When Opus Dei learned that the incident had been taped, they pressured Aguilar to relinquish the cassette. The pressure became so intense that finally the rector handed it over, but not before allowing Berti to make a copy. Claimed Berti, 'When Opus Dei realized I had a copy and wouldn't give it to them, they set out to destroy me. But they were patient and waited for the right moment. You know, in the end they almost succeeded.'[1]

From Caracas, Escrivá de Balaguer went to Guatemala City and stayed a few days with Cardinal Casariego. But the Father did not feel well and cut short his visit, returning to Rome on 23 February 1975. Towards the middle of May he was feeling better again and set off on his last trip to Spain, to view the progress of the basilica at Torreciudad. The following morning, the Municipality of Barbastro conferred upon him the keys to the city, acknowledging him as Barbastro's most famous living son. The Father had finally recouped the family's lost honour.

Back in Rome, he visited the new campus of the Roman College of the Holy Cross at Cavabianca. He described it as his 'second folly', the first being the Villa Tevere, and Torreciudad his last. Cavabianca was in the same sumptuous style as Opus Dei's other architectural achievements.

Then on Thursday, 26 June 1975, he set off after breakfast with Don Alvaro and Don Javier Echevarría for Castelgandolfo, where he visited the Villa delle Rose. Upon arriving at the centre he went into the oratory and knelt in prayer, as required of every member upon entering and before leaving an Opus Dei house. Afterwards, while

[1] Interview with Dr Alberto Jaimes Berti, London, 6 December 1993.

talking with his daughters, he again felt unwell and was immediately driven back to the Villa Tevere. He mounted the stairs to his study, then called out to Don Javier for assistance. He collapsed and died before Don Javier could reach him. He was gazing, we are told, at the portrait of the Virgin of Guadalupe, given to him during his 1970 visit to Mexico. He was seventy-three years of age.

The Father's remains were placed in a mahogany coffin lined with zinc. The municipal medical officer signed the death certificate and gave permission for the body to be laid to rest under the floor of the prelatic church. At six in the afternoon a final Solemn Funeral Mass was celebrated and the coffin, head nearest the altar, was lowered into its tomb, which was covered with a greenish-black slab of marble.

The next morning, Saturday, 28 June 1975, six cardinals, a Papal legate – Archbishop Benelli – and a host of civil dignitaries, among them Giulio Andreotti, attended a memorial service at Sant' Eugenio, the basilica whose construction Opus Dei had helped finance.

Don Alvaro had been at Escrivá de Balaguer's side for forty years, thirty of them as the Father's confessor. Together they had built Opus Dei into a disciplined body enjoying world-wide influence. Together they had fended off the attacks of liberal Catholics and attempts from within the Curia to dismantle the Work. Don Alvaro liked to give the impression that he lived in the shadow of the Father. But he was in fact the real architect of Opus Dei's spectacular growth. By then the Work had 60,000 members in eighty countries. For all of them, Don Alvaro now assumed the role and title of the Father. Around his neck the new prelate general wore the piece of the True Cross which the Founder had wanted passed on to each of his successors.

On 15 September 1975, Opus Dei's General Congress approved Don Alvaro del Portillo y Diez de Sollano – to give him his fully reconstructed name – as the Work's second president general. There was said to have been but one dissenting vote, cast by Don Florencio Sánchez Bella, the regional vicar for Spain. Within the month Don Alvaro banished Sánchez Bella to Mexico, where he became a teacher in one of Opus Dei's local primary schools.

General Franco outlived the Founder by another five months. He died in November 1975, and Prince Juan Carlos de Borbón ascended the throne. During the coming year, a coup d'état in Argentina brought the generals back to power, while in Spain Opus Dei's Banco Atlántico had to be bailed out of trouble by José María Ruiz-Mateos, a secret Opus Dei member and self-made business phenomenon who had become Spain's richest citizen. As a result of Ruiz-Mateos's financial sacrifice, Opus Dei would be able to mount its assault on the Vatican establishment, assuring that at the close of the second millennium it would attain a position of power in the Church unknown since the Knights Templar.

PART FIVE
HIDDEN AGENDAS

20

RUMASA

Ask the Lord for money, because we are in great trouble. But ask him for millions! He owns everything anyway. To ask for five million or fifty million requires just the same effort, so while you're at it . . .

Josemaría Escrivá de Balaguer

SINCE 1857, THE RUIZ-MATEOS FAMILY HAD BEEN INVOLVED IN THE sherry business. And the family enterprise had gradually expanded. In 1958, when José María Ruiz-Mateos was a young sherry broker in Jerez de la Frontera, he succeeded in becoming Harvey's of Bristol's exclusive supplier. Harvey's accounted for approximately 10 per cent of the world sherry trade. Under the contract it had with Ruiz-Mateos the Bristol firm undertook to purchase 20,000 casks of sherry a year at £200 per cask, implying a gross annual turnover of £4 million. The contract left Ruiz-Mateos with enough disposable income to invest in a Spain that was beginning to emerge from decades of economic stagnation. Harvey's, meanwhile, were so pleased with their agent that when the contract came up for renewal they extended it to ninety-nine years.

While José María's father had implanted in the future sherry magnate a deep business sense, his mother had instilled in him an equally religious one, including a deep veneration for the Virgin

Mary, which remained one of the motivating forces of his life. His adoration for the Virgin was reinforced when in the mid-1950s he was introduced to Opus Dei. He regularly attended the Saturday benediction services at an Opus Dei centre on the way to the airport, until 1963 when he and his wife decided to write their separate letters to the Father asking to become members.

After the ministerial changes of 1957, Spain's economy had come to life. The tourist industry led the boom, with more than 6 million holidaymakers pouring $300 million annually into the economy, a figure that would rise to more than $3,000 million a year by the 1970s. With the Harvey's of Bristol 'mine' working well, José María found he had sufficient capital on hand to branch into other fields. He had attracted the attention of Luis Valls Taberner, the newly-appointed deputy chairman of Banco Popular Español. With Valls involved at a top management level, Banco Popular's commercial loan portfolio had increased by 300 per cent in one year and, looking for more business, he requested his assistant Rafael Termes to arrange a meeting with the sherry broker. On the appointed day, Ruiz-Mateos came to Banco Popular's *Presidencia* in Madrid, never dreaming that within two decades he would be acclaimed Spain's most successful entrepreneur.

Two more disparate characters were hard to imagine. Whereas Luis Valls was austere, reserved, not to say icy-cold, the younger Ruiz-Mateos was droll, agile and overflowing with the sun of Andalusia. He was accompanied by his brother-in-law, Luis Barón Mora-Figueroa, like himself an Opus Dei supernumerary. Ruiz-Mateos wanted to acquire the Banca de Jiménez in Cordoba, but although his sherry business was expanding, he lacked the necessary capital. With Banco Popular's assistance he bought the small private bank and later changed its name to Banco de Jerez. Thereafter Ruiz-Mateos joined with Banco Popular's Termes and another associate, Paco Curt Martínez, who although not a member was close to Opus Dei, in several tourist development ventures on the Costa del Sol. They formed a company together under the name of Ruiz-Mateos y Cía.

Luis Valls also introduced Ruiz-Mateos to Gregorio López Bravo, a thirty-seven-year-old naval engineer who in July 1962 was named minister of industry and seven years later became Spain's foreign minister. Valls considered that both Ruiz-Mateos and López

Bravo possessed exceptional qualities. Of Ruiz-Mateos the banker said, 'You are someone capable of creating and maintaining thousands of jobs.' Of López Bravo, whom he called 'Mr Efficiency', he said, 'You will provide the motor for Spain's economic growth.'

That same year, to insure that he possessed sufficient stocks to fulfil the Harvey's contract, Ruiz-Mateos acquired a major sherry producer. But Harvey's had come under new ownership, and early in 1966 changed its commercial strategy and cancelled the contract with Ruiz-Mateos. By then José María had been securely wired into the Opus Dei network and, under the watchful eye of Valls and Termes, he was busily extending his interests into vineyards, food processing, construction and tourism, with the result that he hardly noticed a drop in cash flow. Moreover, Harvey's shift in strategy transformed the Jerez firm from faithful ally into major competitor, as Ruiz-Mateos now directly entered the world sherry market under his own Dry Sack label.

After moving to Madrid, in February 1968 he renamed his holding company Ruiz-Mateos Sociedad Anonima, known in its abbreviated form as Rumasa. Over the next ten years, Rumasa became Spain's largest conglomerate in private hands. José María launched it on a whirlwind acquisition programme, building it into a multinational giant that controlled 350 industrial, shipping, pharmaceutical, tourism and agribusiness enterprises, and twenty banks. It counted 40,000 employees and was one of Spain's most prolific foreign exchange earners, exporting annually goods and services worth in excess of $260 million.[1]

Ruiz-Mateos was not only a devout Catholic but a compulsive workaholic. An image of the Virgin Mary adorned the entrance lobby of every Rumasa building and next to the boardroom he installed a Marian chapel. He chose the bee as his corporate emblem because it was the symbol of the industrious worker. His staff referred to him as the 'King Bee'. On his desktop, among a forest of family portraits – his wife, Teresa, blessed him with seven daughters and six sons – he kept a statuette of the Virgin, two crucifixes and a leather-bound copy of The Way. Living God's Work as a vocation meant keeping a portrait of the Father on his bedside table, confessing weekly to an Opus Dei priest, confiding in his spiritual director,

[1] Memorandum on The Rumasa Group by WW Finance S.A., Geneva, November 1979, p. 2.

attending the weekly circle to which he was assigned and pumping on average $1.65 million a year into the Work's coffers. 'I received money from God,' he said, 'and so I gave money to God.'

RUMASA'S EMBLEM

Whereas Vilá Reyes of Matesa had used Opus Dei for its contacts, Ruiz-Mateos really believed that he was indispensable to God's Work. He allowed the Opus Dei strategists to use his corporate empire, though as far as he was concerned he remained in control. Nevertheless, eight of his fifteen managing directors were Opus Dei members. And because Opus Dei left him 'free' to operate his business as he thought best, he did not perceive the paradox when told by his spiritual mentors that he must remain discreet and deny he was a member of Escrivá de Balaguer's *Corps Mobile*.

He described his spiritual director, Salvador Nacher March, as 'a saint, a wonderful man'. A lay numerary and lawyer from Valencia, 'Boro' Nacher became his alter ego. Ruiz-Mateos trusted him: no subject was too intimate not to be discussed among them. In fact, there was only one person he trusted more and that was Luis Valls Taberner.

With Ruiz-Mateos and Rumasa once again we collide with Opusian double-speak, for the organization claims it does not interfere with the professional lives of its members. 'When Opus Dei has given [members] the spiritual help they need, its job is finished. From then on, as far as the Prelature is concerned, members are *on their own*, as they make up their own mind in all professional, family, social, political and cultural matters – matters which the Church leaves open to the free decision of the faithful. Opus Dei does not get involved, indeed cannot get involved. Even hostile former members agree that this is so, not just in theory, but also and always in practice,' Opus Dei apologist William O'Connor affirmed.[1]

While the entire statement sounds like a denial of reality, the last sentence is particularly striking. Which 'hostile former members'? Not one is named. With good reason. Not one would make such a statement unless a gun was held to his head. But within the context of the 'Spiritual Help/Job Finished' claim, Ruiz-Mateos was a good example of what can happen. Rumasa was all the more carefully controlled because he had created the almost perfect corporate structure for the particular needs of Opus Dei. First, Rumasa was privately owned by Ruiz-Mateos, his four brothers (one of them an Opus Dei priest) and sister. Because it was privately held, Rumasa could do things that publicly held companies, with shares listed for trading on a stock exchange, could not. Second, the Rumasa Group became extremely diversified with its own banks at home and abroad, and large foreign exchange operations. This meant it could be used, on the one hand, to camouflage international transfers, while being milked with the other for contributions. Third, for Opus Dei it was expendable. Thus Rumasa possessed in the green eyes of the Work the qualities of confidentiality, flexibility, availability and expendability, all important considerations for the men governing the finances of Opus Dei.

Optimistic by nature, Ruiz-Mateos became one of the Father's most faithful, obedient and profitable sons. He was fawned upon and spiritually cuddled. He grew to love the Work, and the Work loved him. When told that his help was needed in taking over an ailing Opus Dei auxiliary operation, such as a faltering bank, he did it 'freely' and in good faith. When counted upon to provide $10 million for the University of Navarra, he produced the money willingly and in good faith.

Opus Dei's financial requirements were vast. With five South American universities modelled upon the University of Navarra, a dozen other higher academic institutions in existence or planned

---

[1] O'Connor, *Op. cit.*, p. 34.

around the world, and a $30 million sanctuary at Torreciudad under construction, it needed to draw upon a score of enterprises like Rumasa. A constant pressure existed to find not only new members, but new sources of capital. With such heavy demands the strategists were prepared to bleed a major contributor dry and pass on responsibility for paying off the creditors to the governments concerned. This was high-risk business, for if the failed enterprise was large enough it could place entire sectors of the economy in jeopardy. Even so, it was impossible to imagine that harm might come to a concern as flexible as the Golden Bee. In fact only one major hiccup in the economy was needed. It came in 1974. The economies of the industrial world almost gagged to death over a quadrupling of world oil prices, whose significance – especially in Rome, where Opus Dei was engaged in a battle for greater influence within the Curia – was not realized for many months, and against all expectations the rumblings it brought on continued to cause problems for another decade.

Ruiz-Mateos was sufficiently strong-minded to assume an equilibrium in his relations with the Work that most other brothers in the faith were unable to achieve. On one occasion, when the Opus Dei directors asked him to hire an untested banker, José Ramón Alvarez Rendueles, to run Rumasa's banking division, Ruiz-Mateos refused. This was one Opus Dei suggestion that the King Bee would regret having rejected. Opus Dei was intent on insuring that Alvarez Rendueles's career remained upwardly mobile and, in fact, he later became governor of the Banco de España.

Ruiz-Mateos was well aware that obedience in all matters was the key to being a good son of the Work. He called it 'terrifying obedience'. One of his former advisers and close friend, not an Opus Dei member, remarked, 'Numerary and supernumerary members take vows of obedience. Opus Dei calls them "promises", but they amount to the same thing. Any hesitation to follow the slightest suggestion – in fact an absolute imperative – of one's superiors is interpreted as a refusal to obey God. It is a rejection of God. José María, who for twenty years fought with his conscience to justify the power that the Work holds over its members, said of the people of Opus Dei, "My God, if they adhere to this terrifying obedience they will do nothing without consulting their spiritual director."

'Under such a regime of submission, a member must obey without asking the reason. To question an order is a serious offence. If a spiritual director suggests that it would be a good thing for a member to leave his job and take another, the member must do so immediately. And if a member is asked to move to another country, or never to return to the country where he was born, he must carry out this order without asking for an explanation. To insist otherwise would provoke the anger of his superiors or even a threat of expulsion from Opus Dei.'

Ruiz-Mateos was said to have been devastated by the death of the Founder, to whom he believed he owed everything. By then Rumasa's annual turnover accounted for 2 per cent of Spain's GNP. It was an extremely profitable enterprise and, by juggling its accounts, could fund alone virtually any Opus Dei project, except perhaps the Portillo Option. He religiously paid over the required tithe of 10 per cent of Rumasa's profits, arranging to make quarterly transfers to Opus Dei accounts in Switzerland, though Spain continued to maintain exchange controls until joining the Common Market in 1986. The arrangements were handled directly between Carlos Quintas Alvarez, head of Rumasa's banking division, and Juan Francisco Montuenga, Opus Dei's treasurer for Spain. While Quintas was one of seven top Rumasa executives who were not Opus Dei members, his wife, Mercedes, was a supernumerary.

In addition to these regular payments, Opus Dei made other occasional demands that were destined to have a serious impact on Rumasa's ongoing development. The most significant was Rumasa's 1977 bail-out of Banco Atlántico. The operation proved costly, both to Rumasa and Opus Dei.

Atlántico's problems had begun three years before. The 1974 world liquidity crisis had not been kind to it and by 1977, although its deposits had risen to $730 million, it was experiencing treasury problems and its stock was dropping in the marketplace. Continental Illinois decided to dump its Atlántico shares. Rather than face the possibility of an embarrassing collapse, Opus Dei's Spanish hierarchy asked Ruiz-Mateos – behind the backs of Atlántico's managing directors – to take over the bank and save it from going under. Ruiz-Mateos structured a buy-out by Rumasa that brought Atlántico an immediate infusion of almost $50 million.

With his usual optimism, he highlighted the positive side of the operation. 'It was important for Rumasa to have a strong banking network. Atlántico gave us elements we were lacking. We made

Continental Illinois an offer to purchase their 18 per cent, and it was an attractive offer because the stock was on its way down. Rumasa bought the shares, then we went in and explained the situation to Bofill and Ferrer.'[1]

When informed that Rumasa had acquired Continental Illinois's block of stock, José Ferrer went white and remained speechless for a good ten minutes. Ruiz-Mateos understood that if a man of Ferrer's calibre remained dumbstruck for so long it meant that he was professionally finished. Opus Dei's 'terrifying obedience' demanded that he accept the *fait accompli*, no matter how un-palatable the consequences.

But in order to complete the majority takeover of Banco Atlántico, the Opus Dei directors required Ruiz-Mateos to buy Banco Latino as well, and at a very high price. Banco Latino had advanced signifi-cant loans to Fundación General Mediterránea and other Opus Dei related concerns which had been filed as uncollectable receivables. 'In acquiring Banco Latino, we assumed these liabilities and wrote them off,' the King Bee explained. Thus Rumasa pumped another $13.5 million into Esfina, Fundación General Mediterránea and Atlántico itself to acquire their equity in Latino. With the loan write-offs added, it proved an expensive lifeboat operation. But it permitted Atlántico's former charitable affiliate, the Fundación General Mediterránea, with assets of $100 million, to continue oper-ating for another sixteen years. Finally, by acquiring Atlántico Ruiz-Mateos inherited the services of the Zurich lawyer Arthur Wiederkehr.

Hoping to soften the blow for Bofill and Ferrer, during one of their meetings Ruiz-Mateos passed them a note. He had already told them that he hoped they would remain on Atlántico's board. The note said: 'With me, you will never have problems.' But the 'terrifying obedience' had other intentions for them. Pablo Bofill was sent to London to teach economics at an Opus Dei school. José Ferrer moved to Argentina where his family had important interests, and where also another Fundación General Mediterránea existed that financed the neo-Perónista movement.

With such demands on Rumasa's treasury, it was hardly astound-ing that in 1978 the Banco de España warned Ruiz-Mateos to slow

[1] Interview with José María Ruiz-Mateos, Madrid, 2 March 1995.

its expansion. Moreover, the Banco de España asked Rumasa to supply the state comptrollers with audited financial statements and assigned a deputy governor, Mariano Rubio, to insure that it complied. Although Rumasa was entirely in the hands of the Ruiz-Mateos family, some of the companies it controlled were publicly listed, their stock being held by 100,000 minority investors. But Ruiz-Mateos was unwilling to produce audited accounts as they would show Rumasa's undeclared transfers to the Opus Dei network abroad. Fearing government retaliation, with Arthur Wiederkehr's help he started diffusing Rumasa's assets, an exercise that required several sets of books, but only one of them apparent. Nobody ever accused Ruiz-Mateos of being dumb. He remained as crafty as a fox, and he trusted Luis Valls Taberner.

21

UNITED TRADING

You can't run the Church on Hail Marys.

Archbishop Paul Marcinkus

RUIZ-MATEOS WAS NOT ALONE IN MAINTAINING THAT OPUS DEI controlled a transnational network of banks and financial institutions. In addition to Banco Popular Español and Credit Andorra, he believed that the network included Nordfinanz Bank in Zurich. But one supposes other components existed in Argentina, Peru, Hong Kong or Singapore, wherever the Work did business. Opus Dei did not insist on physical control of the banks in its network, and always the links remained well hidden, almost impossible to detect. One theory we shall now explore is that Opus Dei wanted to control, imagined it controlled, or actually did control Milan's Banco Ambrosiano. As always in these situations, Opus Dei would have worked through a restricted circle of people, some unaware that they were being used, while others, if they suspected, remained unsure as to who was manipulating whom and for what purposes.

One of the key figures in the Ambrosiano affair was Paul Casimir Marcinkus, a priest from Chicago who was known in Rome as a fixer. Marcinkus was ambitious, wanting to become the first American Curial cardinal and grand elector of future popes. He thought he could achieve this by assuming control of the papal purse strings. Early on in his career he had caught the eye of Cardinal Francis Spellman of New York who advised Paul VI to take the young American prelate under his wing. Affable, golf-playing and occasionally cigar-smoking, Marcinkus worked at the time as a translator in the Secretariat of State.

From the outset, financial matters dominated Paul VI's pontificate. The Italian government announced it was going to tax Vatican holdings, which caused the papal money managers to seek ways of diversifying the Holy See's investments. This led to the sale by the IOR of its choicest bank holding, Banca Cattolica del Veneto, which had deposits of $700 million. An option to buy the bank was given to Milan lawyer Michele Sindona, regarded at the time as one of Italy's leading financial wizards. In early 1969 details of Sindona's dealings with the Vatican were leaked to the press and overnight he became a national figure. One of Sindona's closest friends in Rome was Mark Antinucci, an Italo-American businessman who owned the *Rome Daily American*, a newspaper that had CIA connections. Antinucci and Marcinkus played golf together at Rome's Holy Waters Golf Club. As early as 1967, Antinucci talked to Sindona about Marcinkus.

In 1963, when Paul VI began monitoring his career, Marcinkus was supervising the construction of Rome's most luxurious priests' residence, the Villa Stritch. Paul VI asked him to help his personal secretary, Father Pasquale Macchi, organize the Eucharist Congress planned for Bombay at the end of the year. Marcinkus and Macchi hit it off well. For the next few years they virtually ran the papal household, and anyone hoping for a confidential chat with the Holy Father had to pass through them. Marcinkus masterminded the Pope's eight remaining foreign journeys, and saved Paul's life by overpowering a knife-wielding assailant as he lunged through the crowd at Manila's international airport.

After Spellman's death in December 1967, US contributions to the Vatican decreased significantly. Father Macchi suggested that Marcinkus might be the man to reverse the situation. The idea appealed to the pontiff who decided to shift Marcinkus into a vacant position at the IOR, under the octogenarian Cardinal Di Jorio. Marcinkus was an excellent organizer but had no experience as a banker. He requested time off to visit a couple of big money-centre banks, study their systems and see from the inside how they operated. The request granted, he went to Chase Manhattan in New York, in his own words, 'for a day or two ... to see how stocks and stuff operated', and then to Continental Illinois in Chicago, where he was given 'a kind of three-day course, taking me through everything'.[1] He spent another day with the Continental Finance Corporation in Chicago to learn about trust operations, followed by a final day-long tour of a small local bank. In those seven days, Marcinkus became an international banker, equipped to play a leading role in managing the Vatican's finances. On Christmas Eve 1968, Paul VI made him titular Bishop of Orta, and two weeks later confirmed the new bishop's appointment as the IOR's secretary. Marcinkus's starting salary was $6,400 per annum.

Sindona transferred the Banca Cattolica option to Roberto Calvi, a central manager at Milan's Banco Ambrosiano. Calvi became Sindona's understudy in the hidden-hand operations that now evolved between Milan and the Vatican. The two had met some months previously. Sindona, who rarely had a good word to say about anybody, sensed that Calvi wanted to place some of Ambrosiano's offshore funds in joint ventures with him. Sindona implied that Calvi was interested not only in operating offshore, but off-the-books. Not long after getting to know Sindona, Calvi was promoted to general manager.

Founded in 1896, Banco Ambrosiano's statutes stipulated that its operations should be devoted to furthering the Christian virtues of faith and charity. It is difficult to believe that either of these virtues led to the founding in 1956 of a Liechtenstein company called Lovelok. This concern, which became the bank's largest shareholder, was of unknown ownership. It may have been controlled by Carlo Canesi, Ambrosiano's then managing director and Calvi's boss, but this is only speculation. More probably it belonged to a hidden partner whose identity may or may not have been known to Canesi. If taken to the furthest absurdity, the shroud of secrecy surrounding Lovelok meant that it could have been controlled by the Pope himself, or Opus Dei. One year later, Lovelok formed Banca del Gottardo in Lugano, placing 40 per cent of Gottardo's capital with

[1] John Cornwell, *A Thief in the Night – The Death of Pope John Paul I*, Penguin edition, London 1990, p. 73.

the Ambrosiano. Then in May 1963, Lovelok founded a Luxembourg subsidiary called Compendium S.A. to buy more Banco Ambrosiano shares, mainly from cash-squeezed Church institutions, with monies borrowed from the Ambrosiano itself.

Calvi was a character out of a Dostoyevsky novel. Of medium height, balding, with large, brooding eyes, he had served as a cavalry officer on the Russian front, keeping a live chicken under his great-coat during the winter campaigns to warm his hands. In 1943, his tour of battlefront duty ended, he returned home and found work as a clerk with Banca Commerciale Italiana, a state-owned bank where his father was a manager. Because of his war experience, Calvi spoke fluent German. His English and French were less proficient. He joined the foreign department of Banco Ambrosiano in 1947, the same year that Marcinkus was ordained and Escrivá de Balaguer moved permanently to Rome.

For Clara Canetti, Roberto Calvi was the man with a 'Clark Gable moustache'. They met on the beach at Rimini during the summer of 1950 and Roberto courted her while Clara's 12-year-old brother acted as chaperon. She found him not at all shy. In fact she noted that he was even a bit presumptuous. From a well-to-do Bologna family, Clara was an extraordinarily beautiful young woman, an asset for any rising banker. They married a year later and after a honeymoon in the shadows of Monte Rosa they moved into a small apartment in the centre of Milan.

They had two children – Carlo and Anna – and the family's close-ness was the envy of many in their circle of friends. They bought a country estate overlooking the village of Drezzo, near Como; Clara considered it her personal corner of paradise. They were often seen walking through the narrow streets of Drezzo hand in hand, as if on a perpetual honeymoon.

Calvi's first act when promoted Banco Ambrosiano's general man-ager was to bring Compendium out of its secret existence. He renamed it Banco Ambrosiano Holding S.A., and made it the spear-head of the group's offshore operations. This gave Ambrosiano's hidden partner, Lovelok, increased power in the group's affairs. To what extent this was part of a plan agreed to or even devised by Lovelok's true owners can only remain conjecture. Of course even the name of Banco Ambrosiano Holding was ambiguous as at the outset it was only 40 per cent owned by the supposed parent, Banco

Ambrosiano. Another 20 per cent was held by Banca del Gottardo, and the remaining 40 per cent was controlled by still another mystery nominee, Radowal AG of Liechtenstein, through an account at the IOR.

Banco Ambrosiano Holding formed a subsidiary bank in the Bahamas, which began its existence under the name of Cisalpine Overseas Bank, but was eventually changed to Banco Ambrosiano Overseas Limited. To simplify matters, from the outset we will call it Ambrosiano Overseas. Canesi confirmed Calvi's appointment as Ambrosiano Overseas's chairman. In April 1971, the IOR became a minority shareholder of the Nassau bank, acquiring 32 per cent of its voting rights. By then Marcinkus had succeeded Di Jorio as the IOR president.

So ironclad was the IOR's confidence in this untested offshore bank that within a year it had no less than $73.5 million on deposit with it. Furthermore, 'Mr Paul C. Marcinkus' accepted to become an Ambrosiano Overseas director. According to Sindona, Marcinkus enjoyed playing the role of international banker. He also enjoyed golfing on Nassau's Paradise Island championship course. Shortly after Marcinkus attended his first Nassau board meeting, Banco Ambrosiano exercised the option to acquire control of Banca Cattolica del Veneto. This came about in August 1971 but was not made public until the following March.

How Calvi acquired the Banca Cattolica del Veneto option is in itself an interesting tale. He had bailed Sindona out of a heap of trouble by taking off his hands a lame-duck company called Pachetti for $40 million. Sindona had used Pachetti, a one-time leather goods manufacturer, for stock promotion purposes and, hyped out of its corporate socks, it was not worth the quarter of what Calvi paid for it. To sweeten the deal, however, Sindona had thrown in the option to buy 50 per cent of Banca Cattolica del Veneto for $46.5 million. In addition, Sindona was alleged to have paid a $6.5 million commission to Calvi and Marcinkus for taking over Pachetti. Through these operations, Banco Ambrosiano temporarily solved both Sindona's and the IOR's liquidity problems. Very strong! But the question could now be asked whether the Ambrosiano bought Banca Cattolica del Veneto with the IOR's own money? The answer would appear to be yes, unless – another possibility – it was fiduciary money belonging to an anonymous client, for example Lovelok or Radowal.

Before consummating the Banca Cattolica transaction, Calvi asked Marcinkus to arrange a private audience with the Pope. Although the Vatican denies that the meeting took place, in a recorded conversation between the banker and a Sardinian businessman by the name of Flavio Carboni that later fell into the hands of the Milan magistrates, Calvi explained that he had insisted on seeing the Pope in order to be certain that the Holy Father was aware of what Marcinkus was up to. Not only was the Pope informed, Calvi said, but he thanked the banker for Ambrosiano's support.

Unlike Sindona and Marcinkus, Calvi had been a bank employee all his professional life and Carlo Canesi had chosen him as his personal assistant for his discretion, innovation and high integrity. Calvi spoke rarely of professional matters outside of the bank. But he was not given to being oblique with the truth either. When he told his wife that he had dealings with Opus Dei, she certainly believed him. He neglected, however, to tell her when these dealings began and with whom he dealt. But one thing is certain. In 1971 Calvi started travelling regularly to Rome, and his business dealings there intensified in the winter of 1974–75. Among the names he did mention were Dr Francesco Cosentino, secretary-general of the Italian Chamber of Deputies (whom she said advised her husband on political matters), Flaminio Piccoli, chairman of the Christian Democrat party, and Loris Corbi, chairman of Condotte d'Acqua. Both Piccoli and Corbi were known to be close to Opus Dei, or, as in the case of Corbi, close to high-level Opus Dei people. Through Cosentino, Calvi also got to know Andreotti, Ortolani and Gelli. Clara referred to the former as the Great Intriguer, and she called the latter two *il Gatto e la Volpe*, after the Cat and the Fox who stole the gold pieces from Pinocchio.[1]

In 1974, Calvi made the first charted use of Dr Arthur Wiederkehr's Zurich law firm, acquiring United Trading Corporation S.A., a Panamanian shell company. Everything indicates that Calvi was not acting on behalf of the Ambrosiano group but for a confidential client of the IOR, or for the IOR itself, as the IOR took possession of United Trading's entire share capital. But what gives us the greatest insight into the identity of Ambrosiano's hidden partner is that United Trading took over the assets of Radowal and Lovelok, as both were wound up.

---

[1] Clara Calvi diaries, p. 33.

What the IOR wanted to achieve with United Trading, into which Calvi folded about $80 million of existing debt, is an interesting question. A logical explanation would be that the transferred debt had been incurred in a first instance by the IOR's confidential client and guaranteed – as far as Calvi was concerned – by the IOR itself. Otherwise why would the Vatican bank accept such a miserable deal?

United Trading remains one of the great mysteries of the Vatican's financial operations up through the 1980s. The fact that it came out of the offices of Arthur Wiederkehr, who was chairman of Nordfinanz Bank, a Zurich bank suspected of being a turntable for Opus Dei monies, provides us with another clear hint of who stood behind it. United Trading had a subsidiary, Nordeurop AG, registered in Liechtenstein. Over the next few years Nordeurop (note similarity of name with Nordfinanz) came to owe nearly $400 million to Banco Ambrosiano's unit in Lima, Peru. Nordeurop would play an important role in the dealings that followed between Ambrosiano, the IOR and the undisclosed mystery client or, as Marcinkus later expressed it, the 'missing counterparty'.

In trying to cast new light on United Trading's significance, we must look at what was happening in the world financial system, and remember that 1974 was at least the fifth consecutive year in which the Vatican ran a deficit. The year had started well enough. But few bankers or economists foresaw the consequences of the December 1973 decision by the Islamic oil producing states to quadruple the world price of oil. This produced a vast demand for dollars and from a 5 per cent annual growth rate, the world economy shifted in 1974 to a nil or minus growth rate and 12 per cent inflation.[1] The dollar squeeze led to the downfall of the Sindona banking empire, producing a loss to the Vatican estimated as high as $240 million, an earthquake of major proportions. Indeed, the quadrupling of world oil prices was later described as the most destructive economic event since the Second World War, with the Islamic oil producers siphoning out of the world economy an extra $80,000 million a year – equivalent to 10 per cent of all world exports. The rise of Islam in the West can be said to have commenced from this date.

[1] Robert Solomon, *The International Monetary System 1945–1981*, Harper & Row, 1982, p. 316.

Being prudent, Calvi had Banca del Gottardo in Lugano draw up a management contract for United Trading. It was boiler plate, except it stated that United Trading had been formed *on instructions from the IOR*. Monsignor Donato de Bonis and another IOR employee, Dr Pellegrino de Strobel, signed the management contract. But Marcinkus later claimed that the contract was undated when they eventually signed it and then backdated by Calvi once he became executive chairman in November 1975. This assertion was strongly denied by Fernando Garzoni, Banca del Gottardo's chairman, and his general manager. Both assured the Milan magistrates that they had already signed and dated the contract when Calvi took it to Rome, and that '*the IOR knew it was operative as of that date*'.

This automatically cast doubt on the authenticity of a letter on Banco Ambrosiano stationery that was initialled (not signed) by Calvi. In this letter, with the hand-written date of 26 July 1977, Calvi acknowledged that the IOR was holding the United Trading shares on behalf of Banco Ambrosiano. The letter undertook to indemnify the IOR as the fiduciary owner and absolved it of responsibility for United Trading's affairs. At that point the IOR had advanced around $200 million to United Trading.

In the best of cases the letter demonstrated the IOR's awareness that United Trading was a deceptive device. At worst, it was a forgery drafted long after the events to which it related. No copy of the document was uncovered in the files of Banco Ambrosiano, from where it is alleged to have originated. It contains elementary grammatical errors, suggesting it was written by someone whose mother tongue was not Italian. But when the Italian judiciary wished to examine the letter, it was unable to do so as the only extant version of the document was in the hands of the IOR. As the IOR is not domiciled in Italy, but in the Vatican City, the document could not be subpoenaed for scientific examination.

In sworn testimony given in Milan in January 1989, Banca del Gottardo's general manager told magistrates, 'Marcinkus confirmed to me that Calvi had been mandated by the IOR to act on its behalf.'[1] What could be more condemning? He had no reason to commit

---

[1] Raw, *The Moneychangers*, Harvill, London 1992, p. 130. Transcripts of the Bolgiani and Garzoni depositions are contained in the Calvi family archives.

perjury. Marcinkus, on the other hand, refused to give evidence, preferring to hide behind the Vatican's Leonine Walls.

In addition to owning a large block of Banco Ambrosiano shares, United Trading also controlled a rainbow of Latin shell companies that owed Ambrosiano a lot of money. But Calvi would have been unlikely to allow such a heavy concentration of unsecured debt to build up unless he was following the orders of Ambrosiano's largest shareholder and hidden partner. Because of United Trading's growing debt, during the second half of 1977 the first cracks began to appear in Ambrosiano's corporate edifice.

At the time Sindona, then a fugitive from Italian justice, was languishing in his million-dollar suite at the Pierre Hotel in New York, wondering how he was going to pay his legal bills. The Federal Reserve Bank of New York had sunk $1,700 million into his bankrupt Franklin National Bank. Sindona then had the idea of asking Calvi to contribute $500,000 to his defence fund. Calvi prevaricated with the result that when Banco Ambrosiano employees arrived for work on 13 November 1977 they found Milan's financial district plastered with posters accusing their chairman of 'fraud, issuing false accounts, dissimulating assets, illegal export of currency and tax swindling'. The posters also alleged that Calvi had received tens of millions of dollars in undeclared kickbacks from his dubious dealings with Sindona. Calvi sent out a clean-up squad to remove the posters, but the Italian news magazine *l'Espresso* got hold of one and published the story.

Luigi Cavallo, known as *il Provocatore*, was the artist behind this attack on Calvi's integrity. He ran a news service called '*Agenzia A*'. After the *Espresso* story appeared, he wrote to Calvi threatening further disclosures if he did not reconsider 'the possibility of honouring the undertakings so freely made by you some years ago'. Calvi decided to meet Sindona's attorney in Rome, and eventually agreed to pay the $500,000 into a numbered account in Switzerland. The money was transferred from a United Trading account in Nassau.[1]

As a result of Luigi Cavallo's hi-jinx, the Bank of Italy ordered an investigative audit of Banco Ambrosiano. In April 1978, a Bank of Italy inspector, Giulio Padalino, arrived at the Ambrosiano headquarters in Milan with a team of fifty auditors. Calvi seemed

---

[1] Raw, *Op. cit.*, pp. 205–207.

unperturbed. After weeks of digging and sifting, Padalino found that the Ambrosiano's domestic operations were, on the whole, successful and well run. The bank's foreign operations, on the other hand, were of such complexity that he suspected they covered a way of transferring Italian currency out of Italy. Padalino confronted Calvi. The banker denied any wrongdoing. However the audit indicated that breaches of the exchange control laws had occurred. Irked by Calvi's lack of co-operation, Padalino promised further enquiries. Confident that the threat would come to nothing, Calvi left Milan on an extended business trip to South America.

While the Bank of Italy investigations continued, activity at the Villa Tevere centred on preparing a new file for Paul VI concerning Opus Dei's transformation to a Personal Prelature. In June 1978, Pope Paul 'encouraged' Don Alvaro del Portillo to present a formal petition to obtain the 'desired juridical status'. This coincided with a further worsening in the Vatican's finances. Cardinal Villot, now actively on Opus Dei's side, had for two years been pressing Pope Paul to do something about the deteriorating situation.[1] But before Don Alvaro could draft the petition, on 6 August 1978 Paul VI died.

As the cardinals gathered in Rome for the Conclave, Opus Dei's allies made sure that the Vatican's financial problems remained at the forefront of their thoughts. Prior to the Conclave, the new rules decreed by Paul VI before his death required the cardinals to hold daily meetings, called General Congregations, under the chairmanship of the camerlingo (chamberlain) who presides over the Church prior to the election of a new pope. The camerlingo has the task of preparing the *De Eligendo Pontifice* – an oration that praises the qualities of the dead pope and sets out the qualities which the cardinals believe are required of the next pope. At Paul's death the camerlingo was Cardinal Villot.

The Vatican's deficit was now running between $30 million and $40 million annually, and in the first General Congregation Cardinal Palazzini asked whether the status of the IOR should be changed to bring it under greater Curial control. Cardinal Villot hastily conducted an investigation. In theory, the IOR was answerable to a commission of five cardinals, chaired by Villot himself. Villot concluded in his report to the cardinals a few days later that the IOR's

[1] Malachi Martin, *The Final Conclave*, Pocket Books, New York 1978, p. 71.

independent status should be maintained but that a system of stronger internal controls was needed.

In the midst of the General Congregations, Cardinal Wojtyla paid a visit to the Villa Tevere.[1] He entered the Church of Our Lady of Peace, his robes brushing past the seventy-three freshly cut red roses, and knelt to pray beside the tomb of the Founder. This was an unusual gesture for one of the key electors only a week before the Conclave opened.

The election of the Patriarch of Venice, Albino Luciani, was one of the greatest protest votes in the history of papal elections. It marked a rejection of a Conservative-dominated Curia and the Church of Big Business. The new Pope was the son of a bricklayer, quiet, humble and with no diplomatic training nor Curial experience. When the result of the vote was announced, he told his electors, 'May God forgive you for what you have done to me!'

After taking the name of John Paul I, Luciani announced that he wished to be Pastor rather than Pontiff, and that papal pomp was not for him. He told the people of Rome that he intended to commit his Pontificate to applying the teachings of the Second Vatican Council. That by itself, Roberto Calvi later remarked, was a dangerous thing to have said. There was a community within the Church, fundamentalist to the core, that was intent on revising – i.e., correcting – the conclusions of Vatican II.

On Sunday, 27 August, after appearing on the balcony of Saint Peter's to bless the noontime crowds, Luciani lunched with Cardinal Villot. Luciani asked Villot to continue as Secretary of State 'until I have found my way'.[2] Indeed his liberal views on artificial birth control had distressed the traditionalists, and he needed Villot's counsel while forming his 'new-look' administration. The Conservatives reacted to the new Pope's views by assuring the faithful that he was in fact absolutely dedicated to promoting the continuity of the Church's magisterium.

They did this even though they were aware that, when still a bishop, Luciani had wanted the Vatican to relax the rules concerning artificial birth control. Of course, they secretly cursed Luciani's

---

[1] Alain Woodrow, 'Qu'y a-t-il derrière le changement de statut de l'Opus Dei?' *Le Monde*, Paris, 14 November 1979.
[2] Yallop, *In God's Name*, Corgi Books, London 1984, pp. 240–241.

position and immediately after his election a team of trusted priests from the Secretariat of State began cleansing the archives of documents pertaining to the new pope that did not agree with their image of the magisterium. In Venice, according to a former diocesan official, they removed from the Patriarchy's archives all mention of Luciani's views on birth control. Specifically, they were said to have taken with them the notes for a talk Luciani had given to the Veneto region's parish priests during a 1965 spiritual retreat, in which he stated: 'I assure all of you that bishops would be more than happy to find a doctrine that declared the use of contraceptives legitimate under certain conditions . . . If there is only one possibility in a thousand, then we must find it and see if, by chance, with the help of the Holy Spirit, we might come across something that has escaped us to date.'[1]

Some months before *Humanae Vitae*'s publication Luciani again addressed the problem of contraception at a diocesan conference on marriage. This time he said, 'It is our hope that the Pope will utter a word of deliverance.' Weeks later, his superior, Cardinal Giovanni Urbani of Venice, asked him to prepare a reserved text on artificial birth control for Paul VI. Luciani consulted doctors, parents and theologians, and produced a cogent theological argument for a revision of the Church's stand on birth control. Cardinal Urbani sent the document to Pope Paul before the final drafting of *Humanae Vitae*. It reinforced the majority conclusion of the panel of experts appointed by the Pope and was said to have swayed him in favour of a more liberal policy on sexual matters. Only Cardinal Wojtyla's energetic intervention, almost bullying his way into the papal chambers and virtually rewriting some of the *Humanae Vitae* pages himself, saved the day for the Conservatives. All trace of the Luciani text has since vanished, and today the Holy See denies that such a document ever existed.

In the draft of the papal acceptance speech, prepared for him by the Secretariat of State, Luciani excised all suggested references to *Humanae Vitae*. Earlier that year, Opus Dei had organized an International Congress in Milan to celebrate the tenth anniversary of the encyclical's publication. Luciani had refused to address the Congress. Instead, Wojtyla took his place. Then within the first

[1] Andrea Tornielli, 'The Hope of a Pastor', *30 Giorni*, No. 1, Rome 1995.

weeks of his papacy, Luciani told Villot that he planned to see US Congressman James Scheuer, vice-chairman of the UN Population Fund, the world agency that promoted family planning. Scheuer wanted Vatican support for a UN Population Fund plan to stabilize world population at 7.2 billion by the year 2050. An audience for Scheuer was tentatively scheduled for 24 October 1978.[1] This alarmed the Curial Conservatives. By then Opus Dei was regarded as the strongest Conservative force in the Church. It was – and remains – ferociously antagonistic to all forms of family planning other than the natural rhythm method. Shocked by Luciani's intentions, Opus Dei aligned around it all like-minded members of the cardinalate, particularly Höffner of Cologne, Krol of Philadelphia, Sin of Manila, Siri of Genoa, Wojtyla of Cracow and the Curial Conservatives Baggio, Oddi, Palazzini, Poletti, Samoré and, of course, Villot. The outspoken Oddi began openly suggesting that the Holy Spirit had made a mistake in allowing Luciani's election.

Roberto Calvi was in Montevideo when the news of Luciani's election reached him. If anything, he was relieved. Contrary to what was commonly believed, Calvi did not want a cover up of Ambrosiano's dealings with the IOR. At this point he had real grievances and he believed an investigation would result in Banco Ambrosiano receiving the assurances he was seeking. In fact, he regarded John Paul I as one of the few persons likely to instigate a much needed housecleaning at the Vatican bank.

Calvi told his wife and daughter that he no longer trusted Marcinkus. Clara Calvi later testified: 'I knew that he was working on resolving the IOR's problems with the help of Opus Dei. One day he told me that he intended to go to Madrid. "Why?" I asked. He laughed and explained that Opus Dei was very powerful in Spain.'[2]

Apart from the Vatican's deplorable finances, Papa Luciani's two greatest concerns at the outset of his pontificate were to revise *Humanae Vitae* and to convince Giovanni Benelli to become his Secretary of State. Such a move spelled immeasurable danger for Opus Dei. It was said that Alvaro del Portillo feared Benelli more than any other person in the Church.

---

[1] Yallop, *Op. cit.*, p. 246.
[2] Clara Calvi's testimony before Milan magistrates Bruno Siclari and Pierluigi dell'Osso, 25 October 1982, pp. 85–86.

VATICAN COUP D'ETAT

Desperate situations require desperate remedies.
Josemaría Escrivá de Balaguer

ACCOMPANIED BY GIACOMO BOTTA, HEAD OF THE AMBROSIANO'S foreign department, the Calvis stopped in Montevideo on the first leg of their Latin American tour to meet with Umberto Ortolani. The great Vatican door-opener had recently been appointed the Knights of Malta ambassador to Uruguay. Ortolani and one of his sons continued with the Calvis and Botta to Buenos Aires, where Licio Gelli, his wife Wanda, and their two sons were waiting. Calvi was ostensibly in Buenos Aires to discuss with the Argentine authorities the opening of a local Banco Ambrosiano branch. In fact Calvi, Gelli and Ortolani invited the entire naval general staff to dinner. At the end of the meal the admirals asked how they might finance the purchase of fifty AM39 Exocet missiles for their naval aviation. Each Exocet cost $1 million, so the admirals were talking about a $50 million package. As Exocets were manufactured in Italy under licence from the French firm of Aerospatiale, Calvi was able to provide an easy answer. He arranged for financing which, as no record of it was uncovered in the Ambrosiano accounts, one supposes was routed through the United Trading network.

While watching the television news in their hotel on the morning of 29 September 1978, Clara and Anna learned that Pope John Paul I had been found dead in his bed. Roberto was stunned. He had already told Clara that he found Luciani 'very courageous, open to dialogue, but very imprudent. In only a month he made it clear that he intended to adopt his own line at the Vatican. He had shown his intransigence, which surely meant that Marcinkus would be compromised.'[1] With a new pope this was no longer certain.

Calvi had explained to Clara that the reasons for the Vatican bank's troubles were to be found in the vaults of Banca del Gottardo, where the accounting secrets of the United Trading family of companies were kept. Later the IOR's chief accountant, Pellegrino de Strobel, went himself to the Gottardo's offices in Lugano to confirm the extent of United Trading's exposed position. Calvi had wondered what John Paul I knew of these dealings. Probably nothing, he supposed.

What Papa Luciani had intended for the IOR was Marcinkus's replacement as chairman. That Luciani wanted to relaunch Paul VI's *Ostpolitik* also seemed certain. But the opening towards Moscow had been brought to a halt when the Russian Orthodox Archbishop of Leningrad, the forty-nine-year-old Nikodim (widely regarded as a KGB agent), died of a massive heart attack (*infarto miocardico acuto*) in the Pope's antechamber before their meeting could take place.

A week later, Papa Luciani found on his desk a copy of the latest issue of Mino Pecorelli's Rome scandal sheet, *OP*. It revealed that 121 senior prelates were Freemasons. The list included the cardinals Villot, Poletti and Baggio. Shocked, Papa Luciani turned for advice to the only member of the hierarchy he trusted. That was Cardinal Benelli, now Archbishop of Florence, who counselled caution because he suspected Pecorelli of 'sharpening someone else's axe'. Luciani asked Benelli to become his secretary of state. Benelli was moved. His return to the Curia would have meant greater Vatican conciliation towards the Communist bloc and an easing of its stance against artificial birth control, two issues that the Conservative cardinals opposed.

[1] Clara Calvi's diaries, p. 29.

On 28 September 1978, Luciani informed Villot that in addition to removing Marcinkus, he proposed sending Sebastiano Baggio to Venice and the Vicar of Rome, Ugo Poletti, to Florence. Finally, he requested Villot's own resignation, intending to replace him with Benelli.[1] Although Luciani had no way of knowing, the four prelates he wanted to remove from the Curia were essential to the success of Opus Dei's intentions, namely canonization of the Founder, its own transformation as a Personal Prelature, and control of the Vatican finances.

During that night, after only thirty-three days in office, John Paul I died. The scrambling that followed for his succession bore the markings of a minutely prepared *coup d'état*. However much one might wish to believe otherwise, the surprise Pope in whom so many had placed such hope was unlikely to have died from natural causes and – in spite of all that has been written and said on the subject – the indications are strong that a cover up of the real cause of death was engineered by a Vatican clique convinced it was acting to protect the Church and her sacred teachings.

The facts surrounding the discovery of the Pope's death are bizarre to say the least. They prove that the Vatican did not, in the first instance, tell the truth and may not still be telling the truth. The first fact it attempted to hide was that Sister Vincenza found the Pope dead at about 5 a.m. when she brought him his thermos of coffee. She said he was sitting upright in bed, his lips twisted. She noticed that he was clutching a sheaf of papers. An unsettled dispute persists as to the nature of these papers, for they have disappeared. One explanation is that certain members of the Curia did not want the outside world to know that a power struggle was in progress inside the Vatican, engineered by a group that opposed Benelli's return to the centre of power. The papers allegedly detailed the changes that Luciani had intended to decree that same day. But according to Vatican news bulletins, he was holding a copy of *The Imitation of Christ*.

Rumours concerning the missing papers and other anomalies surrounding John Paul I's death continued to surface during the next six years until finally, in June 1984 – intending to dispense with the rumours once and for all – an unsigned memorandum was prepared

[1] Yallop, *Op. cit.*, pp. 302–303.

for a conference of bishops that brushed aside *The Imitation of Christ* story as a pure invention of the press!

This account was just as untrue as the first, produced in an attempt to rewrite history. The same memorandum suggested that the papers seen by Sister Vincenza were nothing more than the Pope's notes for his sermon at the Wednesday audience and the Angelus talk on the following Sunday. But the report neglected to mention that the original Vatican communiqué claimed the Pope had been found by Father John Magee, one of the two papal secretaries.

Sister Vincenza in fact had called Father Magee. His first reaction had been to summon Cardinal Villot from his apartment two floors below. Villot appeared in the papal bedroom a little after 5 a.m. and as camerlingo immediately took charge. According to others present, he did a quick tour of the room, stopping at the Pope's bedside table and at his desk. After his initial visit to the bedroom, a small bottle of Effortil, a liquid medicine used to alleviate low blood pressure, that John Paul kept on his bedside table, went missing. The sheaf of notes also disappeared. No autopsy was requested, and no forensic tests were undertaken.

The Vatican doctor, Renato Buzzonetti, arrived in the bedroom at 6 a.m. and made a brief examination of the body. Buzzonetti informed Villot that the cause of death was *infarto miocardico acuto* – a massive heart attack – and he estimated the time of death at about 11 p.m. on the previous evening. Without further ado, Villot called for the rapid embalming of the body.

Almost immediately the other secretary, Father Diego Lorenzi, who had been Luciani's aide in Venice, telephoned the Pope's personal physician, Antonio Da Ros, who had looked after Luciani for more than twenty years in Venice. 'He was shocked. Stunned. Unable to believe it . . . he said he would come to Rome immediately,' Lorenzi reported. Da Ros had been in Rome two weeks before to examine his patient, and remarked, *'Non sta bene, ma benone'* – 'You're not well, but very well.'[1] But when Da Ros arrived later that same day, he was not allowed near the body.

Benelli was telephoned in Florence at about 6.30 a.m. Overcome with grief and openly crying, he immediately retired to his room and began to pray. When Benelli re-emerged at 9 a.m. to speak to the

---

[1] *Ibid.*, p. 353.

press, he said: 'The Church has lost the right man for the right moment. We are very distressed. We are left frightened. Man cannot explain such a thing.'[1]

Hardly had Benelli spoken than the Vatican information department began creating the legend of the Pope's ill health. But if the Pope's health was so frail, why were no medicines – other than Effortil – to be found in the papal apartments? And whatever happened to that missing bottle of Effortil? Why was Cardinal Villot never questioned about it? Also not to be forgotten, Edoardo Luciani, the dead pope's brother, was on record as stating that Albino had no history of heart trouble.

The controversy surrounding Papa Luciani's death hung over the pre-Conclave General Congregations. As camerlingo, Villot found himself under attack by the more progressive cardinals. He admitted that the Vatican Press Office had given misleading information.[2] The dissident cardinals wanted to know why no autopsy had been performed, nor an official death certificate issued, and they pushed for a collegial statement on the Pope's death. The Conservatives rejected the idea.

No more reactionary figure existed in the Roman Curia than Cardinal Silvio Oddi. He was Opus Dei's cardinal protector. The Italian authorities had demanded an autopsy, but Oddi claimed that he had already carried out an investigation for the College of Cardinals and found no evidence of foul play. Therefore he opposed an autopsy on grounds that it would create a precedent,[3] which was untrue. Papal autopsies had been carried out before. Indeed, Oddi was quoted as saying: 'The College of Cardinals will not examine the possibility of an[other] enquiry at all, and will not accept any supervision from anyone, and it will not even discuss the subject . . . We know . . . in all certainty that the death of John Paul I was due to the fact that his heart stopped beating from perfectly natural causes.'[4]

---

[1] *Ibid.*, p. 320.
[2] Peter Hebblethwaite, *The Next Pope*, Fount (HarperCollins), London 1995, p. 64.
[3] Tommaso Ricci, 'Yallop Debunked', *30 Days*, Rome, June 1988. Ricci was quoting Swiss journalist Victor Willi, who had just written a book titled *Im Namen des Teufels? (In the Devil's Name?)*, refuting Yallop's thesis. The book was 'read and approved' by Joaquín Navarro-Valls, Willi told *30 Days*. But Navarro-Valls denied to John Cornwell that Cardinal Oddi had any official standing as an investigator or spokesman for the Vatican concerning John Paul I's death [see *A Thief in the Night*, p. 291].
[4] Yallop, *Op. cit.*, p. 336.

Then on 12 October 1978, as the second Conclave opened, Father Panciroli, the Vatican spokesman, announced that after all a death certificate had been signed by Professor Mario Fontana and Dr Renato Buzzonetti. The 'certificate' was not, however, a public document. With good reason. It contained a mere five typewritten lines affirming in Italian that the Pope had died in the Apostolic Palace at 23:00 on 28 September 1978 by *morte improvvisa – da infarto miocardico acuto*.[1] Such a document would not have passed muster in jurisdictions where developed notions of civil law existed.

In the second Conclave Siri and Benelli again started as frontrunners. In the opening ballots Benelli almost got the required two-thirds plus one.[2] Then Siri, at the urging of Baggio, Krol, Oddi and Palazzini, asked those who supported him to transfer their votes to Karol Wojtyla. He suggested that Wojtyla would make a 'good doctrinal pope'.

Speaking afterwards about what happened inside the Conclave, Cardinal Enrique y Tarancón expressed disgust for the politicking that surrounded the papal election, while Siri remarked, 'Secrecy can cover some very uncharitable actions.'[3] Siri never specified what those 'actions' might have been, but the election of the first non-Italian pope in 455 years meant that the Holy See embarked upon an apostolic programme that was radically different to the one that John Paul I had begun formulating.

Once elected, Wojtyla wanted to take the name of Stanislaus, after Cracow's first bishop and martyr. But Siri recommended that, to heal the Church's wounds, he should call himself John Paul II. Caracas lawyer Alberto Jaimes Berti, who had known Siri for more than twenty years, was in Rome for the papal inauguration. He said Siri was elated. 'He told me he had backed Wojtyla in the Conclave because he saw him as a providential figure sent to destroy Communism everywhere in the world. "We must help this Pope achieve his mission. He will need money, lots of money",' Berti quoted Siri as saying.

Berti at that time handled the Church finances in Venezuela.

---

[1] A copy of the death certificate was later published by John Cornwell in the appendices to *A Thief in the Night*.

[2] Jan Grootaers, *De Vatican II à Jean-Paul II: Le grand tournant de l'Eglise catholique*, Centurion, Paris 1981, pp. 124–133.

[3] Hebblethwaite, *The Next Pope*, pp. 66–67.

During his visit to Rome, he said Siri drew him aside and mentioned that the Church wanted to create a Latin American bank to promote trade with East Europe. Siri stressed that the bank required a sound capital base and would have to operate with absolute confidentiality.[1]

According to Berti, there was no doubt that if John Paul I had remained alive the Banco Ambrosiano scandal would never have occurred, as Luciani would have uncovered the IOR's secret dealings and put an end to them. On the other hand, there would have been an IOR scandal involving not only Marcinkus, but Opus Dei, the Italian military intelligence agency, SISMI, and others. With Wojtyla as Pope, however, the problems at the IOR were glossed over. Marcinkus continued as the bank's chairman. Villot remained as Secretary of State. It was no secret that Villot was by then Opus Dei's man. And the bottle of Effortil? According to a conspiracy theory still talked about in Vatican corridors, it had been spiked by a clear and tasteless poison that produced the same effect as digitalis, the natural poison that was suspected of being administered to Father Giuliano Ferrari, who died of a massive heart attack only a few months before.

The other results of Papa Wojtyla's election were that Baggio continued as Prefect of the Congregation of Bishops and Poletti kept his job as Vicar of Rome. They were needed to insure the Founder's beatification and Opus Dei's elevation to Personal Prelature. And there was no papal audience for US Congressman James Scheuer, vice-chairman of the UN Population Fund, as Wojtyla, backed by Opus Dei, firmly opposed any change in the Vatican's policy on contraception. Indeed within the first year of his pontificate, Wojtyla used Opus Dei's leading theologian in Latin America, Monsignor Ibáñez Langlois, to pressure Chilean dictator Pinochet into removing from the country $1 million worth of medical equipment supplied by the London-based International Planned Parenthood Federation for a female sterilization programme. Failure to heed the Pope's wishes, Pinochet was warned, would cause Chile to lose papal support in its Beagle Channel dispute with Argentina. Pinochet immediately complied.[2]

[1] Interview with Dr Alberto Jaimes Berti, London, 24 February 1994.
[2] Stephen D. Mumford, *American Democracy & the Vatican: Population Growth & National Security*, Humanist Press, Amherst, New York, 1984, pp. 196–197.

Under Luciani's successor, the same crowd continued to run the IOR and the bank has similarly denied its involvement in other financial scandals. There was no Curial shake-out, and the Jesuits came under increasing pressure to toe the Conservative line or face dissolution. Under John Paul II Opus Dei moved to suppress all dissident opinion on sexual morality. Moreover, with the encyclical *Veritas Splendor* Papa Wojtyla branded abortion, euthanasia, contraception and homosexuality as 'intrinsically evil'. These were all pet Opus Dei phobias. Indeed Opus Dei was accused of indirectly financing the anti-abortion commandos that in the 1990s were formed in France and the United States.[1]

Unaware of the power play in Rome, Roberto Calvi continued his South American travels, visiting Lima before flying to Washington for the annual general meeting of the World Bank and the International Monetary Fund. While in Lima Calvi met the minister of the economy and the president of the Banco de la Nación to discuss the possibility of opening a bank in Peru. To demonstrate the usefulness of such an institution, Calvi had Ambrosiano loan the Peruvian Central Reserve Bank, of which Opus Dei's Emilio Castañón was a director, the necessary funds to pay for a naval frigate ordered from an Italian shipyard. The licence for the new bank was delivered within the year.

John Paul II, meanwhile, made Cardinal Oddi prefect of the Congregation of Religious. The appointment was strategic because the Congregation of Religious was the ministry that held jurisdiction over secular institutes, and therefore Opus Dei. But perhaps more telling was the appointment of Pietro Palazzini as prefect of the Congregation for the Causes of Saints.

John Paul II had been in office for less than a month when he sent Don Alvaro del Portillo a note of warm wishes on the occasion of the Work's Fiftieth Anniversary – its first jubilee. The note was enclosed in a letter from Villot stating that 'His Holiness considers the transforming of Opus Dei into a Personal Prelature as a necessity that can no longer be delayed.' But in the midst of Don Alvaro's rush to have the concerned Congregations issue their *nihil obstat*, Cardinal Villot died, supposedly in his sleep (without disclosing what he had done with the bottle of

---

[1] Réseau Voltaire, Notes d'information No. 15 of 10 April 1995 and No. 23 of 5 June 1995.

Effortil).[1] Villot was replaced as Secretary of State by Cardinal Agostino Casaroli.

In utmost secrecy, Don Alvaro del Portillo forwarded to Cardinal Baggio, Prefect of the Congregation of Bishops, a fifteen-page report on the advantages for the Church of making Opus Dei the first – and only – Personal Prelature. The document was a masterpiece of bureaucratic reasoning, finely constructed and disciplined in style. For once, it gave statistics, including Opus Dei's exact strength – 72,375 members, married or celibate, men and women, representing 87 nationalities, of which about 2 per cent were priests. In addition, it pointed out that Opus Dei was already hierarchically structured as a floating diocese, with what amounted to its own Ordinary, presbyterium, territory and congregation.

Don Alvaro stressed that Opus Dei represented a new pastoral phenomenon in the life of the Church, 'uniquely comparable to the spiritual reality and apostolates of the faithful – clergy and laity – who belonged to the first Christian communities'.

The Transformation Memo devoted an entire section to underlining that 'substantially all of the constitutive elements of a Personal Prelature' already existed in Opus Dei's structure. Then came the clincher: 'The transformation of Opus Dei from Secular Institute to Personal Prelature . . . offers the Holy See the possibility of more efficiently deploying a *corps mobile* of priests and lay persons (specially trained) capable of operating everywhere as a powerful spiritual and apostolic catalyst for Christian action, above all in social and professional domains where today it is often impossible to work decisively in apostolic terms with the means that are currently available to the Church.'[2]

The memo also unveiled some details of Opus Dei's auxiliary activities: 'Members of Opus Dei already work in the following professional enterprises . . . 479 universities and institutes of higher learning on five continents; 604 newspapers, magazines and scientific publications; 52 radio and television stations; 38 news and

---

[1] Cornwell relates in A Thief in the Night, page 87, that a confidential Vatican source told him Villot 'collapsed' outside the Vatican and was taken to the Gemelli Hospital. 'The Vatican people rushed round and snatched the body . . . They pretended the corpse was still alive, took it back to the Vatican, and said he died holily in bed.'
[2] Transformation of Opus Dei into a Personal Prelature; memorandum to the Prefect of the Congregation of Bishops, Cardinal Sebastiano Baggio, 23 April 1979, paragraph 19.

publicity agencies; 12 film production and distribution companies, etc. Moreover, our members, aided by ordinary citizens, Catholic and non-Catholic, Christian and non-Christian, promote in 53 countries the apostolic activities of an educational or social nature: through primary and secondary schools, technical institutes, youth clubs, trade schools, hotel schools, home economics schools, clinics and infirmaries, etc. (See Note 9).'[1]

Note 9 stated that the list was exclusive of the 'apostolate of penetration'. This apostolate was carried out by Opus Dei members within the framework of their normal professional activities by organizing specialized training courses, cultural exchanges, international congresses, conventions and seminars attended by leading economic figures, technicians, teachers and others. The apostolate of penetration specifically targeted countries 'governed by totalitarian regimes that are either atheist, anti-Christian or at least nationalistic in tendency, in which it is difficult or virtually impossible *de jure o de facto* to undertake a missionary or religious activity, and in the end [to establish] an organized presence or activity related to the Church as one of its institutions.'

[1] *Ibid.*, paragraph 20.

23

BANCO OCCIDENTAL

I provided financing throughout Latin America for warships and other military equipment to be used to counter the subversive activities of well-organized Communist forces. Thanks to these operations, the Church today can boast a new authority in countries like Argentina, Colombia, Peru and Nicaragua . . .

Roberto Calvi, 1982

JAVIER SAINZ MORENO, PROFESSOR OF LAW AT MADRID UNIVERSITY, is an acerbic critic of Opus Dei, having formed a very definite view of its *modus operandi* which to him seems more suited to an organization specializing in *pillería* than a branch of the Catholic Church. He has strong opinions.

'Opus Dei distinguishes between its members and the rest of the world. The institution is not afraid to co-operate with people of dubious reputation, outright crooks or even Socialist politicians. But Opus Dei's hierarchy is careful to insure that these persons do not contaminate or come too close to the Work. Once they have been used, Opus Dei washes its hands of them, casts them adrift, abandons and despises them.

'What gives Opus Dei its importance is the influence it wields and also that it deploys its immense financial resources to spread its apostolate . . . Opus Dei knows very well that money rules the world

261

and that religious hegemony of a country or a continent is dependent upon obtaining financial hegemony . . .

'By its audacity, Opus Dei dares to do what other religious orders would never dream of doing: it uses the same weapons as its enemies. For this it will hire people it considers unworthy of respect so that these people do its dirty work. This allows it to achieve its objectives without being directly involved. The end justifies the means. Afterwards Opus Dei pays these people off and forgets them in the same way that one disposes of a dirty handkerchief by throwing it into the dustbin.

'Thus Opus Dei will hire lawyers who counsel them how not to pay taxes – and it's clear that afterwards Opus Dei will claim the money so gained serves to expand its religious works. It will hire architects to find ways of getting around zoning restrictions to obtain building permits – of course the permits are for schools or old people's homes, therefore they serve the social good. It will engage women to create scandals and discredit politicians who oppose the Work. It is clear that because of their low morals, these politicians would succumb to temptation anyway. In short, it hires disreputable persons to carry out its dirty deeds.'

I thought about this for a long while before realizing that Roberto Calvi was one of those 'dirty handkerchiefs'. He had always maintained to his wife Clara that Opus Dei was deeply involved in his dealings with the Vatican. However, according to his wife, he could only recite the names of two persons within the Curia – Cardinal Palazzini and Monsignor Hilary Franco – as intercessors, but neither were, strictly speaking, members of Opus Dei. Of course Calvi was close to Marcinkus, but the Vatican banker was not an Opus Dei member either. He was, on the other hand, a slave for a red hat.

Although not devoutly religious, Roberto Calvi held the Church in esteem. Like Marcinkus, his weak point was his immense ambition. Within the context of the times I believe that Roberto Calvi was not a dishonest person, though his ambition left him open to manipulation. But Calvi had another problem. When he took over as chairman of Banco Ambrosiano he inherited a hidden partner, left behind by Canesi, the former chairman. The hidden partner was, or later became, the bank's largest shareholder, as crazy as that may seem, and whatever Calvi did, as hard as he might have tried – and he did try – he could not get rid of that shareholder.

The identity of the hidden shareholder has never been conclusively proven. The evidence indicates that it was the IOR, or a client of the IOR, but the Vatican bank claimed it was operating on behalf of Calvi, producing copies of suspect or at least 'parallel' letters as 'proof'. And so current wisdom holds that, for lack of better proof, Calvi must have been his own hidden partner. Moreover, the wisdom holds that to have amassed such a large shareholding in the bank, of which he was after all but an employee, he must have used the bank's own money. Therefore he was a crook as well.

The Calvi family has tried for more than a dozen years to convince the world that this was not the case. As a task, it has wholly defeated them. But nevertheless, in my inquiries I developed considerable sympathy for their cause. I might have formed a different view had the people Calvi said were his partners, and those who ran the Vatican bank, consistently told a straight story. But they never have. So it is worth going over the Calvi story as it helps establish the credibility of the very same people who have risen to power within the Vatican.

Calvi claimed it was 'the priests' who were sapping Banco Ambrosiano's capital to finance their covert dealings and he couldn't get them to honour their obligations. Now if that were true it was a very Mephistophelian plan on the part of the 'priests'. As the plan developed, Madrid became the clearing house for many of its operations, which meant that he and his Masonic friends, Licio Gelli and Umberto Ortolani, paid frequent visits there.

During the 1960s the Church decided to soften its stand on Freemasonry. The revised codex of canon law no longer mentioned it as a prohibited institution. Certain sections of the Church even came to view Freemasonry as a viable weapon against Marxism. Italy's Propagande Due (P2) Lodge, not a true lodge in the Masonic sense but a secret grouping of prominent persons useful to Freemasonry's anti-Marxist mission, was evidence of this, as many high-ranking prelates were included among its members. The Church 'invaded' the Freemasonry movement and was 'colonizing' it.

P2 was formed in the late 1960s, allegedly at the behest of Giordano Gamberini, a Grand Master of the Grand Orient of Italy and friend of Giulio Andreotti. But he was much closer to Francesco Cosentino, who also was well introduced in Vatican circles. Either Andreotti or Cosentino, or perhaps both, were said to have suggested the creation of a secret cell of trusted right-wing personalities in key national sectors, but especially banking, intelligence and the press, to guard against what they perceived as 'the creeping Marxist threat'.

The person Gamberini chose to develop the P2 Lodge was a small-time textile magnate from the Tuscan town of Arezzo, midway between Florence and Perugia, who after two years as a Freemason had risen to the Italian equivalent of Master Mason. His name, of course, was Licio Gelli. But the P2's top man, according to Calvi, was none other than Andreotti, followed in line of command by Cosentino and Ortolani.

Andreotti always denied Calvi's allegation. But the fact remains that Calvi feared Andreotti more than Gelli or Ortolani. As for Cosentino, he died soon after the P2 hearings began. The truth of the matter, Javier Sainz said, is that the P2 Lodge was part of a secret right-wing network created with the Vatican's blessing as part of the Occident's bulwark against Marxism. The P1 Lodge was in France and the P3 Lodge was in Madrid. The P3 was headed by a former minister of justice, Pio Cabanillas Gallas.

The sense of all this was that Opus Dei's methodology consisted of using, if necessary, unclean hands to achieve certain of its secular aims and that Calvi, Gelli, Ortolani and the Propaganda network, having similar political aims, were appropriate assets to be exploited and then abandoned. As far as pouring resources into the battle against Marxist subversion in Latin America was concerned, Opus Dei allegedly decided that a secondary Spanish bank would make a good partner for Calvi's Banco Ambrosiano.

In the mid-1970s, Calvi started to show an interest in Banco Occidental of Madrid. Its shares were listed on the Madrid Stock Exchange. A block of 100,000 shares, representing 10 per cent of its capital, was held privately by a Swiss company, Zenith Finance S.A. Dr Arthur Wiederkehr was not on Zenith's board at the time but would become a director in 1980. Calvi acquired these shares for 80 million Swiss francs, *ten times* more than the going market price, which was an unusual thing for an astute banker to do.[1] He placed them in a company owned by United Trading.

Banco Occidental belonged to Gregorio de Diego, an enterprising

[1] Requisitoria of State Prosecutor Dr Pierluigi Dell'Osso in the 1989 Banco Ambrosiano criminal proceedings, Milan, pp. 376 and 381.

freebooter originally from Salamanca. Diego represented everything that Opus Dei admired in the free enterprising ethic. He was clever, aggressively acquisitive and obviously someone gifted for attracting capital. He had made a fortune during World War II by going from village to village, buying rabbit pelts. He sold the pelts to Germany where they were used to line winter uniforms for the Wehrmacht. He also negotiated an important contract to supply German officers with leather boots. But the Germans were upset when they received twice the number of right-footed boots and no left-footed ones. The reason for their displeasure was that they had paid a substantial sum up front and were obliged to renegotiate the contract. Diego ended up selling them a matching number of left-footed boots at double the price. With the capital acquired from the sale of pelts and boots he managed to corner the market in Spanish wolfram, a strategic mineral of which the Germans were in short supply. After the war he found himself with a mountain of money on his hands while the rest of Spain was in the grips of a liquidity squeeze. In the 1960s he bought the Banco Peninsular, which he renamed Banco Occidental. Its headquarters in the Plaza de España had big stained glass windows like a church.

Diego died of a heart attack in the arms of his mistress. Though not a point in his favour, it could hardly be held against the son, also called Gregorio de Diego, who inherited the family empire. Although he had no banking experience Diego II became Occidental's managing director, appointing as chairman the Conde Tomás de Marsal, a Spanish grandee who, like Ortolani, was a secret knight of the papal household.

Under Conde de Marsal, Banco Occidental moved into the investment banking field, taking positions in industrial concerns, such as cement works which fitted well with Diego's property development activities. In the early 1970s, the bank opened a representative office in Rome, primarily for Tomás de Marsal's convenience as frequently he visited the Vatican.

In 1976, Banco Ambrosiano made a loan to Occidental which it used to purchase 1 per cent of Ambrosiano's stock. At the same time, Banco Ambrosiano increased its holding in Banco Occidental to 510,000 shares, for which it paid another 40 million Swiss francs (roughly $18 million), and Calvi went on Banco Occidental's board of directors. In addition to the Conde de Marsal, who insiders described as a religious fanatic, other directors included Pio Cabanillas, the Venerable P3 Master. Like his P2 counterpart, Cabanillas kept secret files on most of Spain's important people. And he was a friend of Luis Valls Taberner.

Diego surrounded himself with Opus Dei members. In this respect his bank was to all intents an Opus Dei bank. His aide-de-camp was supernumerary Eloy Ramirez, for many years the representative in Mexico for Banco Español de Crédito (Banesto), Spain's largest commercial bank. Diego hired him for his Latin American contacts. He always accompanied Diego on foreign trips. When they arrived in a country for the first time, Ramirez would pay a visit to his brothers in the faith and they opened all the necessary doors. But the real *éminence grise* was Diego's brother-in-law, Fernando Pérez Minguez, an art connoisseur and antiques dealer who kept an office in the bank although he was not officially on the payroll. Like the Ramirez couple, Fernando Pérez and his wife were Opus Dei supernumeraries.

Banco Occidental concentrated on developing outlets in Latin America and Florida by acquiring participations in small commercial banks and buying hotels. A member of Occidental's legal department also suspected that Calvi used Banco Occidental as the hinge for arms transactions with Latin American dictatorships. These transactions required Calvi's frequent presence in Madrid. But to stay overnight in the Spanish capital would have attracted attention, so United Trading purchased an executive jet to carry him to and from Madrid in the same day. Instructions were given to Occidental's staff never to mention the Learjet when talking on the telephone with the Ambrosiano offices in Milan, suggesting that the staff in Milan was not supposed to know of the aircraft's existence.

In Madrid, Calvi met frequently with Cabanillas to discuss the possibility of bidding for control of *El País*, because it was feared that Madrid's largest circulation newspaper was leaning too far to the left. The project fitted in well with Opus Dei's Apostolate of Public Opinion and also the P2 and/or Vatican plans to take control of *Corriere della Sera*, Italy's leading newspaper. Matías Cortés Domíngues, a top Madrid lawyer who acted as Banco Occidental's independent counsel, was said to be advising Cabanillas on the takeover plans. Matías's brother, Antonio, also a lawyer, was an Opus Dei numerary.

Some years before, Umberto Ortolani had purchased Banco Financiero Sudamericano, a small Montevideo bank which he called Bafisud. Calvi and Diego began to use Bafisud for some of their South American ventures. In 1976 Ambrosiano Overseas acquired a 5 per cent interest in Ortolani's Bafisud, and Occidental's Cogebel acquired a matching 5 per cent. Ortolani and Diego became good friends. Diego described the Ortolani mansion in Montevideo as 'a museum containing half the Vatican art treasures'.

In 1977, Banco Occidental and Rumasa developed a relationship, engaging in a series of back-to-back deposits. That interlocking relationships existed between the three banking groups – Ambrosiano, Occidental and Rumasa – was demonstrated by a $25 million medium-term loan raised by Rumasa in the marketplace in October 1980. The loan was co-managed by Banca del Gottardo, Ambrosiano's Swiss affiliate, Banque de l'Union Européenne, also partly owned by the Ambrosiano and closely connected with Opus Dei operations in France, and the First National Bank in Saint Louis, Missouri. This latter bank was linked with the Anheuser Busch brewing family, said to have close ties with Opus Dei in the United States.

By then the interest charges on United Trading's debt to Ambrosiano were running at about $50 million a year. As United Trading was domiciled offshore, it had to be fed with offshore money. But as the debt grew, Calvi had trouble finding a supply of offshore money to cover it. Italian banks required special authorization to export capital and to obtain it Calvi would have had to disclose to the banking authorities the existence of the United Trading network. That meant unveiling its covert operations in South America and elsewhere. He became a slave to the open United Trading position – a classic example of the Brazilian economist's adage that if a client owes a bank $1 million and cannot repay, he has a problem, but if the client owes the bank $100 million and does not repay, then the bank has a problem. Calvi had a problem, and its name was United Trading.

Calvi's involvement with Banco Occidental was one indication of his dealings with persons and interests close to Opus Dei. But Opus Dei later denied that Calvi had any dealings with its members, either directly or indirectly. Another indication that he was plugged into an Opus Dei network came when Ambrosiano's offshore resources could no longer support the burden of United Trading's debt and a stopgap solution was found in a South American capital where a director of the central bank and several existing or future government ministers were Opus Dei members.

Calvi opened Banco Ambrosiano Andino in Lima in October 1979. The new bank had a capital of $12.5 million, mostly subscribed by Banco Ambrosiano Holding, Luxembourg, itself partly owned by the United Trading family. Banco Andino now became the innermost sanctuary of the United Trading network. By the end of the first month of operations, Andino's balance sheet totalled in excess of $435 million, virtually all of it in book-scrambling loans conceived to hide the real source and end-use of monies deployed by United Trading and its network of offshore companies.

Strangely Calvi believed that Opus Dei was his ally. A surer ally would have been Cardinal Egidio Vagnozzi, head of the Vatican's Prefecture for Economic Affairs. Vagnozzi was concerned that Opus Dei had proposed to Paul VI, behind his back, to take over the Vatican finances. Vagnozzi was opposed to according Opus Dei any greater influence in Vatican affairs than it already enjoyed. He also mistrusted Marcinkus and spoke to Cardinal Casaroli, the new secretary of state, about his fears. Casaroli, a master of ambivalence, gave him only a minimum of support. He backed Vagnozzi's proposal to call an extraordinary meeting of the 123 cardinals for Monday, 5 November 1979. Vagnozzi wanted to sound the alarm bells, as he maintained that the Vatican was nearing a state of financial collapse. The November 1979 gathering of cardinals was the last major meeting Vagnozzi presided over. He died shortly afterwards and an investigation file he had assembled on Marcinkus disappeared.

At about this time General Giuseppe Santovito, head of SISMI, Italy's military intelligence establishment, hired as his agency's Vatican and Palestinian specialist Francesco Pazienza. Born in 1946 at Taranto, southern Italy, into a staunchly Catholic family, Pazienza held a degree in 'deep-sea physiology'. Blessed with an idiomatic command of five languages, he knew a welter of international celebrities, including Aristotle Onassis, NATO commander-in-chief Alexander Haig, international swindler Robert Vesco, the PLO's Yasser Arafat and a range of Saudi princes. He also had excellent contacts in Latin America, particularly Argentina, where he claimed the nuncio, Archbishop Pio Laghi, was a close friend, as was the

Vatican's permanent representative at the United Nations, Archbishop Giovanni Cheli.

Pazienza had been working for SISMI for almost two years when a new Italian crisis was detonated almost by accident by two Milan magistrates. In mid-March 1981, as part of their investigation into Sindona's criminal activities, the magistrates raided Gelli's home and office. Along with photocopies of various classified state documents, they found what appeared to be the membership list of a secret Masonic Lodge. Several cabinet ministers figured among the list's 962 names. The rest were high-ranking military and secret service officers, prominent industrialists, bankers, journalists, foreign political dignitaries, the pretender to the Italian throne and senior Vatican prelates. Gelli telephoned his office from South America while the raid was in progress and learned what was going on. But the rest of the world remained uninformed for several more months.

Pazienza's boss, Santovito, was one of the names on Gelli's P2 list. He was required to resign. Without Santovito's protection, Pazienza's career as a SISMI agent was at an end. After setting up his own security agency in Rome, he was contacted by Flaminio Piccoli, chairman of the Christian Democrat party. Piccoli, who was Andreotti's friend, suggested that Pazienza meet with Roberto Calvi, as the banker was concerned about the integrity of the people running the IOR. Pazienza proposed to procure for Calvi the missing file on Marcinkus assembled by the late Cardinal Vagnozzi.

Pazienza knew Senator Mario Tedeschi, who published a right-wing magazine called *Il Borghese*, which ran a column on Vatican affairs. *Il Borghese* received most of its Vatican gossip from a Roman blackmailer, Giorgio Di Nunzio. The same Di Nunzio knew that Vagnozzi had deposited the Marcinkus file with a Zurich lawyer, Dr Peter Duft, and claimed that for a lot of money he could get hold of it.

Calvi was becoming an increasingly important factor in the Italian power equation. His bank had assets of nearly $20,000 million and 38,000 shareholders. In spite of its liquidity problems, it remained profitable and was far from bankrupt. But Calvi was attempting to move the Ambrosiano away from its traditional power base – the Catholic Right – into more neutral waters. By the same measure, this would have resulted in diluting the holdings of his hidden partner, and because of this he was showing dangerous initiative. He had begun to do business with the Italian Socialist party. Helping the Socialists to broaden their financial base was not to the liking of Giulio Andreotti. He wanted Banco Ambrosiano brought back into the right-wing Catholic orbit. Pazienza was the person designated to assist in this undertaking.

Pazienza negotiated with Peter Duft, Vagnozzi's 'man of confidence' in Switzerland, for the purchase of the Marcinkus file for $1.5 million. The payment was made from a United Trading account, with one-quarter going to the lawyer and the rest to Di Nunzio's Swiss bank account, and Pazienza delivered the documents personally to Calvi. But the ways of the Lord are wondrous. In 1982, while on a visit to his Swiss account, Di Nunzio died of a sudden heart attack.

Calvi had been working for some months with Gelli and Ortolani on restructuring the Rizzoli publishing empire, which owned the *Corriere della Sera*. By the end of 1980, United Trading had paid out a total of $40.65 million to Ortolani accounts in Switzerland, apparently to engineer a Rizzoli takeover.[1] Calvi supposed that Ortolani was operating for the Vatican and that he had joined the Rizzoli board as the Vatican's representative. By March 1981, the United Trading payments to both Ortolani and Gelli had risen to $76 million. Calvi began pressing the IOR to reduce United Trading's open position. He mistrusted Gelli and Ortolani as much as he feared Andreotti and, believing the right-wing Catholic alliance that formed the bank's traditional power base was hampering the Ambrosiano's expansion, he began to search for new partners. Retribution was swift.

In the midst of the Rizzoli negotiations, magistrates in Milan withdrew Calvi's passport, pending charges for illegally exporting capital. Though he had strong suspicions, Calvi was never able to clearly identify who his enemies were. He suspected Andreotti. And increasingly he came to mistrust Gelli and Ortolani. But he was completely mystified by the opacity of the Vatican. He regarded Opus Dei and Cardinal Palazzini as allies. He looked upon Casaroli, concerning whose private life he claimed to hold some compromising documents, as an enemy, and Marcinkus, by his greed and incompetence, as dangerous.

---

[1] Raw, *Op. cit.*, p. 292.

In an attempt to find out more about the Vatican faction he thought was opposing him, Calvi asked Pazienza – whom he had hired on a retainer of $500,000 – to arrange a meeting with a member of the Casaroli clique. In the week before Easter 1981 Pazienza introduced Calvi to Casaroli's under-secretary, Archbishop Achille Silvestrini. Rather than informing Silvestrini of his dealings with the IOR, Calvi talked about the Rizzoli group, but Silvestrini remained non-committal. Calvi would have liked to have Ortolani's position in the Rizzoli operation clarified. Silvestrini gave nothing away, perhaps because he knew nothing.

The next phase of the $260-million Rizzoli deal took place at the end of April, with a $95-million transfer from Banco Ambrosiano Andino to the account of the Zirka Corporation, Monrovia, at Rothschild Bank in Zurich. This money was labelled as a loan to Bellatrix, a Panamanian company. Bellatrix was a child of United Trading. The $95 million for Bellatrix joined another $46.5 million that had been transferred to Rothschild Bank from Ambrosiano Services, Luxembourg, earlier that year, supposedly to purchase a block of 189,000 Rizzoli shares held at Rothschild Bank, at a price *twenty times* over market value. To these transfers would be added another $8 million, bringing the total amount received by Bellatrix to around $150 million. But there were several anomalies here that only came to light following later investigations. First, although Bellatrix belonged to United Trading, it was Ortolani and Bruno Tassan Din, the Rizzoli managing director, who controlled its operations. Second, Rothschild Bank claimed it had no Bellatrix account on its books. Third, the name of Bellatrix did not appear on Rizzoli's share register.

Marcinkus, meanwhile, was gathering forces to defend himself against the Casaroli group. But as he was planning his counter-offensive disaster struck. 'Something happened that altered the balance of power inside the Vatican. On 13 May 1981, there was an assassination attempt against John Paul II in St Peter's Square. While the Pope was in hospital, Casaroli took charge at the Vatican. This was a serious blow for Marcinkus. Casaroli had every interest in seeing him destroyed,' Pazienza explained.

John Paul II spent four months recovering from the bullet wound. During that time Marcinkus's position was further shaken by a new disaster. On 20 May 1981, Italy's fiscal police, the Guardia di

Finanza, arrested Calvi at his home in Milan for illegally exporting capital through Ambrosiano's offshore network. Operating in the international money markets was, after all, one of the functions of an international banker. But under existing law Italian bankers were restricted in their international operations; to expand their foreign business they had to be artful jugglers. Calvi, perhaps, was a little too artful. The high priest of Italian private banking spent the next two months in prison, treated no better than a common criminal, atoning for his eagerness to assist the Church in her clandestine financial dealings.[1]

Clara Calvi's shock over her husband's arrest was not to be described. Until then she had been convinced that Roberto lived a charmed existence. Naively, she believed that the family was protected from the Italian *combinazione* of graft and patronage that was dragging the country into a moral crisis. It was true that because of the wave of kidnappings in Italy their children were accompanied everywhere they went by personal bodyguards. That was simply a fact of life for wealthy Italians in the 1970s and 1980s. When Carlo Calvi was ordered to report to an army intelligence unit for his military service, he was driven to the barracks in an armour-plated limousine. Their country house at Drezzo, even though perched on a hilltop, was guarded night and day by a private security force. The amount of protection – both political and physical – depended on one's standing: the more prominent the family, the more protection required.

Then suddenly the protection ran out. Italy and Spain were the only western industrialized nations which still maintained foreign exchange controls. This was contrary to Common Market regulations and they would soon be repealed. But for the time being the export of capital remained a criminal offence. And yet, no Italian banker existed who at some point had not sidestepped those restrictions in order to operate competitively in the international marketplace. Calvi was no exception. But he was singled out. His trial was transformed into a media circus.

In Calvi's absence Pazienza took control. He arranged for Clara

---

[1] At a meeting with the author on 2 December 1993, Carlo Calvi said, 'I am still convinced that my father's trial for currency violations was provoked by Licio Gelli to create a serious crisis inside the Vatican.'

to plead her husband's case with Giulio Andreotti. The 'Great Intriguer' told her that Roberto had to step aside. He said he was proposing that the Bank of Italy appoint two 'friendly' commissioners – the financier Orazio Bagnasco, Siri's friend from Genoa, and the president of the Banco Popolare di Novara, a small provincial bank owned by Bagnasco – to take control of the Ambrosiano.

Clara Calvi interpreted Andreotti's reaction as placing him solidly in the Casaroli camp, now preparing its light cavalry for an attack on Marcinkus. But Curial undercurrents are so subtle that it is impossible for an outsider to obtain an accurate overview. Andreotti in fact adhered to what was known as the Rome party, a third force inside the Vatican comprised of arch-Conservatives, aligned doctrinally with Opus Dei and with the Pope. Marcinkus was still useful to them, but in the end he, too, would be eased aside and replaced by other hands.

After Calvi's arrest in May 1981, Banco Occidental found itself in a liquidity bind, and in early July 1981 it went to the wall with a $100 million hole in its accounts. Fraud was alleged. Banco de España took over the failed Banco Occidental, acquiring 51 per cent of its capital for a symbolic one peseta. Banco Ambrosiano Holding sold its Occidental shares to Banco Vizcaya, a Spanish regional bank generally considered to be within Opus Dei's orbit, for a mere $1 million, thereby incurring a $40 million loss. Banco de España then turned around and sold what remained of Occidental's banking business to the same Banco Vizcaya for a nominal price. The Occidental, relieved of its bad debts, thus was reconstituted within Banco Vizcaya, which soon merged with Banco Bilbao to supplant Banesto as Spain's largest commercial bank. By coincidence, Banco de España's governor at the time was Alvarez Rendueles, the young banker whom Ruiz-Mateos had refused to hire.

A few days before Banco de España's intervention, Diego II was advised by a high-ranking official at the central bank, also an Opus Dei member, that if he covered a part of Occidental's losses with a personal guarantee – a guarantee that both knew was uncollectable – he would be permitted to spin Occidental's hotel division off the bank's books into a separate corporation where it would be sheltered from bankruptcy.

Occidental's hotel division owned two prestige hotels in Spain, one in Budapest, about a dozen in the Dominican Republic, several in Portugal, one in Venezuela, the Occidental Plaza in Miami, the Fairmount in San Antonio, Texas, and the Grand Hotel in Atlanta. Forewarned that an arrest warrant was on its way, Diego fled to Atlanta, where he owned a palatial estate with a fleet of luxury cars, swimming pool, baseball diamond, tennis courts and stables for thirty horses. One year later, at fifty-five years of age, he suffered a massive heart attack, but was saved by emergency surgery. Occidental Hoteles S.A., run by his son Gregorio de Diego III, became one of Spain's largest hotel chains.

Ortolani's Bafisud did not long survive Occidental's demise. It became bankrupt and was taken over by the Central Bank of Uruguay. In May 1983 what remained of Bafisud's business was sold to a Dutch bank for one peso. The president of the Uruguayan central bank was Ramón Diaz, an Opus Dei member.

24

BLACKFRIARS

*Had my husband been able to complete his very delicate negotiations
with Opus Dei, he would today be the most powerful man in Italy.*
Clara Calvi

CONVINCED THAT MARCINKUS WAS WITHHOLDING INFORMATION
from the Italian authorities which would have absolved Roberto, the
Calvi family wanted to get a message to the Pope. After Clara Calvi's
meeting with Andreotti, Pazienza flew to New York to confer with
Carlo Calvi. The son was in charge of a Washington affiliate, Banco
Ambrosiano Service Corporation, with offices in the Watergate complex. Pazienza arranged for Carlo to meet the head of the Vatican's
diplomatic mission to the UN in New York, Archbishop Giovanni
Cheli. Pazienza briefed Carlo first, alleging that Cheli was after
Marcinkus's job. Therefore one might have thought that Cheli had
an interest in insuring the message got through.[1]

---

[1] Giovanni Cheli was one of 26 persons to testify at Escrivá de Balaguer's beatification hearings in Rome. He therefore knew the Founder extremely well and worked closely with the
Prelature. After leaving his post at the United Nations, he became one of the powerhouses in
the Roman Curia, serving as co-president of the council of advisers to the papal household
and president of the pontifical council dealing with migrations, was a member of the 'Cor
Unum' and inter-religious affairs pontifical councils and the pontifical commission for Latin
America.

Three of Pazienza's friends accompanied Carlo to his meeting: Father Lorenzo Zorza was Cheli's personal assistant; Alfonso Bove was a Brooklyn businessman; and Sebastiano Lustrisimi was a member of the Italian secret services based in New York. They waited in Cheli's front office at the UN headquarters while Carlo spoke to the Archbishop alone. Carlo thought him arrogant. After listening with evident impatience to Carlo's report on Banco Ambrosiano's dealings with the IOR, Cheli suggested that the 'proper channel' for transmitting such information to Rome would be through the apostolic delegation in Washington. He arranged a meeting for Carlo with the first secretary, Monsignor Eugenio Sbarbaro, and instructed Father Zorza to accompany him.

When Carlo met Sbarbaro, he seemed even less interested than Cheli. Without the IOR's co-operation Calvi was found guilty of exchange control violations, sentenced to four years in prison and fined $13.5 million, pending appeal. 'God's Banker' – as the world press now dubbed him – was released on bail. But he was still without a passport. Moreover, it was of little comfort that during Calvi's sojourn in prison John Paul II had appointed a commission of fifteen cardinals to review the Vatican's finances. At the next board meeting his fellow directors greeted him with standing applause. He then went to Sardinia for a few weeks of rest.

A dozen years after the banker's death new elements continue to surface which contribute to the thesis that he was the victim of a conspiracy involving the Vatican bank and the Ambrosiano's hidden shareholder whose identity, for reasons that were increasingly obvious, the conspirators had wanted to protect. Among the new disclosures were the existence of a Venezuelan connection and the role played by the Italian secret services which knew what was happening step by step but never intervened.

Pazienza, himself appealing a heavy prison sentence for his role in Ambrosiano's subsequent bankruptcy, admitted to feeling used by the 'occult forces' muscling in on Banco Ambrosiano behind Calvi's back. This suggestion of conspiracy was likewise ignored by the magistrates, perhaps because Pazienza was quickly phased out of the picture after introducing Calvi to the man who became the conspiracy's on-the-ground co-ordinator. This was the Sardinian property developer Flavio Mario Carboni.

Clara Calvi liked this 'gentle, sweet-speaking man'. He was

considerate, bringing them gifts of Sardinian goat cheese and olive oil. She did wonder, however, why he always wore loose-fitting jackets until one evening she noticed Carboni carried a revolver tucked into the small of his back.

Clara quickly forgot the incident. Over the next few weeks the Calvis went for cruises on Carboni's yacht. Other guests included Nestor Coll Blasini, the Venezuelan ambassador to the Holy See, and Venezuelan economist Carlo Binetti. A COPEI (Venezuelan Christian Democrat) politician, Coll had close Opus Dei connections, though the Calvis were unaware of this. He had reformed the national business management institute, exorcizing it of all leftist influence, and was a close friend of the COPEI minister of education, Enrique Peres Olivares, a high-ranking Opus Dei numerary. He kept a close eye on the vacationers and talked at length with Calvi. Carboni was accompanied by Manuela Kleinszig, his twenty-three-year-old Austrian girlfriend. He also had a wife and Roman mistress, neither of whom travelled with him.

In the midst of their holiday, Calvi flew to Rome for a meeting with Marcinkus. The night before, Carboni had come to dinner, and Calvi confided that he was having trouble with the 'priests'. At the Rome meeting Calvi wanted to convince Marcinkus to liquidate United Trading because it had got out of hand.[1]

That Calvi had to seek Marcinkus's authority to implement the winding up of United Trading was strong evidence that it did not then or ever belong to Ambrosiano. But the best he could do on this occasion was to persuade Marcinkus to issue two 'comfort letters', acknowledging that the United Trading family, including the parent, were 'directly or indirectly' controlled by the IOR. One letter was addressed to Banco Ambrosiano Andino S.A. in Lima; the other to Ambrosiano Group Banco Comercial S.A. in Managua. Both were dated 1 September 1981.

To obtain these letters, Calvi apparently signed a counter-letter of indemnity, prepared on blank stationery, with a Banco Ambrosiano Overseas Limited heading typed in at the top. It was dated 26 August 1981, the date of his visit to Rome. No copy of it existed in the Ambrosiano files, nor among Calvi's personal papers. It stated that

---

[1] Carboni statement to Examining Magistrate Matteo Mazziotti and Prosecutor Renato Bricchetti at Parma Court House, 15 February 1984, p. 3.

Ambrosiano Overseas held the IOR harmless for issuing the letters of comfort. It also stipulated that the United Trading family would conduct no further operations and its involvement with the IOR – including a $200 million term deposit – would be unwound by no later than 30 June 1982. In spite of this letter, the United Trading shares – the litmus test of corporate ownership – remained with the IOR in Rome. This was in itself a most telling fact.

The counter-letter's intent was to give the illusion that ultimate responsibility for the United Trading family belonged with Banco Ambrosiano Overseas in Nassau. This being the case, Calvi would have been a fool to sign it. Unless he was following orders. The Nassau bank, after all, was one-fifth owned by the IOR and the remainder by Banco Ambrosiano Holdings in Luxembourg which, as we have seen, was at one time 40-per cent owned by Lovelok, the hidden partner. So one could interpret the counter-letter as signifying that the IOR or its unnamed client – the 'missing counterparty' – was simply passing the United Trading position from one hand to the other. By the same measure, the IOR was better protecting itself from the risk of the United Trading network being identified with the Vatican if its existence was discovered by the Bank of Italy.

Another feature of the counter-letter was its insistence on repayment by Ambrosiano Overseas of the $200 million term deposit by the end of June 1982. The IOR has never been terribly explicit about this deposit – one theory being that it was part of a back-to-back operation between the IOR and the Ambrosiano involving a Venezuelan development project with Neapolitan investors. The IOR told Calvi that only once this deposit was retired would 'the rest' – i.e., the monies which the United Trading then owed the Ambrosiano group – be unwound.[1]

When Calvi flew back to Sardinia the same evening he told Clara: 'The priests are going to make me pay for having brought up the name of the IOR. In fact, they are already making me pay.'[2]

With United Trading's usefulness drawing to a close, Marcinkus's importance began to wane. On 29 September 1981, John Paul II promoted him Archbishop and made him Governor of the Vatican City. He still retained his position as head of the IOR, but he spent an

---

[1] Flavio Carboni deposition before Mazziotti and Bricchetti, Parma, 16 February 1984 (p. 14 of English translation).
[2] Clara Calvi diaries, p. 61.

increasing amount of time seeking to improve the administration and revenues of the Vatican City state. If Calvi's hypothesis was right, Opus Dei was about to assume control of the Vatican bank. Six weeks later John Paul II informed Cardinal Baggio that he had decided to elevate Opus Dei to the status of Personal Prelature.

Among Calvi's alternatives for resolving the due-date gap, the two most realistic seemed the sale of 10 per cent of Banco Ambrosiano at an inflated price of $200 a share, or recapturing the $150 million transferred to Bellatrix at Rothschild Bank in Zurich. During the next months he worked on both, relying on Pazienza. Instead of finding a buyer for the Ambrosiano stock, Pazienza reinserted Flavio Carboni into the picture. Pazienza did this by convincing Calvi to approve a $3 million loan to Carboni's Sardinian development company, Prato Verde S.p.A., for which Pazienza received a $250,000 commission.

When Calvi realized that Pazienza was not seriously interested in finding a buyer for the Ambrosiano stock he opened negotiations with Carlo De Benedetti, the man who saved Olivetti from bankruptcy. De Benedetti agreed to buy 1 million Ambrosiano shares – equivalent to 2 per cent of the bank's capital – at $43 each and join the board of directors as deputy chairman. For Calvi, this represented a beginning. It wasn't the moon, but it was nonetheless positively viewed in the marketplace.

The next day Calvi travelled to Rome for an important meeting. At least that is what he told Clara. But he neglected to mention to her – or anyone else – with whom he was meeting. Could it have been with Opus Dei's Grand Exchequer? Clara had no way of knowing. The same day, however, *La Repubblica* broke the news of De Benedetti's entry into the Ambrosiano.

Calvi was furious. De Benedetti's association with the Ambrosiano was supposed to have remained for the moment confidential. Calvi waited two days before informing De Benedetti that the *Repubblica* interview had met with a 'negative' reaction in Rome. But it is difficult to imagine why a man of De Benedetti's calibre becoming deputy chairman might have been dimly viewed. Perhaps it was because De Benedetti, indisputably an asset for the bank, was Jewish, and the people who Calvi saw in Rome did not want a Jew in a position of authority inside a Catholic bank that was handling covert financial operations for the Vatican.

De Benedetti put back his shares and left. His seat on the Ambrosiano board was filled by Orazio Bagnasco, who seven months before had been proposed by Andreotti as Calvi's replacement. Bagnasco had made a fortune selling shares in property-based mutual funds, prompting Clara Calvi to call him 'the door-to-door financier.'[1] Bagnasco had with a friend purchased in the market 2 per cent of Ambrosiano's stock and demanded to be admitted to the board. The conclusion was hard to dispel that Bagnasco was the Roman party's replacement for De Benedetti.

Calvi was now desperate. He thought he had found an ally in De Benedetti, only to have him replaced by a man of lesser stature whom he mistrusted. This led him to play his last remaining card, sending Pazienza to Zurich to trace the Bellatrix monies. Pazienza referred to the Bellatrix assignment as 'Operation Vino Veronese', because one of the companies through which $14 million of the missing Bellatrix money had transited, Recioto S.A., bore a name similar to an Italian wine called Richiotta, from the region of Verona.

Operation Vino Veronese ran into a blank wall, or rather it ran into Jurg Heer, a man of one thousand secrets. He was Rothschild Bank's credit director. After speaking with him, Pazienza concluded that the $150 million had completely volatilized. 'I drew a big zero,' he reported. 'This guy [Heer] was real spooky.' Calvi was not impressed; Operation Vino Veronese was Pazienza's last assignment. This left the field free for Flavio Carboni, who now became Calvi's closest confidant.

Earlier that month Calvi had asked Carboni to transmit a message to his contacts at the Vatican that unless the 'priests' faced up to their obligations, both Banco Ambrosiano and the IOR would go down the tubes. Carboni took this message to Cardinal Palazzini. This might have seemed strange, as Palazzini had nothing to do with finance. But Carboni knew that Palazzini was Opus Dei's staunchest supporter in the Curia and that Calvi's problems lay with Opus Dei, not Marcinkus. From this point forward, the Vatican and Opus Dei deny the description of events put forward by either Carboni or the Calvi family.

Carboni arranged for Calvi to meet Palazzini. Afterwards, Calvi

[1] *Ibid.*, p. 46.

told his wife that he was accorded a secret audience with John Paul II, who asked him to help straighten out the situation at the IOR. The Pope, said Calvi, assured him that if successful the rewards would be great.[1] Heartened, Calvi began planning a restructuring of the Banco Ambrosiano group, while drafting a proposal for over-hauling the IOR which he believed Opus Dei would present to the Pope.[2]

Palazzini got back in touch with Carboni in March 1982 and told him that the IOR was 'impenetrable'. He suggested that Calvi see Monsignor Hilary Franco, who knew Marcinkus better since they both lived in the same Villa Stritch residence. A quick glance in the *Annuario Pontificio* indicated that Franco – incardinated in the arch-diocese of New York – was a research assistant with the Congregation of the Clergy. The *Annuario Pontificio* did not disclose that Franco was also Palazzini's personal secretary.

Like Marcinkus, Hilary Franco aspired to a grand career in the Curia. He had recently been named an Honorary Prelate of the Papal Household. Such recognition raised him to a Grade 1 Minor Official (Step 2) in the Vatican's arcane bureaucratic machinery. According to Carboni, Hilary Franco agreed to act as Calvi's intermediary with the IOR and Opus Dei.

At the end of April 1982, Roberto Rosone, Ambrosiano's deputy chairman, was shot in the legs by a man riding pillion on a motor scooter. A security guard fired two shots that hit the fleeing gunman in the head. He toppled into the roadway, dead as a doornail, but the driver got away unscathed. The assassin turned out to be Danilo Abbruciati, a member of a Roman underworld association known as the Banda della Magliana. He had disappeared some months before, having decided to run the Banda della Magliana's money laundering operations from London. But why was Rosone on an underworld hit list? Pazienza claimed a police report alleged that Rosone was laundering money for the underworld. This was never substantiated and Rosone strongly denied it. Within days, however, it was rumoured that Calvi had put out the contract on Rosone's life because he believed his deputy chairman was plotting behind his

---

[1] *Ibid.*, p. 69.
[2] Clara Calvi deposition before Examining Magistrate Bruno Siclari and Public Prosecutor Pierluigi Dell'Osso, 24 October 1982, p. 86.

back. But Calvi was terribly shocked by the attack which he took as a warning for himself. It left him brooding and sleepless.

Two weeks later, Calvi wrote to Hilary Franco, requesting an urgent meeting to discuss ways of raising $250 to $300 million for the Ambrosiano. In this letter the chairman of a $20,000 million bank literally grovelled before the Grade 1 Minor Official (Step 2) of the Vatican, and he would only have done so if he believed there was some overriding reason, such as Franco's proximity to Opus Dei and to the Pope.

The wildest stories circulated about this prelate. Clara Calvi was told that he was the Pope's confessor.[1] Carboni's assistant, Emilio Pellicani, thought Franco had an office at the Opus Dei headquarters. Carboni claimed that Franco had excellent White House contacts.[2] He also maintained good relations with South Africa and its client state, the black homeland of Bophuthatswana, where he was said to be interested in investing Vatican funds in a gambling casino and race track. Franco's other South African interest was reported to be Cape Town's President Hotel, at which was held the annual Miss Seapoint beauty contest.[3]

Franco informed Carboni that Opus Dei was willing to front a loan for the Ambrosiano group so that it could repay the $200 million to the IOR on deadline. 'Monsignor Franco knows everything; he knows that I asked him whether Calvi could obtain from Opus Dei a $200-million loan . . . and he assured me that these matters would be resolved, and that in a month or a month and a half everything would be all right,' Carboni told the Milan magistrates two years later.[4]

In spite of Calvi's grovelling, the tone of the 12 May 1982 letter to Franco, thanking him for his 'valued intervention with the Vatican authorities', was relatively up-beat because the banker at last believed a solution was in sight. He told Clara and his daughter that Opus Dei had presented to the Pope a new plan whose centrepiece was Opus Dei's assuming control of the IOR, and that if accepted it

[1] Clara Calvi diaries, p. 69.
[2] Pellicani testimony before the Chamber of Deputies P2 Commission, 24 February 1983, Vol. CLV, Doc. XXIII, No. 2, Ter 9, pp. 344–345 and 643.
[3] 'Sierra Leone/South Africa: The Strange Story of LIAT', *Africa Confidential*, London, 24 June 1987, Vol. 28, No. 13.
[4] Statement of Flavio Carboni to Examining Magistrate Mazziotti and Prosecutor Bricchetti, Parma Court House, 16 February 1984 (p. 14 of English translation).

would create 'a completely new balance of power within the Vatican.'[1]

After talking with the Calvi family I am convinced that the banker sincerely believed he was dealing with representatives of Opus Dei. Of course it is possible that he was being purposely misled. But his trips to Madrid and his restructuring plan for Ambrosiano which involved Carlo Pesenti, an Ambrosiano board member known to be close to the Vatican and also to members of Opus Dei, were not figments of Calvi's imagination. They really existed. Moreover he was led to think that if he resigned from the Ambrosiano he would be named a financial adviser to the Vatican.

But Calvi's optimism was short-lived. On his next visit to the IOR on Thursday, 20 May 1982, Marcinkus refused to see him. Instead, Calvi met his assistant, Dr Luigi Mennini. The encounter was glacial. Marcinkus wanted Calvi to appear before the commission of cardinals that was looking into the Vatican's finances. The commission, according to a Calvi memorandum later recovered from his briefcase, wanted to know why the Milan banker had used United Trading monies without prior approval to support the Ambrosiano stock.[2]

That the cardinals were aware of United Trading's existence is of itself revelatory. In any event, Calvi suspected that Marcinkus was preparing a criminal complaint against him just as his appeal of the currency violations conviction was due to be heard. This caused Calvi to lose his cool. He shouted at Mennini, 'Be careful! If it comes out that you gave money to *Solidarnosc*, there won't be one stone of the Vatican left standing on another.'

The details of this meeting, denied by the Vatican, came to light because Carboni secretly recorded his conversations with Calvi who told him about it when they met at Drezzo that weekend. Calvi by then had sent Clara to Washington to be with their son Carlo as he claimed her life was in danger in Milan. Anna had refused to accompany her mother because she was about to sit for her final exams at the University of Milan.

---

[1] Testimony of Anna Calvi to the Milan Magistrate Bruno Siclari and Prosecutor Pierluigi Dell'Osso, 22-23 October 1982, EM3 f4, pp. 265 ss.

[2] The undated, unheaded document refers to 'these companies' and the reproach was made by Marcinkus before the Commission of Cardinals. 'These companies' can only refer to the United Trading complex. [Source: *Tribunale di Roma, Sentenza nella causa di primo grado n. 168/92 contro Carboni e altri*, 23 March 1993, pp. 102–104.]

At the end of May, Calvi wrote to Cardinal Palazzini, pleading with him 'to intervene once again with those who, like yourself, have the best interests of the Church at heart.' After claiming to possess evidence that Casaroli and Silvestrini had taken bribes from Sindona, he asked Palazzini to arrange another audience with the Pope, so that he could explain the problem 'in its entirety, above all to prevent the projects of the enemies of the Church . . . from succeeding'.

On the first weekend of June, Calvi returned with Anna to Drezzo. Having heard nothing from either Palazzini or Hilary Franco, he drafted a last letter to the Pope in which he accused the IOR bankers of negligence and misdealing. In part the letter stated:

> The policy of always working from the shadows, the absurd negligence, the obstinate intransigence and the other incredible attitudes of some senior Vatican officials make me certain that Your Holiness has been little or not at all informed about the nature during these long years of my group's relations with the Vatican . . .
>
> At the specific request of your authorized representatives I have provided financing for many countries and politico-religious organizations in the East as in the West. It was I who, at the request of the Vatican authorities, co-ordinated throughout South and Central America the creation of numerous banking entities with the aim, in addition to everything else, of containing the penetration and extension of Marxist ideologies.
>
> After all of this, I am the one who has been betrayed and abandoned by those same authorities to whom I always paid maximum respect and obedience.

Before closing, Calvi said he wanted to turn over to the Pope 'a number of important documents that are in my possession, and to explain to you in plain language how these dealings, about which you certainly are not informed, happened and could happen again'.

By this time Licio Gelli had returned clandestinely to Europe. He was sighted at the beginning of May by an Italian secret service agent dining in a Geneva restaurant with Hans Albert Kunz, a business associate of Carboni. Soon after, the still powerful Venerable Master of the dismantled P2 Lodge contacted Calvi to demand money. The pressure never stopped. Seeing her father distraught, Anna asked him to explain what was really happening. Calvi told her that to deal with the IOR problems 'we have drafted and put forward a plan which provides for the direct intervention of Opus Dei,' and that Opus Dei 'was due to supply an enormous sum . . . to cover the IOR's open position at Banco Ambrosiano.'

As Ambrosiano's restructuring plan progressed, Calvi had told his wife, 'If Andreotti does not throw a spoke in the wheels in the next couple of weeks, all will be well.' Two days later, he again told Clara: 'What Andreotti had to say to me today gave me no pleasure at all.' Then he claimed that Andreotti was threatening to kill him. 'We lived in a perpetual climate of terror and subject to constant presages of death,' she said. One of his last comments was, 'If they kill me, the Pope will have to resign.'[1]

On 7 June 1982, Calvi informed the Banco Ambrosiano board for the first time that $1,300 million was at risk in his dealings with the IOR. The next day Calvi removed from the bank two cartons of documents which he regarded as essential in proving that he had been misled by the 'priests' sending them to an unknown destination, possibly Drezzo.

Calvi flew to Rome on Wednesday evening, 9 June 1982. His chauffeur in Rome, Tito Tesauri, picked him up at the airport and noted that his black briefcase, bulging with documents, was heavier than usual. Calvi spent the night at his flat in the old part of the city. Next morning over the phone he told Mennini that he declined to meet the commission of cardinals because the documents he needed to explain his dealings with the IOR were stored abroad and without a passport he was unable to retrieve them. He nevertheless agreed to meet Mennini on the following morning.

Sometime during his Thursday round of meetings, Calvi was shown a copy of a forged warrant for his arrest. The idea for the false warrant, according to a Guardia di Finanza undercover agent, came from Licio Gelli. The agent, codenamed 'Podgora', claimed that Gelli was waiting in London under an assumed name. Italian magistrates, as Calvi had already learned, have sweeping powers of detention. Believing the warrant to be authentic, he had every reason to be concerned. He disappeared that night.

According to Carboni, Calvi moved to the apartment of Emilio Pellicani in Rome's Magliana suburb. Pellicani was Carboni's

---

[1] Testimony of Clara Calvi, 19–26 October 1982, p. 88.

batman. Tito Tesauri went to pick up Calvi early next morning – Friday, 11 June 1982 – and drive him to his meeting at the IOR. The chauffeur found Calvi's flat empty, the bed ruffled but unslept in, and a note in the kitchen written by his boss in a trembling hand: 'I have returned earlier than expected.'[1]

At 1.30 p.m., Calvi called Mennini to apologize for missing that morning's appointment, but promised to meet him the following week. Then, accompanied by Pellicani, Calvi supposedly took an Alitalia flight from Rome to Venice, and was driven by Pellicani from Venice to Trieste, where he was entrusted to Silvano Vittor, a petty smuggler whose mistress, Michaela, was Manuela Kleinszig's twin sister. Vittor would arrange for Calvi's clandestine passage into Austria during the night. But the only problem with this version of events is that Tina Anselmi, head of the P2 parliamentary commission, as well as several other persons well known to Calvi, were on the same flight and none noted the banker's presence aboard the aircraft. So it is possible that he arrived in Trieste by other means.

In fact the mayor of Drezzo, Leandro Balzaretti, claimed that Calvi and Carboni arrived in Drezzo by car late Thursday night. Balzaretti, an insurance agent, knew Calvi well. The Calvi family originally came from nearby Como, and the two spoke the Como dialect together. Had Calvi returned to Drezzo to pick up the two cartons of documents deposited there earlier in the week?

'Calvi called me from his house and said he wanted to pass by the office at midday to discuss insurance for a small bank he had bought in the south. He said he was leaving afterwards for Rome and would not be back in Drezzo until the twenty-sixth. I waited, but at noon he called on the car telephone to say he couldn't make it. I never heard from him again,' Balzaretti said when we met at his home in Drezzo.[2]

Como is 530 kilometres from Trieste. Travelling by car, the journey could easily be made in six hours. Calvi and Pellicani arrived at the Hotel Excelsior in Trieste in the early evening. Calvi was alleged to have only his bulging briefcase with him. But if he had come from Drezzo he almost certainly had the two cartons of documents as well.

Calvi initially had planned to go to Zurich, where Anna was

[1] Statement of Tito Tesauri to the Direzione Centrale della Polizia Criminale, Rome, 3 December 1991.
[2] Interview with Leandro Balzaretti, 10 February 1994.

waiting for him, as he wanted to make inquiries about the missing $150 million at the Rothschild Bank. But the conspirators did not want Calvi in Zurich. They wanted him in London. Calvi's hilltop property at Drezzo was within 50 metres of the Swiss frontier and after picking up documents and money, he could have walked out of the front gate, crossed a dirt track and made his way down the wooded north slope of the hill to the Swiss village of Pedrinate, on the outskirts of Chiasso. Or indeed he could have gone by road because the customs post on the Italian side of the border at Pedrinate was unguarded and to cross into Switzerland all he needed, as an Italian citizen, was an ID card which he carried with him. But Carboni evidently convinced him to drive with Pellicani to Trieste while Carboni went back to Rome aboard his private Cessna. By the time they arrived at their respective destinations the cat was out of the bag. Rome's chief prosecutor, Dr Domenico Sica, had been informed that the banker was missing. Sica immediately raised the alarm.

Vittor arranged for a Yugoslav associate to drive Calvi during the night to the home of the Kleinszig sisters at Klagenfurt, Austria. Vittor explained that he would use another route to smuggle Calvi's briefcase and, one assumes, the two boxes of documents over the border, joining up with the banker in Klagenfurt to await Carboni's arrival. Calvi spent the day in Klagenfurt nervously waiting for the Triestine smuggler to arrive with his bulging briefcase and boxes of documents.

Vittor only appeared around midnight with the briefcase, but the two boxes of documents are never again mentioned. The delay in Vittor's arrival meant that he had unrestricted possession of the briefcase and perhaps the boxes for twenty-four hours, giving him ample time to photocopy the contents. One can only surmise that, among other items, the briefcase and boxes contained the missing accounting for United Trading, perhaps also the books of the defunct Lovelok and Radowal, and the Vagnozzi file on Marcinkus. The accounting items would certainly have provided evidence as to the real ownership of the Lovelok-Radowal-United Trading complex and therefore might have vindicated Calvi in the event of litigation.

Calvi remained intent on meeting Anna in Zurich. After Carboni arrived with Calvi's two suitcases – packed in Drezzo the previous weekend and handed to Carboni in Milan before Calvi left for Rome – it was decided that Vittor would drive him to Bregenz, on the Austrian border with Switzerland, while Carboni, Manuela and her sister Michaela flew to Zurich to judge whether a Swiss border crossing on a forged passport that Carboni had procured for him might be attempted. In fact Carboni met in Zurich with two other conspirators, Swiss businessman Hans Kunz and Roman restaurateur Ernesto Diotallevi, an associate of the late Danilo Abbruciati. Six weeks previously, Carboni had paid Diotallevi, a member of the Banda della Magliana, $530,000 for purposes unknown and in Zurich he promised to pay Diotallevi's mother-in-law a further large sum.

From Zurich, Carboni phoned Pellicani in Rome and asked him to check flight schedules from London to Caracas. He and Kunz then drove to Bregenz, arriving about 9 p.m., where they had a long meeting with Calvi. Only their version of what transpired exists, but it was clearly more tense than either Carboni or Kunz were prepared to admit. Carboni pressured Calvi to come up with $200 million so that the money could be transferred to Caracas before the end of the month.

According to Carboni, during the meeting Calvi told them he had been asked 'on behalf of Opus Dei and other religious orders in South America to form by September 1982 a banking institution to finance trade between Latin America and eastern bloc countries'.[1] Caracas was foreseen as the bank's headquarters. Carboni then claimed that Calvi put forward a plan for raising $350 million within the next few days. Calvi said he had $150 million in a strongbox at the Banque Lambert in Geneva, another $50 million at a bank in the United States, and he believed he could obtain $150 million from a contact in London. Carboni added that after raising the necessary cash Calvi proposed to fly to Caracas.

Had Carboni let slip something that he should never have mentioned? To cover up this gaff, Carboni claimed that he and Venezuelan economist Carlo Binetti were planning to go to Caracas and Calvi, with nothing better to do, proposed to join them there. In any event, this was the first mention of a Caracas connection and suddenly it loomed large in Calvi's plans for the few days that remained to him.

Carboni proposed that Calvi fly directly to London on a private

---

[1] Carboni deposition taken by Milan Examining Magistrate Mazziotti and Prosecutor Dell'Osso at Parma Prison on 7 April 1984.

charter (private flights are subject to less stringent immigration controls) while he went to Geneva to recover the $150 million from the Banque Lambert strongbox. He knew by then that Calvi had several bunches of strongbox keys in his briefcase and supposed one was for 'San Patricio's well', as he now called the Lambert cache. He also proposed that Kunz fly to the US and pick up the $50 million.[1] This would leave Calvi free to deal with his London contact.

Calvi must have realized by then with whom he was dealing. Apparently he had no intention of turning over the Banque Lambert strongbox key to Carboni, believing perhaps that it was the last insurance policy he possessed. He claimed instead that his wife's power-of-attorney was needed to gain access to the strongbox. Carboni was not pleased. He had an apparent fixation on a sum of $200 million and, it seems, an urgent need to be in Caracas before the end of the month. Calvi assured Carboni he could handle everything from London. He may have mentioned that Baron Lambert, owner of the Banque Lambert, had a top-drawer solicitor who could manage to have the contents of the Geneva strongbox delivered to London. He asked that Kunz arrange for the rental in London of a luxury town house or apartment so that he could discreetly meet his third source of funds, the supposed high-level contact.

Carboni and Kunz returned to Zurich. Next morning Kunz arranged for a taxi jet to pick up two 'directors of Fiat' at Innsbruck airport and fly them to Gatwick. In the confusion at Gatwick, they missed the driver of a hired car sent to collect them and took a taxi to Chelsea Cloisters, a residential hotel in Sloane Avenue, where Kunz's London solicitor had made a reservation under the name of 'Vittor plus one'. Calvi was not pleased with the eighth-floor convenience flat that he was required to share with his minder, and complained bitterly. But the banker was no longer the master of his movements. Vittor told him nothing could be done until Carboni arrived in London the following afternoon.

Next morning, Calvi contacted Alberto Jaimes Berti, Cardinal Siri's friend. Since May 1980 Berti had lived mainly in London where he owned an apartment in Hans Place, behind Harrods. Calvi had

---

[1] Details of this plan and Calvi's intended travel to Caracas are given by Carboni in his deposition taken by Mazziotti and Dell'Osso at Parma Prison on 7 April 1984, on pp. 12 and 16 of the English translation.

first met the Caracas lawyer in 1975 or 1976 at a reception at the Grand Hotel in Rome for the Venezuelan president, Carlos Andrés Pérez.

Berti agreed to see Calvi at the beginning of the afternoon, and when he arrived at the Chelsea Cloisters, Calvi was waiting for him in the lobby, dressed in a dark suit and tie, his moustache well trimmed. They sat down in one corner and Calvi removed from his briefcase a notebook which he consulted once at the beginning of their half-hour discussion. Calvi apparently knew that Berti was the custodian of a sealed envelope containing the shares of a Panamanian company that held $2,200 million belonging to as many as six principals who he suspected included the IOR, the Spanish branch of Opus Dei, Ruiz-Mateos's Rumasa, Banco Ambrosiano and, perhaps, the Camorra. When last in Rome, Berti had spoken to Donato De Bonis, the IOR's priest secretary, who advised him that he could openly discuss the matter with Calvi, reinforcing his impression that the IOR and Ambrosiano were no strangers to the transaction.

At one point Berti surmised that the money was intended to capitalize the Latin American trade bank that both he and Calvi had been told about, though by different sources. In the interim, the money was invested in blue chip bonds in New York. Calvi asked if the portfolio could be used to guarantee a loan. Berti thought this possible, but for technical reasons it would require several days to arrange. Calvi seemed relieved and observed, 'So the matter is resolved'. He told Berti he would be back in touch.

While waiting for Carboni to arrive, Calvi telephoned Clara. She said he sounded elated. 'Something mad is about to happen. It's marvellous. It could change our lives,' he told her. He also asked Vittor to get him a British Airways flight schedule.

Accompanied by the Kleinszig sisters, Carboni booked into the Park Lane Hilton that same afternoon and called Calvi shortly after 6.15 p.m. They met at about 8 p.m. and spent the next two hours walking in Hyde Park. Again, only Carboni's version exists of what transpired, but Calvi returned to the Chelsea Cloisters a shaken man. At 7.30 a.m. next morning he called Anna in Zurich. He said she was no longer safe in Zurich and must leave immediately for Washington. Anna later testified that her father sounded very nervous 'and he said terrible things would happen if I didn't leave'.

Carboni did not attempt to contact Calvi at all on the following day – Thursday – until late in the evening – around 11 p.m. He claimed that Calvi refused to see him. Instead Vittor came down to the lobby and together they went for a drink to a nearby pub, The Queen's Arms, where the Kleinszig sisters were waiting. When Vittor returned to the Chelsea Cloisters at about 1 a.m. he had no key and had to be let into flat 881 by the night manager. The TV set was on, but there was no Calvi. Undisturbed, Calvi's supposed bodyguard turned in for the night.

By the sworn affidavit of another eighth-floor resident, who was only questioned about these events seven years later, it was clear that both Vittor and Carboni were lying. Cecil Coomber, a South African artist then in his early seventies, was a resident in flat 834, down the corridor from the one occupied by Calvi and Vittor. At about 10 p.m. that evening, Coomber and a companion decided to go out for dinner. Waiting at the lift were three men. The two younger ones spoke in Italian, while the third – whom Coomber identified as Calvi – looked apprehensive and remained silent. All five took the lift to the ground floor. As Coomber crossed the lobby to the front entrance, he saw the three turn towards a service entrance at the rear of the building, where another resident had noticed a black car with driver parked. Coomber's sideways glance made him the last person to see Roberto Calvi alive. The banker carried no briefcase; he was wearing a necktie, and he still had a moustache.

Calvi's body was found hanging from scaffolding under Blackfriars Bridge early next morning. He was wearing a two-piece light grey suit but no necktie. And no moustache. Only his feet were in the water. The River Police were called and removed the body, conveying it by launch to the Waterloo Police Pier. The policemen found four large stones in the victim's pockets and a brick inserted so roughly inside the six-button trouser fly that it had ripped off a button. The autopsy performed that afternoon found the victim had died about 2 a.m. of asphyxia due to hanging. No body injuries were noted.

The corpse carried a forged Italian passport in the name of Gian Roberto Calvini, a wallet with £7,000 in various currencies, two watches, four pairs of spectacles, but no keys. In one pocket was a slip of paper with the handwritten address of the Chelsea Cloisters, the business card of Colin McFadyean and a page torn from an address book on which appeared the telephone numbers of Monsignor Hilary Franco.

Detective Inspector John White of the City of London Police was called to the Snow Hill Police Station around 7 p.m. that evening. A telex had come in from Interpol announcing the arrival in London of Rome prosecutor Domenico Sica, accompanied by three Italian police officers. As the reserve inspector on duty that night, White was delegated to meet the Italians at Heathrow at 3.30 a.m. and he drove them directly to the morgue. Dr Sica identified the body as Calvi. The Italian magistrate needed no convincing that he was dealing with a homicide. Immediately back in Rome, he issued an international warrant for the missing Carboni.

Unknown to White, Calvi's travelling companions had already skipped the country or were preparing to do so. Acting on the scrap of paper found in Calvi's pocket he went to the Chelsea Cloisters on the Saturday morning to inquire if Calvi had been registered there. He drew a blank. Because Calvi's death was regarded as a suicide, no scientific examination was made of the scaffolding under Blackfriars Bridge.

Clara Calvi learned of her husband's death on the Friday morning. Her brother, Luciano Canetti, called after hearing a newsflash on Italian radio that the missing banker had been found dead in London. The shock was devastating. She collapsed. A doctor was called. The family did not know what would happen next.

'After the sharp, wounding pain of the first days when we sought refuge in the Watergate under the protection of armed guards, our spirit remained strong. We were guided by a constant faith in him and a determination to use the judicial systems as diverse as Italy and England to uncover the truth. It was our duty, no matter the cost or risk, because we knew that suicide was out of the question,' Carlo Calvi later explained.

PART SIX
CORPS MOBILE

25

'WITH VERY GREAT HOPE'

It is only by Beelzebub, prince of the demons, that this man casts out demons.

Matthew 12:24

THAT THE 'NEW BALANCE OF POWER WITHIN THE VATICAN' DID come to pass – as Calvi had predicted it would – was confirmed by events in Rome during the next three years. A resuscitated Ambrosiano was placed under new ownership, as Andreotti had wanted. The United Trading family descended into a corporate hell, never to be heard from again. The IOR was bailed out of trouble, with persons close to Opus Dei assuming control over it and the papal purse strings.

But as these events unfolded it became more than ever apparent that Calvi, even in death, held the key to a bundle of secrets that remained a threat to the new power group at the Vatican. Possession of those secrets and their selective destruction had to be assured at any cost. The secrets were of course contained in Calvi's bulging black briefcase and missing cardboard boxes, and provided the only evidence linking the dead banker to those associated with the Vatican's new power group.

For information about what happened to the briefcase we have to rely on an Italian secret service report.[1] It disclosed that on the same day that Calvi's body was discovered a courier had flown on a private jet from Geneva to Gatwick where Carboni handed him a part of the briefcase's contents. These were flown back to Geneva and taken to a secluded lakeside villa where Gelli and Ortolani were waiting to examine them. The briefcase itself – with the remainder of the documents and the several bunches of keys – was flown by another private jet on Sunday from Edinburgh to Klagenfurt where the next day it was deposited in a strongbox at the Karmoner Savings Bank.[2]

On the Monday some of the conspirators gathered in Zurich to compare their alibis, and to consult by telephone with a lawyer in Rome, Wilfredo Vitalone, brother of Andreotti's closest confidant, Senator Claudio Vitalone. They decided that Vittor would give himself up to the authorities in Trieste, while Carboni went into hiding. Financially, at least, Carboni could afford to take some time off. Between January and May 1982 Calvi had authorized a series of payments to Swiss accounts under the Sardinian businessman's control totalling £16.3 million. This was not bad income for a man who the previous October had bounced cheques in the amount of £352,000.[3]

On 2 July 1982 the three commissioners appointed by the Bank of Italy to take control of Banco Ambrosiano met Marcinkus at the IOR offices in Rome. Marcinkus maintained that the IOR was not bound by the two comfort letters it had issued under the date of 1 September 1981 and therefore the Vatican bank would not pay the $1,300 million (£730 million) the commissioners insisted it owed the Ambrosiano. On 13 July 1982, Cardinal Casaroli tried to calm international criticism of the Vatican's lack of financial scruples by appointing a committee of 'three wise men' to unravel the true nature of the IOR dealings with Banco Ambrosiano: Philippe de Weck, former chairman of Union Bank of Switzerland who was involved in the 'sniffing aircraft' scandal, Joseph Brennan, chairman of Emigrant Savings Bank of New York, and Carlo Cerutti, a senior executive of STET, the Italian state-owned telecommunications company.

---

[1] Message No. 22582/1X/04 di prot. Re: Roberto Calvi to the Ministero dell'Interno (UCIGOS) and Comando Generale Arma CC., 2° Rep. S.A. – Uff. Operazioni.
[2] Mario Almerighi, *Ordinanza de rinvio a giudizio nel procedimento penale contro Flavio Carboni e altri*, Rome, pp. 93–94n.
[3] Convicted on the cheque-bouncing charges by the Criminal Court in Rome on 24 October 1986, Carboni was sentenced to nine months' imprisonment.

Meanwhile Carboni was arrested near Lugano. His briefcase contained a stack of documents relating to various aspects of Calvi's disappearance and the co-ordinated alibis of the key co-conspirators for the period around the time of the banker's death. The same day in Milan subpoenas were issued for Marcinkus, Mennini and de Strobel. Fearing arrest, Marcinkus moved into the Governor's Palace inside the Vatican City. On 5 August 1982, John Paul II approved raising Opus Dei to a Personal Prelature, though the decision was not announced for another two and a half weeks due to strong dissent within the Curia. The dissent showed that four years into John Paul II's papacy resistance to the clique that had worked for his election remained significant and a period of further consolidation was needed.

On 6 August 1982, the Bank of Italy placed Banco Ambrosiano in liquidation. Nuovo Banco Ambrosiano, formed by seven leading Italian commercial banks, immediately took over the operations of old Banco Ambrosiano, paying £252 million for Ambrosiano's remaining £1,460 million in deposits and its domestic network of one hundred branches. The foreign network, which contained most of the liabilities, was severed from the parent and therefore was not included in the buy-out operation. Its various components went into liquidation under separate procedures in the jurisdictions concerned. The new Ambrosiano opened its doors for business on the following Monday as if nothing had happened.

On 23 August 1982, the Vatican spokesman, Father Romeo Panciroli, announced that Opus Dei would be transformed into a Personal Prelature. Panciroli added, however, that publication of the relevant document – entitled *With Very Great Hope* – had been postponed for 'technical reasons'. Vatican sources claimed that foremost among the 'technical reasons' was Cardinal Giovanni Benelli's continued and determined opposition.

With Carboni in custody, dissension broke out among the conspirators just as the Calvi family was moving to have the suicide verdict handed down by the first London inquest quashed. The verdict had been based on the coroner's contention that the body bore no signs of violence, when in fact there were marks to the face consistent with thumb scratches made as the noose was slipped rapidly over the banker's head from behind. One of the hitherto unnamed conspirators was pressing for a larger payoff. But before appropriate measures were taken, Gelli decided it was time to come in from the cold. On 13 September 1982, he attempted to withdraw £30 million from his account with the Union Bank of Switzerland in Geneva: hardly an inconspicuous operation. The bank manager politely asked his client to wait while the withdrawal was processed and called the police. Gelli was arrested on an Italian warrant.

Sergio Vaccari and Licio Gelli were said to know each other. Gelli was an ardent collector, and Vaccari had excellent contacts in the London antiques trade. Originally from Milan, he spoke four languages and was described by his former landlord as an elitist with an enormous hatred of humanity. 'He would murder for a price and that was known in the underworld. You see, he found an ecstasy in violence. He loved other people's fear,' claimed Bill Hopkins. He was so frightened of Vaccari that in the spring of 1982 he asked the 'antiques' dealer to move out. Vaccari agreed, provided Hopkins found him something of equal standing in the same neighbourhood. Hopkins did, at 68 Holland Park. When he moved out, Vaccari left behind a file of Calvi press clippings. Thinking nothing of it, Hopkins tossed it out. Then a few weeks later Vaccari returned to ask Hopkins for details about renting a convenience flat at the Chelsea Cloisters, where Hopkins knew the management.

According to 'Podgora', Vaccari was the point-man. He conveyed Calvi from the Chelsea Cloisters to the final rendezvous with his killers. But Vaccari thought his work deserved a better price. In early September 1982 he flew to Rome for a few days. When he returned, according to Hopkins, he was in 'a sunny mood'. He told his cleaning lady to take a few days off. When she returned to clean the apartment on the morning of 15 September 1982 – two days after Gelli's arrest in Geneva – she found her employer half sprawled across a white leather sofa in a pool of blood. He had been stabbed eighteen times about the face and chest. The Metropolitan police, when they arrived, assumed that Vaccari had known his killers. The curtains were drawn. Three half-filled whisky glasses and a box of 'After Eight' chocolates were on the coffee table. An open briefcase which contained an Italian Masonic document was on one of the two matching armchairs. There were traces of drugs and electronic weighing scales in the kitchen. His antique desk had been rifled and two drawers spilled open.

One of Vaccari's neighbours reported seeing two men leave the building at about the presumed time of the murder and believed they were speaking Italian. Among the suspects questioned by the police was Giuseppe 'Pippo' Bellinghieri. The thirty-six-year-old Bellinghieri admitted knowing Vaccari and having visited the Holland Park apartment several times. But Bellinghieri claimed to have been on a pilgrimage to Poland when Vaccari was murdered. The investigation was closed and the crime remains unsolved.

With Gelli and Carboni in prison, Vaccari out of the way, and a suicide verdict on Calvi that the City of London Police seemed determined to uphold, the conspirators were secure. One of the conspiracy's essential features had been to paint Roberto Calvi's reputation as black as possible. It was said that he had embezzled money, accepted undisclosed commissions, consorted with crooks and kept a high-class mistress in Rome – in other words that he was a man of no morals. Suddenly Opus Dei and the Vatican entered the fray, also implying that Calvi was a liar and a cheat. How could anyone believe such a man? His reputation was thoroughly sullied, in spite of the family's efforts to vindicate him. By association, his family also became tainted. It was suggested, for example, that their only interest in having the suicide verdict overturned was to collect the £1.75 million in insurance money due on the banker's death.

While the campaign to slander Calvi continued, the Vatican's 'three wise men' delivered a preliminary report. By their own admission it 'did not have a conclusive character' because they had not been given full access to the relevant documents. Consequently, they recommended a joint investigation by the Vatican and Italian governments, to be conducted 'on the basis of the documents in the possession of the two parties, in order subsequently to draw from them consequences that seem legitimate.'[1]

This started a new flood of rumours that so alarmed the Vatican it felt compelled to publish an editorial in the 8 October 1982 issue of *l'Osservatore Romano,* denying that Opus Dei or any of its members had dealings of any sort with Calvi or Banco Ambrosiano. Then on 17 October 1982 *l'Osservatore Romano* published a denial that the IOR had received any funds from the Ambrosiano.

[1] Raw, *Op. cit.*, p. 13.

This was repeated in its weekly English language edition of 28 October 1982.

I.O.R. – AMBROSIANO

Recently a Rome daily newspaper published some conclusions . . . concerning the relations between the Institute for the Works of Religion (IOR) and the Ambrosiano group. It presented them inexactly as the 'results arrived at by the international committee of experts instituted by the Vatican to determine the actual participation of the IOR in the activities of the Banco Ambrosiano of Roberto Calvi'.

These are, in fact, the conclusions of a long and accurate study carried out by the IOR and its legal advisers on the basis of the documentation in the possession of the same Institute and summarized with reference to contrary statements made publicly and authoritatively.

Since great publicity was given to the conclusions and they were the subject of numerous comments, our paper also deems it opportune to publish their exact text:

1. The Institute for the Works of Religion did not receive any funds either from the Ambrosiano group or from Roberto Calvi, and therefore is not bound to restore anything.

2. The foreign companies which are in debt to the Ambrosiano group were never managed by the IOR, which had no knowledge of the operations carried out by those companies.

3. All the payments made by the Ambrosiano group to the aforesaid companies were made at a time prior to the so-called letters of patronage.

4. These letters, because of their date of issue, did not exercise any influence on the payments in question.

5. Should eventual verification be required, all this will be proved.

These assertions were misleading. To maintain that 'the IOR did not receive any funds from the Ambrosiano group . . . and therefore is not bound to restore anything' was untrue. At that very moment the IOR was in the process of repaying £60 million in lira deposits to the Ambrosiano group. But the statement insisted that the conclusions were based on 'a long and accurate study carried out by the IOR and its legal advisers on the basis of documentation in the possession of the Institute'. Very well, but what study? Why was it never made public or, for that matter, made known to the three wise men?

The study was anything but accurate. It would have been interesting, therefore, to have seen the documentation that the experts relied upon in making their conclusion. Were they forged documents? Based on the fact that in another nineteen months the Vatican would own up to a 'moral responsibility in the affair', the question of forgery became relevant. The other relevant question remained who, really, was running the IOR?

One can only wonder, therefore, which legal advisers conducted the investigation and whether they were members of Opus Dei. Moreover, the language seemed to have an all too familiar ring to it. Certainly Cardinal Benelli, who had at least some of the facts at hand, should have known the statement to be false. But for the moment the energies of the Roman Curia were focused on preparing for the triennial plenary session of the College of Cardinals that was scheduled to open towards the end of November.

On Friday, 22 October 1982, Opus Dei's most implacable opponent in the College of Cardinals, Archbishop Benelli of Florence, suffered a massive heart attack – *infarto miocardico acuto,* the medical bulletin said. But the sixty-two-year-old Benelli – a hearty, good-living Tuscan – had been in robust health, claimed his personal secretary. He worked long hours and rarely slept more than four hours a night. The first signs of heart trouble began only two days before and he died on 26 October 1982. His passing was said to have been a miracle as important for Opus Dei as the unexplained cure of Sister Concepción which had paved the way for the Founder's beatification. Benelli had been preparing to oppose Opus Dei's becoming a Personal Prelature at the meeting of cardinals.

Four days before the convocation opened, Opus Dei's regional vicar for Italy, Don Mario Lantini, wrote a one-page letter to Clara Calvi and her son Carlo to complain about their declarations to the

press. The tone of the letter was obsequious. Other than its posturing, one wonders why a doctor of theology and philosophy such as
Lantini would have bothered. The obvious answer must be that by
insisting the banker had been murdered, the Calvis were embarrassing more than a few people. After offering his 'Christian
condolences', Lantini referred to three recent articles in the *Wall
Street Journal*, *La Stampa* and *l'Espresso* in which the Calvis
affirmed that Roberto Calvi had been in contact with Opus Dei
before his death. Lantini continued:

> *In my capacity as counsellor of Opus Dei for Italy I should like to
> confirm what has already been communicated and published in all the
> press, namely that no one representing Opus Dei has ever held any
> connection or contact, either directly or indirectly, with Roberto Calvi
> or with the IOR over share transactions with the Ambrosiano or in
> any other operation (or planned operation) of an economic/financial
> character of any kind or relevance.*
>
> *Given this absolute distancing of Opus Dei – and in order that full
> light may be brought to bear on this aspect – the necessity becomes
> apparent of knowing to which elements you are referring when you
> speak of Opus Dei. The intention, among other things, is to provide
> evidence of who could have wrongly used the name of Opus Dei or
> attempted to attribute false intentions to it.*
>
> *I would therefore ask you, Signora and Signore Calvi, to be so kind
> as to furnish me in particular with indications of people, facts and cir-
> cumstances and to specify any other material which would serve to
> clear up the facts you have referred to in the interviews quoted.*

Lantini gloated over the fact that he was never graced with a reply
and Opus Dei brushed off the widow Calvi's statements as
'emotional speculation'. But what she said was only a factual rendering of what her husband had told her. She never claimed anything
more than that. Moreover, Don Mario Lantini's letter was con-
tentious. Clara Calvi had at all times been clear about her source and
had given testimony about it under oath on several occasions. Don
Lantini knew this, so why did he bother to trouble her? The fact that
she never replied was therefore neither surprising, nor material. But
the real point was that Don Lantini's letter might have been more

appropriately addressed to the persons who had led Roberto Calvi to believe he was talking – directly or indirectly – to Opus Dei.

With Benelli's death, the last opposition to Opus Dei's elevation to 'floating diocese' status evaporated in the College of Cardinals and three days after the meeting closed Cardinal Casaroli and Cardinal Baggio issued on behalf of John Paul II the Papal bull, *With Very Great Hope*, including the Apostolic Constitution known as *Ut sit*, which transformed Opus Dei into a Personal Prelature.

The Pope declared:

With very great hope, the Church directs its attention and maternal care to Opus Dei, which – by divine inspiration – the Servant of God Josemaría Escrivá de Balaguer founded in Madrid on 2 October 1928, so that it may always be an apt and effective instrument of the salvific mission which the Church carries out for the life of the world.

So now it was official. According to this declaration the Pope agreed that Opus Dei was not Escrivá de Balaguer's invention, but God's. Escrivá de Balaguer had only been the messenger. But just as significant, *Ut sit* legalized Opus Dei's status under canon law as a state within a Church.

Not only did *With Very Great Hope* and the Apostolic Constitution *Ut sit* make Don Alvaro del Portillo the 'little pope' of Villa Tevere, it confirmed that he reported to no-one save the Big Pope across the Tiber, though as far as the Big Pope was concerned he was rather more dependent on Opus Dei than met the eye. Should for any reason the Prelate of Opus Dei not wish to take orders from the Pontiff of Rome, he would then be responsible only to God. But if the Pontiff chose not to listen to the Prelate he risked finding his finances reduced by a significant amount.

The confirmation contained in *With Very Great Hope* that Opus Dei was founded 'by divine inspiration' bestowed upon the Prelature justification for its supreme arrogance as it placed the Work above all other institutions of the Church, being that it was the only one – aside from the Church herself – that claimed to be founded by God and not by man. This was exploited as a divine licence permitting Opus Dei to practise a *modus operandi* that in certain matters placed it close to the outer fringe of social custom and legality.

The official ceremony raising Opus Dei to the Church's only Personal Prelature took place in mid-March 1983 in Sant' Eugenio. Dramatic though it was, crowning a half-century of hope and planning, the ceremony was overshadowed by an unsettling event. Two weeks before, the Rumasa group was expropriated by Spain's newly elected Socialist government and placed in liquidation.

26

PARAPARAL

Faithful, docile. We want this to be our disposition and we will tell Jesus, using the words of the Father: 'Yes, Lord . . . I will be faithful, and I will let the hands of my Superiors mould me so as to have this distinctive supernatural polish of our family.'
Josemaría Escrivá de Balaguer, 'In the Hands of the Potter',
Crónica X, 1958

JOSÉ MARÍA RUIZ-MATEOS HAD NOT ONLY TRUSTED LUIS VALLS LIKE A brother but he considered him one of the Work's leading strategists. But for two persons who shared similar views, their lifestyles were vastly different. Ruiz-Mateos was outgoing, while Valls was reflective, almost monkish. Ruiz-Mateos was accessible to his staff, and enjoyed talking with them; Valls secreted himself away on the top-floor-but-one of Banco Popular Español's new *Presidencia* in Madrid's Edificio Beatriz. Banco Popular's name appeared nowhere on the building's exterior, nor was it displayed in the entrance lobby. The topmost floor was reserved for Luis Valls's penthouse and roof garden. Even though an inscribed numerary, for many years he had refused to live in an Opus Dei residence.

Valls could never understand why Ruiz-Mateos insisted on displaying his octagonal bee emblem on all of Rumasa's four hundred enterprises. In this Valls was not alone. Alvaro del Portillo, when he came to Madrid, inevitably complained to Ruiz-Mateos, 'I see too many bees. Seriously, why do we have to see this little bee everywhere?' It was another way of saying that Ruiz-Mateos, for an Opus Dei person, was too up-front, too image-conscious, and that he didn't 'let the Lord shine through'.

This was a curious reflection from the prelate general of an organization that had the reputation of being madly narcissistic and extravagant in feathering its corporate nests, whether in Rome, Madrid or the high Andes. By the 1980s, Opus Dei in Spain had an annual budget of £6 million. Modest though this might seem, it only covered the operating costs of the regional vicariat and the nine provincial delegations. In reality, through its corporate network and full-time fund raisers, Spanish Opus Dei reportedly takes in on average £160 million a year.[1] This represents twice the annual budget of the Catholic Church in Spain. But what does the *Obra*, which claims to be a purely 'religious organization with no material assets', do with all this undeclared money? That is what the Spanish Socialist Party wanted to know.

For some time it had been apparent that Spain's next general elections, scheduled for October 1982, were likely to bring in the first Socialist government since the Civil War. Some Socialists blamed Opus Dei for fomenting an attempted *coup d'état* that had occurred on 23 February 1981, delaying the party's return to power, and expected Felipe González, the Socialist leader, to take retaliatory action. Luis Valls, for his part, feared the Socialists would seek to nationalize the banking sector. He made himself the unofficial spokesman of Spain's privately owned commercial banks in defending the right of free enterprise.

The Socialist threat could not have come at a worse time. Anticipating the Holy See's acceptance of the Portillo Option, Opus Dei's need for funds at this stage was immense. Spain, as usual, led the way when it came to raising cash for God's little needs. Ruiz-Mateos suspected that Gregorio López Bravo, who after serving as Spain's foreign minister became deputy chairman of Banesto, the country's largest commercial bank, was given the task of cover-

---

[1] Santiago Aroca, 'The Godfather of Opus and its Strawmen', *Tiempo* 217, 7 July 1986. (Exchange rate of 190 pesetas to £1.)

ing the Portillo Option. But because of Opus Dei's insistence on discretion, even though they were the best of friends López Bravo would never have admitted it. Nevertheless, in June 1980 he formed the Instituto de Educación e Investigación (IEI), with himself as chairman and Enrique Sendagorta Aramburu, another supernumerary, as deputy chairman. Sendagorta served on the board of Banco Vizcaya, and was deputy chairman of Indubán, Vizcaya's investment banking arm. He personally contributed more than £1 million to the cause. Ruiz-Mateos was 'indexed' for a special payment to IEI of 1,500 million pesetas (£7.9 million). He was told that the money was for the University of Navarra but he suspected it was really to help underwrite Opus Dei's takeover of the IOR.

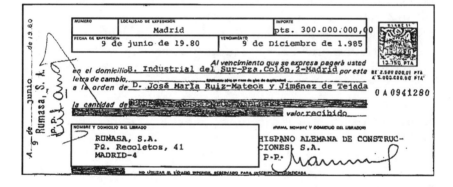

Unable to meet this indexation at one go – it was over and above Rumasa's quarterly *decimus* transfers – Ruiz-Mateos proposed to pay the full amount over five years in annual instalments of 300 million pesetas (£1.6 million) each, plus 10 per cent annual interest on the outstanding balance. To do this he issued five promissory notes to an intermediary, Hispano Alemana de Construcciones S.A., so that the notes could be discounted. The notes were issued on 9 December 1980, payable by the Banco Industrial del Sur in favour of Hispano Alemana on the same date each year. The first year's draft carried interest of 150 million pesetas (£789,000), giving it a total face value of 450 million pesetas (£2.4 million). In addition, Ruiz-Mateos furnished the Opus Dei directors with a written undertaking to renew this arrangement every five years for seventy-five years. The contract stipulated that the payments to Hispano Alemana were for IEI's account.

After Rumasa's takeover of Banco Atlántico, the Rumasa banks – all twenty of them – collectively moved into the prestige group of the top eight commercial banks in Spain, directly behind Luis Valls's Banco Popular Español. There was a fear among establishment bankers that Ruiz-Mateos had discovered some sort of new formula and if allowed to continue unchecked he would transform Rumasa into Spain's number one bank. The Banco de España reacted by pressuring Rumasa to open its books for inspection.

Ruiz-Mateos concluded that the most influential person in Spain's financial establishment was Luis Valls. He had noted that a majority of the central bank's directorate and board of governors were 'Vallses' – people who owed their allegiance to the chairman of Banco Popular Español – including the governor, José Ramón Alvarez Rendueles, and his deputy, Mariano Rubio, who was responsible for insuring that Rumasa complied with the central bank's executive order. But Ruiz-Mateos was only too aware that if he opened Rumasa's books to Banco de España's inspection, the undeclared transfers to Opus Dei would be uncovered, causing both the Work and Rumasa a lot of problems. On the other hand, if he refused he risked provoking Rumasa's expropriation. He therefore decided to broach the matter with Valls.

Ruiz-Mateos claimed that Luis Valls assured him the Banco de España problem 'could be solved with money, by paying money'.[1] Ruiz-Mateos said that Valls instructed him to hire a political payoff specialist, Antonio Navalón Sánchez, and for legal work to retain the services of Matías Cortés Domíngues. 'Both are people who enjoy my entire confidence,' Valls said.

'How much cash is needed?' Ruiz-Mateos asked.

'One thousand million pesetas [£5.3 million] for now,' Valls allegedly replied.[2]

Matías Cortés was Spain's leading criminal lawyer. Among his

---

[1] Ruiz-Mateos Open Letter to Luis Valls Taberner, February 1995.
[2] Unpublished memorandum of 2 February 1994 in the files of Kroll Associates, London, and Ruiz-Mateos Open Letter to Luis Valls, February 1995. Luis Valls disputes Ruiz-Mateos's version of the expropriation scenario. While he acknowledges meeting Ruiz-Mateos on many occasions, and notably during 'six or seven lunches', he said the only time they ever discussed Rumasa's problems was in early 1982 at a reception given by King Juan Carlos for Prince Philip, Duke of Edinburgh. He said Ruiz-Mateos asked him for the name of a good lawyer as he was unhappy with how his solicitors were handling the Banco de España probe. Valls gave him one name – Matías Cortés – and thought the matter closed.

clients were Emperor Jean Bedel Bokassa of the Central African mock empire, the local representative of Rothschild Bank, a couple of Spain's leading publishers and Manuel de la Concha, president of the Madrid Stock Exchange who later, along with Mariano Rubio, went to prison for corruption. Cortés exuded influence; the king's private telephone number was in his agenda and he dined with cabinet ministers and dukes. He owned a public relations agency and an Italian restaurant, and did business with Dr Arthur Wiederkehr's convenience company factory. Although on close terms with Valls, on one occasion he noted under a reference to Opus Dei's senior banker and another person identified only as Pedro the comment *'soberbio, obsceno y chuleta de barrio'* (arrogant, obscene and a neighbourhood hood).[1]

In March 1982 Ruiz-Mateos hired Navalón as a consultant. Ruiz-Mateos said he paid Navalón, who had previously worked as political bagman for Valls, a monthly retainer of £31,560 without ever asking for a receipt. Cortés, Navalón and Valls were friends of Pio Cabanillas, the ubiquitous notary public and justice minister in the transitional government that brought democracy to Spain. Cortés was experienced in the school of hard-knocks lawyering. As Banesto's outside counsel, he had helped negotiate the 1978 takeover of Banca Coca. Ignacio Coca, who had risen to prominence under Franco, sold the bank for a substantial cash payment and 7 per cent of Banesto's share capital. Only afterwards did the Banesto board discover that Coca had over-valued the assets, using the crude device of fictitious property and securities holdings. Cortés asked Coca to make good the missing 8,000 million pesetas (£42 million). Coca committed suicide.

The Socialists obtained an absolute majority in the October 1982 elections. With González in the prime minister's office, Ruiz-Mateos asked Luis Valls what was going to happen. He said Valls told him to give Navalón another 1,000 million pesetas, presumably for central bank officials or members of the new Socialist government. The money was handed over by Ruiz-Mateos's personal secretary, either in cash or bearer cheques. A delighted Navalón called the bribe money his 'candies'.[2]

---

[1] Note in Matías Cortés's agenda for 5 August 1983.
[2] 'The Rumasa Affair Soils the Vatican and Opus', *Tiempo*, Madrid, 1 August 1983.

A few months later, Opus Dei sent two emissaries to question Ruiz-Mateos about who in Rumasa knew of the transfers to Switzerland. He told them the transfers were handled by the head of his banking division, Carlos Quintas. That seemed to satisfy them but, reflecting on this later, Ruiz-Mateos concluded that, knowing what was about to happen, the emissaries wanted to make sure Quintas had cleansed the books of all Opus Dei-linked transfers. Also in early 1983 his two supposed friends, Banco Popular director Rafael Termes and Paco Curt Martínez, put back their shares in Ruiz-Mateos y Cía, a Rumasa subsidiary, to Ruiz-Mateos who, unsuspecting, bought both of them out according to a generous book-value formula. Reflecting on these events long afterwards, it seemed to Ruiz-Mateos that he was the only person in Madrid who didn't know that the government was going to seize Rumasa, apparently with Luis Valls manipulating the levers from behind the scenes.

Ruiz-Mateos came away from a meeting with Cortés and Navalón on the morning of Wednesday, 23 February 1983, confident that a solution to Rumasa's problems was about to be found. But in the late afternoon Cortés met Petra Mateos, chef de cabinet of Miguel Boyer Salvador, the Socialist super-minister of economy and finance, who reported back to her boss that Rumasa definitely refused to comply. Boyer immediately gave orders for a para-military force to invest the Rumasa buildings in Madrid. The date was significant, being the second anniversary of the aborted *coup d'état* that Ruiz-Mateos suspected had been financed by Valls. Ruiz-Mateos was at home when the expropriation was announced in a TV newsflash that evening and until then had no inkling that Rumasa's fate had been sealed.

'I learned of Rumasa's expropriation at the same time as the Spanish people – at home, watching television. For days I had received no word from Valls. Some weeks before he had mysteriously called to tell me that Rumasa's expropriation was one of the alternatives under consideration by the Socialists, but not to worry as Rome was not lost, and for this reason I still trusted him,' Ruiz-Mateos later wrote to Don Alvaro del Portillo.[1]

All of Navalón's candies had come to nothing. Miguel Boyer explained to the nation that Rumasa had refused to submit to a

[1] José María Ruiz-Mateos letter to Don Alvaro del Portillo, 31 May 1985.

government audit. Boyer said he feared that, having over-extended itself, the Ruiz-Mateos empire was about to collapse. While a privately owned holding company, he pointed out that Rumasa controlled many publicly traded banks and corporations. If suddenly the empire collapsed he feared it would provoke a national crisis. This danger justified his intervention.

A dejected Ruiz-Mateos asked Luis Valls, 'What do I do now?'

'You keep your mouth shut and get out of the country,' he said Valls advised him. 'We'll help you, but you must do what Matías Cortés tells you.'

And so, in a move reminiscent of Calvi's flight from Italy, Ruiz-Mateos disappeared from sight. He arrived in London accompanied by his private secretary Pepe Díaz, banking director Carlos Quintas and a bevy of private bodyguards. He was exhausted and depressed. He was told on no account to disclose his membership in the Work. To insure his obedience, he was assigned a new spiritual director, Frank 'Kiko' Mitjans, a Catalan for whom he never felt much warmth, and a permanent minder, Benedict Whyte, who Ruiz-Mateos described as 'a very gentle but obedient person'.

Ruiz-Mateos's whereabouts remained a mystery to the Spanish press, fuelling all sorts of rumours concerning his dishonesty and criminal responsibility in provoking the Rumasa crisis. He felt isolated, but his faith remained strong. He attended Mass daily at Saint Mary's Church in Codogan Street, Belgravia, around the corner from Sloane Street. He always arrived in a black limousine, preceded by an identical vehicle containing his bodyguards. He sat at the back of the church. When he wished to celebrate the marriage of his eldest daughter, the pastor of Saint Mary's was asked to turn over the church to Opus Dei for the occasion.

As the weeks passed, Ruiz-Mateos became convinced that Valls had betrayed him to save Banco Popular Español from nationalization. The authorities and press painted him more of a scoundrel each day. Boyer claimed there was a $2,000 million hole at Rumasa. According to Ruiz-Mateos's reckoning, the group should have shown a net worth of $3,300 million. From London he instructed one of his lawyers, Opus Dei supernumerary Crispín de Vicente, to sue the government, seeking the return of his assets. The government retaliated by charging Ruiz-Mateos with fraud, keeping false books and illegally exporting capital. A warrant was issued for his arrest.

Investigators found copies of Rumasa promissory notes for £9.3 million (interest included) in favour of IEI. López Bravo confirmed that the IEI – which he said provided financial assistance to students and researchers – had received 870 million pesetas (£4.6 million) from Ruiz-Mateos but denied that the institute transferred the money to Opus Dei, which, had it been destined for the IOR, was of course correct. Opus Dei also denied that it had *ever* received monies from Ruiz-Mateos.[1]

'I am not a member of Opus Dei, though I sympathize with its objectives,' Ruiz-Mateos told Stephen Aris of the London *Sunday Times*.[2] A week later he told *The Financial Times* banking correspondent, 'I never met Calvi, but some people say I will end up like Calvi.'[3]

His declarations brought two Opus Dei supernumeraries to London to counsel him to remain silent. One of them, Luis Coronel de Palma, governor of the Banco de España from 1970 to 1976, hinted that the expropriation had been a deal to save Banco Popular Español from nationalization. Coronel was followed by López Bravo. As a friend, López Bravo was upset. He had already warned Ruiz-Mateos in an elliptical manner not to trust Valls. Opus Dei members are forbidden to speak badly of another member. This time López Bravo, who was beginning to have his own doubts about certain Opusian ethics, assured Ruiz-Mateos, 'Luis Valls owes you an explanation.'

Over the next four months Luis Valls called twice. 'He told me that if I remained patient the future would be fascinating. He also said that we would meet soon with our brothers in a country yet to be determined to talk over everything . . .' Then, after a visit from Navalón, Valls came to London to meet with his unhappy friend.

'You betrayed me,' Ruiz-Mateos told him.

'What are you talking about?' Valls replied.

Valls avoided any kind of explanation. At that point Ruiz-Mateos decided there were two *Obras*: *Opus Dei*, spiritually spotless, as originally intended by the Founder, and *Opus Homini*, the *Obra* that some men made of it. He decided to sever all ties with *Opus Homini*.

[1] 'Rumasa – Search and Destroy', *The Economist*, 16 April 1983
[2] Stephen Aris, 'How Mateos Rose and Fell: the End of a Reign in Spain', *The Sunday Times*, 24 April 1983.
[3] 'This is only the start of a very long film', *The Financial Times*, London, 30 April 1983.

He fired Matías Cortés, refused to have anything more to do with his London 'minder', Ben Whyte, and stopped giving his confidences to Kiko Mitjans. Opus Dei sent his former spiritual director of fifteen years, Boro Nacher, to London to try to reason with him. But Ruiz-Mateos refused to see him, suspecting Nacher of knowing all along that Valls and the Madrid directors were plotting to sacrifice Rumasa to the Socialists.

Ruiz-Mateos claimed he had never heard mention of the Caracas lawyer Alberto Jaimes Berti or the Paraparal property venture. If both he and Berti were telling the truth, then Opus Dei had been operating behind his back well before the expropriation, running money through Rumasa's banking sector without his knowledge or consent. According to Berti, the agent for this operation was Ruiz-Mateos's brother-in-law, Luis Barón Mora-Figueroa.

Ruiz-Mateos described his brother-in-law as '100-per cent Opus Dei. He is a wonderful man, but a fanatic of Opus Dei. To talk with him today is like talking to a brick wall.' Luis Barón likewise denied that he ever met Berti, and Ruiz-Mateos doubted that his brother-in-law had travelled to Caracas in 1980 on an investment mission.

Until the early 1980s, in addition to handling the Church finances in Venezuela, Berti acted as legal council to the Apostolic Nunciature in Caracas. He had set up a clerical pension fund through a company he founded under the name of Inpreclero and, at Archbishop Benelli's behest, he used another company – Inecclesia – for anonymously investing Church money in American blue chip securities or specially designated projects. Although managing director of both companies, they were controlled by the Venezuelan Conference of Bishops through its finance committee. Inecclesia had audited assets of $1,400 million.

Now Berti is the first to admit that he was never a great admirer of Escrivá de Balaguer or the organization he founded. As counsel to the Apostolic Nunciature Berti had been called upon over the years to carry out some disagreeable tasks that were a source of embarrassment to the Prelature. The first occurred in 1970 when the nuncio in Caracas received a complaint from the parents of two teenaged boys in the diocese of Margarita, a group of islands off the Venezuelan coast. The parents were threatening criminal action against the local bishop for molesting their sons and the nuncio feared a scandal. He asked Berti to intervene. The Bishop of Margarita was Francisco de Guruceaga, Opus Dei's first vocation in Venezuela.

Berti flew to La Asunción on the Isla de Margarita and through the help of a woman prosecutor in the sexual offences department got hold of and shredded the Guruceaga file. He then negotiated a $160,000 payment for the parents. The nuncio sent Guruceaga to London on an extended sabbatical, where he lived a secular existence for the next three years, travelling extensively.

In 1973 the new nuncio, Monsignor Antonio del Giudice, gave Guruceaga another chance and appointed him Bishop of La Guaira, a small diocese and port city in the federal district of Caracas. According to Berti, Guruceaga considered himself a mercantile prelate, licensed to make money for God's work. One of Guruceaga's deals had been the 1975 sale for $2.5 million of a tract of land belonging to the diocese of La Guaira. The money disappeared. Del Giudice's successor asked Berti to investigate. Berti said he gathered the documentary evidence and the nuncio sent his report to the secretary of state, Cardinal Villot, in Rome. Nothing more was heard of the affair.

At Benelli's request, Inecclesia also helped people connected with the Church to invest monies anonymously on the American stock markets. For Berti to handle the operation, however, the client needed to supply him with several letters of introduction from important ecclesiastic authorities or organizations like the Knights of Malta. He would tell the client to transfer the money to an Inecclesia account in Panama City. The money would then be assigned to a shell company in whose name the US securities were purchased. Once the money was fully invested, Berti furnished the client with the bearer share certificate of the Panamanian company.

This was the procedure used when Berti said he was contacted at the end of 1980 by Luis Barón Mora-Figueroa, chairman of Banco del Norte, one of the twenty banks belonging to the Rumasa group, and also a member of Rumasa's board of directors. He said Luis Barón presented him with several letters of recommendation from the Vatican and other Church authorities, including Villot's successor as secretary of state, Cardinal Casaroli, and the IOR's prelate-secretary Donato de Bonis. Luis Barón told Berti that he represented a syndicate of investors involved in a long-term project.

At first Berti thought the project might have been the Latin American trade bank that Cardinal Siri had mentioned. Only later, when plans for the bank were shelved, did Berti suspect that the project was Paraparal, Venezuela's largest property development venture.

Paraparal was a planned 14,000-home residential city, on the shores of the Lago de Valencia, launched in 1976 by developer, Giuseppe Milone, who had arrived from Naples the year before. The cost of bringing Paraparal onto the market was estimated at around $2,000 million. Berti was Milone's Caracas attorney. As Berti pointed out, there were not a great many investors around with $2,000 million lying idle. The Church was one; the Mafia (or Naples's crime syndicate – the Camorra) another. As for the former, Berti, a manager of Church money, was certainly qualified to give an opinion.

Luis Barón knew the precise distribution of liquidities inside the Rumasa group. His Banco del Norte assembled and collated the financial data required by the Banco de España for Rumasa's banking division, and it also prepared the regular reports sent to the monetary authorities detailing the group's foreign exchange positions.[1] Berti claimed that Luis Barón entrusted to Inecclesia's safekeeping $2,000 million, later increased by another $200 million. Berti said he followed the normal procedure. The money was transferred in several instalments to a Panamanian shell company and sent for investment to designated brokers in New York. The money in fact came in with some delay, requiring adjustments in the investment schedules. During this time Berti went to Rome on business and met the IOR's de Bonis. Berti claimed he discovered that de Bonis knew all about the Barón transaction. His familiarity with it convinced Berti that the IOR was also involved. Moreover, according to Berti, de Bonis mentioned that Roberto Calvi was another insider with full knowledge of the operation.[2] This made sense as Berti had noted that some of the monies received in Panama came through the Ambrosiano network.

At about this time, a palace revolution occurred within the Conference of Venezuelan Bishops. Francisco de Guruceaga took over the Conference's finance committee and immediately brought

[1] WW Finance *Memorandum on The Rumasa Group*, Geneva 1979, p. 12.
[2] Monsignor Donato de Bonis has denied knowing Alberto Jaimes Berti or being in any way aware of the 'Barón' operation.

Inpreclero and Inecclesia under his control. Berti drew his mandate from a six-member board of directors – of which he was one of the three lay members. Guruceaga bypassed the directors and in February 1983 appointed himself president of both companies in a procedure that Berti considered illegal. Berti refused to hand over the books. In retaliation Guruceaga accused him of embezzling up to $50 million from the clerical pension fund.

Assuming control of the two companies was consistent with Opus Dei's policy of monopolizing management of the Church's finances wherever and however it could. Opus Dei, for example, was said to have done the same under Pinochet, with its members taking over the Chilean Church's finances.[1] But it was their tactics that shocked Berti: 'Opus Dei was unscrupulous and immoral in their campaign to remove me. They tried to destroy me. For eight months they used the radio, TV and newspapers in a well orchestrated campaign of lies and hate that was impossible to counter.'

During his fray with Opus Dei, Berti uncovered what he considered was further evidence that the $2,200 million was destined for the Paraparal project. He knew that in 1981 the project faced one of its innumerable liquidity crises and risked going under. At the time Milone had been desperate to raise another $200 million. It was then, Berti said, that Calvi was asked to invest in Paraparal. But the Ambrosiano had treasury problems of its own, thanks to its United Trading exposure. Nevertheless Calvi agreed but as a show of good faith he requested that the syndicate make a compensatory deposit of $200 million with the Ambrosiano network. This was apparently done through the IOR, but Berti concluded that Calvi did not complete his side of the bargain because he said the banker called him in Caracas and asked him to get Milone to stop pressuring him for money.

Because of the Ambrosiano's deepening problems, Calvi was unable either to put up the $200 million or reimburse the 'compensatory' deposit. As a result, the Paraparal operation risked going under and other monies had to be found. This explained for Berti the delay in receiving the last slice of the $2,200 million, with one of Milone's backers stepping in to save the project from going under.

---

[1] 'Chile's monetarist model starts to come apart', *Latin America Economic Report*, 14 January 1977.

If true, this would have made a marked man out of Calvi. While this description of events made sense, Berti's reasoning was based on deduction rather than hard facts, until one day he had to go to Rome to settle legal matters with Milone, and was threatened by a 'Mr Tortola', who identified himself as a Camorra associate. Tortola told him: 'We reached Calvi in London and we can reach you any place you go.'[1]

Berti supposed an entry in Rumasa's books related to the Barón operation. But when Rumasa was expropriated, to prevent the government liquidators from tracing it, ownership of the Paraparal development was transferred to a new company called Cali S.A. Formed in Panama on the same day as Rumasa's nationalization, it acquired the litigation rights of a plaintiff who had brought an action against Paraparal. Cali won the case, placing the Paraparal development company in default, thereby enabling it to assume ownership. 'This was a very unusual form of sale,' Berti observed wryly. That it was, and very clean, too, as nothing linked Cali to the original investment syndicate.

Berti's story was based on a mixture of conjecture and insider knowledge. The Vatican and Opus Dei had also consistently denied involvement in Calvi's 'misdealings'. But towards the end of 1983, the Vatican realized it was going to be taken to court by the creditors of Banco Ambrosiano. This prodded the Vatican to take its first hesitant steps towards a settlement. In January 1984 the Vatican indicated through a Rome lawyer that it would consider making a $250 million (£140.3 million) payment to settle the Ambrosiano affair. But the IOR did not have such a sum available. Some thought was given to raising a commercial loan for up to $90 million (£50.5 million). Then at the end of January, Marcinkus claimed, the IOR arranged 'other financing'.[2]

The source of the 'other financing' has never been disclosed. But on 25 May 1984 the IOR agreed to pay $244 million (£137 million) in settlement of all claims against it. When this amount was added to the time deposits and other assets it had forfeited, and the $99 million (£55.6 million) in lira deposits that it repaid, the IOR's total loss in the Ambrosiano fiasco amounted to $510 million

[1] Memo to the Files of Kroll Associates, London, by Jeffrey Katz, 16 November 1993.
[2] Raw, *Op. cit.*, p. 37.

(£286.3 million).[1] The settlement, in effect, left the IOR bankrupt. Marcinkus protested. 'It didn't kind of clear us out completely; we had to kind of lower our capital level,' he said.[2] But the IOR had no capital level, in that it had no share capital *per se*. It may have had reserves, and it had deposits. The IOR was kept in being, therefore, by the loyalty of its depositors. The largest depositor was Opus Dei.

There was a 'codicil' to the settlement whereby the IOR agreed to hand over to the creditors an assortment of bearer shares belonging to the United Trading family of companies – those mentioned in the comfort letters. These included the entire share capital of the parent United Trading itself, and also 53,300 shares, representing 23 per cent of the share capital, of Banco Ambrosiano Holding, Luxembourg.

On the earthquake scale of financial disasters, by the payment to the Ambrosiano creditors, 1984 was definitely a volcanic nine for the Vatican. Where the money came from to cover this enormous hole was disclosed in the fuzziest of terms to the cardinals in a meeting that took place nine months later. They were informed that the IOR's $244 million payment 'was covered entirely by the [IOR] itself, without contributions from the Holy See and without drawing on the funds entrusted to the administration of the Institute.'

José María Ruiz-Mateos was still denying any connection with the Prelature. But he was beginning to come out of a long decompression period with the certainty that he had been betrayed. Shortly after he fired his UK solicitor, the British Home Office refused to renew his residence permit, obliging him to leave the country. He was eventually arrested on a Spanish warrant in Frankfurt and held for three months before being freed on £2.7 million bail. He applied for political asylum, which was refused, and spent the next year and a half fighting extradition.

In the midst of the extradition proceedings, on 31 May 1985 Ruiz-Mateos composed a 45-page hand-written letter to Don Alvaro del Portillo that was frank, touching, full of hurt, but without bitterness, as a son unburdening his soul to a father, hoping for

[1] *Ibid.*, p. 16.
[2] John Cornwell, *Op. cit.*, p. 132.

understanding, guidance, and some form of human warmth. It began:

> I assure you, Father, that all the facts I tell you are true, and God knows it. My only aim is to inform you of what happened and, if convenient, to receive your advice. Everything has been taken from me. They didn't value anything. I have been dishonoured, discredited in my work and thrown out of Spain. I have been persecuted and slandered. I went to gaol and was separated from my family. Is there anything left? . . .
>
> I beg of you, Father, to put yourself in my situation and try to understand me. I'm sure you will feel compassion . . . and that if only you understand what I am suffering it would help so much to alleviate the pain . . .

He recited the parade of senior Opus Dei members who had come to see him in London and, later, while in prison in Frankfurt. They asked him to remain silent, but, he reflected, 'who really benefits if I keep silent . . . ? You can be assured, Father, that at no time did I wish to involve the institution and I believe that I have demonstrated that heroically . . .' But how was he rewarded for his silence? He claimed that the regional vicar for Germany had warned him, 'You could die tomorrow of a heart attack . . .' The letter continued:

> [M]y personal entourage is intimately linked to the Work: wife, children, brothers, brother-in-law and even my lawyer [Crispín de Vicente]. How many times I cried before them about my situation, only to receive a sepulchral silence and I noted that all of them looked at me with reserve, and finally I understood that they did not understand . . .

He then cited a letter he had received from Luis Valls, denying any involvement in his problems with the Banco de España. 'If someone deceived you, it was not me,' Valls claimed.

To insure that his letter got into the hands of the prelate general, Ruiz-Mateos had his eldest son, Zoilo, deliver it in person to the Villa Tevere. Ruiz-Mateos never received a reply. But one day Amadeo de Fuenmayor came from Rome to see him.

'How is your soul?' Fuenmayor asked. 'Have you been following the norms?' Ruiz-Mateos brushed off the question and wanted to know what had happened to his letter.

'What letter?' Don Amadeo replied. 'Do you know that you could die tonight? Have a heart attack? Or die of cancer?'

In November 1985, the German authorities agreed to Ruiz-Mateos's extradition and he was flown to Madrid by military jet. He spent the next seven weeks in a maximum security wing of Alcalá-Meco Prison, which gave him more time to reflect. He appeared at a remand hearing early in the New Year and escaped custody by donning a false moustache, wig and trenchcoat in the courthouse toilets, only to reappear a few days later at a well-publicized press conference to complain about the conditions of his detention. Thereafter, the red-faced authorities agreed to place him under house arrest.

By then he did not see why, on top of everything else, he should be charged with illegal export of capital when those who pressed him into doing it were not accused with him. And so he informed the Madrid magistrates that three national directors of Opus Dei – Alejandro Cantero, Juan Francisco Montuenga and Salvador Nacher – not only pressured him into making enormous contributions to Opus Dei but also had him transfer abroad the money for them. He said that he had diverted to Opus Dei abroad almost £40 million out of Rumasa's cash flow. His allegations were promptly denied by Opus Dei's national headquarters, though it was now admitted that Ruiz-Mateos had been an *Obra* member after all.

In May 1986 the directorate of Opus Dei in Spain issued an ulti-matum to Ruiz-Mateos, threatening to expel him if he did not withdraw his accusations against the three directors. But rather than back down, Ruiz-Mateos produced fifteen photocopies of trans-actions involving Rumasa transfers through Nordfinanz Bank, Zurich, for a 'River Invest' account at Union Bank of Switzerland in Geneva. While the state prosecutor's office puzzled over what to do next – the state prosecutor, Francisco Jiménez Lablanca, was an Opus Dei member – Opus Dei had the aplomb to deny that it was in any way connected with Ruiz-Mateos's business activities, and in fact countered the bad publicity with an eight-page interview with Tomás Gutiérrez Calzada, the regional vicar for Spain, in *Epoca*. The interview was headed 'The Enemies of Liberty Are Attacking Us'. 'Liberty' in this Opusian usage was interchangeable with 'Church'.

The 'enemies' of the Church, it turned out from the next line, was Ruiz-Mateos, because he was 'threatening us with public scandal.'[1]

Realizing he was now well outside of the road, Ruiz-Mateos began to fear for his life.[2] 'Not only am I aware that something could happen to me, I'm surprised it hasn't happened yet. Many Spaniards have died mysteriously for much less and history is plagued with crimes committed in the name of God,' he said in a 1986 interview.[3] Three months previously Michele Sindona had died in a Milan prison after drinking a poisoned cup of coffee, and the incident, like Calvi's murder, was fresh in his mind.

He was freed from house arrest after a first fraud charge was dropped for lack of evidence. But by then his Rumasa empire had been liquidated. The state patrimony office sold Banco Atlántico to an Arab group at a fire-sale price, prompting a Barcelona newspaper to claim the winding up of Rumasa had cost the Spanish taxpayer more than twice the £1,000 million that the public prosecutor alleged Ruiz-Mateos had defrauded from the state. Other charges were still pending.

By this point one had the impression that Felipe González would have been happy to see the Rumasa affair buried and forgotten. But Ruiz-Mateos was not going to let that happen. His counter-action against the government claimed £842 million in damages. He put across key points in his case by calling press conferences in front of government buildings and turning up dressed like a pirate or Superman. It was the only way, he said, to keep his case in the public eye.

In June 1989 he obtained temporary immunity from prosecution by being elected to the European parliament. Before he could celebrate his victory, however, he was rushed to hospital and had one metre of his intestines removed as a result of a mesenteric thrombosis. This type of thrombosis, usually fatal, can only result from a vascular obstruction, eating a venomous fish, a spider bite or poison. Ruiz-Mateos went to the Mayo Clinic for post-operatory convalescence. The doctors there considered it likely that he had been poisoned. On the basis of their report, back in Madrid he brought an attempted murder charge against persons unknown.

[1] *Epoca*, Madrid, 11 August 1986.
[2] 'Opus Dei in plot to kill me', *The Sunday Press*, Dublin, 25 May 1986.
[3] Phil Davison, 'A brush with death for "Superman",' *The Independent*, London, 1 June 1993.

Spain's Constitutional Court was asked to rule on the legality of the Rumasa expropriation law. It has eleven judges and a president, whose vote counts double. After lengthy consideration, six of the judges voted against the law's legitimacy; five were in favour. The president, Manuel García-Pelayo, then approaching 80 years of age, decided – after receiving a call from Felipe González – to vote with the minority. Two years later García-Pelayo retired to Venezuela. Before dying of a stroke, he stated that in rendering the Rumasa judgement the integrity of the Constitutional Court had been debased.

Ruiz-Mateos appealed the ruling to the European Court of Justice in Strasbourg which upheld his claim that the Spanish government had acted unconstitutionally and failed thereafter to accord him a fair trial. But the Strasbourg court said it was not competent to rule on his claim for compensation.

Twelve years after Rumasa's expropriation, Ruiz-Mateos still had not been given his day in court – a 'day' that some experts feared might last for several years and would be exceedingly embarrassing for Opus Dei. When asked who was responsible for his downfall, he replied, 'I think the same people who organized the *coup d'état* also organized the expropriation of Rumasa.'

But who were these 'same people'? I asked.

'*Los "Vallses"*,' he replied.[1]

---

[1] After Ruiz-Mateos published an open letter to Luis Valls in February 1995, the banker sent the following note to leading Spanish newspaper and magazine publishers:

> Ruiz-Mateos has been lying for five years. He has now forged something for the first time: a letter and a signature. Now he is no longer in disguise. Besides, he has started off on a new stage of informative terrorism. Never up to date have his suits and reports succeeded. His accusations are but plain lies. Yet he keeps on playing this game since he is aware that the defendant cannot materially prove he is not guilty. Thanks to such a *divertimento*, the man in the street becomes confused with [the] accusations on the one part, and the defendant's pleas of not guilty on the other. Ruiz-Mateos is just trying to arouse doubt. Could you make your editors keep a close eye so that they may not be caught unawares by those inventions that the overactive and wicked minds of Ruis-Mateos and his cronies work up?

27

BISHOP OF RUSADO

If Opus Dei is guilty, so is the entire Church.

William O'Connor

THE OUTLINE OF A PLOT WAS LAID OUT IN THE RECORDS OF Carboni's phone calls while shadowing Calvi's progress from Trieste to London, which were produced in evidence at the second inquest in London. Obtained from the hotels in which Carboni had stayed, they confirmed he had been in daily contact with Hilary Franco, Rome lawyer Wilfredo Vitalone and the main Vatican switchboard. There seemed no doubt that the orders had come from Rome.

The next breakthrough occurred when lawyers acting for the Calvi family stumbled across criminal proceedings in Trieste involving Silvano Vittor's attempt to sell agent 'Podgora' part of the contents of Calvi's missing briefcase. The undercover agent's real name was Eligio Paoli, and he worked in Trieste for the Guardia di Finanza, and probably SISMI. He was only one of at least four agents working for different Italian agencies who knew details of Calvi's flight. It was Podgora who learned that Sergio Vaccari had been hired to assist in Calvi's murder.

By then Gelli decided he had been behind bars long enough and succeeded in bribing a guard to smuggle him out of prison in a laundry hamper. Within a few days of his escape, a Spanish passport was waiting for him at the home of Ferdinando Mor, the Italian consul general in Geneva and a former P2 member.[1] Days later Gelli left for South America, stopping off in Madrid on the way. In Madrid it is said that he had talks with Gregorio López Bravo.[2]

Following Calvi's death, Francisco Pazienza had assured Clara that she could always turn for help to two of his closest friends in New York, Father Larry Zorza and Alfonso Bove. They were partners in a Brooklyn funeral parlour and Bove also owned two travel agencies in Manhattan. He called once or twice to ask Carlo about transferring funds from Sicily to Nassau. In the course of their conversations, Bove never sought to hide his Mafia connections.

Father Zorza, on the other hand, was required to resign as Archbishop Cheli's aide at the United Nations after his arrest for smuggling stolen paintings into the United States. On the way to his arraignment, he told a US Customs agent, 'I hope this doesn't take long. I have to say Mass at 5 o'clock.' Zorza then explained to the judge that it had all been a mistake. 'I did it sincerely to help somebody, and now I am terribly sorry . . . I have learned a lot.' He was given a three-year suspended sentence. Not long afterwards he was again arrested while trying to sell $40,000 worth of tickets for the Broadway hit 'Les Miserables' back to the box office from where they had been stolen. 'My friends never told me the full story about those tickets,' he assured the judge this time. While the judge deliberated on sentencing, Zorza was arrested a third time, on this occasion for his involvement with the second Pizza Connection that imported Sicilian heroin into the United States.

Pazienza himself was arrested in New York on an Italian warrant for his involvement in Banco Ambrosiano's fraudulent bankruptcy. The police nipped him as he was transmitting 'highly valuable information on terrorism and other matters' to American intelligence agents. A US Customs officer testified in his favour, claiming that before becoming involved with Banco Ambrosiano Pazienza had been one of his country's top intelligence operators and that an 'unidentified group of people' wanted him dead.

[1] Ferdinando Mor testimony before the Chamber of Deputies P2 Commission, Vol. CLVII, Doc. XXIII, No. 2 Ter 13, pp. 554–555.
[2] *Ibid.*, p. 555.

While being held in New York, Pazienza made some startling revelations that might have had something to do with the threats on his life. He alleged that the Ambrosiano monies advanced to the United Trading family had been intended for various causes of the Vatican. He added that one-third of the money was stolen by middlemen. The names of Gelli, Ortolani and Tassan Din were given in a Dublin affidavit filed by the liquidators of Banco Andino. Another third went into shoring up the IOR's control of Ambrosiano itself. The final third, he asserted, actually went into the Vatican's covert political causes. In each case he was talking about $450 million, more or less.

And what were those 'Vatican causes'? He mentioned Poland's Solidarity movement, of course, and the Irish Republican Army, as well as various groups or dictatorships opposing the spread of Marxism and Liberation Theology in Latin America.

In the reorganization of the Vatican finances that followed, a new five-member supervisory board of lay experts was created for the IOR. Its president was Angelo Caloia, head of the Mediocredito Lombardo bank. The vice-president was Philippe de Weck. The other three were Dr José Angel Sánchez Asiain, former chairman of Banco Bilbao, Thomas Pietzcker, a director of Deutsche Bank, and Thomas Macioce, an American businessman. The new managing director was Giovanni Bodio, also from the Mediocredito Lombardo.

Caloia and Bodio were both associated with Giuseppe Garofano, the onetime chairman of Montedison and top executive at Ferruzzi Finanziaria S.p.A., Italy's second largest private industrial group after Fiat. Garofano, an Opus Dei supernumerary, served with Caloia on the Vatican's Ethics and Finance Committee, until arrested in 1993 in connection with a $94 million political kickback scheme, a substantial amount of the money for which passed through Ferruzzi's account at the IOR, in the name of the 'Saint Serafino Foundation'. Sánchez Asiain was described by Ruiz-Mateos as one of the 'Vallses'. He was close to Alvaro del Portillo and a boyhood friend of Javier Echevarría, though Opus Dei denied he was a member.

The time for tidying up had come. With Calvi dead, Ruiz-Mateos discredited and Jaimes Berti out of circulation, the secret machine had triumphed. In Italy an interminable round of litigation linked to the Ambrosiano and P2 affairs (note, no 'IOR' affair), the likes of which the republic had never known, was getting under way and probably would not conclude before the end of the millennium. In Spain, all was quiet on the juridical front, but there were problems in the upper ranks of *Opus Homini*.

At the same time a restructuring of the Spanish banking industry was set in motion with a proposal by the country's fourth-rated Banco Bilbao to take over the first-rated Banesto. But Banesto's deputy chairman, López Bravo, backed by his friend and investment partner, Ricardo Tejero Magro, and another associate, steel magnate José María Aristrain Noain, successfully opposed the merger. Instead the smaller Bilbao merged with Banco Vizcaya to become Spain's largest commercial bank, under the name of Banco Bilbao-Vizcaya, while Banesto slipped to third position, just ahead of Banco Popular Español.

López Bravo, according to Professor Sainz Moreno, was going through a crisis of conscience. After more than thirty years as a loyal member, he wanted to leave Opus Dei. 'He had finally understood that Opus Dei was not a spiritual organization but a financial multi-national, and he was in profound conflict with Luis Valls,' the professor said. But López Bravo knew many of the Work's darkest secrets. In fact his deception with Opus Dei began soon after his meeting in Madrid with Licio Gelli at the end of August 1983, as the fugitive was on his way to Montevideo. What had Gelli told him? And who else had Gelli seen in Madrid? Both Swiss and French intelligence sources reported that he had met 'friends in Opus Dei'.[1]

Had Gelli spoken of the secrets contained in Calvi's missing brief-case? Or of the murder of Sergio Vaccari? Strangely, the Italian magistrates had been informed that a high-ranking member of Opus Dei from Spain was in London at the time of Calvi's death. In the same vein, it also would have been interesting to know whether López Bravo spoke about his concerns to his closest associates at the time, Ricardo Tejero and José María Aristrain. Tejero was not known to have any particular Opus Dei ties, but he was one of the few Spanish bankers who dared stand up to Luis Valls.

Whatever the reasons for his disillusionment, on 19 February

---

[1] Isabel Domon, 'L'arme qui aurait permis à Gelli de quitter la Suisse', *24 Heures*, Lausanne, 21 October 1983.

1985 López Bravo planned to go to Bilbao on business. He had a first-class reservation aboard the 9 a.m. Air Iberia flight. He arrived at the airport late, carrying only a briefcase, and was the last person to board the aircraft. The Boeing 727 took off from Madrid fifteen minutes behind schedule, with 148 passengers and crew aboard. As the flight made its approach in bad weather towards Bilbao's Sandica Airport it exploded in mid-air and crashed. Everyone aboard perished.

The first reports spoke of an ETA bomb. But the technical commission investigating the crash later found that the aircraft was off course and had struck the television antenna atop Mount Oiz. It was suggested in the press that the pilot had been seen drinking before takeoff. The crash was attributed to pilot error. The strange thing, commented Professor Sainz Moreno, was that of all the victims, López Bravo was the only one for whom no remains were found. 'Not even his Rolex watch,' he said.

Eight minutes after the Iberia flight had departed Madrid, Ricardo Tejero left his apartment and went down to the underground garage where he kept his car, directly opposite the Edificio Beatriz, home of Banco Popular Español's *Presidencia*. As he paused to unlock his car door, two men approached and shot him in the head. The assassins fled undetected. The police affirmed that it was the work of the Madrid Commando of ETA Militar. They apparently based their conclusion on the fact that the assassins had identified themselves to the doorman of the building by producing outdated badges of the Dirección General de Seguiridad. Similar badges had been found among ETA material seized by an anti-terrorist squad in France a few weeks before.

Barcelona's *La Vanguardia* was the only newspaper to link the two incidents. The *Vanguardia* reporter who covered the Tejero assassination walked across the street from the garage to the Banco Popular *Presidencia* hoping to elicit some comment from the bank's chairman. He was told that Luis Valls had left the bank's premises and returned to his apartment on the floor above. When finally the reporter reached the banker, Luis Valls told him, 'Everyone is completely shattered. It could have happened to me.' Luis Valls kept his two sports cars in the same garage.

The third partner in a Basque shipping venture that López Bravo and Tejero had structured was José María Aristrain. He and his wife were reportedly Opus Dei supernumeraries.[1] But Aristrain was said to have been expelled from the Work because he had left his wife and taken the glamorous Anja Lopez, wife of France's leading composer of operettas, as his mistress. Aristrain survived his two friends by a little more than a year.

He and Anja Lopez spent their last weekend together at the May 1986 Monte Carlo Grand Prix. They chartered a helicopter to take them back to Cannes-Mandelieu airport where Aristrain had his private aircraft waiting. The helicopter, a four-place Squirrel, rounded Cap d'Antibes into the Golfe de Juan and within sight of the Croisette spun out of the air, exploding upon impact with the water. There were no survivors. An investigation was immediately opened by the public prosecutor of Grasse. Eye-witness reports indicated that the crash was consistent with rear-rotor failure, causing the helicopter to spiral into the sea. The rear rotor is the easiest part on a Squirrel to sabotage. Some media reports suggested the ETA was responsible.

Six weeks before the Cannes accident, Roberto Calvi's black brief-case mysteriously reappeared in a Milan television studio. This media scoop was the assiduous work of the Sardinian property developer Flavio Carboni who was now portraying himself as a protector of Vatican interests. Carboni's brand of protection, how-ever, cost money – a lot of money. Of course he had very high legal bills as well.

After his arrest in Lugano, Carboni was extradited to Italy at the end of October 1982 and while the charges against him were investi-gated he was transferred to the prison in Parma. He remained under 'preventive custody' in Parma until August 1984, when his detention was changed to house arrest within the precincts of the city. He rented a suite at Parma's Maria Luigia Hotel and, outside of prison walls for the first time in two years, he lost no time in getting down to work.

In May 1984, Carboni's lawyer in Rome, Luigi D'Agostino, had laid the groundwork by contacting a Polish Jesuit who worked for the Vatican. D'Agostino asked Father Casimiro Przydatek to visit Carboni at Parma prison 'for pastoral reasons'. D'Agostino had

---

[1] Both *Golias* (No. 30, Summer 1992, p. 126) and *Tiempo* (No. 218, 20 July 1986, p. 32) iden-tify José María Aristrain Noain as an Opus Dei member.

excellent Vatican connections since he originally helped Carboni set up the meetings with Cardinal Palazzini and Monsignor Hilary Franco. It is interesting that, as far as is known, rather than unveiling his new mission to Hilary Franco, Carboni chose a Polish priest who spoke Italian haltingly.

Carboni told Father Casimiro that he was not in need of a confessor but wished to make known to the Church hierarchy that he had important documents to sell. Carboni did not state it quite that way, but the intent was the same. 'Carboni proposed himself as a defender of the Church. He said he wished to launch an international press campaign that would clear the Vatican's name in the Ambrosiano affair, because he knew where the Calvi documents were hidden. He assured me the documents proved the Vatican's innocence and he could arrange for their purchase,' the Polish priest said.[1]

Back in Rome, Father Casimiro spoke to Bishop Pavel Hnilica, who was his confessor and the real target of Carboni's strategy. Hnilica was portrayed as the Pope's closest adviser on Church affairs in East Europe. Originally from Trnava, in the heart of Catholic Slovakia, he had been ordained as a Jesuit in secret in 1950, at a time when the Czech authorities were actively persecuting priests as traitors. Paul VI elevated him in secret to the non-existent bishopric of Rusado (located in what was Mauritania Caesariensis, today Algeria). After moving to Rome during the height of the Cold War, Hnilica became the head of Pro Fratribus, which smuggled relief funds and bibles behind the Iron Curtain and assisted Catholic refugees.

Hnilica sent Father Virgilio Rotondi, who was also said to have the Pope's ear, to Parma to meet Carboni. Over the next two months Carboni and Rotondi outlined an international campaign, supposedly designed to gain worldwide sympathy for the Vatican, based upon selected documents from Calvi's briefcase. It was codenamed 'Operation S.C.I.V.' after the Italian initials for the Vatican city state. But Carboni wanted almost £20 million to set the operation in motion. He said the money was needed to acquire the Calvi documents, as well as to corrupt politicians, journalists, publishers and magistrates. Moreover, he was asking for £6 million up front to

[1] Almerighi *Ordinanza*, Section 6.2, p. 141.

cover 'anticipatory expenses and fees'.[1] Rotondi took the proposal back to Hnilica and they consulted their superiors.

The Bishop of Rusado's first contact with Carboni occurred in November 1984, after the terms of his house arrest were altered to permit him to return to his villa in Rome. Hnilica claimed he had received approval from his superiors to explore Carboni's proposal further. As a sign of good intentions, Carboni handed the bishop three letters written to Roberto Calvi in 1980 by the Turin black-mailer Luigi Cavallo, two of which were originals. He told Hnilica that he knew the whereabouts of other documents but to acquire them he needed cash.

While the Cavallo documents reflected poorly on Calvi, they were not material in proving the Vatican's innocence in the Ambrosiano affair. A further meeting was scheduled for early January 1985 with Father Rotondi. At this meeting Carboni provided copies of two let-ters written by Calvi – one on 30 May 1982 to Cardinal Palazzini, and the other on 6 June 1982 to Monsignor Hilary Franco – as well as a somewhat scissored document which began with the words, 'Monsignor Marcinkus Reproaches Me . . .'[2] For these three docu-ments, Father Rotondi gave Carboni a cheque for £190,000.[3]

To help convince Hnilica that the deal was legit, Carboni allied himself with an engaging underworld character by the name of Giulio Lena. Carboni told Hnilica that Lena had put up the money to recover part of the Calvi documents. Lena was one of Rome's more innovative narcotics dealers. But the Bishop of Rusado did not know this. On the contrary, he found Lena charming and cultured. To obtain a percentage of the action, Lena actually bought into Carboni's deal, paying him £600,000. This was a heavy burden for Lena, as his own financial situation was far from rosy.

In May 1985, Lena gave Hnilica an undated letter signed by Calvi with the name of the addressee removed, but certainly intended for the person who – like Beelzebub, prince of the underworld – he believed could cast out the demons. In it he criticized Gelli and Ortolani, calling them agents of the Devil. He said he was convinced that a collapse of the Ambrosiano would cause the collapse of the Vatican, adding:

[1] *Ibid.*, Section 9.3, p. 226.
[2] *Ibid.*, Section 11.2, p. 283.
[3] *Ibid.*, Section 11.2, p. 278n., and Section 11.4, p. 305n.

Since I am abandoned and betrayed by those I regarded as my most reliable allies, I cannot help but remember the operations I undertook on behalf of the representatives of St Peter's . . . I provided financing throughout Latin America for warships and other military equipment to be used to counter the subversive activities of well organized Communist forces. Thanks to these operations, the Church today can boast a new authority in countries like Argentina, Colombia, Peru and Nicaragua . . .

He ended the letter by saying:

I am tired, really tired, too tired . . . The limits of my long patience have been largely overreached . . . I insist that all the transactions concerning the political and economic expansion of the Church must be reimbursed; I must be repaid the $1,000 million that I furnished at the express wish of the Vatican in favour of Solidarity; I must be reimbursed the monies used to organize financial centres and political power in five South American countries, an amount totalling $175 million; that I be retained on conditions still to be determined as a financial consultant because of my work as a go-between in many East European and Latin American countries; my peace of mind must be restored . . . ; that Casaroli, Silvestrini, Marcinkus and Mennini leave me alone! I will attend to the other obligations on my own!!![1]

After receiving this document, Hnilica issued Carboni two cheques drawn on the IOR for a total of £61,000. In the meantime, as Lena's financial position was causing some concern Carboni suggested he ask Andreotti for a loan. There had already been some prior discussion between Carboni and his brother Andrea about whether some of the documents recovered from Calvi's briefcase should be sent directly to Palazzini and also, through Senator Claudio Vitalone, to Andreotti.[2]

Lena was told that a letter introducing him to Andreotti had been delivered by Sister Sandra Mennini, daughter of IOR director Dr Luigi Mennini. This she later denied. In any event, within a few days of the letter being drafted, Lena received a four-month loan of

---

[1] *Ibid.*, Section 1.3, pp. 11-14.
[2] *Ibid.*, Section 2.2, p. 29.

400 million lire (£168,000) at the Rome Savings Bank. To cover the loan, on 15 November 1985 Hnilica gave him two IOR cheques which the Bishop signed and left blank, with instructions to hold them until told for what amount they could be cashed. A few weeks later Lena was instructed to fill them out for 600 million lire (£252,000) each and present them for payment twenty days apart.[1]

Lena's joy was short-lived as both cheques were refused. When informed, the Bishop of Rusado was beside himself. He assured Carboni that the cheques were covered and that the IOR was blocking them for political reasons. Carboni accepted this, but demanded that Hnilica replace the cheques, which the bishop did, issuing at the end of March 1986 another twelve cheques drawn on different accounts at different banks for a total of £458,000. When later questioned, Hnilica said that Carboni had told him that 'the famous Calvi briefcase which he had already shown me' would be unveiled to the public on the SPOT TV show. 'Carboni told me that after the broadcast he would be obliged to hand over the briefcase to the Milan magistrates.'[2] SPOT was a magazine programme hosted by political commentator Enzo Biagi.

With the Pro Fratribus replacement cheques in hand, Carboni assured Hnilica that the SPOT transmission, to which he was committed, would be a triumph for the Vatican, as it proved that the Vatican had nothing to fear from the ghost of Roberto Calvi. On camera Enzo Biagi introduced the neo-Fascist Senator Giorgio Pisano to his viewers as the person who had uncovered the briefcase. Pisano, who had written a book entitled *The Calvi Murder*, claimed he had bought it for £20,000 in an after-dark encounter with two unknown individuals. The reason for his interest, he affirmed, was because he wished to put this key piece of evidence into the hands of the authorities. Carboni and Silvano Vittor were present on the set as well to attest that it was the same satchel they had seen in Calvi's possession in London. 'He held onto it like a drowning man clutches a life-saver,' Carboni delicately recalled.

What Calvi's Rome driver had described as a 'bulging, heavier-than-usual' bag appeared empty-cheeked before the cameras. As it was opened – allegedly for the first time since its disappearance – the

[1] *Ibid.*, section 12.1, p. 310.
[2] *Idem.*

cameras zoomed in to discover its contents. Predictably, it contained no notebook, no agenda, no address book, and no bunches of strong-box keys. It did contain Calvi's driving licence, a Nicaraguan passport in his name and the keys to the Calvi apartment in Milan and the house at Drezzo. It also contained eight documents – not exactly an arsenal of ammunition for God's Banker to use against Beelzebub's demons. The documents were the following:

1. Letter of Calvi to Cardinal Palazzini, dated 30 May 1982
2. Letter of Calvi to Mgr Hilary Franco, dated 6 June 1982
3. Letter of Carboni to Calvi, dated 6 June 1982
4. Undated note: 'Mgr Marcinkus reproaches me . . .'
5. Undated memorandum headed: 'Re: Conversation with Roberto Calvi, banker of the Ambrosiano and launderer of dirty money . . .'
6. Letter from Luigi Cavallo to Calvi, dated 9 July 1980, 'As you might imagine . . .'
7. Letter from Luigi Cavallo to Calvi, 'Among the tribes of Uganda . . .'
8. Letter from Luigi Cavallo to Calvi, 'A few days ago I was on holiday by the sea . . .'

The prying by state television into a dead man's briefcase for the financial gain and prestige of the show's promoters, with two of the principal conspirators in the banker's disappearance on the set, seemed the height of bad taste. But, after all, it was April Fools' Day 1986. The general public, meanwhile, was unaware of the dealings between Carboni and the Bishop of Rusado. These only came to light two years later following the forced boarding off the Italian coast of a yacht flying a Spanish royal standard. Customs police found on board the yacht 1,800 kilos of Lebanese hashish. The consignee was Dr Giulio Lena. In charge of the investigation was Rome examining magistrate Dr Mario Almerighi, who obtained a warrant to search Lena's villa in the Alban hills outside of Rome.

Almerighi not only turned up evidence of a major narcotics ring and also the counterfeiting of Central African Republic banknotes but he uncovered Lena's dealings with the Bishop of Rusado. This led the magistrate to search the Pro Fratribus offices. Hnilica at first denied everything, but the evidence was overwhelming. The documents uncovered at Pro Fratribus showed that Hnilica had acted with the knowledge of the highest Vatican authorities, even though the Vatican's financial support had been withdrawn in mid-stream, forcing him to turn instead to underworld loan sharks to raise the funds that Carboni demanded.

Among the evidence sequestered at Pro Fratribus was a SISMI file on Flavio Carboni, 12 Calvi documents, a letter from Hnilica to the Cardinal Secretary of State, Casaroli, explaining his negotiations with Carboni and cashed cheques totalling £1.5 million. But the most condemning item was Cardinal Casaroli's reply to Hnilica in which the Vatican's number-two disclosed he had informed the Pope of the latest developments. Casaroli's letter stated:

Most Reverend Excellency,

I have received and read with great attention your letter of 25 August concerning your efforts with others relative to the problems of the IOR.

Appreciating the importance and gravity of the situation which you set forth, I thought it important before replying to you to inform the Holy Father.

In his name I am able to convey to you the great pain and pre-occupation caused by what we learned from your letter. Neither the Holy Father nor the Holy See were aware of the activities that you summarily set forth.

It is first necessary to mention, in order to avoid all misunder-standing, that your efforts were undertaken without any order, authorization or approbation from the Holy See.

Moreover, one cannot deny that the notable economic situation into which the Holy See – seriously in deficit – has fallen would render it extremely difficult, in any case, to meet the request formulated by Your Excellency and to be thus relieved, the Holy See as well as your-self, of the burden of the immense indebtedness which you have revealed to us.

Concerning the causes and modalities of your efforts to shed full light on this apparent indebtedness it is, of course, necessary to esti-mate the legal consequences that your intervention, based on the best of intentions, could encounter.

By this letter I profit from these circumstances to confirm the dis-tinguished esteem which we hold for you before Our Lord.

It was a strange letter for the secretary of state to have written. It attempted to distance the Holy See from Hnilica's endeavours. 'We had no idea . . .' But was this posturing for the record, as the secretary of state was worried about the legal consequences of Hnilica's actions? It also inferred that Rotondi's initial cheque for £190,000 had directly come from the Vatican coffers. But more striking was that the letter contained no order to desist, only to proceed with extreme caution, without directly involving the Holy See, and with whatever resources Hnilica himself could mobilize – and all this with the 'distinguished esteem' of the two highest authorities of the Catholic Church. Casaroli's letter was therefore Hnilica's authorization to proceed, but at his own risk and peril.

Casaroli's letter begged a number of questions:

1. The 'esteem' of the Pope and the secretary of state for the results that Hnilica had already achieved made one wonder what other documents the Bishop of Rusado had acquired from Carboni. Almerighi was fairly certain that for the £1.5 million which the Vatican and Pro Fratribus had already paid, Carboni must have delivered more than Hnilica was willing to admit. 'Hnilica', Almerighi said privately, 'was not telling *all* the truth.'

2. What happened to the United Trading documents? The secret accounting kept by Calvi for the United Trading family was his first line of defence. The banker had made it clear that only with these documents could he defend himself against the allegations by Marcinkus that he had breached the IOR's trust. An up-to-date accounting for United Trading existed. Carlo Calvi had seen his father working on one. In his testimony, Carlo Calvi said, 'I recall in March 1982 seeing my father in his study at Drezzo working on a 1982 version of those accounts . . . These tabulations have never been found, neither in the house at Drezzo, nor the apartment in Milan, or anywhere else. My father always carried these accounts with him. We can suppose that they were with him in his briefcase during his last trip to London . . . I remember in fact having seen my father place those tabulations in his briefcase . . .'[1]

---

[1] *Ibid.*, section 12.2.2, p. 330.

3. What were the reasons for the IOR's sabotage of Hnilica's initiative? Was it because the IOR's directorate had done a separate deal with Carboni to get hold of the missing accounting documents it wanted? The absence of these documents suggest that the IOR – by then controlled by Opus Dei, if we can believe Calvi's last words – had indeed come to a separate arrangement.

4. The moral implications of the Vatican's involvement in these machinations were unsettling. Did the Holy See have such terrible things to hide that it needed to resort to Carboni's services? In Calvi's letter to the Pope of 5 June 1982 he referred to his role in financing arms shipments to Latin American dictatorships, providing financial support to Solidarity and financing other dissident groups in East Europe. Calvi would not have made this claim if he did not have the documentation at hand. What happened to those documents?

5. By leaving Hnilica out in the cold, did the Secretary of State realize he was pushing the Bishop of Rusado into dealing with underworld loan sharks? With Carboni threatening, on 17 March 1987 Pro Fratribus mandated Vittore Pascucci to raise a $10-million six-month loan. Pro Fratribus received an advance of £1.26 million from Pascucci at usurious rates. Pascucci was described by a secret Guardia di Finanza report as the 'dominus' behind Eurotrust Bank Limited of Crocus Hill, capital of the break-away island state of Anguilla, in the Lesser Antilles. Although not licensed to operate abroad, Eurotrust Bank had an office in Rome under the name of Eurotrust S.p.A. Eurotrust Bank was under investigation for alleged laundering of narcodollars on behalf of the Mafia.[1]

6. Most important of all, how much did the Pope know? Were his Opus Dei advisers, the men who handled – according to Calvi and others – the Vatican finances, keeping him in the dark? According to Hnilica, the Pope's mail was filtered by the Secretariat of State. Other sources have indicated the Pope was told only what his advisers wanted to tell him.

[1] Nucleo Centrale Polizia Tributaria della Guardia di Finanza, VII Gruppo, 1° Sezione, Report No. 1429, Rome, 12 October 1990.

Hoping to learn some of these answers, Almerighi subpoenaed Monsignor Hilary Franco. He had discovered that Franco's real (baptized) name was Ilario Carmine Franco, born not at all in New York but in Calabria. He questioned Franco for forty-five minutes before giving up. He found the Grade 1 Minor Official (Step 2) of the Roman Curia 'evasive and untruthful'.

Moreover, Opus Dei in Rome had put out another statement by then repeating that the Prelature 'has absolutely no connection with the Calvi affair' and that Hilary Franco 'has never had any contact with Opus Dei, nor with any of its members'. This seemed unlikely, if for no other reason than Franco had been on the staff of the Congregation of the Clergy, to which Alvaro del Portillo was a consultor and Opus Dei's Alberto Cosme do Amaral, Bishop of Leira, a member of the directorate.

The statement also trotted out the, by then, well-worn refrain that Don Mario Lantini, regional vicar for Italy, had 'invited' Calvi's widow by registered letter 'to justify, with full details, the basis on which she made her assertions' that her husband had dealings with Opus Dei. 'He has yet to receive a reply.'

It appeared that Carboni had used the contents of Calvi's briefcase at his convenience, removing from it scores of documents while leaving only those he supposed would further his plan, and inserting others that originally had not been there. It is difficult, for example, to understand why Calvi would carry with him on his last journey documents relating to his alleged treachery against Sindona. Nor would he have wanted to carry with him the document, 'Conversation with Roberto Calvi, banker of the Ambrosiano and launderer of dirty money'.

The presence of such documents in his briefcase when shown on TV logically suited the objectives of Carboni and those who found it expedient to maintain that Calvi was a man of low morals and no credibility – a man who, when he said, 'Opus Dei was in control of the IOR,' was not to be believed. 'The object was to dirty the image of Calvi . . . and make him appear as the number-one defrauder of the Vatican bank,' concluded Almerighi.[1]

Almerighi recommended that Carboni, Lena and Hnilica be sent for trial under article 648 of the criminal code. Article 648 concerns

---

[1] Almerighi *Ordinanza*, Section 12.2.2, p. 328.

the relatively minor offence of dealing in stolen goods, the maximum punishment for which, if found guilty, is a five-year prison sentence. It was not much, but it was a beginning. In March 1993, all three were found guilty, but the verdict was later overturned because of 'faulty legal procedure'.

28

MONEYBAGS THEOLOGY

If we're not guilty, we don't pay.
                                        Archbishop Paul Marcinkus

OPUS DEI IS A POOR FAMILY WITH MANY CHILDREN. FOR ANYONE WHO
has relations with the Prelature, this theme is repeated with the regu-
larity of monks reciting a mantra. Opus Dei has no money. It refuses
to publish a balance sheet, even though one is prepared every three
months by the *Consulta Técnica* for the prelate bishop and his inner
council. In 1992, Opus Dei was so deprived of cash that it requested
members invited to attend Escrivá de Balaguer's beatification gala
for a contribution, in addition to travel costs, of $3,000 each to cover
expenses.

One Opus Dei priest in Argentina who received an invitation
wished to attend the ceremony so badly that he asked his family in
Venezuela to advance the money for him. They sent a cheque to an
auxiliary society, as instructed. Overjoyed, the priest planned his
travel so that he could stop over in Caracas on his return to see
his parents. But the priest's superior said no, that would not be
appropriate, and the invitation was withdrawn. Needless to say, the
auxiliary society never returned the money, and the family, realizing
it would be a hassle to get it back, never bothered to ask. Even if one

took the lower estimate of pilgrims who attended the beatification proceedings, a quick calculation at $3,000 a head supposes that Opus Dei took in a minimum of $450 million on the extravaganza, audience with the Pope included.

This was a shining example of Opus Dei's special combination of Capitalist ethos and traditional religion, which it successfully deployed to counter Liberation Theology. The combination might be called Moneybags Theology. It offered strong affirmation that Opus Dei was not exclusively concerned with the salvation of souls but also with big-numbers finance.

Opus Dei is a reflection of its *modus operandi*, which provides the Prelature with the necessary resources to sustain its expansion. But above all Opus Dei's success was made possible by its unique juridical status. In spite of recent revisions, the Vatican's *Codex Iuris* remains based on the Gregorian canons of the thirteenth century, when commerce and banking were not highly developed, Johann Gutenberg had not yet invented movable type, and Machiavelli was still two hundred years away from publishing his handbook on human deceit as an instrument of government and diplomacy.

Opus Dei operates in an almost medieval vacuum. Because of the insufficiency of its institutions the Vatican is not equipped to regulate a worldwide conglomerate. Canon law was never designed to govern an organization whose roster of activities is unknown even to a majority of its members. The Vatican's lack of oversight gives Opus Dei unrestrained freedom; its incorporation as an enterprise of pontifical right provides it with the necessary standing to function in other jurisdictions without submitting the sum, or even certain of its parts, to the laws and regulations of those jurisdictions.

This renders Opus Dei as dangerous as it is unique. It is dangerous because it operates as if its members believe God is the chairman of the board, giving it the divine right to insert itself between the laws of nations and the canons of the Church. Rather than a floating diocese, Opus Dei functions like a compact, tenacious mercantile state, with its own councils, foreign policy, finance ministry and state religion, even its own territories – the dioceses entrusted to its care. All this might seem somewhat quixotic if not for the fact that Opus Dei members have been accused of fraud, designing sophisticated weapons systems, being involved in *coups d'état*, consorting with crooks and collaborating with military anti-insurgency operations.

Opus Dei is dangerous because it makes no disclosure, because it is confrontational and because it is an association that includes a high percentage of zealots. Opus Dei's inscribed numeraries, the inner circle, believe they are morally right, doctrinally unassailable and the guardians of the Christian conscience. Josemaría Escrivá de Balaguer promised Opus Dei members salvation if they followed his norms and customs. *Crónica,* the internal publication whose access is forbidden to mere supernumeraries, quotes from Ecclesiasticus (Apocrypha 44:20–21), applying to the Blessed Josemaría this passage: 'When tested he was found loyal. For this reason, God promised him with an oath that in his descendants the nation would be blessed . . .' The reference is, of course, to Abraham, but *Crónica* is not ashamed to interpret Biblical passages as prophecies of Opus Dei's own destiny. Novices are taught that Opus Dei is God's perfect instrument, sinless and incapable of error, and that they have been called to execute God's Plan and protect the Church.

At the evening reflection in Opus Dei residences the Father's words take precedence. They are more often quoted than the Gospel, which they interpret freely in any event. Thus, on one occasion the Father told his children, 'It is understandable that the Apostle should write: *"all things are yours, you are Christ's and Christ is God's"* (1 Corinthians 3:22–23). We have here an ascending movement which the Holy Spirit, infused in our hearts, wants to call forth from this world, upwards from the earth to the glory of the Lord.'[1]

Opus Dei is an 'ascending movement'; its members are Christ's soldiers, and everything they do is for the Father's glory. And so for the Father everything is permitted. John Roche stated that when he was at the University of Navarra in 1972, Opus Dei numeraries were still talking about the Matesa scandal, in which $180 million apparently volatilized without trace into the international monetary system, a masterpiece of financial dissimulation. Said Roche, 'Members could see nothing wrong in the misappropriation of this money. They thought it was clever. Opus Dei has very little social or business morality.'

Opus Dei is not above kidnapping members (Raimundo Panikkar), sequestrating them (María del Carmen Tapia, Gregorio

---

[1] Homily given by Josemaría Escrivá de Balaguer on the campus of the University of Navarra, 8 October 1967.

Ortega Prado), threatening priests it suspects of activities more political than pastoral (Giuliano Ferrari), bullying members who get out
of line or inciting them to lie (José María Ruiz-Mateos) and mis-
informing parents of young recruits about the true intentions of the
Work (Elizabeth Demichel). Why, therefore, should it be above using
other forms of *pillería*?

A Catholic International Press Agency editor said he had been
informed on 'high authority' – i.e., Bishop Pierre Mamie – that when
Opus Dei priests went knocking on episcopal doors to ask for letters
in favour of Escrivá de Balaguer's beatification they made it clear
that a positive response would engender Opus Dei's support – in the
form of a cheque – for a worthy diocesan project of the local bishop's
choice. Fully one-third of the world episcopacy had no hesitation in
providing such a letter.

Opus Dei is a poor family with many children. And yet Opus Dei
invested $300,000 to cover the costs of the beatification proceedings,
which the postulator general allowed was a bargain. Did this include,
one wonders, the contributions to the favourite charities of those
bishops who supported the cause of raising Escrivá de Balaguer to
the altars? Did it also include the costs of the medical assessment that
confirmed the miraculous cure of Sister Concepción Boullón Rubio?

Among the non-paying pilgrims in St Peter's Square for Escrivá de
Balaguer's beatification were Monsignor Wolfgang Haas, the newly
appointed Bishop of Coire, Switzerland's largest diocese, Monsignor
Kurt Krenn, whom John Paul II had named Bishop of Sankt Pölten,
not far from Vienna, and Monsignor Klaus Küng, Bishop of
Feldkirch, also in Austria. Küng is an Opus Dei prelate; Haas and
Krenn are so much in favour of the Prelature that they are thought
to be associate numeraries. In each case their episcopal appointment
provoked a rebellion among parishioners.

When in December 1986 John Paul II first named Klaus Küng,
Opus Dei's then regional vicar for Austria, to head the see of
Feldkirch, the public outcry was so fierce that the Vatican was forced
to suspend the appointment. The Pope waited another two years,
hoping that the storm had blown over, before reconfirming Küng's
elevation. But when his consecration was held, 5,000 parishioners
marched in silence through the streets of Vorarlberg. Nationwide
protests occurred in 1991 when Küng's friend and associate Kurt
Krenn, who claims he stands 'solidly behind Opus Dei', was named

auxiliary bishop of Vienna. Krenn immediately appointed Opus Dei's new regional vicar, Monsignor Ernst Burkhardt, as his chaplain of students.

Krenn was accused of refusing dialogue, of overspending on personal comforts and of maligning opponents. When asked on national television why he didn't resign, he replied: 'If I did, then God Himself would have to resign, as I only represent the truth that God gives us.' Fifteen thousand demonstrators for Krenn's removal gathered in Sankt Pölten, carrying banners that said, 'Resign, so God can stay', and 'We want a shepherd, not a dictator'. According to an opinion poll by the weekly *News,* an estimated 66 per cent of Austrian Catholics believed Krenn should go, and 82 per cent thought his arrogance damaged the Church's standing.[1]

Among New World dioceses none preoccupied John Paul II more than San Salvador. It was here that in 1975 an attempt was made to poison the Liberal Swiss priest Giuliano Ferrari. Five years later – on 24 March 1980 – Archbishop Oscar Romero was assassinated by the death squads of Colonel D'Abuisson. Then in December 1981, the parishioners of El Mozote were massacred. In 1989, six Jesuit priests at San Salvador's Catholic University were killed, and in June 1993 the Vicar of the Salvadoran armed forces, Bishop Joaquín Ramos Umana, was shot in the head.

The man picked to succeed Oscar Romero was Arturo Rivera Damas, a Salesian who served as apostolic administrator after Romero's death. In spite of opposition from the Conservatives, who felt he was too left-wing, Rivera Damas was elevated to archbishop in 1983. He was soon characterized by Conservatives as 'a troublesome bishop' because he spoke out for the Church against the abuses of the military. In November 1994, Rivera Damas was called to Rome as John Paul II was about to create thirty new cardinals. Some expected he would be among them. As it turned out, he was not: he suffered a massive heart attack and died instantly. In his last interview the day before, the 'troublesome bishop' let it be known that he had received death threats some months before and that they emanated from 'those groups known as the dinosaurs because they do not accept the peace agreement with the leftist guerrillas'.

When asked by his interviewer if Liberation Theology was dead,

---

[1] 'Church Liberals Protest', Associated Press, 22 June 1993.

Rivera Damas replied, 'The salvation brought by Our Lord includes the concept of liberation from all oppression. This fundamental vision of salvation must always be kept in mind. That is why I believe that this form of theology is not over but still has a lot to say.'[1] Ignoring diocesan wishes that Rivera Damas be replaced by his auxiliary, five months later John Paul II named Opus Dei's Fernando Saenz Lacalle, El Salvador's interim military Ordinary, as the new Archbishop of San Salvador.

Underworld dons and certain prelates within the Church, though guided by different theologies, frequently intermingled in a twilight zone where Christian morals and the ethics of power become blurred. We have already seen the case of Archbishop Cheli, co-president of the papal household's council of advisers, whose assistant at the UN was involved in the Pizza Connection affair and who laundered money on the side, while Cheli himself associated with secret service officials. In fact the Calvi case in its *ensemble* was a good example of this intermingling of power, priests and organized crime. High officials inside the Vatican, it is now known, were informed of the conspiracy against Calvi and still continued to deal with the likes of Flavio Carboni.

The Theology of Organized Crime was all that Francesco Marino Mannoia had ever been taught. The Sacraments of the Black Hand he knew well. He also knew some chemistry, for he was very good at distilling opium base into heroin. He was one of the persons arrested in the first Pizza Connection case in New York in 1985. The Pizza Connection was a Mafia ring that sold Sicilian heroin through pizza shops in the US. Rather than spend the rest of his life in prison, Mannoia turned state's evidence. In July 1991, five Italian magistrates flew to New York to hear what he had to say.

According to Mannoia, the Mafia's 'finance minister' Pippo Calò was told that Calvi had become 'unreliable'. Calò handled liaison between the Mafia and the Camorra, and he was well acquainted with Carboni and Gelli. From that moment the conspiracy coalesced around three men. Gelli was the brains; Carboni the co-ordinator; and Calò provided the brawn. For strategic reasons, Calò felt that London would be safer than Italy for what they had in mind. He ordered Francesco Di Carlo to carry out the task.

---

[1] Andrea Tornielli, 'A Troublesome Bishop', *30 Giorni*, No. 1, 1995.

To his neighbours in Woking, Surrey, Frank Di Carlo seemed a mild-mannered businessman who commuted daily into London where he ran a small hotel, travel agency and money changing operation near King's Cross. In Sicily, however, he was known as the 'Butcher of Altofonte'. And to Her Majesty's Customs inspectors he represented the biggest prize of 'Operation Devotion', which in May 1985 netted 60 kilograms of pure heroin on the Southampton Docks. In March 1987, Di Carlo was sentenced to twenty-five years in prison. Seated in the public gallery during the proceedings was Pippo Bellinghieri, one of Di Carlo's runners and a suspect in the unsolved Sergio Vaccari murder.

After Mannoia's disclosures, Detective Superintendent White of the City of London Police went to see Di Carlo in prison. Di Carlo said he had an iron-clad alibi for the night of Calvi's murder but that he would tell everything he knew about the banker's death if transferred to an Italian prison. A request was made through proper channels. The Italian prison authorities, however, were not interested.

As a result of Mannoia's story Carlo Calvi and his mother decided to hire an international firm of private detectives to investigate further. In New York, Carlo was introduced to Steven Rucker, a senior managing director of Kroll Associates Incorporated, which describes itself as 'a corporate investigation and consulting firm with over 200 employees and nine offices at worldwide locations'. Kroll requested a $1 million deposit. He told Calvi, 'We have a small army of informers walking the streets of London who could be working for you.' Calvi blinked, and reached for his cheque book. Kroll assigned the investigations to Jeffrey M. Katz, a former US Air Force intelligence sergeant. Katz assigned a team of researchers to the project and, ten years after the crime, discovered that evidence in the hands of the police appeared to have been disposed of or mislaid.

Katz assumed that the weak link in the Calvi case was Silvano Vittor. Kroll's informers reported that Vittor was engaged in smuggling arms into Croatia, a country at the edge of the Spiritual Curtain and one of the newest centres of Opus Dei activity. Katz also discovered in the files of Calvi's solicitors a copy of a Swiss hotel registration slip supposedly filled out by Hans Albert Kunz when he checked into the Holiday Inn at Zurich airport to meet with Carboni on 20 June 1982, two days after the Calvi murder.

Hans Albert Kunz had never been extensively interviewed by the police. He knew Ernesto Diotallevi of the Banda della Magliana was believed to do business with arms traffickers in association with Licio Gelli, and to be a consultant to Carboni's company, Sofint, in Rome. His wife had given Anna Calvi, when waiting in Zurich for her father, £14,500 so that she could fly to Washington on the morning that Calvi was found dead.

Although the registration slip was in his name, it obviously had been filled out by someone else. Kunz was born on 14 February 1923. The slip showed a date of birth of 10 December 1923. The signature was not Kunz's. And it gave a London address when Kunz lived on the outskirts of Geneva. The address was 80 Grove Park Road, London SE 9. When Katz checked it out, the family who lived at that address had never heard of a Hans Albert Kunz. Katz discovered another Grove Park Road at Strand-on-the-Green, Chiswick. The house numbers, however, ended at 78. Where 80 should have been was a slipway to the Thames. Strand-on-the-Green was a twenty-minute drive from the Chelsea Cloisters. Katz took a boat from Chiswick downriver under tidal conditions similar to the night of 17 June 1982. Fighting the tide, it took two hours. Calvi was seen leaving the Chelsea Cloisters at about 10 p.m. Allowing an hour for the drive to Chiswick and his transfer to a boat, this would have put him on the scaffolding at Blackfriars within the time frame suggested by the coroner for his death.

Kroll Associates hired Dr Angela Gallop, a former head of the Home Office's Forensic Science Laboratory, to conduct a forensic review of the existing evidence. She was assisted by her associate, Dr Clive Candy, who for many years had been the head scientist at the Metropolitan Police Forensic Science Laboratory. They concluded: 'The proposition that Roberto Calvi was murdered seems inescapable.'

A scientific examination of Calvi's clothing and shoes showed that he could not have walked on the scaffolding, as surmised by the police. This implied that he had been brought there in a boat and, already dead, strung up on the scaffolding. The staining on the back of his clothing suggested he had been laid out on a damp surface before being hung from the scaffolding. Dr Gallop also pointed out that the pathologist who performed the first autopsy had 'failed to notice the scratches on Calvi's cheeks'. When these were examined at a second autopsy in Milan, Professor Fornari said they had been made before death, perhaps by the fingernails of the person who slipped the noose rapidly over Calvi's head. Crucial police evidence was unavailable – the microscopic samples of green paint scraped from the soles of Calvi's shoes. The only paint trace that remained on the shoes those ten years later was not of the same colour as the narrow green band on some of the scaffold poles. In any event, these poles were mostly painted orange and were rusty, which showed no traces on his shoes. From where, then, had the green paint come? The answer will never be known as the remaining traces are too small to be adequately analysed.

The Forensic Access Scientific Investigation into the Death of Roberto Calvi cost the Calvis more than £150,000. It told them that the City of London police had conducted "no proper scientific examination" at the death scene itself. But more to the point, it diplomatically ridiculed the police theory that Calvi, a 62-year-old physically unfit banker taking medication for vertigo had on a suicidal urge discarded his belt and necktie – never found – thrown away the key to his hotel room, shaved off his moustache in the middle of the night, filled his pockets with 5.4 kilograms of rocks and stuffed a building brick in the crotch of his pants which supposedly he had picked up on a nearby building site, walked more than 100 metres along Paul's Walk, climbed over a high parapet, descended some three metres on a metal ladder towards a dark and swirling river, jumped a metre-wide gap onto an unstable scaffolding, shimmied along it to the far end, took out three metres of marine rope which he happened to have in his pocket, tied a noose around his neck, slipped the other end of the rope through an eyelet in one of the pole fasteners, then launched himself into the river to die in a most demeaning manner.

To insist that Roberto Calvi had not been murdered defied logic. It also demonstrated a lack of familiarity with the sign language of the Mafia and Italian Freemasonry. Stones in a dead man's pockets is a warning to others that stolen money produces a barren return. A brick in the crotch is the reward for unfaithfulness. The Rome magistrates had tried to locate the sultry Neyde Toscano, a forty-one-year-old Brazilian who was said to have been Calvi's Rome mistress. She was known to have had ties with the Banda della Magliana and the Camorra, having been the former mistress of a

Neapolitan underworld boss, Nunzio Guida. But Roberto Calvi was not known as a man who threw money away on entertaining courtesans in Rome's nightclubs. It was possible that the beautiful Miss Toscano had been placed in his arms, or even his bed, with the intention of later blackmailing him, but the police never were able to question her. She disappeared and has never been found.

Carlo and his mother sent a copy of the Forensic Access report to the British home secretary, then Kenneth Clarke. In their covering letter they noted that recent revelations affecting the case indicated a renewed police effort might achieve an important breakthrough. 'We believe that if further official inquiries are now made . . . it will be possible to gather enough admissible evidence, even after ten years, to bring the killers to justice.'

Three weeks later the home secretary replied by letter that he had 'no authority to intervene in these matters'. Carlo could not believe Kenneth Clarke's response. If the home secretary had no authority to intervene in police matters, then who did?[1]

Opus Dei has 80,000 members in the world. According to Professor Sainz Moreno, when operating its strategy of discretion in the secular world, it relies upon 'men of trust'. That was the praxis of its Moneybags Theology. In Italy, Opus Dei's 'men of trust' were said to include Giuliano Andreotti, Flaminio Piccoli and Silvio Berlusconi. Cavalière Berlusconi's publishing house Mondadori – Italy's largest – put out a big print-run edition of *The Way*, his

---

[1] After more than ten years battling to uncover the truth, the Calvi family was finally forced to give up for lack of money. Their last setback came when Kroll Associates, claiming its investigators were on the edge of an important breakthrough, stopped work on the case for nonpayment of $3,119,972.52 in back fees and expenses.

A year later Kroll sued the Calvis in New York for breach of contract. Kroll requested the court hearings be held *in camera* due to the 'highly sensitive' nature of the investigations, alleging that Carlo Calvi's disclosures to the author had endangered the life of a confidential source – identified in the proceedings as 'Mr X, a UK citizen'. Kroll further asked that the Calvis be enjoined from discussing the investigation or litigation with 'any journalists or other persons associated with the print, television, film, radio or broadcast media, without Kroll's prior consent'. The judge accepted both motions. The judge was not informed, however, that 'Mr X' had at all times spoken freely with the author and had even asked that his photograph, which he thoughtfully supplied, appear in the book.

In August 1995, the prestigious New York law firm of Cadwalader, Wickersham & Taft, representing the Calvi family, asked to withdraw from the proceedings. This was granted. The Calvis were requested to appoint new lawyers to represent them. When they failed to respond, Kroll Associates asked for a default judgement in the amount of $3.8 million. This was accorded in May 1996.

When contacted immediately afterwards, Cadwalader's Grant B. Hering refused to discuss why he and the firm had withdrawn, citing client-attorney confidentiality.

television networks gave prime-time transmission to Opus Dei documentaries and Berlusconi himself was warmly solicited for funds, among them a £20,000 contribution in 1994 for an Opus Dei theological institute for women.

Before Berlusconi became prime minister, Giulio Andreotti had been the Work's strongest political supporter. He prided himself on being the first person to petition Paul VI to have Escrivá de Balaguer raised to sainthood. That was in 1975, the year of the Founder's death. Andreotti has said that in his political career spanning four decades he never betrayed his Christian principles. He kept a copy of *The Way* on his bedside table and he attended Opus Dei's main retreat centre in Italy. He has been friends with three Popes – Pius XII, Paul VI and John Paul II – all of whom helped promote his career. He was a minister in thirty Italian governments and seven times prime minister. Andreotti's influence was well known. The Socialist Party leader Bettino Craxi, his arch-opponent in the Chamber of Deputies, dubbed Andreotti the Beelzebub of Italian politics.

Andreotti was certainly Beelzebub as far as Clara Calvi was concerned. The years of stress unbroken, she had developed Parkinson's Disease and was almost unable to walk. Her hands contorted by the effects of the illness, she spent much of each day seated on one of the two giant sofas in her living room, reading the Italian press and digesting every piece of material that in any way related to her husband's death. She had surrounded herself with mementoes of happier times: photos of her and Roberto, and the children, on holidays by the sea, at dinner parties in Milan, Christmas at Drezzo. Her mind never seemed to rest.

The manipulation of political power in Italy through graft and corruption, necessitating a parallel economy dominated by intrigue and double bookkeeping, left the door open for organized criminals to become the partners of politicians in the administrative machinery of the State. For Carlo Calvi, Banco Ambrosiano's demise and his father's death was the first institutionalized manifestation of this trend. If his father had been able to defy the 'occult forces' rather than being consumed by them, Carlo wondered whether the 'Clean Hands' investigations that swept Italy in the early 1990s might not have been brought on ten years earlier.

Certainly it appeared that Andreotti was well acquainted with Italy's *bustarella* (bribes) syndrome. The 'Clean Hands' investigations uncovered allegations that he had received $1 million to engineer a cover-up of a major loan scam involving Italy's savings loan federation. Two things happened. Mino Pecorelli, publisher of the Rome scandal sheet *OP*, informed Andreotti he had proof that the payment was laundered through Carboni's Sofint company and he intended to disclose it in *OP*'s next issue. He never got the chance. On the evening of 20 March 1979 he was found behind the wheel of his car, shot four times in the head.

In 1994 Andreotti's friend and former foreign trade minister, Claudio Vitalone, brother of the lawyer Wilfredo with whom Carboni had been in almost hourly phone contact while shadowing Calvi's flight to London, was charged with ordering Pecorelli's slaying. Accused with him were Mafia bosses Gaetano Badalamenti and Pippo Calò. Andreotti, friend of three popes who claimed never in his long career of public service to have forsaken his Catholic principles, joined them at trial, accused of issuing the contract against Pecorelli. Magistrates in Palermo had already stunned the world by accusing 'Uncle Giulio' of 'protecting, assisting and consorting with the Cosa Nostra' in return for electioneering support that helped maintain the Christian Democrat Party and Andreotti at the apex of Italian political life for more than three decades.

'This is really a blasphemy that has to be erased,' Andreotti told reporters.

Other blasphemies requiring attention included those made by Swiss banker Jurg Heer. He had been credit manager at Rothschild Bank in Zurich, responsible for managing the Bellatrix account until fired by his superiors. Put out by his rough handling, Heer lifted the lid on Pandora's box. He claimed that in 1982 he had received a phone call from Licio Gelli requesting him to fill a suitcase with $5 million in bank notes and hand it over to two men who arrived at the bank in an armour-plated Mercedes. Heer said he later asked for an explanation. 'The money was for the killers of Calvi,' he was told.

Rothschild Bank, it should be remembered, was where $150 million transferred from Banco Ambrosiano's offshore network to Bellatrix, a member of the United Trading family, became side-tracked. Less than 20 per cent of that money was recovered by the Ambrosiano liquidators. Heer's revelation raised an interesting question: were Calvi's killers paid with monies belonging to United Trading?

Heer was questioned by an examining magistrate in Zurich and then disappeared. He was last seen in Madrid around Christmas 1992. He purchased an air ticket for Thailand, where charges against his credit card ended a few months later. Heer's disclosure raised considerable interest among investigators working on the Calvi case. They would like to interview the banker. But there is real concern that he may no longer be alive.

As Ruiz-Mateos had said in London more than ten years before, this was only the beginning of a very long film. The conviction against Carboni, Lena and Hnilica in the Calvi briefcase trial was overturned because of 'faulty legal procedure'. By then Lena, like Toscano and Heer, had gone missing and also was feared dead. Almerighi had been hoping to use all three of them as material witnesses in the newly reopened Calvi murder enquiry. Almerighi notified Gelli, Carboni, Pippo Calò and Frank Di Carlo that they were official suspects, but he was totally dumbfounded when informed that Di Carlo's transfer to an Italian penitentiary was refused by the Italian Prisons Authority for 'not serving the cause of justice'.

'There are still people in this country who do not want the killers of Roberto Calvi brought to justice,' Almerighi commented.[1]

But it was Pazienza who pointed out one of the strangest anomalies. He maintained that in 1982, when the Bank of Italy commissioners moved in, Banco Ambrosiano was not bankrupt. 'Banco Ambrosiano may have had liquidity problems, but there was no "black hole". That was bullshit! When placed in liquidation Ambrosiano was still a viable bank. How could a bank that supposedly was bankrupt show a profit one year later of $300 million?' he asked.

Gelli, meanwhile, had given himself up to the Swiss authorities on condition that he be extradited forthwith to Italy, where more than five years later all judgements against him remained under appeal. His return to Italy and Andreotti's eclipse marked the passing of an era. The generation of Cold Warriors to which they belonged had

---

[1] Within weeks of Romano Prodi's election as Italy's new centre-left premier, the Italian Prisons Authority reversed itself. In June 1996 Francesco Di Carlo was extradited to Italy and began co-operating with the Rome magistrates.

become obsolete and was no longer needed. The Occident was facing a new constellation of forces that required new minds and different faces. As the end of the second millennium approached the words of André Malraux seemed more prescient than ever: 'The twenty-first century will be a century of religion or it will be not at all.'

PART SEVEN

JUST WAR

29

THE POLISH OPERATION

A militia old like the gospel and like the gospel new to arise with the divine command to propagate Christian perfection among people of all social classes.

Crónica VIII, 1959

AS FAR AS IS KNOWN, POLAND WAS OPUS DEI'S FIRST DEEP-PENETRATION operation. It got under way as Banco Ambrosiano in Milan was beginning to develop its offshore network and increased in momentum after United Trading was formed. It reflected to perfection Escrivá de Balaguer's affirmation that Opus Dei was a 'disorganized organization'. By that he did not mean an unstructured organization, for with its praxis manuals, norms and customs, constitutions and codex, Opus Dei was almost stiflingly structured. But in reacting to threats against the Church it remained flexible, mobile, alert.

The architect of Opus Dei's penetration into Eastern Europe was said to have been Laureano López Rodó, who served as Spanish ambassador to Vienna from 1972 to 1974. His strategy predated the founding of *Solidarnosc*, the Polish free trade union, by seven or eight years. Because of it, the Austrian capital became the most frequently used gateway into Eastern Europe for Opus Dei's *milites Christi*, and still today Opus Dei maintains an active presence in

Vienna, overseen by Monsignor Juan Bautista Torello, its leading psychologist, working alongside political scientist Martin Kastner, member of a wealthy mercantile family, and Dr Ricardo Estarriol Sesera, a foreign correspondent for Barcelona's *La Vanguardia* newspaper. Estarriol and Kastner actively attempted to recruit members of the Polish community in exile who gravitated around the Institute for Human Sciences, set up during López Rodó's ambassadorship by two of Karol Wojtyla's closest friends from Cracow, Krzysztof Michalski and Father Josef Tischner. Wojtyla himself made frequent visits to the Austrian capital during the mid-1970s.

Vienna was also well known to Pavel Hnilica, Bishop of Rusado, as it was the western terminus of Pro Fratribus's bible-smuggling route into southern Poland. Hnilica, who in the 1980s enjoyed the Pope's confidence, became to this extent a rival of Opus Dei, when the Prelature began extending its influence inside the papal administration. According to some Vatican-watchers, this may have led to Hnilica's entanglement and later entrapment in Flavio Carboni's devious Operation S.C.I.V.

While in the 1960s Poland was nowhere to be seen on Opus Dei's political horizons, by the 1970s and 1980s it loomed large. When John Paul II made his first papal visit to Poland in June 1979 for the 900th anniversary of the martyrdom of St Stanislaus – Cracow's first bishop – he was accompanied by an Opus Dei staff, including his personal secretary, Father Stanislaw Dziwisz. *Vanguardia* correspondent Estarriol was also in the papal entourage, reporting the delirious greeting that more than a million Poles gave the Pope when he arrived there.

Opus Dei's *milites Christi* brought to Poland the financial means to form a Catholic underground that would act, if not in outright defiance of, at least in parallel to the government. Its objectives were twofold: to create a strong Catholic press; and to put in place a network of intellectuals and professionals – few would become actual members, but all were considered doctrinally sound – to lead a national revival. One of these was a young electrician at the state-owned Lenin shipyards in Gdansk, Lech Walesa. But there were others and out of their efforts grew KOR, a Workers' Defence Committee headed by Jacek Kurón. It was provided with a fund, financed by anonymous grants from the West, to assist families of workers imprisoned or thrown out of their jobs by the government.

A key person in transmitting their needs to Rome was Estarriol.

By the end of the 1970s, Poland was no longer able to service its $14,000 million bank debt to the West and the economy ground to a virtual standstill. In August 1980 the government ended food subsidies, which raised prices overnight by 40 per cent. In Gdansk, workers occupied the shipyards and formed an illegal strikers' committee that was baptized *Solidarnosc*. Support for *Solidarnosc* spread across the country, forcing the government to negotiate the 21-point Gdansk Agreement. Estarriol was there, filing detailed despatches throughout the three-week crisis. He was the first informed when the government accepted to negotiate with *Solidarnosc*. When the negotiations were interrupted five days later, his paper *La Vanguardia* ran an exclusive interview with Walesa, and at the end of that August Estarriol reported that the authorities had caved in to the workers' demands. He also revealed that the Church under Cardinal Wyzynski had played a critical role in the final phase of negotiations.

The concessions won in Gdansk for all Polish workers included the right to form free trade unions, elect their own representatives, strike in support of grievances and publish union newspapers free of government control. *Solidarnosc* immediately planned to launch its own national weekly. But *Solidarnosc* had no funds, and certainly no printing plant. The capital to buy plant, newsprint and pay salaries had to come from somewhere. Again, Estarriol was said to have relayed *Solidarnosc*'s requirements to Rome.

The Solidarity movement revolutionized Polish politics. But, explained Walesa, 'nothing would have been possible without the election of Papa Wojtyla, his travel to Poland and the continuous, obstinate and smart work of the Church. Without the Church nothing could have happened.'[1] Jerzy Turowicz, who became editor of the Catholic weekly *Tygodnik Powscechny*, one of the country's most influential publications, said that because of John Paul II's visit, 'for the first time the Polish people felt strong.'

When a distraught Walesa visited Rome in January 1981 Estarriol came with him. The Solidarity rank and file was out of control, refusing to obey the central directorate and the Soviets were concerned. Estarriol reported weeks before that Leonid Brezhnev had called a secret meeting of the Warsaw Pact in Moscow. Walesa

---

[1] Oriana Fallaci, interview with Lech Walesa, Warsaw, 23–24 February 1981.

feared a Soviet move to crush *Solidarnosc*. He was said to have met senior Opus Central and CIA strategists in Rome. Three weeks later – on 9 February 1981 – General Wojciech Jaruzelski assumed control in Warsaw and prepared to tear up the Gdansk Agreement. Solidarity planned a nationwide protest strike that threatened to turn into general insurrection. Brezhnev responded by ordering a Soviet invasion. When the Pope was informed, he called the Kremlin and told Brezhnev that the strike would be shelved if he called off the invasion. A report by 'Department 20' of the East German Ministry of Public Security recorded that 'within an hour, Brezhnev informed the Pope there would be no military intervention'. John Paul II called Cardinal Wyszynski, then gravely ill. Wyszynski summoned Walesa to his bedside and told him he must obey the Pope's order. Without consulting Solidarity's directorate, Walesa cancelled the strike. And so John Paul II was said to have saved Poland from Soviet invasion.[1]

The mood at factories throughout the country turned grim. Uncertain whether they would be able to feed their families or heat their homes during the winter, workers responded by organizing factory sit-ins. With the situation deteriorating, in December 1981 Jaruzelski imposed martial law. Responding to pressure from Moscow, he was determined to force the country back to work and, to show he meant business, overnight he arrested 5,000 Solidarity activists.

Financing Solidarity had initially been undertaken by United Trading through the Banco Ambrosiano's offshore network. But by now it meant in effect subsidizing the entire Polish economy. Opus Dei, therefore, turned to Washington. At about this time the Work was said to be seeking to draw closer to President Reagan's Director of Central Intelligence, William J. Casey. A street-smart Irish-American Catholic from Queens, Casey was one of Reagan's most heeded foreign policy advisers. He had made his mark during the Second World War with the OSS, parachuting agents into Germany. After the war he entered private law practice in New York and had made his first million dollars on Wall Street by the age of 40. This qualified him to become Nixon's head of the Securities & Exchange

---

[1] Jonathan Luxmoore, 'The Pope Saved Poland from Soviet Invasion', *The Tablet*, London, 15 October 1994.

Commission. Under Reagan, Casey was called upon to co-ordinate Washington's response to the Polish crisis.

Casey's first reaction was to fly to Rome and consult the Pope. He and two other members of Reagan's inner team, Alexander Haig and Vernon Walters, were Knights of the Sovereign Order of Malta, which gave them instant and confidential access to the papal apartments. But when the Polish crisis broke, Casey's moral fitness to head the CIA was being questioned by the Senate Select Committee on Intelligence and he was unable to leave Washington. He despatched General Walters in his stead. Over the next five months Walters made a dozen visits to the Vatican.

The Walters shuttle prepared the way for a meeting between Reagan and John Paul II that took place on 7 June 1982. The US president agreed to underwrite the Vatican's plan for keeping Solidarity alive. Through Opus Dei, the Church had already spent many millions on the Solidarity cause – $1,000 million, if you believe Calvi; something less than $450 million, according to Pazienza; or $40 million according to the left-wing American magazine *Mother Jones*.[1] While President and Pope reviewed the Polish situation, in another corner of the papal apartments Reagan's secretary of state Alexander Haig and national security adviser William Clark were conferring with Cardinal Casaroli and Archbishop Silvestrini on Eastern Europe and the Middle East.

According to Vatican sources, Casey had also intended to attend but at the last moment was confronted with a triple intelligence crisis and had to cancel. On 6 June 1982, Israel invaded Lebanon. The following day, opposition leader Hissan Habré seized power in Chad, successfully concluding a long-planned CIA operation that ended Qaddafi's influence there. Also the CIA expected Iran to launch an offensive against Baghdad within days that it feared would result in the setting up of a fundamentalist Shiite state in southern Iraq. All three emergencies highlighted the US administration's concern with radical Islam. Consequently, the discussions with Casaroli and Silvestrini focused mainly on how to contain the Islamic threat, though this was never reported.

In addition to the informal agreement over Poland, Reagan's

[1] Reference to $40 million is made by Martin A. Lee in 'Their Will Be Done', an article appearing in *Mother Jones*, San Francisco, July 1983.

Vatican meeting was important for two other reasons. First, it came about as a result of Opus Dei's growing influence both in Washington and on a policy level inside the Vatican. Opus Dei had played a determining role in shaping the Vatican's reaction on Poland, giving rise to almost Byzantine rivalry and jealousy between Portillo and Casaroli. But the second key point that resulted from the meeting was the realization that while the Pope's attention remained fixed on Poland the emphasis of American foreign policy had tilted towards dealing with radical Islam. To be sure, the last spasms of Soviet imperialism – the Kremlin's threat to send the Red Army into Poland and its invasion of Afghanistan – preoccupied the Reaganites, but they were more concerned with security of the Middle Eastern oilfields should Islamic extremists take over the region.

A Reagan White House aide at the time was Dr Carl A. Anderson, who served as liaison officer for special interest groups – e.g., Opus Dei – at the White House. Anderson was an Opus Dei member and as such his apostolate was to attract others in his milieu into the Work. But he was unlikely to have been the only one working inside the Reagan administration, though Opus Dei refuses to provide information on such matters. Nevertheless, with Casey running the CIA, the agency took up the war against Liberation Theology in Latin America like never before. And as Reagan's senior East Europe and Middle Eastern expert, Casey rarely undertook a trip to Europe or the Middle East without first stopping in Rome to exchange views with the Pope.[1]

The change in foreign policy focus was brought on by the downfall of Shah Mohammad Reza Pahlavi, the US's principal ally in the Persian Gulf, through which 70 per cent of the West's oil passes. The Shah's ouster by Ayatollah Ruhollah Khomeini, who like the Pope had no armoured divisions, no squadrons of F-4 Phantoms, and no battle fleet, marked a dramatic turning for modern Islam. As long as the Cold War raged, Communism had been the common enemy of the West and most political commentators refused to take the word of the Prophet all that seriously. But they were wrong; a second confirmation of radical Islam's new assertiveness came two years

---

[1] Carl Bernstein, 'Holy Alliance', *Time*, 24 February 1992, and *National Catholic Reporter*, 28 February 1992.

later when another group of fundamentalists, inspired by the same Ayatollah Khomeini, assassinated Egyptian president Anwar Sadat and very nearly succeeded in transforming America's second major ally in the region into an Islamic theocracy hostile to the West. This prompted a reformulation of McNamara's domino theory, giving it a radical Islam dynamic. Reagan's advisers feared that if Egypt fell to Islamic extremists, Saudi Arabia and the other Gulf kingdoms would soon follow.

Washington's concerns would have been passed on to the Opus Dei establishment at the very least by Carl Anderson, and Opus Central – with intelligence contacts throughout Europe – if not already aware of the extremist menace would have begun to react. Indeed it was not long before Estarriol was in Moscow, reporting on Brezhnev's intentions for Afghanistan. In any event, the Spanish ambassador in Moscow, supernumerary Juan Antonio Samaranch, would have kept Opus Dei informed of Soviet preoccupations.

After the Vatican agreement, Casey was said to have been 'positively rejuvenated at the prospect of flooding Poland with expensive equipment and cheap agents. He was delighted to take advice from Cardinal John J. Krol [the Polish-American Archbishop of Philadelphia], and to use priests in Poland to spread subversion.'[1] Others he listened to were New York Cardinal Terence Cooke and the new Apostolic Delegate in Washington, Archbishop (now Cardinal) Pio Laghi, formerly the Vatican's top man in Buenos Aires: all strong Opus Dei supporters. Cooke, moreover, was the Grand Protector and Spiritual Adviser of the Knights of Malta. And in 1977, he had travelled to Poland to discuss Paul VI's succession with the Archbishop of Cracow.

After the Pope's visit to Poland, Opus Dei's *milites Christi* became active in organizing training courses, conferences and debates among Polish intellectuals. In 1986, it arranged the first student exchange programme between Poland and the West. That summer the Vienna-based European Forum for Students sent 400 students from ten European countries to work on a half-dozen church construction sites. While in Poland, the volunteer workers participated in a series of seminars on the theme of 'Europe 2000 – A New Image for Man'.

---

[1] Peter Hebblethwaite, 'Time's Papal Plot', *Tablet*, London, 29 February 1992.

In June 1989, the Polish Communist party was defeated in the country's first free elections since the Second World War. Democracy's return to Poland signalled the death of Communism throughout eastern Europe. A month later, Warsaw re-established diplomatic relations with the Vatican and Opus Dei officially opened a regional vicariat in Warsaw.

After the fall of the Berlin Wall in November 1989, Opus Dei quickened its march into Eastern Europe, consolidating with an official presence what previously had been a hidden one. On 15 April 1990, Alvaro del Portillo visited Warsaw. He was met at the airport by his regional vicar, an Argentinian electrical engineer, Esteban Moszoro, who had been ordained in St Peter's by John Paul II eight years before, and by the newly appointed nuncio, Monsignor Joseph Kowalczyk. The next day the Opus Dei prelate bishop met Cardinal Jozef Glemp, the new primate.

By then Gdansk had its own mosque, and authorization was about to be granted for the construction of an Islamic centre and mosque in the north-eastern city of Bialystok, financed by a Saudi grant, to mark the 600th anniversary of the settling of Tartars in the region. About 20,000 of their descendants remained.

Once the target of Ottoman expansion, as the end of the second millennium approached Poland was again a focus of Islamic regard, but for different reasons. With the collapse of the Warsaw Pact, the Polish capital became the nerve centre of an international bazaar dealing in surplus Soviet arms and the merchants of death did a brisk business selling the cast-off weapons to Allah's troops. The arms were primarily destined for Islamic fundamentalist groups in North Africa, the Middle East, the Horn of Africa and Bosnia.

According to author Yvon Le Vaillant, Opus Dei was involved in espionage up to its ears.[1] The Spanish magazine *Tiempo*, maintained that espionage – and particularly the 'counter-revolution' branch of Spain's CESID – was 'the pretty girl of Opus Dei'.[2] Opus Central was therefore well placed to monitor the international arms trade and reportedly at about this time it began to develop corridors of proximity with the more moderate face of Islam.

Shortly after Germany's re-unification, Escrivá de Balaguer's sons

---

[1] Le Vaillant, *Op. cit.*, p. 135.
[1] *Tiempo* No. 219, 21 July 1986.

opened centres in Prague, Brno, Budapest, Riga and Stettin. But the Prelature was particularly concerned with developments in the Balkans where Father Stanislav Crnica established the Work's first centre in Zagreb. The distance between Rome and the Croatian capital is only 535 kilometres. Chaos in the Balkans could flood Italy with refugees, inevitably bringing with them the scars of conflict and promise of increased tension as local resources became over-stretched. A shrinking resource base breeds insecurity, and insecurity leads to conflict. The formula had been proven in the Horn of Africa and by the 1990s it was being exported by Iran to the Balkans where all the ingredients existed for a descent into a fundamentalist inferno: three religions with a legacy of mutual hatred eyeing each other, certain that the opening skirmishes of the next Crusade had already begun.

Before the Church can proclaim a new Crusade, the moral guidelines of the Just War doctrine must be met. But the Just War doctrine had not been invoked in the West since the Battle of Lepanto in the sixteenth century. During the Reagan administration, with their own legate in Baghdad and monitors elsewhere in the Arab world, the Pope's 'intransigent hussars' began revamping the Just War doctrine. With the eruption of conflict in the Balkans their efforts became more urgent. But before the doctrine could be invoked, the updated version had to be accepted by the Church hierarchy. After beatification of the Founder and control of the Vatican finances, this became Opus Dei's most pressing objective.

30

THE MORAL DEBATE

Islamic fundamentalism is an aggressive revolutionary movement as militant and violent as the Bolshevik, Fascist and Nazi movements of the past.
  Professor Amos Perlmutter, American University, Washington, DC

SOON AFTER BEING NAMED HEAD OF THE CIA, BILL CASEY ADOPTED the idea of harnessing radical Islam to counter the Soviet invasion of Afghanistan and he convinced the Saudis to bankroll the project. Casey never dreamt that the undisciplined extremists would actually succeed in defeating the Communists, only that they might contain them in the mountains of the Hindu Kush. By involving Islam's fanatic fringe in what he considered a never-ending mission, Casey hoped to distract the fundamentalists from undermining Arab governments that were the West's allies in the region.

As the holder of several papal distinctions, Casey would have shared the Pope's view of Islam, considering it a religion that denies the Divine Revelation. However the wily CIA chief appeared not to have taken into account that, since its founding in the seventh century, Islam has succeeded like no other force known to history in motivating men to kill or be killed in the cause of propagating their faith.

The extremist leaders were only too happy to take advantage of Saudi petrodollars and American logistics to form a strongly motivated army of militants. The *Mujahedin-e Islam* – Combatants of Islam – were so successful in bleeding the Soviets in Afghanistan that they contributed in a major way – and in their view more so than the Christian Pope – to the disintegration of the Evil Empire. But once unleashed there was no stopping them. The Evil Empire had gone, but what became known as 'Islam's Floating Army' kept on returning to haunt its creators.

For Christendom one of radical Islam's most dangerous beliefs is that Allah has promised them Europe as *Dar al-Islam* – the Land of Islam. They regard the defeat that Charles Martel handed the Moors near Poitiers in 732 as only a temporary setback – albeit one that has dragged on now for more than 1,200 years. According to the Anglo-Islamic writer Ahmad Thomson, the most radical believe that the forces of Allah are again poised to harvest the fruit of the Almighty's promise.

With its 2,000 years of institutional memory, the Vatican would not have forgotten that only 100 years before Charles Martel's victory at Poitiers the old Roman province of Syria was one of the wealthiest corners of Christendom. Its towns and cities possessed magnificent churches and a well-endowed clergy. But its agriculture and industry were increasingly dependent upon migrant labour to perform the more menial tasks, much as in Germany today with its 3.5 million guest workers and their families. The migrant workers around the year 600 were more often than not Arabs. Treated little better than slaves, they became increasingly discontent while realizing as they grew in number that they constituted a social force in their own right.

Then one August day in 636 a ragtag army of 6,000 scimitar-wielding horsemen rode out of the desert to defeat the finest fighting force in the world, a 50,000-strong Byzantine army under Emperor Heraclius, and within a decade Christianity had all but disappeared from the region.

Everything learned about Opus Dei suggests that the question which today most concerns Villa Tevere is whether the West faces a similar fate. Participants at one of its closed-door seminars near Barcelona concluded that 'a parallel exists between the present situation in the Occident and the fall of the Roman Empire, whose citizens were unaware of their own decadence.'[1] Now this was an alarmist, not to say scaremongering conclusion. But it was perfectly in line with Opus Dei's use of the psychology of fear.

For a religious autocracy the Vatican City State supports a surprisingly broad diversity of views. Obedience to the pope is absolute, but one quickly learns that papal absolutism comes in varying degrees and sometimes along differing paths. Once elected, a pope rules until death or until he chooses to resign. The same is true of Opus Dei's prelate bishop. This means that the two strongest religious leaders in the West can develop political strategies over longer periods – up to ten or twelve years if necessary – which is a luxury that no elected political leader enjoys. Quite clearly a long-term perspective was necessary to engineer the Roman Curia's acceptance of an updated Just War doctrine. But before it could directly influence Vatican policy, Opus Dei needed to consolidate its power base within the Curia.

Former numeraries stress that part of Opus Dei's *modus operandi* is to maintain a constant feeling of anxiety among the troops. 'Opus Dei obtains the loyalty of its members not through love, nor through belonging to a close-knit community, but through the element of fear. Fear controls better than love, better than money, better than faith. The fear element and Opus Dei are happy bedfellows,' affirmed Father Felzmann.

Fear for the Church's survival was certainly present at Opus Dei's founding in pre-Civil War Spain. Fear for the Church remained constant throughout the Cold War. With the fall of Communism, the fear factor remained strong in the Work's culture. After John Paul II's election, Opus Dei began attempting to condition the Roman Curia in the same way it conditions its members. By hammering home the notion that the Church is threatened *from within* as well as *from without,* Opus Dei convinces members that they are engaged in an ongoing crusade. One observer has described John Paul II's papacy as representing a return to 'Ultramontanism', the extreme Conservative force that dominated the Church at the time of the First Vatican Council. 'The central government of the Church thinks it is still defending *a fortress of faith against the besieging forces of*

---

[1] 'Immigration: le Cardinal de Barcelone craint une proliferation des délits en Europe', APIC No. 40, 9 February 1995.

barbarism', claimed a religious affairs commentator.[1]

As far as Opus Dei is concerned, history has shown that there is nothing like an external threat for producing a reaction of 'genuine exaltation' that brings believers back to the basics of their faith. Surely every thinking Christian believes that militant Islam must be met by a measured, morally appropriate Christian response. But what constitutes a morally appropriate response? Opus Dei is certainly one of the few agencies actively studying the question. In the final analysis the difference between what is right and what is wrong, between a Just War or just a war, boils down to a question of moral authority. But does Opus Dei possess sufficient moral currency to shape Christendom's response to radical Islam?

As we have seen, Opus Dei's hierarchy has consistently acted as if all means are appropriate. It has been accused of lying, forging documents and employing disinformation, sanitizing its records and using threats and physical coercion. A case in point was that of John Roche who when he sued Opus Dei for a return of funds was confronted with forged documents in court.[2]

Raimundo Panikkar told a Jesuit editor in Zurich that a highly placed member of the Roman Curia had discovered two priests from the Villa Tevere in the archives of his Congregation removing or replacing documents relating to Opus Dei or its Founder.

'In the Congregation of Religious we no longer find certain letters and documents about Opus Dei that we know should be there. In some cases only empty file folders remain,' one Vatican researcher, Dr Giancarlo Rocca, claimed. 'Several times we have found files where the original document has been removed and another substituted in its place . . . It is very serious. Their way of writing history is false.'

---

[1] Clifford Longley, 'Unfinished business', *The Tablet*, London, 20 May 1995, p. 622 (emphasis added).

[2] After leaving Opus Dei, in 1975 John Roche brought suit in the High Court of London to recover £4,500 he said he had loaned the institute and £25,000 representing that part of his salary paid by the British government into a London account on his behalf during the eleven years he spent as a teacher at Strathmore College in Kenya. Opus Dei maintained that the account had never belonged to Roche but to Opus Dei Registered Trustees, producing supporting documents to this effect and also showing conclusively that no loan had been made. On the basis of these documents, the judge ruled against Roche. Only after the judgment was handed down did Roche realize that some of Opus Dei's evidence had been 'fabricated'. When he threatened an appeal, in October 1982 Opus Dei's solicitors acknowledged that thirteen of the documents purporting to reflect 'the sequence of transactions . . . were not written on the dates they bear, but in 1976' – i.e., after the action was filed. The solicitors proposed an out-of-court settlement if Roche would forgo further litigation and remain silent.

We have also seen that all members of Opus Dei do not share the same knowledge of the Work's structure. The 1982 *Codex Iuris Particularis Operis Dei* is not commonly handed out to subordinate members.[1] These constitute an army of professional workers who by their discipline, good appearances and sincere faith can be usefully deployed by the Work in government offices, prison administrations, tax bureaux, the FBI or the French presidency. It has been alleged that numeraries provide an ideal screen for the special 'apostolic tasks' of the Work, as decreed by the central hierarchy and permitted by its internal statutes.[2] Ah, the statutes! Even here there is confusion.

Has the *Codex Iuris* replaced the much more detailed and still secret 1950 Constitutions?[3] 'The 1950 Constitutions are, of course, no longer in force,' Andrew Soane affirmed. 'They are completely superseded by the 1982 Statutes.'[4] But are they, really? Article 172 of the 1950 Constitutions states: 'These Constitutions are the foundation of our Institute. For this reason they must be considered holy, inviolable and perpetual . . .' Moreover, Opus Dei numeraries like John Roche were told that, like the Ten Commandments, the 1950 Constitutions were intended to last *in aeternum*. Paragraph 2 of the *Codex Iuris*'s Final Dispositions seems to imply this as well. It states:

> This Codex, to be made known to all members of Opus Dei, priests and lay people, as well as priests, aggregate and supernumerary, of the Priestly Society of the Holy Cross, enters into force from 8 December 1982. All members remain subject to the same obligations and maintain the same rights existing under the previous juridical regime, unless the prescriptions of this Codex expressly establish otherwise, or unless they are derivatives of norms repealed by the new Statutes.

This is an unusual declaration, uncommon in law. In as much as the 1982 Codex does not mention any article pertaining to the 1950 Constitutions, it therefore appears to abrogate none of them.

[1] The *Codex Iuris* was published in Latin in Fuenmayor et al., *The Canonical Path of Opus Dei*, Scepter Publishers, Princeton, 1994 (originally published by Ediciones Universidad de Navarra, Pamplona, 1989), and Pedro Rodríguez et al., *Opus Dei in the Church*, Four Courts Press, Dublin 1994 (originally published by Ediciones Rialp, Madrid, 1993)
[2] Dr Robert Meunier, research physicist, *Reflections on Opus Dei*, Geneva [unpublished].
[3] *The Canonical Path of Opus Dei* only publishes the first chapter, with its 12 articles, of the 1950 Constitutions, when there are 20 chapters in all with a total of 480 articles.
[4] Andrew Soane, 9 November 1994.

To call Opus Dei a secret society is calumnious, spokesmen for the Prelature maintain. They point to the investigation conducted by the Italian Minister of the Interior in 1986, Dr Oscar Luigi Scalfaro, who became President of the Republic. After eight months of consideration, Scalfaro, described as a 'rigorous and fundamentalist Catholic' and 'suspected' member of Opus Dei,[1] came to the conclusion that Opus Dei was not a secret association and to support this assertion he quoted from the 1982 *Codex Iuris*. 'These statutes, which the minister [Scalfaro] quoted in detail, were what the critics had claimed to be Opus Dei's secret rules . . . However to demonstrate that there was nothing to hide, the prelate of Opus Dei approached the Vatican to have the statutes made public. The Vatican agreed and copies were made available. None of the critics took up the offer to examine them,' an Opus Dei apologist claimed.[2]

According to Vatican sources, Don Alvaro del Portillo did not *ask* but was *ordered* by the Secretary of State, Cardinal Casaroli, to provide the parliamentary commission with copies of the statutes to save it from being branded a secret organization, which would have reflected poorly upon the Church. But what Opus Dei spokesmen never mention is that Switzerland's supreme court – the Swiss Federal Court which sits in Lausanne – issued a judgement on 19 May 1988 – two years after Scalfaro's 'investigation' – in the matter of Verein Internationales Tagungszentrum, an Opus Dei auxiliary society, against the *Tages Anzeiger* newspaper of Zurich. The judgement characterized Opus Dei as a 'secret association' that operates 'covertly', with a maximum of opacity in its affairs.

The use of threats by the captains of Opus Dei's *milites Christi* was hardly subtle. Their recruiting practices have been criticized. And their financial dealings, as the record shows us, have been attacked as unethical and underhand.

These, then, were the morals of the men who were preparing the doctrinal instruments needed to rearm Christendom against radical Islam. But to insure the doctrine's acceptance by the Roman Curia, and then by the leaders of the West, they first had to consolidate their power base inside the Vatican.

[1] Massimo Olmi, 'L'Opus Dei à l'assaut du Vatican,' *Témoinages Catholiques*, Paris, 7 December 1986, p. 9.
[2] William J. West, *Opus Dei – Exploding a Myth*, Little Hills Press, Crows Nest, Australia 1987, pp. 21–22.

CONSOLIDATION

Religious freedom is the cornerstone of all freedoms.

John Paul II

IN MAY 1984 THE PONTIFICAL COMMISSION FOR SOCIAL Communications, the official Vatican media and public relations office, was taken over by a forty-nine-year-old American prelate, Archbishop John Patrick Foley. This marked a final phase in the palace revolution that began in the autumn of 1978. It was one of consolidation that would place Opus Dei at the centre of power, giving its senior policy planners unimpeded access to the papal apartments on the *terzo piano* of the apostolic palace.

Not very much was known in Rome about the bald and pudgy Monsignor Foley. He was portrayed as a media specialist who had been brought from the New World to overhaul the Vatican's communications machinery. A protégé of the archly conservative bishop-maker Cardinal Krol, since 1970 Foley had been editor-in-chief of the *Standard and Times*, Philadelphia's archdiocesan newspaper.

In December 1984, Foley stated in an article for the International Catholic Union of the Press that Catholic journalists 'should be like candles, communicating the light of Christ's truth and the warmth of Christ's love, and being consumed in the service of God'.[1] That same month, the Vatican spokesman, Father Romeo Panciroli, a known Opus Dei detractor, was banished from Rome, being assigned a posting in the boondocks of Liberia. He was replaced by Dr Joaquín Navarro-Valls. By then the Roman Curia was absolutely certain on which side of the Tiber lay the sectarian sympathies of Archbishop Foley.

Navarro-Valls's appointment represented a first bit of house cleaning by the dynamic new president of the Commission for Social Communications. The person he had chosen to become emperor of the Sala Stampa – the Press room – was the first professional journalist to hold the job, having been for several years Rome correspondent for the Madrid daily *ABC*.

'He was presented to his colleagues as a modern Leonardo da Vinci, being a medical doctor and having done his apprenticeship as a bullfighter. But the great breakthrough, we were told, was that Navarro-Valls was the first layman to be director of the Vatican Press Office. What was not revealed was that Navarro-Valls is a member of Opus Dei. So the attempt to palm him off as an "ordinary layman" simply did not wash. No ordinary layman has to report regularly to his "director" (Opus Dei term for superior). And no ordinary layman may go to confession only to an Opus Dei priest . . . That Navarro-Valls is personally charming, a vast improvement on Panciroli, and understands deadlines, may be splendid as far as it goes, but it cannot alter the fact that he is unlikely to promote the cause of truth-gathering in the Vatican,' were the prescient words of Peter Hebblethwaite.[2]

Alvaro del Portillo was a consultor to the Council for Social Communications. Associate numerary Enrique Planas y Comas, a diocesan priest from Avila, was raised to the rank of honorary prelate to the Holy See and became one of Foley's chief assistants. In June 1988, Foley's Council was reorganized. By order from above, the Sala Stampa was detached from it and made a 'special office' of the Secretariat of State, a significant upgrading. As a result, the Council for Social Communications became primarily responsible for the audio-visual image of the Pope. Foley's star had paled

[1] Hebblethwaite, *In the Vatican*, Oxford University Press, Oxford 1988, p. 187.
[2] *Ibid.*

somewhat. On the other hand, the influence of the 'ordinary layman' was on the rise. Navarro-Valls had the Pope's ear, and he was destined to become one of the powerhouses in the Vatican administration with backstairs access to the *terzo piano*.

With these changes, the whole aura of the papacy would be revitalized as John Paul II was increasingly surrounded by professional image-makers. Needless to say, the image-makers were Opusian, having attained the summit of their Apostolate of Public Opinion – AOP – by taking in hand the media packaging of the Pope. By the end of the 1980s Opus Dei's AOP specialists were responsible for overseeing the Vatican Radio, *l'Osservatore Romano*, the Vatican publishing house and were considering adding a fourth pillar to the Holy See's communications outreach programme, a Vatican television network. Foley himself became head of the Filmoteca Vaticana, the official film and video archives, though it was Monsignor Planas y Comas who ran it for him.

John Paul II has always been outspoken in his views about the duties of Catholics in defending their faith. In 1976, while still Archbishop of Cracow, he led a procession from the Metropolitan Cathedral into the city's central square, filling it with a sea of worshippers, many more than could fit into the cathedral, in flagrant disobedience of the civil authorities. In the square under pelting rain he delivered the fieriest of the day's quartet of homilies, *The Courage to Profess One's Faith*, that would be reprinted by Opus Dei in its CRIS series. 'The cause of man's spiritual freedom, his freedom of conscience, his religious freedom, is the greatest of human causes,' he said. Five years later Papa Wojtyla developed the same theme, this time for a world audience, in his World Peace Day message, traditionally delivered on the first day of each new year. Christians, he said, were bound under moral law to defend themselves against evil. 'Even as they strive to resist and prevent every form of warfare, Christians have a right and even a duty to protect their existence and freedom by proportionate means against an unjust aggressor,' he explained.[1]

With Communism defeated, Papa Wojtyla turned his attention to Christian rights in the front-line countries with Islam. According to his Opus Dei spokesman, the Pope was alarmed by the rise of

[1] 'Must Defend Rights, Pope Says', *Boston Globe*, 22 December 1981.

Islamic fundamentalism in the wake of the Second Gulf War. Resistance to UN operations in Somalia was a case in point. In July 1993, he worried that combat missions by US Marines in Mogadishu would fuel a violent reaction from radical Islamists. Within six months of a US helicopter raid in which sixteen Somalis were killed, the Catholic Cathedral in Mogadishu was blown up. Mogadishu's last bishop, Pietro Salvatore Colombo, had been gunned down outside the cathedral in July 1989. Radical Islam's reaction, therefore, was such that Christians could no longer practise their faith in what once had been a European city on the Indian Ocean.

Oppression of Christian rights in front-line countries remains a leading concern of the Vatican as it approaches the Millennium Jubilee, a celebration intended to bear witness before world consciousness that the Christian faith is the only religion capable of revealing the mystery of salvation to all mankind. 'This Good News impels the Church to evangelize,' the Pope told his bishops in Manila. In other words, the Church cannot renounce her duty to proclaim Christ to all peoples. While repeatedly underlining that 'the Church's mission and destiny is to save man, the whole man,' he would also state, 'Evangelization must never be imposed. It involves love and respect for those being evangelized ... Catholics must carefully avoid any suspicion of coercion or devious persuasion.'[1]

There was little Christian love or charity to be found in the Balkans. John Paul II had repeatedly warned that a generalized Balkans conflict could spell disaster for the West. He called for the 'disarming of the aggressor'. He stressed many times that legitimate defence against aggression was a Christian duty. 'In Church teaching, each military aggression is judged morally wrong. Legitimate defence, on the other hand, is admissible and sometimes obligatory,' he said.[2]

An unnamed papal aide – Navarro-Valls, according to some sources – added that the Vatican would support 'precise, proportionate and demonstrative' military action in Bosnia to stop aggression. But the official stated that such an intervention would have to respect the Church's teachings on Just War.[3] The Just War

---

[1] L'Osservatore Romano, Weekly Edition, 25 January 1995, p. 6.
[2] 'Pope Warns of Spread of Yugoslav Conflict', Reuters, 12 January 1994.
[3] Ibid.

label was now launched onto the market, like a 'green label' for natural foods, ecologically sound and biologically pure. The label had been refused to George Bush for Operation Desert Storm, perhaps because it still required the last doctrinal touching up, or perhaps because the Vatican, whose nuncio in Baghdad was solidly Opusian, believed that the Allied reaction to the Iraqi invasion of Kuwait was not so 'precise' and 'proportionate' as it should have been.[1] In any event, a little more than three years after the Iraqi aggression against its oil-rich neighbour, for the first time since the Crusades of old the Just War doctrine was unveiled for public consumption in an updated form, and placed on display in the spiritual marketplace.

With its emphasis on universal love, Christianity has always struggled with the idea of war. After Constantine the Great embraced the Cross in the fourth century, St Augustine of Hippo (354–430) first elaborated a limited argument in favour of military action. The North African bishop allowed that under certain conditions wars might be waged by command of God. He wrote: 'War should be waged only as a necessity, and waged only that God may by it deliver men from the necessity and preserve them in peace.' Eight hundred years later St Thomas Aquinas put forward his three prerequisites for a Just War:

- Combat must be waged by a competent government or authority;
- The cause must be just;
- There must be a 'right intention' to promote good.

Subsequent theologians have added new notions such as war should be a 'last resort' and that the anticipated good results must outweigh the suffering incurred to win them. Overlaid on these notions was John XXIII's doctrine of 'Avoidance of War'. In 1994,

---

[1] On 9 April 1994, the papal nuncio in Baghdad, Opus Dei's Bishop Marian Oles, was transferred to Almaty, becoming nuncio in Kazakhstan, Kyrgystan and Uzbekistan. Shortly after Oles took up his appointment, FBI director Louis J. Freeh announced that the FBI would extend its foreign training programme to Kazakhstan and Uzbekistan. Freeh also announced that the FBI would open offices in the Baltic republics, where Opus Dei's Archbishop García Justo Mullor had recently been named papal nuncio and apostolic administrator of the See of Tallin, capital of Estonia. Freeh is reported to be an Opus Dei member, a fact that he has neither denied nor confirmed.

however, the Avoidance of War concept was side-stepped for a reworked formulation of Just War.

The new Catechism published in that year gave a tentative definition of Just War, pending further refinement, which stated: 'All citizens and all governments are obliged to work for the avoidance of war. However, as long as the danger of war persists and there is no international authority with the necessary competence and power, governments cannot be denied the right of lawful self-defence once all peace efforts have failed.' It gave the four moral parameters needed for a conflict to be considered a Just War:

- The damage inflicted by the aggressor on the nation or community of nations must be lasting, grave and certain.
- All other means of putting an end to the aggression must have been shown to be impractical or ineffective.
- There must be serious prospects of success.
- The use of arms must not produce evils and disorders graver than the evil to be eliminated.

The unnamed papal aide – i.e., Navarro-Valls – implied that under the redefined doctrine not only was it the right of individual governments to defend their people from unjust aggression, but it was the 'duty' of the international community to intervene, within the limitations of the four parameters, should a people, nation or ethnic minority be unable to guarantee its own freedoms and human rights. Such a broad palette for intervention could just as well be used for protecting the Holy Sepulchre, or the Marian shrine of Medjugorje in western Bosnia, as for the survival of the oppressed. The unnamed aide was not far from hinting that under the Just War doctrine Christian princes who acted as white knights in defence of basic freedoms – Muslim as well as Christian – would receive full papal honours and the stamp of moral legitimacy for their military actions.

The new Just War parameters were fashioned against a background of exploding nationalism in the Balkans. In the spring of 1990 both Slovenia (98 per cent Catholic) and Croatia (then 75 per cent Catholic) organized multi-party elections that led a year later to their declaring independence. No sooner had Franjo Tudjman, the new Croatian president, revived the Croatian chequerboard flag that had been a Ustachi (Croatian Fascist) symbol during the Second World War than the Yugoslav federal army invaded the country from bases in Serbia. Croatia at the time had barely enough military equipment to outfit a battalion.

Sandwiched between Croatia and Serbia, Bosnia's 2 million Muslims reacted by unleashing their own nationalist aspirations, rallying to the banner of Alija Izetbegovic, a philosopher recently released from federal prison. Izetbegovic was by no means a fundamentalist. But twenty years before he had written a short treatise concerning the condition of Islam in the world, titled simply *An Islamic Declaration*. It was credited with renewing interest in the study of Islamic theology in Bosnia, resulting in a Saudi grant that permitted the 1977 opening of an Islamic theology faculty at Sarajevo University.

In the early 1980s, Izetbegovic wrote a more important work, *Islam between East and West*. In it he presented Islam as a tolerant religion that had been positively influenced by the spiritual values of the West. He described Christianity in flattering terms as 'a near-union of supreme religion and supreme ethics'.[1] Had the Serbs listened to Izetbegovic there might never have been religious warfare in the Balkans, and the rest of Europe would have been spared the shock of finding itself on the brink of a new Crusade. Instead, the Serb leader Slobodan Milosevic threatened to annex both Bosnia and Croatia. With Milosevic arming the Bosnian and Croatian Serbs, the Croatian government established contacts with the Warsaw arms bazaar and with professional arms traffickers in the West, including Silvano Vittor.

The war's first major battle was the siege of the Danubian city of Vukovar, which ended with a Serb victory. Not a building was left standing. David Bourot, a Frenchman who had been arrested in Pristina on charges of spying for the Croatians, described the Serb tactics. 'They systematically attacked churches, hospitals and civilian targets. They waged a war of terror against the civilian population, not against opposing military forces.'

In prison at the time, Bourot watched a programme transmitted by TV-2, a private Belgrade channel, detailing how the Croats were receiving arms shipments supposedly financed by the Vatican. The

[1] Noel Malcolm, *Bosnia – A Short History*, Macmillan, London 1994, p. 221.

documentary followed one $3 million transaction filmed in Zagreb by a Croatian who worked for Serbian intelligence. While Bourot was aware that the airwaves were humming with disinformation, he found the documentary convincing.

One of the next Serb targets was Banja Luka in central Bosnia. The ethnic cleansing that began there in April 1992 was described by one UN official as 'a scorched-earth policy to erase any trace of Muslim or Croatian culture in the region.'

During Ottoman rule Banja Luka had been the seat of the Bosnian pashas. It had two sixteenth-century mosques, an Ottoman clock-tower, three other mosques and a Muslim cemetery, all demolished in a single night. Banja Luka's non-Serbs were expelled wholesale. Of the district's forty-seven Catholic churches, within a year only three were left standing.

The early Croatian campaigns against Serb and Muslim were no less brutal. In December 1993 the Croatian authorities announced that Islamic militants were planning an all-out *jihad* against the West. The warning came after Muslim fundamentalists had slit the throats of twelve Croatian engineers at Chiffa-Habril, 60 kilo-metres south-west of Algiers.[1]

A few months earlier three Bosno-Muslim soldiers captured by Croats had been turned into human bombs and sent back toward their own lines. One of the doomed men had cried out to his com-rades, 'Don't shoot, don't shoot: we are Muslims,' as he stumbled up the slope towards the Bosnian trenches above Novi Travnik.

Anti-tank mines had been strapped to the soldier's chest and back. Rope bound his hands to his sides, and wire ran from his torso back towards the Croat positions. His two companions had been identi-cally converted into walking, stumbling bombs. Panic seized the trench defenders. A Bosnian officer ordered his men to open fire: they refused. Then there were three huge explosions. The deputy com-mander of the Tomasevic Brigade, a crack Croatian unit, later admitted that one of his soldiers, crazed because the remains of his

[1] Outraged by the killing of the Croatian technicians, John Paul II said: 'One can only deplore these crimes which . . . appear to be expressions of hostility against believers – Christian believ-ers' [source: 'Pope Says Christians Targeted in Algeria', Reuters, 22 December 1993]. The Chiffa-Habril site was only a few kilometres from the Trappist monastery of Our Lady of the Atlas, where in 1996 seven monks were abducted and murdered in the same manner. This time a more emotional John Paul II said, 'No one may kill in the name of the Lord.'

dead brother lay between the lines, had committed this act of human depravity.[1]

The Croatians by then had placed their country under the Pope's protection as Sancho Ramírez of Aragon had done in the eleventh century. The Vatican was the first to recognize Croatia's independence, followed by Germany and the European Community. Diplomatic recognition may have helped end the war in Croatia – having by then claimed at least 10,000 civilian lives – but it permitted the Serbs to turn their attention to Bosnia.

The morally indefensible onslaught against Bosnia by the Serbian Christians – followers of the Eastern Orthodox rite – stirred up centuries-old enmities between Muslims and Christians. The Pope, through his Opus Dei spokesman, let it be known that the West could not allow the Serb injustice to stand unopposed. Left unstated but strongly implied was that a Serb victory over the Bosnian Muslims would turn the Islamic world against the West. 'You must understand the reaction of Islam. Because Americans and Europeans do not see religion as a factor in the development of state policy, they overlook the fact that the Islamic world views the West's inaction in Bosnia as Christians letting other Christians oppress Muslims,' one military expert explained. Indeed the Pope's advisers argued that the Serb massacre of Bosnians had to be stopped to prevent militant Islam from transforming the Balkans into a European Afghanistan. This cause was taken up by the Pope and became the Vatican's most pressing foreign policy issue.

As usual, Vatican intelligence in the Balkans was first rate. Its agents reported that Izetbegovic had carefully prepared his strategy for an independent Muslim state. Already in May 1991 he visited Tehran to develop ties that later would save his fledgling state from being overwhelmed by the militarily superior Serbs. In early 1992 Iran sent $10 million in 'humanitarian' aid through Hungary and Zagreb to Bosnia. Other arms shipments were in the pipeline and two hundred Revolutionary Guards already were present in the country under the guise of military instructors. 'We have two duties: the first is *jihad*, and the second *da'awa* – to spread the call of Islam,' their leader was quoted as saying.[2]

---

[1] Anthony Loyd, *The Times*, 24 November 1993.
[2] Andrew Hogg, *The Sunday Times* (London), 28 June 1993.

Opus Central, according to one Vatican observer, was convinced that to prevent Iran from expanding its foothold in Europe the Serb aggression in Bosnia had to be rolled back. 'The strategists at Villa Tevere were obsessed with this idea,' he affirmed. But forcing the Serbs to hand back Bosnian territory was not a proposition the political leaders of the Western Alliance were eager to accept. It would take three years of 'obstinate and smart' manoeuvring by the Pope's 'intransigent hussars' to convince them.

32

THE 'CLOAK AND CRUCIFIX' BRIGADE

All that the Pope and his men in the media want is social lawlessness resulting in economic collapse in Muslim countries – as is the situation in Sudan due to the Christian lawlessness – so as to exploit it under the pretext of the 'only political task of the Church' to evangelize Muslims. The Church needs to give up its love for lawlessness, anarchy and economic ruination as a means to proselytize the victimized people.

Saudi Gazette, Riyadh, 13 February 1993

PROPONENTS OF A MIDDLE PATH AMONG THE PAPAL ADVISERS HAD counselled against John Paul II's February 1993 visit to Khartoum. They saw it as a no-win encounter. They argued that the Holy Father's presence in the Sudanese capital would give a degree of legitimacy to one of the sponsors of international terrorism that certainly was not deserved. According to the bishop of El Obeid, Monsignor Macram Gassis, the visit was organized by the pro-Opus Dei nuncio in Khartoum, Archbishop Erwin Josef Ender, against the advice of the Sudanese episcopate. 'He denies it, and he is angry with me for saying so,' Bishop Gassis reported. The other bishops backed Gassis. 'Remember,' they told the Pope on his way through Kampala, 'the hands of the men you will be shaking in Khartoum are covered in blood.'

Opus Dei, on the other hand, regarded Africa, where over-population, shrinking resources and ecological degradation were causing insecurity, conflict and migration, as the first battleground in the spiritual wars. From Ceuta to the Cape, Islam was rapidly gaining ground. They believed, therefore, that it was imperative for the most political pope of modern times, the spiritual warrior who defeated Communism, to show the papal colours in Khartoum, from where radical Islam was being exported not only to the rest of Africa but to spiritual hotspots around the world.

When he arrived in the Sudanese capital, John Paul II was already looking ahead to the third millennium, the preparations for which – the Great Jubilee, as he called it – provided one of the central themes of his pontificate. It was, he said, an event *deeply charged with Christological significance*.[1] From his writings it is clear that John Paul II was fascinated by the millennium view contained in the Revelation to John, with its mystical symbolism: the seven bowls of wrath, the judgement of Babylon, the defeat of the beast and the false prophet, and the founding of the new Jerusalem. 'The world needs purification; it needs to be converted,' he said,[2] but for him the only way to salvation was through Christ the Redeemer. 'Islam,' for Papa Wojtyla, 'is not a religion of redemption.'[3]

If the intent of his millennium jubilation was to bring the mystery of Christian salvation to all mankind he was brewing a dangerous formula. The focus of his Great Jubilee was the Holy Land, the common heritage of the three great monotheist religions. But to anyone who lived in the region, it was evident that no devout follower of Islam, nor anyone who holds sacred the teachings of the Talmud, could be expected to treat 'world purification' as defined by John Paul II with anything but hostility.

Indeed none viewed the Pope's formula with greater scorn than the slight, lightly bearded Hassan al-Turabi, who did not give the impression of being a radical. In fact he appeared as a most reasonable man, holding degrees in international law from Khartoum, London and the Sorbonne. A charismatic speaker, he was eloquent in Arabic, and fluent in English and French. Turabi rejected Christian

[1] Apostolic Letter *Tertio Millennio Adveniente*, 31; Rome, 10 November 1994 (emphasis in original).
[2] *Tertio Millennio Adveniente*, 18 & 32.
[3] John Paul II, *Crossing the Threshold of Hope*, Cape, London 1994, p. 92.

salvation, because he knew that only those who follow the prophet Mohammed can reach the Garden – the Muslim equivalent to eternal salvation in Paradise.

By admonishing the regime in Khartoum to stop killing Christians, John Paul II was edging closer to his own showdown with Islam. However, the exercise almost backfired. The Sudanese leaders had been poised to show the world, through the offices of the Vatican press corps, that theirs was a tolerant regime after all, having cleaned up the dilapidated Khartoum Cathedral and making a large square nearby available for an open-air papal mass that was attended mostly by refugees from the south who lived precariously in shanty towns around the capital and whose children were threatened daily with forced conversion.[1]

With a population of only 25 million, but covering a huge territory, Sudan's strategic importance in the religious conquest of Africa was undeniable. By wiping out or converting by force the 7 million Christians and animists in the south, the fundamentalist Islamic front that ran the country would be able to drive a wedge into the heart of black Africa, separating the Christian communities in the east from those in the west and leaving them more vulnerable than ever to political assault. Only three factors were holding the Islamic forces back: the resistance of the Sudanese People's Liberation Army (SPLA); economic chaos in the north; and the hostile natural environment of the south.

Africa's largest country offers an interesting portrait of a radical state. Its per capita GNP is around $55, the world's lowest. Annual inflation runs at about 120 per cent.[2] The chronic famine in a land watered by both the Blue and White Nile is man-made, a weapon of repression and genocide. Foreign debt is so high that servicing it eats up all of Khartoum's foreign exchange earnings. Bashir's answer has been to repress all forms of dissent, banning trade unions and muzzling the press. In its first year in power, the military council executed five times more people than during the whole post-independence period. At Dr Turabi's insistence, Islamic law – *Shariah* – was re-introduced, first in the north and then extended to

---

[1] 'Sudan Forces Christian Youths to Follow Islamic Indoctrination', Associated Press, 8 January 1994.
[2] *The Economist, The World in Figures*, 1995 edition.

the whole country, and the holy war against the south was intensified with the help of Iranian military aid.

This, then, was the regime that the Pope wanted to engage in a constructive dialogue. But it mattered little if he was unsuccessful. In his attempt to reason with the naked face of Islamic fanaticism, he was building reserves of moral currency, showing the world that he had in fact tried – that his efforts to end aggression against Christians in the south had been ineffectual, one of the parameters required for a Just War. But the Pope's principal interlocutor, Dr Turabi, was for many the most dangerous figure in the Islamic world today. Egyptian officials describe Turabi as 'the anti-Christ' of Islamic renewal. Western intelligence sources claim that he and his chief of staff, Saudi entrepreneur Osama Binladen, are financing Islamic extremists accused of fomenting anti-government unrest in Egypt. In addition, the US State Department alleges that with Iranian support they have set up more than a dozen extremist training camps in Sudan and Iranian weapons are shipped through Khartoum to insurgent groups in Algeria, Egypt, Eritrea and Uganda.

A member of one of Saudi Arabia's leading merchant families, Osama Binladen answered *jihad*'s call in 1985, spending two years fighting for Allah in Afghanistan. In addition to his own presence on the front lines, he provided travel funds for Arab volunteers from a half-dozen countries who wished to join the mujahedin. 'Not hundreds, but thousands,' Binladen said. With his Iraqi engineer, Mohammed Saad, he blasted tunnels into the Zazi mountains of Afghanistan's Bakhtiar province for mujahedin hospitals and arsenals, then cut a mujahedin trail across the country to within 25 kilometres of Kabul.[1]

Binladen moved to Khartoum in 1991 and his Bin Laden Company is Sudan's largest contractor, building roads and airports for the Bashir regime. He also built a guest house on the outskirts of Khartoum for itinerant veterans of the Afghan conflict and lectures on revolutionary Islam.

It is alleged that Turabi, with Binladen as his banker, stands behind a group of Afghani war veterans known as the *Gama'a al-Islamiya* (Islamic Group), who organized several assassination

---

[1] 'Anti-Soviet warrior puts his army on the road to peace', *The Independent* (London), 6 December 1993.

attempts against Egyptian president Hosni Mubarak and his ministers and have begun extending their activities to Europe, with a base
in Bosnia and an operations centre in London.

When the Pope visited Khartoum, I was in Dammam, on the Saudi
Arabian Gulf coast, studying the after-effects of Saddam Hussein's
eco-terrorism. Damage to the Gulf's eco-systems caused by 700
burning oil wells and 11 million barrels of crude floated onto the
waters of the Gulf far surpassed earlier predictions. In terms of
man-made disasters, nothing quite like it had been experienced
before. But the local press made no mention of Saddam's ecological
time bomb. Instead it concentrated on what 'that man from Rome'
was up to in Khartoum.

The Saudi reaction surprised me. Saudi Arabia, after all, was supposedly the West's strongest ally in the turbulent Middle East. Even
bigger than Sudan – most of it sand – it sits on top of the world's
largest known oil reserves, which earn the royal treasury around
$40,000 million a year. The kingdom's 17.5 million people do not
know poverty. But under the surface of a brand new industrial infrastructure, with all the gadgetry that the gods of Western technology
could possibly bestow, there is unrest, indicating a growing dis-
enchantment with the Saudi royal family and the kingdom's
dependence on Western allies.

'The animosity between Islam and the West is a matter of fact,' a
Saudi engineer working on the oil clean-up told me. 'Many of us feel
it was wrong for the King to have asked the West to defend us. More
and more we are convinced that the Gulf War was a Western plot to
install a permanent military presence in Saudi Arabia. Otherwise,
President Bush would never have left Saddam sitting in Baghdad. The
Americans actually need Saddam. They keep him in power so that
we feel afraid.

'But then we ask ourselves, with all the money our government
spends on armaments – $16 billion last year – why do we need the
Americans to protect us from Iraq? Many friends in the university
feel that King Fahd has allowed Islam's holy land to be defiled by
foreign troops,' he said.

A curious kingdom, this Saudi Arabia. Its citizens appear to have
everything that rapid modernization can bring, while in reality they
lack basic freedom. Civil rights groups are repressed, censorship is
stifling, and the *Mutawah*, the religious police, are everywhere alert,

hustling improperly dressed women off the streets and forcing merchants to close their shops during the five daily prayer periods. But if the Saudis themselves enjoy little freedom, the foreigners who live in the kingdom have none. And there are almost 5 million guest workers, technical advisers and scientific experts, fully 3 million of whom are non-Muslim. The non-Muslims are not permitted to practise their religion. There are no churches in Saudi Arabia. Churches are forbidden. In Rome, however, the Saudis financed the construction of one of the largest, most opulent mosques outside the Muslim world. No bibles are permitted in the land of the Prophet either, nor Christmas cards or rosaries, and obviously priests and clergymen are *persona non grata*. Saudi Arabia has never been visited by a pope. It is one of the few countries where the greatest pilgrim of the century, John Paul II, has not knelt to kiss the soil. Nor would he ever be invited to do so.

And yet I knew from a previous visit that the Vatican has a 'cloak and crucifix' squad of travelling priests who, under the guise of visiting businessmen, bankers or chemical engineers, come to celebrate Mass in secret and administer the sacraments at Catholic homes located in the compounds that in every Saudi city are set aside for foreigners. Never at the same place two Sundays in succession. Always indoors and behind drawn curtains, out of view from informers and above all the *Mutawah*. The penalty for being caught is arrest and expulsion.

I was unable to ascertain at the time whether the priests who entered Saudi Arabia disguised as engineers, bankers and businessmen – 'dressed like everyone else, though not *like* everyone else' – were men from the Villa Tevere. But for many expatriates in the land of the Prophet their presence provided real comfort. Subsequently I learned that Opus Dei did have 'friends' who passed through the kingdom from time to time. Its *milites Christi* were indeed an evangelizing force that Arab extremists had reason to fear. In Christendom, Opus Dei had become the equivalent of Islam's *Mutawah*, solemn guardians of Catholic orthodoxy, the Pope's secret police.

The West did not have long to wait for radical Islam's response to the Pope's nine-hour stopover in Khartoum. A fortnight later an Islamic terrorist group bombed the World Trade Center in New York, killing six people and injuring 1,000. Six of the twelve terrorists were from Sudan and Sheikh Omar Abdel Rahman, the Egyptian cleric who was their spiritual leader, had received his visa to enter the United States in Khartoum. From his headquarters in a Jersey City mosque located over an electrical appliance shop, Abdel Rahman maintained contact with Muslim activists from Brooklyn to St Louis. And as if the twin towers of the World Trade Center were not enough, his followers planned to blow up the United Nations, the FBI's New York headquarters, two commuter tunnels and the George Washington Bridge.

Nor were the Sudanese authorities long in launching a new offensive into the south. It was as if the pontiff's visit had never occurred and the Provincial of the British Jesuits, who had undertaken a fact-finding mission the year before, had been right all along. 'My visit to Khartoum and Port Sudan has done much to convince me that dialogue with an Islamic fundamentalist regime is a lost cause,' stated Father Michael Campbell-Johnston.[1]

The Pope again appealed to the Sudanese leaders to stop their harvest of death. But nothing changed. The Holy Father was informed of Khartoum's response by the bishop of the southern city of Rumbek: 'I have no words to describe the plight of my people other than – believe me – it is apocalyptic.'[2] The Vatican's chief representative in the south, Bishop Cesare Mazzolari, later disclosed that four Christians in his diocese had been 'crucified because they refused to reconvert to Islam, a faith they had left twenty years before'.[3]

Whereas most Western liberals view with suspicion anyone who talks about God in public, the followers of Islam consider Allah's word as central to their existence. This has always been so and therefore offers little insight into why the approximately 16 million Muslims in Europe and the 6 million in North America have suddenly become more assertive. But one factor unquestionably was the Shah of Iran's demise.

While he was in exile in France, Khomeini discovered that with the revolution in modern communications he could fuse the temporal and spiritual worlds into an unstoppable alliance that within less

[1] Michael Campbell-Johnston, 'Cross and Crescent in Sudan', *The Tablet*, 1 February 1992.
[2] 'Bishop Pleads for Pope's Help', Reuters, 24 May 1994.
[3] 'Four Christians crucified in Sudan, says Bishop', Reuters, 5 December 1994.

than a year had brought about the Shah's downfall. Audio cassettes smuggled into Iran carried the voice of Khomeini directly to the Iranian people, circumventing the Shah's control of the media and undercutting the authority of the literate classes who, except for the clergy, were secular in outlook.

The audio-visual revolution in the service of religious fundamentalism paved the way for Khomeini's return. After fourteen years of exile he was welcomed by a delirious crowd of millions that massed along the route to the cemetery of martyrs, where he proclaimed the formation of an Islamic Republic. Those who opposed him were threatened with the 'punishment of Allah' and in less than two weeks all opposition ceased, enabling him to announce 'Shah Mat!' – in Persian literally 'the Shah's dead', but also 'Check Mate!'

Khomeini's victory over the Shah, who boasted that under his rule Iran had become the world's seventh military power, changed the course of modern Islam. It provoked a spontaneous movement to re-organize society according to the customs and teachings of the Koran. The roots of Islam's revival spread among the academic and professional élite, and – like their counterparts in Opus Dei – they were intent on detaching the wisdom of science from the values of a secularized society in order to promote a social system that was submissive to the one and true God.

It could be said that since Karol Wojtyla had become pope at exactly the same moment the Catholic Church also changed course. Wojtyla's election ended the hesitancies of the post-Vatican II period. Opus Dei supported the Pope's plan for re-evangelization of the West, which in many respects was similar to the re-Islamization movement. The major difference was that Opus Dei operated its apostolate from the top down, while the Islamic movements worked more generally from the bottom up.

Although their aims are quite different, radical Islamic groups bear similarities to Opus Dei and other Christian fundamentalist organizations in terms of structure and discipline. Committed members live in their own communities according to the precepts of Koranic law. Those qualified for higher employment turn over their earnings to the movement. Many are sent to work in the Persian Gulf or Europe to proselytize, recruit and establish parallel financial structures. Their aim is to destroy the *jahiliyya* – an Arabic word describing the period of 'ignorance' and 'barbarism' that existed before the Prophet Mohammed preached in Arabia and has been reapplied to the secular societies of the twentieth century.[1]

For the radicals, *jahiliyya* was reimposed on the Muslim world by Christian Crusaders and later by Christian missionaries. They regard twentieth century missionaries as modern Crusaders who use physical and spiritual coercion to proselytize with results often 'no less horrific' than the Inquisition. 'We can regretfully say "no less horrific", since Christianity still plays a ruthless and dynamic political role, particularly in Africa,' claimed the Anglo-Islamic writer Ahmad Thomson.[2]

The point is, however, that a more tolerant Islam does exist, one that would have the world believe it is not all that different from early forms of Christianity, and that consequently on both sides of the Spiritual Curtain there is room for conciliation and co-operation. But the cause of conciliation can hardly be helped when a pope affirms that Islam is not a salvic religion. This is certainly not what Islamists believe. According to the Islamic Da'awa Centre in Dammam, Islam has its own formula for salvation and at first glance it would appear to be much less dogmatic: 'Anyone who says: "There is no god but God," and dies holding that belief will enter paradise.'[3]

Nothing very radical about that. It did not mean, however, that Islam and early Christianity matched each other all the way down the line. But there was at least a theological basis for dialogue, and for understanding. Wrong, countered John Paul II. 'The theology . . . of Islam is very distant from Christianity.'[4]

All the same, John Paul maintained that the Church remained open to dialogue. And this in spite of the existence of Islamic countries dominated by fundamentalist regimes that seek to destroy Christianity. In these countries, he said, 'Human rights and the principle of religious freedom are unfortunately interpreted in a very one-sided way – religious freedom comes to mean freedom to impose on all citizens the "true religion". In these countries the situation of

[1] Gilles Kepel, *The Revenge of God*, Polity Press, Cambridge 1994, p. 20.
[2] Ahmad Thomson, *Blood on the Cross – Islam in Spain in the Light of Christian Persecution through the Ages*, TaHa Publishers, London 1989, p. 346.
[3] Abu Ameenah Bilal Philips, *The True Religion*, Islamic Da'awa and Guidance Centre, Dammam, p. 8.
[4] John Paul II, *Op. cit.*, p. 93.

RANKS OF ISLAM*

* For countries with Islamic populations of 2 million or more

	Population 1992	Islamic (in millions)	Christian (in millions)	Annual Pop. Growth (All) %	GNP per person $
Indonesia	184.3	160.3	16.6	1.9	670
Pakistan	119.3	115.7	1.2	2.7	353
Bangladesh	112.8	98.1	1.1	2.8	155
India	883.5	97.2	17.7	2.0	330
Iran	64.6	60.0	0.64	2.3	4,720
Turkey	58.5	57.9	0.08	2.1	1,954
Egypt	54.8	51.5	2.7	2.6	630
Nigeria	101.9	45.85	48.9	3.0	268
China	1,203.1	30.0	12.0	1.04	2,500
Algeria	26.4	26.1	0.26	3.0	1,832
Morocco	26.3	26.0	0.26	2.5	1,036
Uzbekistan	23.0	20.5	0.01	2.08	2,400
Sudan	26.6	19.4	2.4	2.7	349
Afghanistan	21.6	19.2	-	2.3	218
Iraq	19.2	18.6	0.58	3.8	12,104
Saudi Arabia	15.9	15.9	-	4.0	7,942
Yemen	13.1	13.1	-	3.1	731
Syria	13.0	11.8	1.2	3.8	1,718
Malaysia	18.6	9.86	1.1	2.0	2,790
Tunisia	8.4	8.3	0.08	2.3	1,284
Somalia	8.3	8.3	-	3.2	119
Kazakhstan	17.4	8.2	8.0	0.62	3,200
Mali	9.0	8.1	0.09	2.9	221
Azerbaijan	7.8	7.3	0.37	1.3	1,790
Senegal	7.8	7.1	0.5	3.1	780
Niger	8.2	6.6	-	3.2	292
Tadjikistan	6.1	5.2	0.35	2.6	1,415
Guinea	6.0	5.1	0.48	2.5	510
United States	255.4	5.1	224.75	0.9	23,119
France	57.3	5.0	45.84	0.3	22,300
Libya	4.9	4.9	-	3.1	5,637
Jordan	3.9	3.7	0.16	3.6	1,527
Germany	80.5	3.5	74.86	0.6	22,917
Turkmenia	4.0	3.5	0.4	2.0	3,280
Kirghizia	4.8	3.3	0.7	1.5	1,790
Philippines	64.2	2.6	56.5	2.7	711
Mauritania	2.1	2.1	-	3.0	530
United Kingdom	57.7	2.0	52.2	0.2	17,760
Lebanon	3.8	2.0	0.9	1.1	1,170

Christians is . . . terribly disturbing. Fundamentalist attitudes of this nature make reciprocal contacts very difficult.'[1]

One of the most troublesome aspects of radical Islam is that in spite of the Koran's special regard for 'People of the Book', which is nevertheless tempered by an underlying suspicion – 'Neither the Jews nor the Christians will ever be satisfied with you until you follow their sect'[2] – imams like Sheikh Omar Abdel Rahman steadfastly maintain in their preaching that the West is Islam's enemy. According to Abdel Rahman, the Koran 'permits terrorism as among the means to perform *Jihad* for the sake of Allah, which means to terrorize the enemies of God . . . We must be holy terrorists and terrorize the enemies of God.'[3]

The West is becoming increasingly multi-cultural. Both the United States and France have Islamic populations of more than 5 million, while Germany has 3.5 million and Britain 2 million. The day is not far off when France will have her first Muslim-majority cities – Metropolitan satellites of the great *Umma*, with their own police, schools, exorcist imams and Islamic institutions. Already today a visitor sees almost as many North Africans as French in the centre of Grasse, the perfume capital in the Alpes Maritimes, and the Gothic old town of Cardinal Siri's Genoa, where Christopher Columbus's father once tended shop, is now populated by Maghrebian immigrants living under miserable conditions, many without proper papers.

With the longest Mediterranean coastline of any NATO country, Italy is infiltrated by hundreds of illegal immigrants each month. There are 85,000 Muslims in Rome alone. After twenty years in the making, in 1995 the Islamic community in the Eternal City inaugurated their new mosque, not far from the Viale Bruno Buozzi. A polemic had arisen over the height of the minaret. Originally planned for 43 metres, it would have been taller than the dome of St Peter's and had to be scaled down. Then finally, £35 million later – 75 per cent donated by Saudi Arabia – the project that 'bestowed a new legitimacy on Islam in Italy' was completed. At which Cardinal Silvio Oddi let fly a string of vicious comments that made Muslims bristle. 'I consider the presence of a mosque, and the attached Islamic Centre,

---

[1] *Ibid.*, p. 94.
[2] *Cf.* Sûrah II.120, the Cow.
[3] Gail Appleson, 'Koran Allows Terrorism', Reuters, 2 February 1995.

to be an offence to the sacred ground of Rome,' he remarked,[1] forgetting that Vatican II teachings on religious liberty had paved the way for the mosque's coming. Cardinal Oddi, among many others, pointed out that in Saudi Arabia churches were not allowed and people were imprisoned for celebrating Mass.

Among the world's approximately fifty-two Islamic states, Turkey is the only one that remains fully secular and fully democratic. But for how much longer? In 1994 municipal elections the militant Islamic Welfare Party took control of local governments in Ankara, Istanbul and seventy other municipalities. Months later extremists in Istanbul attempted to blow up the city's Orthodox cathedral, seat of the Ecumenical Patriarch Bartholomew. This was followed by the passing of a motion in the municipal council – quickly disavowed after it created a storm – to tear down the 1,600-year-old Theodosian Walls, stretching almost 30 kilometres from the Golden Horn to the Marmara shore, because they symbolized the bulwark of Christendom in the region. The Welfare Party again triumphed in the December 1995 legislative elections, winning a plurality that did not augur well for the future of democracy in NATO's only Islamic member state.

Christian communities that have existed in south-east Turkey since before the Battle of Manzikert are today threatened with extinction, having been caught in the latest fighting between the Turkish army and Kurdish separatists. Increasing harassment by Islamic fundamentalists, particularly in university centres, has brought about a Christian exodus, so that in all the country only an estimated 80,000 remain. Since the Gulf War, those Turkish Christians who have chosen to remain are no longer permitted to disseminate the Bible or learn traditional liturgical languages.

[1] Gabriel Kahn, 'Facing East', *Metropolitan*, Rome, 9 April 1993.

33

AFRICA'S BURNING

Without peace between religions, there can be no peace at all.

Hans Kung

There are places today where Christians fear for their lives as a result of the activities of Islamic extremists.

George Leonard Carey, Archbishop of Canterbury

IN MID-MARCH 1994, ALVARO DEL PORTILLO MADE A PILGRIMAGE TO the Holy Land, where Opus Dei was moving closer to assuming an active role in protecting the Holy sites. He spent a week 'following the footsteps of Jesus Christ. During those days he had pastoral meetings with numerous Christians there whom he encouraged to be promoters of peace . . .'[1]

Christianity was endangered in the Holy Land, and that concerned Opus Dei. 'In a world which is witnessing the re-emergence of hitherto dormant religious and ethnic identities, this situation is extraordinary and demands attention,' wrote Said Aburish, a Palestinian Muslim. He believed that 'a Jerusalem without believers in Christ would be more serious than Rome without a pope.'[2]

[1] Javier Echevarría, 'A Priest and a Father', *L'Osservatore Romano*, 24 March 1994.
[2] Said K. Aburish, *The Forgotten Faithful: Christians of the Holy Land*, Quartet Books, 1994.

392

The latest in a long series of burdens that the Christian community had to endure was *Intifada* – the Palestinian rebellion in the territories occupied by Israel. It had brought with it an increase in Islamic extremism, which seemed only natural, but it was a pervasive extremism that made Palestinian Christians fear for their future when the territories – especially Bethlehem – came under control of the Palestinian National Authority in December 1995. The *Jerusalem Post* reported 'dozens of cases' of Christian clergy being attacked by Muslims and concern was felt that after the first Palestinian elections Christians in Bethlehem could become 'second-class citizens with no protection for their religious rights'.[1]

That Christianity would be impoverished without a strong presence in the Holy Land was undeniable. Opus Dei seemed to be giving the problem the attention that Aburish suggested was needed when it opened a new centre in Bethlehem. Only 4,000 Christians then remained in Jerusalem and in the whole of the Holy Land there were perhaps not more than 130,000. Property that had been Christian for hundreds of years, including Saint John's Hospice in the Christian quarter of the Old Town, had been expropriated or sold. The imposing Notre Dame of Jerusalem centre (formerly the Notre Dame de France) opposite Jaffa Gate was itself facing seizure for non-payment of taxes. Opus Dei's solution for that centre's financial problems, if accepted, would make the Prelature the dominant Christian organization in the Holy Land.

But these plans were not to be fulfilled under Don Alvaro's prelatureship. After his week-long visit to the Holy Land, on the evening of 21 March 1994 he celebrated Mass for the last time in the Church of the Cenacle and returned to Rome on the following day. That night he died of a heart attack. He was eighty. The vicar general, Don Javier Echevarría, was at his side and took possession of the piece of the True Cross originally worn by the Founder. Within the next twenty-four hours, John Paul II visited the prelatic church of Our Lady of Peace and knelt before the funeral bier of Don Alvaro. This bending of protocol – a pope only kneels before the earthly remains of a cardinal – was more than papal esteem for the prelate general of Opus Dei but a sign of fidelity to the organization that had done everything in its power to raise him to Peter's throne. The Pope

---

[1] 'Christians fear Muslim takeover', *The Tablet*, London, 28 October 1995.

immediately confirmed Don Javier as the new Prelate and within eight months elevated him to titular Bishop of Cilibia, once a town in the African Limes of North Africa.

Days after thousands of mourners had filled the Basilica of Sant'Eugenio for Don Alvaro's funeral, the first-ever Synod of African Bishops opened in Rome. Vatican communicators said it burst into life amid 'the sound of drums, the singing of hymns, the burning of incense, and the expression of feelings through motions of dance'. More accurately, it opened to bursts of machine-gun fire, rape and looting that erupted in Kigali after the assassination of Rwanda's Hutu president, Juvenal Habyarimana, supposedly by Tutsi rebels.

Cardinal Francis Arinze, a Nigerian convert from the African animism of his parents, described the Synod as an opportunity for 'exchanging gifts' between the Church of Africa and the universal Church. There was little mention of the Church's dialogue with Islam in spite of pre-Synod expressions that this was one of Africa's most urgent needs. Some Vatican observers believed that Arinze had been primed to play down interreligious strife because of the delicate contacts then in progress between the Vatican's AOP specialists and certain Islamic fundamentalist regimes. Cardinal Arinze's pre-Synod message did reveal that the gathering of African bishops 'looks toward the year 2000 when the continent is expected to be divided roughly equally between Christians (48.4 per cent) and Muslims (41.6 per cent)'. The Synod's working paper stated that Islam was an 'important but often difficult partner in dialogue'.[1] But that was all. A curtain of silence descended over the question of Christian-Islamic relations as if intrigues were afoot about which the faithful should not be informed.

Members of the Vatican press corps have expressed dismay that since it came under Opus Dei's domination the public information policy of the Holy See has been one of reducing news that comes out of the Vatican to a level of relative banality. 'This appears to be a conscious policy of Navarro-Valls. The press corps is told nothing meaningful about what is actually taking place inside the closed sessions of the Synods,' complained Father Nikolaus Klein, editor of a Jesuit magazine.

---

[1] Cardinal Francis Arinze, 'An Agenda for Africa', *The Tablet*, 9 April 1994.

'Press conferences feature participants selected by Navarro-Valls because they have nothing to say. This was especially the case at the Synod of African Bishops,' he noted. His sources told him that relations with Islam were, in spite of official mutism, one of the most seriously debated topics. He found only one person – Archbishop Henri Teissier of Algiers – willing to talk of the danger represented by radical Islam. Islamic fundamentalism is 'the gravest problem facing the Church in Africa today'.

The 1994 African Synod closed as it had opened, under the sign of death. In Algiers, a French Marist priest and a Little Sister of the Assumption, who ran a library in the Casbah, were shot dead in broad daylight. Archbishop Teissier called it a 'senseless crime', and said it was 'more important than ever to increase the number of places where Christians and Muslims can meet and get to know and like each other'. His words provoked the anger of the Armed Islamic Group, whose leaders declared him an 'enemy of Islam'.

Navarro-Valls's reasons for not drawing attention to Christian-Islamic strife during the African Synod became discernible in the meeting's closing document. It said the Synod had been concerned that the UN Population Conference – scheduled for Cairo that September – was planning to promote unrestricted abortion and contraception. The document, apparently approved by the African bishops, stated: 'We all condemn this individualistic and permissive culture which liberalizes abortion and makes the death of the child simply a matter for the decision of the mother.' Calling the UN's agenda an 'anti-life plan', the bishops appealed to all countries to reject it. Meanwhile, Africa was burning and bleeding.

The undermining of the UN Population Conference demonstrated one area where John Paul II was diametrically opposed to the intentions of Papa Luciani, who had been hoping to work out a common strategy with the UN Population Fund, sponsor of the Cairo conference. It was said that John Paul II – or his Pro-Life policy-makers – were prepared to wreck the UN Population Conference unless references to artificial birth control and pregnancy termination were removed from all conference literature.

To defeat the UN's 'anti-life plan' the Vatican strategists had decided it would be smart to form, for this one issue only, a common front with Islamic fundamentalists. But because it is a sovereign city-state, the Vatican is the only representative of a world religion to have permanent status with the United Nations. While this does not give it a seat on the Security Council, its delegates can attend General Assembly sessions, and, by extension, meetings of other UN bodies, such as the UN Population Conference. No Islamic organization enjoys a similar status which meant that in forming its one-time alliance the Vatican would have to deal with those radical Islamic states that shared the same rabid abhorrence of abortion and contraception.

A month before the Cairo conference opened, the Holy See sent an envoy to Tehran to drum up support for its Cairo position. The Iranian deputy foreign minister Mohammed Hashemi Rafsanjani concurred: 'Collaboration between religious governments in support of outlawing abortion is a fine beginning for the conception of collaboration in other fields.'[1]

One week later, the Vatican ambassador to Algeria, Monsignor Edmond Farhat, an Arabic-speaking Lebanese, went to Tripoli to sew up Libya's participation in the fundamentalist alliance. Farhat had already been there a few weeks before with the deputy secretary of state, Monsignor Jean-Louis Tauran, who, in addition to discussing the UN's 'anti-life plan', informed his Libyan hosts that 'the Holy See is against maintaining the UN's economic and political sanctions against Libya'. Navarro-Valls denied, however, that any deal had been struck with either the Iranians or Libyans. Nevertheless both hard-line regimes reaped propaganda benefits from the attention shown them by the papal envoys. The official Libyan news agency, Jana, quoted Archbishop Farhat as stating: 'The dialogue to find a peaceful solution to the Lockerbie crisis is continuing.' He added, 'an identity of views emerged on the UN Conference on Population and Development, and notably as far as concerns the family.' So by linking the controversy over Libya's supposed role in the December 1988 mid-air bombing over Scotland of Pan Am flight 103, in which 270 people were killed, and the UN Population Conference, it was logical to assume that a deal had been struck after all.

On population questions, then, the Vatican made common cause with Islamic extremists. This opportunist plan – the forming of an alliance of convenience – Pro-Life insiders affirmed, was the work of

[1] Jim Hoagland, 'The Pope Sups with Two Devils', *The Washington Post*, 23 August 1994.

Opus Dei, once again demonstrating that the Prelature was capable of directing Vatican policy.

The Cairo strategy was crafted within the Pontifical Council for the Family, assisted by the Pontifical Academy for Life and the John Paul II Institute for the Family. All three were under Opus Dei's influence. The Council for the Family was headed by its ally, Cardinal López Trujillo, and among the Council's consultors were two members of Opus Dei's priestly hierarchy and their close associates, Bishop James Thomas McHugh and Monsignor Carlo Caffarra.

The founding of the Pontifical Academy for Life in February 1994 was made possible by the financial backing of the Prelature and the Knights of Columbus,[1] whose supreme knight, Virgil Chrysostom Dechant, had since the mid-1980s drawn close to Opus Dei. Dechant had hired as the Knights' public information officer senior Opus Dei supernumerary Russell Shaw. As the chief executive officer of the world's largest Catholic fraternal society, with 1.5 million members, Dechant paid himself a princely salary, declaring income of $455,500 in 1991. Most of this, he said, was contributed by the Knights of Columbus insurance operation, which has policies in force totalling more than $20,000 million. Such wealth enabled the Knights to give away in excess of $90 million each year to Catholic causes, including those of Opus Dei. For example, it supported the US Bishops Conference anti-abortion campaign with $3 million annually. In addition to his Academy for Life duties, Dechant is a member of the Pontifical Councils for the Family and for Social Communications, the central directorate of the IOR, and an honorary consultor to the Pontifical Commission for the Vatican City State.

The Academy for Life's directorate is headed by Professor Gonzalo Herranz Rodríguez of the University of Navarra, and among its members are Professor Caffarra and Cristina Vollmer, a French-born countess who was married to Venezuela's ambassador to the Holy See, Dr Alberto J. Vollmer Herrera, both supernumeraries. She headed the World Organisation for the Family which in 1986 organized an international conference to promote family solidarity in Paris under the presidence of Princess Françoise de

[1] Hebblethwaite, *The Next Pope, Op. cit.*, p. 119.

Bourbon-Lobkowicz and Bernadette Chodron de Courcel, wife of French president Jacques Chirac. Countess Cristina's husband, a lay consultor to the administration of the Holy See's Patrimony, also served on the Pontifical Council for the Family.

The John Paul II Institute for the Family, founded in October 1982 with funding raised by Opus Dei, is headed by Professor Caffarra, with former White House aide Carl Anderson as vice-president and director of the Institute's US campus in Washington, DC. Another member of the Institute's Washington staff is the Knights of Columbus spokesman Russell Shaw.

The Vatican delegation to the Cairo Population Conference was solidly in Opus Dei hands. Its number-three man was Bishop McHugh, whose Pro-Life lobbying in the US is financed by the Knights of Columbus. However McHugh and his two superiors deferred to Joaquín Navarro-Valls, who had set aside his duties as head of the Vatican's Sala Stampa to insure that Rome's directives were followed to the letter in Cairo. McHugh and Navarro-Valls were assisted by the Academy of Life's Cristina Vollmer.

By adopting the Opus Dei's Cairo strategy, the Vatican went against the common position of the Western powers not to deal with states that sponsor international terrorism. For some Catholics, dealing with international renegades seemed a stratagem imagined by the Devil. Navarro-Valls later issued a justification, claiming that at Cairo 'the future of humanity was at stake', which even he might admit was an exaggeration. He denied that the Vatican had been intent on blocking a population-control consensus. 'We were interested in a consensus on the true well-being of men and women, not in a consensus on words and, even less, on slogans,' he said.

The issues dealt with at the Cairo Conference were everyone's concern. It would have been immoral to impose the permissive standards of Western secular societies, particularly in matters of abortion, upon the Third World. Nevertheless acceptable ways of solving the world population crisis have to be found. The world population could burgeon from 5.5 billion in 1995 to 10 billion within twenty years. The UN Population Fund had hoped that from Cairo would emerge a plan to stabilize world population at 7.2 billion by the year 2050. Instead of constructively working towards an acceptable stabilization programme, the Opus Dei-inspired Vatican strategy was negatively geared to do maximum harm. Disgusted US officials

qualified the Holy See's manoeuvring as 'the most vehement and con-
certed diplomatic campaign the Vatican has launched in recent years
to influence international policy'.[1]

Opus Dei indirectly boasted its structuring of the Vatican's
alliance with radical Islam. While the Cairo Conference was in
progress, the Prelature's AOP specialists organized conferences with
members of local Islamic communities to affirm support for the joint
anti-Cairo line. By being seen publicly to participate in these meetings Opus Dei could hardly be accused of having an anti-Islam bias.

'The Work is not against anyone and will never start a Crusade,
however that word is taken, against any religion. Nor would it take
part in one. Blessed Josemaría wrote: "A Christian lay outlook . . .
will enable you to flee from all intolerance, from all fanaticism. To
put it in a positive way, it will enable you to live in peace with all
your fellow citizens, and to promote this understanding and
harmony in all spheres of social life" (Conversations, no. 117).
Respect for the dignity and freedom of other persons is fundamental to Opus Dei,' maintained Andrew Soane.

Five months after Cairo, Opus Dei organized a seminar on illegal
European immigration at one of its retreat centres outside Barcelona
that was closed to the public. The Barcelona seminar supported a
view opposed to the one expressed by Andrew Soane. The seminar
concluded that the growing rate of Islamic emigration to Europe
risked provoking serious social conflict in the years ahead.

'By the year 2000 all major European cities will be multicultural.
The traditional European population is ageing, while the immigrants
are young and proliferating,' Opus Dei ally Cardinal Ricard María
Carles, the Archbishop of Barcelona, pointed out. 'Such a demo-
graphic rift can only bring instability and strife for future
generations,' he added. Therefore it was felt that if these trends
continued, a relatively affluent and secularized European society,
being capricious and morally bankrupt, would be unable to stand up
to a more motivated, spiritually disciplined and determined immi-
grant population.

'Cardinal Carles drew a parallel between the present situation in
Europe and the fall of the Roman empire, whose citizens were

---

[1] Alan Cowell, 'Vatican Finds Sin in Text for UN Population Session', *International Herald
Tribune*, Paris, 9 August 1994.

unaware of their own decadence. In our day, the Cardinal pointed out, the three Christian values of work, liberty and love have been debased,' a report on the seminar concluded.[1] The Barcelona seminar was clearly concerned with the Islamic threat to Europe and the fact that, being more dynamic, Islam was winning recruits among European Catholics by the hundreds each year. After smothering Christian belief in its historic cradle-lands – the Middle East and Asia Minor – Islam was now challenging Christianity in Europe, and in times of a shrinking world economy it was doing not too badly. For the protectors of the Church, these were worrying signs.

If Cairo offered one example of how Opus Dei conducted its AOP, and Barcelona another, yet a third was provided by the Institute for Human Sciences, a think-tank that had been founded in Cracow under Wojtyla's guidance. Later, while López Rodó was Spain's ambassador to Austria, the Institute moved to Vienna. After Wojtyla's election as Pope the Institute began holding regular symposiums at the papal summer palace in Castelgandolfo, chaired by John Paul II himself. In August 1994 the Institute organized its fourth Castelgandolfo symposium. The focus of the three-day meeting was the 'Next Crusade', though it was given the more anonymous title of 'Identity'. The Pope sat slightly apart at a small wooden table, listening intently. He was planning a trip to Croatia, and the Vatican – in preparation for the Millennium Jubilee – had just established diplomatic relations with Israel.

The Institute's president, philosopher Krzysztof Michalski, put forward the view that the collapse of the Soviet empire made it necessary 'to search for a new order'. The search implied that one of the West's first priorities was to turn back the wave of Islamic migration. Six months later, NATO's Secretary General Willy Claes confirmed that a strategy to protect Europe from radical Islam had become the Western Alliance's primary concern. Coincidence? Other topics covered were the Islamic world's attitude to its own identity, and also whether Europe would be able to absorb its growing Islamic minorities.

The participants concluded that unless centuries of mutual hostility and misunderstanding were overcome the West's collision with

---

[1] 'Immigration: le Cardinal de Barcelone craint une proliferation des délits en Europe', APIC No. 40, 9 February 1995.

Islam would dominate world relations at the beginning of the third millennium. They noted that it had become fashionable to talk of the Middle East as a 'Crescent of Crisis'. But what if one of the Crescent powers developed a nuclear capacity? What if Algeria turned seriously fundamentalist? According to Rabah Kebir, the exiled Islamic Salvation Front president, Islamic rule in Algeria was inevitable. 'Western nations must understand that, sooner or later, Muslim countries will be governed by Islamists. This is the wish of the people,' Kebir told the French religious daily *La Croix*.[1] Bosnia's Izetbegovic would have agreed. But neither Kebir nor Izetbegovic were invited to the Castelgandolfo symposium.

John Paul II believed he had made an important step towards a 'Crusade of Understanding' when he spoke out against US policy during the 1991 Gulf War, refusing to accord Operation Desert Storm the Just War label because it did not meet 'the rigorous conditions of moral legitimacy'. He thought his stance had impressed the Islamic world. That seemed doubtful as Islamists continued to regard him as a political agent who – in the words of his would-be assassin Mehmet Ali Agca – though 'disguised as a religious leader is the Crusade commander'.[2] The depth of the Islamic hardliners' hatred and mistrust was sadly brought home in December 1994 by the killing of four White Father missionaries – three French and one Belgian – in Algeria. In a fax sent to news agencies in Nicosia, the Armed Islamic Group said their killing was part of a campaign 'for the annihilation and physical liquidation of Christian crusaders' in Arab lands.[3]

[1] *La Croix*, Paris, 20 January 1995.
[2] Brodhead, Frank, and Herman, Edward S., *The Rise and Fall of the Bulgarian Connection*, Sheridan Square, New York 1986, p. 52.
[3] Three of the 'crusaders' were aged 69, 70 and 75. They were, respectively, Father Jean-Marie Chevillard, Father Charles Deckers and Father Alain Dieulangard. The fourth victim, Father Christian Chessel, was 36.

34

THE CROATIAN WAR MACHINE

To make war against wars is a just and rightful war.

Pope John Paul II

OPUS DEI AND JOHN PAUL II SHARE AN EXTRAORDINARY DEVOTION TO the Virgin Mary. The Prelature has adopted the Pope's motto *Totus tuus* ('All for you, Mary') as its own. Opus Dei members turn out at all papal appearances waving *Totus tuus* banners. According to the doctrine of the Virgin, she co-operated in man's redemption by becoming the Mother of God. Papa Wojtyla believes that she has a major millennium role to play, and that Marian apparitions signify her journey through space and time on a pilgrimage towards the second coming, which marks 'the close of the age' – i.e., the end of the world. But before the Parousia – the second coming – Christ ordered that the Gospel must be preached in all nations; 'and then the end will come'.[1]

Mary also had special significance for Rwanda's Hutu rebels, a number of whom were newly converted Muslims. Until the civil war there, Rwanda was regarded as one of Africa's most Christianized countries. Only 10 per cent of its population was Muslim. The Hutus

[1] Matthew 24:3 and 24:14.

comprised more than 80 per cent of the population, but paradoxically almost half of Rwanda's Catholic clergy was Tutsi.

'This was unbearable to Hutu extremists,' explained Father Octave Ugiras, a Tutsi priest who ran the Christus Centre in Kigali. During the troubles, Hutu militiamen came to the centre and slaughtered seventeen priests and nuns, believing them to have supported the Tutsi-led Rwandan Patriotic Front, which later won the civil war. 'The militiamen told us we had nothing to do with God. They said the Virgin Mary was a Tutsi woman and she had to be killed.'[1] The Hutus then riddled Mary's statue with bullets. During the four weeks that the African Synod sat in Rome, more than 200,000 Rwandans – including the Archbishop of Kigali, two bishops, 103 priests and 65 nuns – were slaughtered by the extremists.

Thirteen years before the Rwandan massacres, the Virgin Mary made her first appearance in the Bosnian Croat village of Medjugorje with a plea for peace and reconciliation. Judging by the tragic events that followed, the message was not understood, and yet Medjugorje became the fourth most popular pilgrimage for Christians of all faiths, attracting before the outbreak of war in the Balkans hundreds of thousands of people each year.

In 1986 the Vatican began to show an interest in Medjugorje and the Congregation for the Doctrine of the Faith was asked to investigate the 'authenticity' of the apparitions. A rumour swept Medjugorje that the Pope had secretly come to see for himself. When asked in January 1987 by an Italian bishop how to react to the events at Medjugorje, the Pope replied: 'Aren't you aware of the marvellous fruits they are producing?'[2]

A few days later, the Virgin spoke through one of the local mediums of her sadness about what was happening in the world. 'You have allowed Satan to take the upper hand . . .' she is quoted as having said. Four years later the region was inflamed in bitter inter-religious conflict. With overwhelming superiority in arms, the Serbs dominated the battlefield, carrying out medieval-style warfare that threatened to reduce Sarajevo to cinders and spark the beginning of

---

[1] Edith M. Lederer, 'The Church and Rwanda', Associated Press, 23 January 1995.
[2] Robert Faricy and Lucy Rooney, *Medjugorje Journal – Mary Speaks to the World*, McCrimmons, Great Wakering, Essex, 1987, p. 146.

the Tenth Crusade. One-third of Croatia and nearly three-fourths of Bosnia fell to the Serb aggressors.

The Serbs, it seemed, feared the 'Croat lobby' in Rome more than the Croatian army. The Serb media branded Vatican policy as 'dishonest and untrustworthy'. Belgrade was convinced that the 'obstinate and smart work' of the Holy See – guided by Opus Dei and the newly appointed nuncio in Zagreb, Archbishop Giulio Einaudi – enabled Croatia to dote its newly formed national army with an impressive arsenal of modern weaponry. Indeed, Serb sources alleged that Father Stanislav Crnica, the Opus Dei regional vicar in Zagreb, had direct access to President Franjo Tudjman's office.[1]

Archbishop Einaudi took up his posting six weeks after the Vatican – on 13 January 1992 – became the first foreign 'power' to recognize Croatia's independence. He had previously been nuncio in Chile where he had come under the spell of Opus Dei's former regional vicar, Adolfo Rodríguez Vidal, who had been elevated to Bishop of Los Angeles di Chile. During Einaudi's nunciature the number of Opus Dei bishops in Chile rose to four. Einaudi was not only a friend of the Prelature, he saw eye to eye with Regional Vicar Crnica on all important issues.

Belgrade's suspicions of Vatican collusion seemed confirmed when Serb intelligence purloined from the files of the Croatian finance ministry a draft $2,000 million loan agreement which the Vatican had purportedly arranged through the Sovereign Military Order of the Knights of Malta. The loan was for 10 years and it carried no interest. Even though the 12-page document was undated and unsigned, the accompanying correspondence – between the Croatian government and Monsignor Roberto Coppola, who described himself as a Knights of Malta plenipotentiary minister and extraordinary ambassador – was dated in early October 1990, eight months before Croatia declared independence.

After receiving a copy of the loan agreement, the Serb newspaper *Politika* charged that the Vatican was assisting the break-up of Yugoslavia. Possibly from a partisan position, *Politika* reported that

---

[1] According to reports from Zagreb, one of President Tudjman's daughters-in-law – he has two, Ivana Moric, wife of Dr Miroslav Tudjman, and Snjezana, wife of Stjepan Tudjman – is an Opus Dei supernumerary.

Cardinal Franjo Kuharic of Zagreb helped arrange the loan, which had been negotiated on the Croatian side by prime minister Josip Manolic, his deputy Mate Babic, finance minister Hrvoje Sarinic and a councillor at the French finance ministry, Madame Mirjana Zelen-Maksa.[1] But what the Serbs did not realize was that in Zagreb's haste to finance the first arms purchases from abroad it had fallen victim to a hoax.

No mention of 'Monsignor' Coppola appeared in the Vatican yearbook and the Knights of Malta, embarrassed by the unwanted publicity, maintained that the loan document was bogus, part of a confidence trickster's attempt to harvest an up-front commission of $200,000 from the Croatians. The fraud was uncovered in time and the perpetrator – although he claimed immunity from prosecution by virtue of holding diplomatic passports from several eastern countries – was said to be in jail in Italy. In fact the Knights of Malta's anti-fraud department, headed by Count José Antonio Linati, possessed a lengthy file on Roberto Coppola, an enterprising Neapolitan with a history of past misrepresentations dating back to the 1970s, and had warned the Order's embassies abroad to be on the lookout for the unworthy 'monsignor'.

Politika nonetheless noted that the Vatican financiers had also backed the founding of an embargo-busting cargo airline that operated between the Adriatic port of Split and Malta. It claimed that the money for the airline had been transferred to the Croatians through a Luxembourg bank that formerly had been used in some of the United Trading transactions.

Politika's disclosures apart, the evidence suggests that the Opus Dei network, in contravention of the UN arms embargo imposed in 1991, was instrumental in easing Croatia's task of forging a well-armed, efficient war machine, first by improving Croatia's image in the West so that it escaped international sanctions, and then facilitating its contacts with the Clinton administration. The efforts to arm Croatia began even before the Vatican's recognition of the Tudjman republic.

When the federal Yugoslav forces abandoned their barracks around Zagreb in 1992 they left behind two old Yugoslav Air Force

---

[1] Radivoje Petrovic, 'The Holy See is providing loans to help Croatia and the break-up of Yugoslavia', *Politika*, Belgrade, 2 February 1991.

MiGs and a few disabled tanks. By September 1993, the Croats had purchased twenty-eight MiG 21s from surplus stocks in the Czech Republic. The MiGs were transported to Croatia in kit form by truck through Hungary. Zagreb was also successful in obtaining a piece of the American foreign aid pie. Opus Dei's Washington network, which by then extended from the papal nunciature on Massachusetts Avenue to the White House, the FBI and the Pentagon, provided the Croats with the right contacts so that they knew exactly what to ask for and how to formulate their requests.[1] The Serbs were hit with international sanctions, but the Croats, perpetrators of their own depredations in western Bosnia, successfully avoided them.

In a move that perplexed observers, Alvaro del Portillo spent several weeks during the summer of 1993 at the Prelature's Warwick House in Pittsburgh. Its director, numerary John Freeh, was the brother of Louis J. Freeh, since 1993 Clinton's director of the FBI.[2] Officially Bishop Portillo was in Pittsburgh to address prominent local Catholics. But unremarked was that Pittsburgh is the headquarters of the Croatian Fraternal Union of America, a life insurance association with assets of $150 million but also the largest Croat emigrant organization in the world. The Union's national president, Bernard M. Luketich, was so highly viewed by Rome and Washington that he accompanied the official White House delegation that greeted John Paul II on his visit to the United States in 1995.[3]

Opus Dei's operations in Pittsburgh were assisted in the 1980s by an energetic young priest, Father Ron Gillis, who had been recruited while a law student at Boston. Gillis had known the Founder in Rome and witnessed some of his famous tantrums. On one occasion he reported that Escrivá de Balaguer started banging chairs about, screaming that he needed more 'saints' – i.e., new vocations. Gillis told a friend he never wanted to be a priest but the Father convinced him he had a vocation as big as a house. Gillis confided that Opus

---

[1] The nuncio in Washington, Archbishop Agostino Cacciavillan, began his diplomatic career in 1976 as the nuncio in Kenya, where he first came into contact with Opus Dei's Corps Mobile.
[2] John Freeh resigned as a numerary and left Warwick House in 1994 to marry. Attempts to reach him were unsuccessful and it is uncertain whether he remains an Opus Dei member.
[3] *The Pittsburgh Post-Gazette*, 1 October 1995.

Dei was attempting to recruit inside the Pentagon and that he himself regularly gave lectures there on 'military ethics'. Soon after, he left Pittsburgh and by 1992, as the Balkans crisis hotted up, he was back in Washington.

In the summer of 1993, plans to arm Croatia in spite of the UN embargo took on greater urgency. According to the Stockholm International Peace Research Institute, which monitors arms transfers in the region, Croatia created its own armaments industry and refurbished equipment left behind by the Yugoslav army. Other arms were acquired from Ukraine, among them 200 T-55 battle tanks, 400 armoured personnel carriers, 150 heavy artillery pieces, 35 multiple rocket launchers and 45 assault helicopters. But the Croatians lacked basic battlefield management skills.

In January 1994 the Croatian Fraternal Union was instrumental in founding the National Federation of Croatian Americans as a registered lobby in Washington. Luketich had White House contacts at the highest level, extending to Bill Clinton, Al Gore and Anthony Lake, the National Security Adviser.[1] Lake, who describes himself as a 'pragmatic liberal', had served in two previous administrations – Nixon's and Jimmy Carter's. A former political science professor at Holyoke College in Massachusetts, he had received his PhD from Princeton, where he could have encountered Opus Dei's Father John McCloskey III, an assistant chaplain who left the Princeton chaplaincy in 1990 after creating a firestorm by advising students not to take courses which he deemed doctrinally dangerous.

Two months after the Croatian lobby's formation, Zagreb's defence minister, Gojko Susak, requested Washington's assistance in educating the Croatian general staff 'in military-civilian relations, programming and budgeting'. Susak's extreme Croat nationalism – he was originally from the region of Mostar – had caused him to flee Yugoslavia in 1967, settling with two brothers in Ottawa, where he worked in a Kentucky Fried Chicken

---

[1] *Zajednicar* (Fraternalist), 'the official organ of the Croatian Fraternal Union of America', reported in its 6 January and 3 February 1993 issues that Mr Luketich was invited to a private dinner at the Old State House Building in Little Rock with Hillary and Bill Clinton and Al Gore. See also, *inter alia*, *Zajednicar*, 7 April 1993, and 'Special Report From Washington' concerning an American-Croatian delegation headed by Mr Luketich that met at the White House on 27 February 1995 with Anthony Lake and Alexander Vershbow, the NSC's senior adviser for European Affairs, *Zajednicar*, 8 March 1995.

franchise. Later he bought a pizza parlour and staffed it with Lebanese while putting all his energies into organizing Canadian Croats for the Croatian Fraternal Union of America. In 1991, Brother Susak was listed as president of the board of trustees of the Ottawa chapter, when he returned to Zagreb to beef up Croatia's military punch.

Susak specifically asked the Clinton administration for permission to employ a group of retired US army officers who operated from offices in Alexandria, Virginia, under the name of Military Professional Resources Incorporated.[1] The only problem was the 1991 UN arms embargo imposed on all of Yugoslavia. But this problem faded with John Paul II's visit to Zagreb in September 1994 to celebrate the ninth centenary of the See of Zagreb. Tudjman was said to be ecstatic. He told a press conference that the first papal visit to the Balkans since 1117 signified Vatican backing for Croatia's bid to regain its Serb-held territory 'by war if necessary.'

'The Holy Father is coming as an apostle of peace, the preacher of co-operation and friendship among nations,' he said. 'His arrival . . . signifies moral support from the supreme international moral authority for Croatia's demand that it has the right to establish its legal system over its entire territory.' To show Croatia's 'everlasting gratitude' for the Holy See's protection two bootlegged MiG 21 fighters escorted the papal airliner into Croatian airspace and when it landed on Croatian soil church bells pealed throughout the country.

In 1519, Leo X had bestowed on the Croats the title of *Antemurale Christianitatis* – the Bulwark of Christianity – for their defence of Europe against endless hordes from the East. Almost 480 years later, John Paul II was again exhorting the Croats to stand firm for Christendom. Within days of the papal visit, Military Professional Resources (MPRI) received the green light from the US State Department to sign a consulting agreement with the Croatian defence ministry. Clinton, after conferring with his national security adviser, approved the decision. MPRI was no fly-by-night organization. It employed 140 persons and reported an annual

---

[1] David B. Ottaway, 'US General Plays Down Bosnia Role – "Non-Lethal Advice" Is All He's Giving', *The Washington Post*, 28 July 1995.

turnover in excess of $7.5 million. Among those working on the Croatian contract – nondescriptly referred to as the 'Democratic Transition Assistance Programme' – were former US Army chief of staff General Carl Vuono, former US Army Europe commander General Crosbie 'Butch' Saint, and former Defence Intelligence Agency chief Lieutenant General Ed Soyster.

'The mission was to convert the eastern-style army they had . . . to a western-style army based on democratic principles,' Soyster said. 'We are talking about totally changing a system, converting their eastern-style military to a western one with democratic values and methods.' MPRI's assistance 'has no correlation to anything happening on the battlefield today,' he added.[1] Otherwise stated, MPRI was assisting Croatia to train a professional officers corps. Leading the Croatian programme on the ground was retired Major General Richard B. Griffitts. His 15-strong group was staffed by former Pentagon colonels. The Croats were accorded State Department clearance to attend special courses at US bases and schools.

Under a separate arrangement, retired Major General John Sewall, former deputy director of strategic planning for the Joint Chiefs of Staff, spearheaded a State Department effort to improve military co-ordination between the Bosnian and Croatian governments and the Bosnian Croat militia – in other words, to make the three forces more combat efficient. Sewall took over the job of special adviser to the Bosnian and Croatian militaries from General John Rogers Galvin, the former Supreme Allied Commander in Europe.

Although the Americans denied it, French and British intelligence sources claimed that the Croatians were receiving advanced US computer technology and fire-control systems designed to give them battlefield superiority. This know-how, however, was not passed on to the Bosnians. It seems that by then Lake had counselled Clinton to silently assent to a Tudjman proposal – put forward in the spring of 1994 – to allow Iranian arms for Bosnia to transit Croatia.[2] It has since been alleged that by turning a blind eye to the

---

[1] Sean D. Naylor, 'Retired Army General Helps Balkan Militaries to Shape Up', *Army Times*, Washington, 12 June 1995.

[2] James Risen and Doyle McManus, 'Despite his public opposition to lifting embargo, Clinton reportedly let shipments go through', *Los Angeles Times*, 5 April 1996.

Iranian arms shipments to Bosnia, the Americans permitted Tehran to expand its foothold in the Balkans. But the evidence suggests otherwise. The Iranians already had their foothold. They had been shipping their arms through the Croatian ports of Split and Rijeka since 1993, with Zagreb routinely exacting a 'transit tax' on the 30- to 50-truck convoys before they left the ports for destinations inside Bosnia. Opus Dei's strategists seem to have realized that if Bosnia did not receive a minimum of military aid to defend itself, without permitting Sarajevo an offensive capability that might threaten Croatia – a proposition that the Bush administration had refused – Islamic guerrillas would soon be present in the Balkans in uncontrollable numbers and Bosnia would fully become an Iranian client state. At least this way Croatia could exert some control over the weapons flow, thereby guaranteeing Zagreb's military superiority over its beleaguered neighbour.

The plan worked well enough, although it was rendered more complicated than expected by the fact that American military gear was soon being spotted in the battle zone. How did it get there? That mystery remains unsolved. Possibly the Iranians, having some left-over American equipment from the time of the Shah, introduced it in an effort to sour relations between the US and its European allies. The subterfuge almost succeeded, because the French and British governments became unhappy about the apparent violation of the UN embargo. Their peacekeeping contingents reported seeing Bosnian Croat and Muslim soldiers dressed in American battle fatigues and carrying M-16 rifles. UN officials were in fact convinced that the US used NATO patrols enforcing the 'no-fly zone' over Bosnia to shield private contractors sending contraband arms cargoes into Bosnian-held Tuzla airport. They claimed that the deliveries were made at night using just-off-the-ground airdrops, a technique developed when Butch Saint was commander of the US Army in Europe and Sewall was the army's deputy chief of planning.

In spite of allegations that the US was breaking the arms embargo, there was no FBI investigation, even though the British and French brought their embargo-busting evidence to the attention of US Joint Chiefs of Staff chairman General John Shalikashvili and Richard Holbrooke, the assistant secretary of state for European affairs. It perhaps should be pointed out that FBI director Louis Freeh, appointed by Clinton in July 1993, and his wife Marilyn have been named as supernumerary members and that their two eldest children attended The Heights, Opus Dei's school in Washington.[1]

By July 1995, when John Paul II officially invoked the Just War doctrine to defend Bosnia, it was clear to the Vatican that the Serb aggression risked transforming what had been the world's most secularized Islamic community – a model for future relations between Christians and Muslims – into a radical theocracy, not far distant from Rome. If Bosnia turned radically Muslim, the very existence of the Catholic Church in that part of the Balkans would be threatened. Tudjman, therefore, was primed to follow the Vatican's lead. His advisers proposed the opening of peace talks with the Serbs of Krajina, which were predestined to fail, thereby qualifying for application of the Just War doctrine. Meanwhile, the commander of the Croatian armed forces, General Janko Bobetko, and his American advisers put the final touches on Operation Storm. The Serbs helped at the end of July 1995 by overplaying their hand, seizing control of Srebrenica, a UN 'safe zone' in eastern Bosnia, once again turning international opinion against them. In quick succession the UN abandoned Zepa, another Muslim 'safe area', and Sarajevo came under intensified bombardment. Serb General Ratko Mladic then moved his troops against the Muslim enclave of Bihac, where 180,000 Muslims were encircled, in the west of Bosnia.

Four years after the Serbs had set up on Croatian territory the autonomous Republika Srpska Krajina, one supposed that they were solidly dug in and ready for a fight. As part of Greater Serbia, the Krajina Serbs believed they enjoyed the solid backing of Belgrade. The joint attack on Bihac by Bosnian Serbs and those of Krajina provided the pretext for General Bobetko to begin Operation Storm. His streamlined, Americanized army launched a lightning attack against Krajina. Within eighty-four hours Krajina's capital of Knin had fallen and the siege of Bihac was lifted.

As the Croatian war machine started rolling through Krajina, a mortar attack – supposedly carried out by Serbs – against Sarajevo

---

[1] The Inspector in Charge of the FBI's Office of Public and Congressional Affairs, John E. Collingwood, stated in reply to the author's queries to the director: 'While I cannot answer your specific questions, I do note that you have been "informed" incorrectly by whomever your sources might be.'

killed thirty-seven civilians, bringing almost instant NATO retaliation: in two weeks 3,500 bombing sorties (two-thirds of them
by American warplanes) destroyed over 100 strategic targets in
Serb-held territory. The Serbs were unable to counter-attack. Within
days they had lost more than 3,000 square kilometres of terrain and
their routes were clogged with 60,000 new refugees. Bobetko's
troops were within shelling distance of Banja Luka when they
announced a unilateral ceasefire. Belgrade never budged.

The coincidence of a Croatian blitzkrieg and the NATO bombing forced the Serbs to admit defeat. The Vatican newspaper
L'Osservatore Romano portrayed the NATO air raids as a warning
to the psychopaths of Pale, intended to 'restore hope to the martyred
people' of Bosnia. The bombings were not an act of war, the Vatican
paper said, but demonstrated 'a determination to protect the rights
of those populations, the unfortunate Bosnians – Croats, Serbs and
Muslims – and all the other ethnic groups dragged into the madness
of a lengthy and ferocious war.'

Cardinal Kuharic of Zagreb proclaimed Operation Storm 'a legitimate action of Croatia to liberate her own territory'. When he
pointed out that the rebel occupation of Krajina had been illegal, that
Knin had rejected Tudjman's offer to negotiate, making military
action a necessary last resort, and that the international community
was unable to protect the victims of Serb aggression, he was reciting
the four prerequisites for receiving a Just War label.

More importantly, Operation Storm had momentarily short-
circuited radical Islam's call for total *jihad*, issued after the fall of
Srebrenica. Iran's foreign minister Ali Akbar Velayati had pledged at
a private meeting to give the Bosnian Muslims all the military assistance they needed, forcing more moderate nations like Turkey, Egypt,
Malaysia and Jordan, whose troops participated in the UN human-
itarian force, to back the Bosnian government openly rather than
leave the Iranians to hold Islam's high moral ground.

Backed by its new military might, Croatia was determined to exert
a moderating influence over its neighbour and made it clear that
imported Islamic extremism would not be tolerated. By then a couple
of brigades of non-Bosnian Muslims, numbering about 4,000 fighters
qualified by US officers as 'hard-core terrorists', were operating
within and sometimes in parallel to the Bosnian government forces.

Although the Dayton peace agreement that followed the Serb

defeat called for all foreign fighters to leave Bosnia, defence officials acknowledged there was little hope of persuading them to depart, even in spite of Bosnian affirmations that they would be out of the country within thirty days. 'These guys are mean. They've got to be controlled,' an American adviser to the Bosnian government said.[1]

According to a Sarajevo newspaper, a handful of the volunteers left for Chechnya, where war with the Russians had broken out again. But many simply faded into the snow-covered Hercegovina mountains to prepare for the next round of fighting. They were only too aware that the 1995 Dayton agreement had brought about the *de facto* partition of Bosnia, and this was not acceptable to them. They called it a betrayal.

Instructors at a 'Martyrs Detachment' training camp in central Bosnia, according to an intercepted report to their headquarters in Tehran, told European recruits that they were engaged 'in a *jihad* to defend Islam and its sacred principles against a *crazed, spiteful Occidental Crusade.*' For members of the 'Seekers of Martyrdom' battalion, then, the Tenth Crusade had already begun. A Croatian flag flew over western Bosnia, where the Croatian kuna and not the Bosnian dinar was in use, and those inhabitants who remained considered that part of the country to be solidly Croatian. As further proof, Medjugorje was under the control of the apparently Opus Dei-assisted and Catholic-led Croatian Army.

Zagreb demonstrated its determination to bar imported Islamic extremism from the region when in September 1995 it arrested Sheikh Tala'at Fouad Qassem, a leader in exile of the *Gama'a al-Islamiya* terrorist organization. Sheikh Tala'at had been foolish enough to cross Croatia on his way to Sarajevo to offer the Bosnian army more mujahedin volunteers. The Croatian authorities claimed they had expelled him, but he and his bodyguard disappeared and were presumed dead.

Days later *Gama'a* exploded a car bomb in Rijeka, killing the bomber and injuring twenty-nine. A statement faxed to the Reuters news agency announced that *Gama'a al-Islamiya* had carried out its first terrorist attack against Croatian interests. 'This historic operation is to assure the Croats that the fate of Tala'at Fouad Qassem

[1] Dana Priest, 'Foreign Muslims Fighting in Bosnia Considered "Threat" to US Troops', *The Washington Post*, 30 November 1995 (emphasis added).

will not pass without floods of blood running through internal and external Croatian interests,' *Gama'a* said.

A month later the Croatians answered *Gama'a*'s threat by inter-cepting and killing the 'Emir of the Mujahedin', Sheikh Anwar Shaaban, and four other Muslim volunteers serving with the Bosnian Third Army Corps. The ongoing hatred and fear prompted one Serb observer to remark that even with 60,000 NATO troops acting as guardians of the Dayton agreement, 'there will be no real peace in Bosnia for a long time to come.' Nevertheless the lull before the next round of fighting enabled the Pope's secret warriors to focus their attention elsewhere along the Spiritual Curtain.

35

HOPELESS DIALOGUE

Both Islam and Christianity are missionary faiths . . . Can believers who really believe passionately in their hearts that theirs is a missionary faith which calls people to holiness and truth really be committed to dialogue?

Dr Carey, Archbishop of Canterbury

A FORMER HIGH-RANKING OPUS DEI MEMBER IN SPAIN BELIEVES THAT the next Crusade – the Tenth Crusade – will be a cybernetic one, not fought with bombs or bullets, or even Middle Eastern oil, but with the latest computer technology and electronic communications. In his view, the words of the Prophet will be drowned in the fantasies of the cyberspace revolution – a revolution directed and controlled by the West. When the Muslim masses – poorly educated, semi-literate and dependent upon what their own media and mullahs tell them – obtain unrestricted access to Western information, culture and, above all, the Good News of the Gospels, they will be liberated from the bondage of medieval tyranny which now makes them fundamentalist fodder.

This view was to an extent echoed by John Paul II in early 1991 when, in response to a suggestion that development was no longer applicable to a country's state of industrialization but, today, to the strength of its banking sector and, tomorrow, its command of advanced communications systems, he smiled and noted, 'That is the thesis of Opus Dei.'[1]

Radical Islamic leaders are only too aware of the threat to their authority posed by the West's mastery of communications and information-transfer technology. Satellite-beamed TV transmissions expose the true believers to Western materialism and profane images of unveiled women. While laws can restrict individual freedoms, there is no technology that can place the communications genie back in the bottle once it has escaped.

One of the characteristics of a theocratic state is that in order to survive it must rigidly control the basic freedoms of its citizens, enforcing its edicts with spiritual tyranny that denies human rights. Freedom of choice is the enemy of fundamentalism in all its forms. Opus Dei's propagandists tell us that one of Escrivá de Balaguer's fundamental concerns was social justice in the world.[2] He maintained that Christians have a duty not only to expose social injustice but to find solutions that better serve mankind – i.e., their oppressed brothers or sisters 'in nations burdened with totalitarian regimes that are either anti-Christian, atheist or dominated by extreme nationalist fervour'.

This concern for social justice was said to have led to the founding by Opus Dei of its own human rights non-governmental organization (NGO) in Geneva, with UN Economic and Social Council observer status. Its task was to monitor access to basic education, as enshrined in the Helsinki Human Rights Charter. Nowhere was Opus Dei's name associated with the new NGO so that the Prelature can in no way be accused of stirring up animosity against Islamic states, the primary target of the 'access to education monitoring'. The International Organization for the Development of Free Access to Education is headed by an Opus Dei numerary but its staff includes non-Opus Dei members. One of its undertakings is the publication of a yearly report on the application of the Helsinki Charter in the field of education in all UN member states. In 1995, the Free Access to Education organization received approval from

---

[1] *Le Monde Diplomatique*, Paris, January 1995.
[2] 'Centre for Research and Communication, Manila', Opus Dei Newsletter No. 9, published by the Office of the Vice-Postulator of Opus Dei in Britain, p. 10.

CRUSADE FLASHPOINTS

Key to Hotspots

1 Algeria
2 Bosnia
3 Chad
4 Chechnya
5 East Timor
6 Egypt
7 Gaza
8 Horn of Africa
9 Nagorno-Karabakh
   (Armenian enclave in Azerbaijan)
10 South Philippines
11 Sudan

Islam's Holy Land

Saudi Arabia No churches,
            No Christian clergymen,
            No bibles,
            No religious tracts
            allowed

Key to Confrontation Points

1 Tadjikistan
2 Ethiopia
3 Eritrea
4 France
5 Iran
6 Istanbul
7 Kenya
8 Kosovo
9 Lebanon
10 Mali
11 Nigeria
12 Niger
13 Pakistan
14 Tanzania
15 Turkey
16 Bradford (UK)
17 Glasgow (UK)
18 Northern Iraq
19 Uganda
20 Zimbabwe

the Geneva authorities to open a summer University of Human Rights.

The Free Access to Education organization is another example of Opus Dei's use of the guile of snakes and innocence of doves. The NGO's concern is not targeted at Catholic countries, to be sure, but primarily the access of Islamic women to equal-rights education. In Afghanistan, Sudan and the Yemen, for example, literacy among women is abysmally low and the local *ulema* – the clergy, which is male by definition – insists on it being kept that way. Opus Dei's Geneva NGO, therefore, is one small way of applying pressure on traditional Islamic countries to become more amenable to change. This carries with it a destabilizing component. It is part of Opus Dei's strategy for countering Islam – albeit the 'soft' part, but nevertheless hidden, because Opus Dei does not want to be seen, indeed cannot be seen, as an enemy of Islam.

This segment of Opus Dei's strategy to shake up Islam and make it more open and less aggressive to the ways of the West emerged at the Fourth UN Conference on Women in Beijing in August 1995. Joaquín Navarro-Valls appeared on television at the opening of the conference to inform the world that there was no Vatican alliance with Islam at Beijing. Left unsaid was that it was part of Opus Dei's double-handed strategy to use women's rights to discredit traditional Islam. The need to improve education for women, the connection between poor education and poverty, and the fact that women bear the 'heavier burden' of poverty, were central to the Vatican platform at Beijing.

Faced with the hostility that the obstructionist performance in Cairo had earned it, the Vatican changed tactics. Its Beijing delegation was officially headed by a *liberal* Harvard law professor, Mary Ann Glendon. But Navarro-Valls was also present, more as a negotiator than spokesman. When some 2,000 of the 4,500 delegates signed a petition asking the UN to withdraw the Holy See's permanent observer status, Navarro-Valls remarked nonchalantly, 'That was already decided in the twelfth century.' The twelfth century was when the Second, Third, German and Emperor's crusades were fought, marking the height of the Crusading movement.

The Vatican negotiators emphasized that the Holy See's views on the role of women were quite different from those of many Muslim countries. But Rome had 'toned down' its approach, according to Navarro-Valls, because it felt the issues were 'peripheral to the main dialogue'. Instead, the Catholic thrust came from the Latin American and Philippine delegations, which, if not actually led by Opus Dei militants, all had strong Opus Dei components. But even this back-door approach risked being counter-productive. A survey conducted by Costa Rica's Arias Peace Foundation found that of the 290 Central American NGOs polled, 71 per cent described Opus Dei as an organization of religious bigots comparable to Islamic fundamentalists, 80 per cent said it did not represent the needs or aspirations of women in their countries, 51 per cent that it kept women in a subordinate position, 78 per cent that it pressured official delegations to the conference to adopt the Opus Dei stance on key issues, especially reproductive rights (e.g., forbidding contraception or the use of condoms, either as a family planning measure or in HIV/AIDS prevention programmes), and 18 per cent felt that its efforts ran counter to freedom of expression.[1]

Nevertheless, there are many Christians who agree with Opus Dei's 'soft' approach. The fact that Opus Dei is known, vaguely, to be doing something to counter radical Islam earns it the sympathy of those who want a stronger Western response to the Prophet's 'crazies'. In general, the concept of Just War as a last resort against unprovoked aggression has been largely accepted by traditionalists and other right-wing groups. The fact that Opus Dei was the principal proponent of a dusted-off Just War doctrine has brought it their admiration.

One of the front-line countries in the Spiritual Wars is the Philippines. With a 1990 population of 65 million, 84 per cent Catholic, the country has a vociferous Muslim minority. Its birth rate is just over 3 per cent, giving it a projected population by the end of the millennium of 90 million. Opus Dei's operations in the Philippines are important and enjoy the full backing of Cardinal Jaime L. Sin, described as the Richelieu of south-east Asia.

The first Opus Dei centre was opened in Manila in 1964, after a number of Filipino students who were recruited into the Work while attending universities in the United States returned home 'with a

---

[1] 'Central American Women – Fundamentalist Bulwark', Inter Press Service, 4 September 1995.

desire to introduce Opus Dei's apostolic ideals in their country'. Their 'unavoidable duty . . . to find Christian solutions to the problems of society' led them to found the Centre for Research & Communication in Manila as an institute of higher studies in business administration and economics. 'By providing at the same time the basic principles of the social teaching of the Church, it seeks to imbue human, economic and social development of the Philippines with a Christian spirit', an Opus Dei publication stated.[1] Such a concept, needless to say, clashes with radical Islam.

The Spiritual Curtain in the Philippines descends somewhere south of the Jintotolo Channel which roughly divides the archipelago in two. During the 1970s about 50,000 persons were killed in sectarian conflict in the south. By the 1980s the government more or less had the situation in hand and the killings receded until 1991, when rival Muslim groups began banding together under a new organization, Abu Sayyaf, which received Libyan and Iranian support. In April 1995, they unleashed their first large-scale operation, an attack on the southern Philippine town of Ipil, on Mindanao Island, that killed 100 people and left the centre of the town of 50,000 in smouldering ruins.

'Abu Sayyaf is doing everything in its power to create a situation where Christians and Muslims will go to war . . . as a prelude to setting up an Islamic state in the southern Philippines,' announced the minister of the interior, Rafel Alunan. Abu Sayyaf, he said, was part of a global network radiating from the Middle East, with tentacles extending to the United States and Asia. They have been laying the groundwork in the Philippines for at least four years, as it was an obvious staging point for expanding into other parts of south-east Asia, Alunan added.

'It's a Christian country, the only one in Asia. They have an axe to grind against Christians. These guys are a throwback to the Middle Ages. They want to see the resurgence of the Islamic Empire . . . They want theocratic rule,' he said.[2]

Abu Sayyaf, which means 'Father of the Executioner' in Arabic, was founded by Abdurajak Abubakar Janjalani, a Libyan-educated high-school teacher. It operates throughout the southern Philippines

---

[1] Opus Dei Newsletter No. 9, *Op. cit.*, p. 11.
[2] Alistair McIntosh, 'Extremists Want Philippine Religious War', Reuters, 8 April 1995.

and has kidnapped scores of Catholic priests and missionaries. According to Alunan it is linked to an international fundamentalist organization, *Harakat al Islamiya*, of which very little is known. *Harakat al Islamiya* was said to be allied with Sheikh Omar Abdel Rahman, the blind Egyptian cleric found guilty of instigating the 1993 World Trade Center bombing, and to Ramzi Ahmed Yousef, leader of the Manhattan bombers and mastermind of a plot to kill the Pope during his January 1995 visit to Manila. US and Philippine authorities also accused Yousef of carrying out the December 1994 bombing of a Philippine Airlines flight that killed a Japanese passenger and of planning to blow up in quick succession eleven American airliners.

Abu Sayyaf defectors have disclosed that Filipino recruits are sent to Pakistan and Afghanistan for religious and military training. The government claims that Abu Sayyaf has also incorporated elements of Islam's Floating Army into its ranks. A few days after the Ipil attack, Philippine intelligence was informed that four Hamas militants had entered the country to make contact with Abu Sayyaf.

While Abu Sayyaf terrorists were wreaking havoc in Ipil, Muslim delegates from eighty countries gathered in Khartoum to attend a four-day meeting hosted by Dr Hassan al-Turabi's Popular Arab and Islamic Conference. It attracted delegates from the Islamic Salvation Front, the Armed Islamic Group, Hamas, Hezbollah, Islamic Jihad, Tabligh, Egypt's Muslim Brotherhood, *Gama'a al-Islamiya*, the US Nation of Islam and other militant groups. At the outset of the conference, Turabi accused NATO and Western intelligence agencies of 'instigating a new Crusade against Islam and against Islamic revival'.

'The West is trying to extinguish the light of Islam,' Turabi charged. But he had another design in mind. Turabi wants to restore Islam to a central role in world affairs. To do this he needed an Islamic forum that was linked neither to governments nor political persuasions. The Khartoum conference backed him, voting to create the Islamic Popular Congress, intended to be a Vatican for the Islamic world.

With the Islamic Popular Congress, Turabi argued, the followers of the Prophet would be better equipped 'to defend Islam from Western aggression'. Needless to say, the Saudis and other traditional Islamic powers did not approve, but in the restructured dynamics of the post-Cold War Islamic world leadership was escaping from the royal autocrats of the Arabian peninsula and drifting towards the more radical members of the Central Islamic Axis. This was bad news for the world of salvation.

Once the conference voted in favour of the Islamic Popular Congress, Turabi could afford to talk moderation. The conference's final resolution urged co-operation with Christian fundamentalists, stating that they shared common ground with Islamic conservatives. 'The conference supports . . . a dialogue with the West and recommends that Muslims try to start a debate with the Christian world to begin co-operation with people of the faith against the forces of corrupt materialism,' the statement said.

Turabi was more than ever the man to watch in the Islamic world and the priests at the 'parish on the far side of the Tiber' were surely measuring him as a possible counterpart in the West's 'dialogue' with Islam. At an earlier press conference Turabi had gone directly to the heart of what he alleged was the basic malaise. 'There is a need for leading figures in the West to learn about Islam, directly . . . The West cannot govern the world. There is no God called "the West",' he said.

'Humanity is very close, the means of communication are great. We should have . . . dialogue. Let's talk to each other. One or two languages can serve for that communication, and let everyone contribute his own share, his own culture, to the common stock of human culture.

'My values dictate that I should dialogue even with someone who is hostile to me . . . The Koran tells me, "talk to him". My religious model is the Prophet, who created the first state with a written constitution, a state established between Muslims and Jews . . . And he invited the Christians and allowed them to pray inside his mosque. So my model, which I call perfect, is such that I'll do my best to talk to him who is hostile to me. If you don't want to talk to me, you'll never speak Arabic, so I will learn English, and learn French, and some German perhaps, and some Italian. He doesn't want to talk to a black man, but I'll talk to him. He doesn't want to share wealth evenly between North and South in the international economic dialogue, but I'll try to share human wealth with him, or freedom . . . But, of course, if he commits aggression against me, I'll use force. I'm told in the Koran to respond exactly . . .'[1]

Fine, Dr Turabi, but what of the Sudanese record? When in October 1995 the German ambassador Peter Mende sought information from the authorities in Khartoum about the killing of gaoled students who took part in anti-government protests he was threatened with expulsion.

Opus Dei never makes an idle threat; nor would it allow its pope to make one either. When John Paul II told his hosts in Khartoum to cease 'the terrible harvest of suffering' in the south of Sudan or risk the wrath of the God of Abraham he was not expressing a wish but a statement of force. Six months after the Pope's visit to Khartoum, a little-known interdenominational human rights organization – Christian Solidarity International – made an entry into the south of the country, not only bringing aid to the decimated Christian and animist communities, but also whipping up political support for south Sudanese autonomy in the neighbouring Christian states, backing a National Democratic Alliance against Khartoum and launching in Western capitals a campaign to promote the autonomist cause. After one visit to the south, Christian Solidarity's Baroness Caroline Cox, a trained nurse, reported that Sudanese troops regularly raided Dinka villages, abducting children and young women to provide labour and sexual services. Some were given Muslim names and forced to attend Koranic schools, while others were sold on the Manyiel slave market in Bahr el Ghazal province.

A new Christian Sudanese newsletter, *Light and Hope for Sudan*, reported in July 1995 that since the beginning of the ten-year-old civil war, 'nearly 2 million have died, most from starvation and disease, and 5 million have fled their homes'. Khartoum, the newsletter said, was using starvation to facilitate 'its programme of Islamization and Arabization'. The Christian Solidarity mission called for human rights monitors to visit all areas of Sudan. Turabi made it clear that such a proposal was not on his agenda for dialogue. Christian Solidarity had, by then, highlighted the existence in southern Sudan of all the necessary elements for a 'Just War'.

---

[1] Dr Hassan al-Turabi press conference, Inter-Religious Dialogue Conference, Khartoum, 8–10 October 1994, downloaded from Internet, 'Contemporary Islamic Political Views', from: Ben.Parker@unep.no.

Weeks later the Sudanese rebels, revamped into a disciplined fighting force, launched their first major offensive since the Pope's visit to Khartoum. They wiped out an élite mechanized division, killing or capturing 7,000 government soldiers and seizing all of its equipment. Using tanks for the first time and supported – Khartoum alleged – by regular units of the Ugandan and Tanzanian armies, the rebels recaptured most of Western and Eastern Equitoria in spite of attacks by Iranian-piloted helicopter gunships.

Within weeks the morale of the southern forces had been transformed. What had made the difference? I asked John Eibner, Christian Solidarity's Sudan operations director. 'Because they are no longer isolated,' he answered.

Christian Solidarity is an interesting study in operational anonymity. Its origins and resources are untraceable. It claims that its accounts are audited by a recognized auditing firm and that the annual financial statements are available to the public. But this is not the case. The public is shown a skeleton balance sheet that is unsigned and ambiguously labelled. While purporting to be the Christian Solidarity International accounts, it appears to be those of the Swiss branch only – and gives no indication of the direct source of its funds, only general headings.[1]

Following the October 1994 murder in Algeria of two Spanish religious sisters, the Pope remarked, 'I feel it my duty to remind all men of goodwill that an authentic solution can only be reached by distancing themselves from the abyss of violence, so as to follow instead the way of dialogue . . .'[2]

But the Pope had really touched on the bottom line of the spiritual balance sheet when he stated in *Crossing the Threshold of Hope* – the royalties from which he pledged to rebuild the destroyed churches of Croatia – that '*Islam is not a religion of redemption . . .* Jesus is mentioned, but only as a prophet who prepares for the last prophet, Muhammad.' By affirming his Millennium Jubilee

---

[1] Christian Solidarity International, headquartered in Zurich with antennae in 21 countries, claims to help 'persecuted Christians of any denomination in any country, by prayer, campaigning and practical action'. It has NGO status with the UN in Geneva, and is active in such spiritual hot spots as Nagorno Karabakh, Armenia, Bosnia, Iraq and Pakistan. It claims that 90 to 95 per cent of its income comes from individual donors, the remainder from churches, foundations, businesses and governments. It is headed by a Reform pastor, Dr Hans Jürg Stückelberger.

[2] 'We cannot kill others in the name of God', *L'Osservatore Romano*, 2 November 1994.

intention of bringing the mystery of Christian salvation to all mankind – to 'purify the world' through Christian conversion – he sends out a contrary message to Islam that he is not interested in placing his vision of salvation – his 'genuine religious belief' – on an equal footing with the teachings of the Koran, which demand total submission to the word of Allah, as interpreted by the Prophet.

A year after the separate calls by John Paul II and Hassan al-Turabi for a dialogue between religions, Islamic *jihad* had been exported to Croatia, France and Germany, with bombings and terrorist threats. Algeria's outlawed Armed Islamic Group in a message carried on Internet from an address in San Diego, California, boasted that 'with pride and strength our *jihad* has made military hits in the heart of France . . . in its largest cities. Let it be our promise that we will disturb your sleep, and tear [you] up, and Islam will conquer France.'

'We are at war,' declared French interior minister Jean-Louis Debré, after the eighth 1995 bomb attack had spread fear and suspicion. 'It is the war of modern times, and I tell you that the government is determined to win that war and will make no concessions,' he said.

After the German police broke up an Islamic arms network by arresting nine people, Abdelkhadar Sahraoui, supposedly a neutral Algerian businessman living in exile, warned on German TV, 'If we see that you are neo-colonialists, that you want to destroy our people, that you want not partnership but domination in the Mediterranean, then we will fight you.'

Either the Pope and Turabi had not heard the other's call for dialogue or they lacked sincerity. The Iranians, on the other hand, felt no need for dialogue, and this in spite of their opportunistic alliance with the Vatican during the 1994 UN Population Conference. The Iranians had an altogether more straightforward approach. 'Christianity is truly lacking in divine and religious spirituality, and is an arid and useless movement,' Ayatollah Ahmed Jannati, the country's second-ranking religious figure, announced, reflecting the radical mood that transfixed his country. Christianity, he said, had created a centralized power in the person of the Pope, whom all Catholics are obliged to follow. 'Through this system they have maintained that lifeless corpse, while Islam possesses so much spirituality, so much depth, with such strength for administering the world.'[1] As Ayatollah Jannati pointed out, you can't dialogue with a corpse.

With its unbending dogmatism, Opus Dei has been credited by its supporters with putting life back into the Church and accused by others of polarizing the Church. Many Catholics, however, do not want to know about the Curial battles between Progressives and Conservatives, or between the Rome party and the *Ostpolitikers*. They want to worship in peace and with confidence in their pope. But as the Millennium Jubilee approaches, this may no longer be possible. The 'smart and obstinate' work of the Pope's secret warriors risks bringing about a polarization of religions. It was Turabi who first drew attention to it.

'Islamic renaissance has reminded some Christians who have been oblivious to religion that they have to define themselves in contrast to this phenomenon. They say they are Christians, even if they are not necessarily very religious. But the danger is that some people may try to exploit religion . . . for their own economic and political interests, [and] try to mobilize Christianity against the Islamic renaissance. That's why I think we need to communicate.'[2]

---

[1] 'Christianity dead, says Iran cleric', Reuters, 2 December 1994.
[2] Dr Hassan al-Turabi press conference, Khartoum, 8–10 October 1994.

EPILOGUE

The relationship between Christianity and Islam is . . . one of the great fault lines running between and through civilizations, with recurrent tremors reminding us that destruction can burst forth again where such deep divisions lie beneath the surface crust.

Dr Carey, Archbishop of Canterbury

OPUS DEI'S DRIVE TO DOMINATE THE ROMAN CATHOLIC CHURCH IS OF a determination not seen since the Counter-Reformation. Because it is so determined, in whatever form the Prelature develops during the years ahead it will not be without friction, both inside and outside the Vatican. This makes its existence a matter of concern to everyone, whether the holder of a Catholic baptismal certificate or a simple pedestrian in the secular city.

Opus Dei is no doubt sincere in its desire to protect the Church. Its members include many dedicated and outstanding people. Its founding principles centred upon a Christian work ethic are laudable. But Opus Dei has been in constant evolution since 1928. Because of the tactics it employs to achieve its goals, including the use of *pillería*, and the fact that it is subject to no disclosure and very little oversight, some observers have compared it to 'a Mafia shrouded in white.'

Every signpost indicates that behind the black-stained doors at the Villa Tevere Opus Dei's senior strategists are hard at work, plotting to combat with a 'just and rightful' response what they regard as the deteriorating moral values of society and religious radicalism wherever it threatens their vision of the Church. Former high-ranking members confirm that such a reaction is consistent with the Prelature's philosophy and goals. But the outsider is barred at every turning from learning anything meaningful about Opus Dei's inner intentions. It is therefore essential that the experiences and testimonies of former members be made known as they provide the only available insight of what really goes on in the minds of Escrivá de Balaguer's sons and daughters.

Opus Dei is a secret sect that has successfully removed itself from the hierarchic control of the Church. Secrecy is the enemy of an open, democratic society. If Opus Dei is not secretive, as it repeatedly maintains, why does it refuse to publish the quintennial reports on its apostolic work that Article VI of *Ut sit* requires it to submit to the Pope? The answer: 'Neither Opus Dei nor the Holy See would make public a document prepared for the Pope.' That essentially tells us everything we need to know about Opus Dei's moral authority. Opus Dei defends a just cause but employs unscrupulous methods for achieving its ends.

While Opus Dei might be listed, *inter alia*, in the *Vatican Yearbook*, the *Catholic Directory for England and Wales*, other diocesan directories around the world, and in the telephone directories of the cities where it operates, the fact remains that it covers its workings with an opacity intended to render them inaccessible to public scrutiny. Opus Dei does not want the rest of the world to know what it is doing. Article 190 of the 1950 Constitutions requires that 'whatever is undertaken by members must not be attributed to our Institution, but to God only'. By virtue of Article 190 Opus Dei's role in forging a more aggressive political policy for the Vatican remains shrouded in secrecy.

A higher political profile for the Church apparently brings increased financial dividends in the form of contributions from the faithful, as once again the Holy See was running at the break-even point. This does not mean that the financial insecurity of the 1980s is over, as one financial hiccup would be sufficient to put the Vatican back in the red. But the record shortfall of $87.5 million reported in

1991, which decreased to $3.4 million in 1992, was followed by a small $1.5 million surplus in 1993 (the first since 1981). Another small surplus of $419,000 was posted in 1994. Then a deficit of $22.5 million was at first predicted for 1995, again sending financial shivers through the Curia. But the Vatican later reported that the expected shortfall was wiped out by increased income from investments, mostly bonds and real estate. In other words, one Roman prelate remarked off the record, Opus Dei had again come to the rescue. Another small surplus of $330,000 was predicted for 1996.

Opus Dei ally Cardinal Edmund Szoka, who left the archdiocese of Detroit to take charge of the Vatican's Prefecture for Economic Affairs, confidently stated that the refloating of the Holy See's treasury meant the 'image problem' caused by the Banco Ambrosiano scandal was behind it. But with Andreotti on trial for conspiracy to murder and associating with the Mafia, new revelations were expected that made Szoka's assertion seem less than certain. In any event, vulgarizing the Church's central 'mystery' by linking it to earthly parameters, portraying the Holy See as a multinational enterprise concerned with such things as price/earnings ratios and cash-flow requirements, Cardinal Szoka risked committing the error of 'reductionism', a serious theological offence.

One of the Vatican's largest property holdings outside Italy was the Notre Dame of Jerusalem centre. When faced with a 1995 operating loss, having incurred cumulative deficits of $330 million during the previous decade,[1] the Vatican was forced to divest itself of non-revenue producing properties. Ownership or usufruct of the Jerusalem centre, according to Rome sources, was finally transferred to Opus Dei, thereby wiping out the anticipated 1995 deficit. Assuming control of the huge Notre Dame complex meant that the Prelature had extended its influence to the Via Dolorosa and access to the Holy Sepulchre, where for 2,000 years Christian pilgrims have flocked to touch the tomb of 'the God made flesh'. But officially Opus Dei is not present in Israel, not having registered with the Ministry of Religious Affairs, as its headquarters in the Holy Land remains in Bethlehem, which is under Palestinian control.

[1] By comparison, King Fahd of Saudi Arabia announced that his government had spent $18.7 billion developing Islam's two holy cities of Mecca and Medina during the same period, with the result that the Grand Mosque in Mecca could accommodate one million worshippers at one time, vastly more than St Peter's.

Opus Dei's activities in the Holy Land allowed plans for the Millennium Jubilee to proceed with confidence. In September 1995, President Yasser Arafat of the Palestinian national authority called on John Paul II at Castelgandolfo and invited him to celebrate the year 2000 in Jerusalem and Bethlehem. According to the press release issued by Navarro-Valls, Arafat wanted to thank the Pope for the support 'which the Palestinian cause has always received from the Holy See'.[1]

Jerusalem was to be the centrepiece of the Millennium celebrations and Opus Dei wanted to be well implanted there to insure the Pope's safety. But Dr Turabi, the ayatollahs of Qum, Hezbollah and Hamas were all said to look unfavourably upon the planned millennium visit. Jerusalem was after all Islam's third holiest city and the radical fringe saw no reason for the papal incursion. Confronted with a possible hostile reaction to the Pope's presence in the holy city, the prized goal of every Crusade since the eleventh century, Opus Dei's acquisition of the fortress-like Notre Dame centre seemed like prudent forward planning. It also confirmed Villa Tevere's authority over the Supreme Authority of the Rock.

Opus Dei denies it meddles in Vatican politics. But can it be believed? Perhaps part of the answer – revealing of the inner nature of the Catholic Church's leading sect – is contained in two passages from the Prelature's confidential internal publication, *Crónica*:

- *The lesson is clear, crystal clear: all things are lawful for me, but not all things are expedient.*[2]
- *Dirty clothes are washed at home. The first manifestation of your dedication is not being so cowardly as to go outside the Work to wash the dirty clothes. That is if you want to be saints. If not, you are not needed here.*

---

[1] The Holy See's Sala Stampa Bulletin No. 319/95, issued on 2 September 1995. Two months later Arafat issued the same invitation to foreign ministers of 26 countries attending the Mediterranean co-operation conference in Barcelona. 'I invite you to participate in this great world religious and historical event – the second millennium of the birth of Our Lord Jesus Christ, peace be upon Him – and to make Bethlehem a beacon of peace and co-existence of all faiths in the whole world . . .' Arafat said.

[2] In this editorial, 'The Confession', in *Crónica* VI, 1962, Escrivá de Balaguer was paraphrasing I Corinthians 6:12. Paul is quoting in this passage 'the Lord Jesus Christ'. But as used in *Crónica*, the reader is left with the impression that the 'me' refers to Escrivá de Balaguer himself.

'All things are lawful for me' explains in six words Opus Dei's arrogance and gives it the writ to interpret legislative texts as it sees fit, or even ignore them altogether. One might imagine that an organization founded by 'divine inspiration' would not have dirty linen. But apparently from time to time Opus Dei does. The strict order that dirty linen must be washed at home illustrates its mania for secrecy. Inevitably, this mania must lead to a collective 'siege mentality' common to many sects. Opus Dei is uncommon in that for half a century it has been developing its apostolate by amassing unprecedented financial power for a religious institution. No other Christian sect has met with such success.

The *Crónica* affirmations are worth bearing in mind at a time when the reign of the present Pope is coming to an end. Never has the papal succession been so important. There are those within the Curia who believe that if the Catholic Church is to retain significance and not become irrelevant in the twenty-first century, she must again wield power in a temporal as well as a spiritual sense. They support the notion that religion is a missing dimension in the dialogue between peoples and nations. In the end analysis, however, Opus Dei prelates are not open to dialogue because no meaningful dialogue is possible with a group or organization that is convinced it possesses the divine truth and therefore knows all the answers.

On most issues of direct interest to it, Villa Tevere can count on the support of at least sixty cardinals. To insure that the episcopate is favourably disposed towards it, Opus Dei arranged for an 'independent' American foundation – the Wethersfield Foundation of New York – to finance scholarships for African bishops to study in Rome. A majority of Catholics live in the Third World, making it a Third World Church, and therefore Opus Dei's move to improve the theological standards of key Third World prelates seemed generous and wise. Interestingly, however, the foundation's cheques were made out not to those who received Opus Dei's invitation but to Prelature's theological institute in Rome, the *Ateneo Romano della Santa Croce,* thereby insuring that tuition for each of the beneficiaries was paid up front. Nevertheless, the idea was genial, permitting Opus Dei to spiritually wine and dine the Africans at someone else's expense. But behind this seemingly charitable offer was said to lie a more devious plan: having decided that the next pope will in all probability be Spanish, Opus Dei was reportedly looking two popes ahead, when the time might be opportune to elect the first black African pontiff. Just as a Polish pope was needed to defeat the Evil Empire of Communism, so Opus Dei apparently believes that a black pope will be needed to reverse Islam's march in Africa. From today's bishops come tomorrow's cardinals, and Opus Dei was already insuring that those on its list of possible candidates were properly indoctrinated with the true teachings of the Church.

In addition to its influence over the cardinalate (by the end of 1995, 122 of the 165 cardinals had been appointed by John Paul II), the following eighteen prelates and nine lay people – by no means a complete list – are part of Opus Central's power base inside the Curia:

- Monsignor Joaquín Alonso Pacheco, consultor to the Congregation for the Causes of Saints;
- Dr Carl A. Anderson, vice-president, John Paul II Institute of the Family;
- Reverend Professor Eduardo Baura, consultor to the Congregation for the Evangelization of Peoples;
- Reverend Doctor Cormac Burke, member of the college of assessors of the Tribunal of the Roman Rota;
- Monsignor Ignacio Carrasco de Paula, professor at the Ateneo Romano della Santa Croce, member of the Pontifical Academy for Life and consultor to the Pontifical Councils for the Family and Pastorale per gli Operatori Sanitaria;
- Archbishop Juan Luis Cipriani, consultor to the Congregation for the Clergy;
- Monsignor Professor Lluis Clavell Ortiz-Repiso, magnifico rettore of the Ateneo Romano della Santa Croce, consultor to the Congregation for Catholic Education and under-secretary for the Pontifical Council on Culture;
- The Honourable Virgil C. Dechant, central director of the IOR, member of the Pontifical councils for the Family and Social Communications, and adviser to the Vatican City State; his wife, Ann, also serves on the Pontifical Council for the Family;
- Monsignor Stanislaw Dziwisz, capo ufficio, first section, general affairs, Secretariat of State, and personal secretary to the Pope;
- Reverend Professor José Escudero Imbert, consultor to the Congregation for the Causes of Saints;
- Monsignor Amadeo de Fuenmayor, consultor to the Pontifical Council for the Interpretation of Legislative Texts;

- Monsignor Ramón García de Haro, consultor to the Pontifical Council for the Family;
- Monsignor José Luis Gutiérrez Gómez, member of the college of relators at the Congregation for the Causes of Saints and consultor to the Pontifical Council for the Interpretation of Legislative Texts;
- Dr John M. Haas, president of the International Institute for Culture and a faculty member of the John Paul II Institute of the Family. Founded in response to John Paul II's call for the re-evangelization of culture, Haas's cultural institute guides groups of prominent intellectuals from Europe and the Americas on tours of Catholic sites in Europe. Its activities are tied in with the International Academy for Philosophy in Liechtenstein and it is used by Opus Dei as a high-level recruiting vehicle;
- Archbishop Julián Herranz Casado, consultor to the Congregation of Bishops, president of the Council for the Interpretation of Legislative Texts, member of the Supreme Tribunal of the Apostolic Signature, and co-president with archbishops Cheli and Foley of the Council of Advisers to the Papal Household;
- Reverend Professor Gonzalo Herranz Rodríguez, head of the Bioethics Department at the University of Navarra, president of the directors' council of the Pontifical Academy for Life and consultor to the Congregation for Catholic Education;
- Monsignor José Tomás Martín de Agar y Valverde, judge on the Ordinary Tribunal of the Vicariat of Rome;
- Professor Jean-Marie Meyer, a French philosopher, and his wife, Anouk Lejeune, members of the Pontifical Council for the Family (Anouk's mother, Birthe Brinsted Lejeune, widow of Jerome Lejeune, the brilliant bio-geneticist who was lauded by science for his discovery of an extra human chromosome related to mental retardedness, is an honorary member of the Pontifical Academy for Life);
- Euro-MP Alberto Michelini, media consultant to the Vatican;
- Reverend Antonio Miralles, consultor to the Congregation for the Doctrine of the Faith and former dean of the theology faculty at the Ateneo Romano della Santa Croce;
- Monsignor Fernando Ocáriz, Opus Dei's new vicar general, consultor to the Congregation for the Doctrine of the Faith and permanent member of the Pontifical Commission 'Ecclesia Dei', formed in 1988 to bring members of the Econe movement of Archbishop Lefebvre back into the fold;

- Monsignor Enrique Planas y Comas, director of the Filmoteca Vaticana;
- Professor José Angel Sánchez Asiain, central director, the IOR;
- Ambassador Alberto Vollmer, consultor to the Administration of the Holy See's Patrimony, and his wife, Countess Cristina Vollmer, members of the Pontifical Council for the Family;
- Monsignor Javier Echevarría, grand chancellor of the Ateneo Romano della Santa Croce and consultor to the Congregation for the Causes of Saints. In March 1995 John Paul II appointed him consultor to the Congregation for the Clergy, reinforcing Opus Dei's voice in directing the careers of diocesan priests around the world;
- Another fifty Opus Dei priests carry the honorary titles of chaplain of the Papal Household or prelate of the Holy See.

With less than four years remaining before the great millennium jubilee, the careers of some of the key players in this long-running film of intrigue have been touched by a series of disquieting events. Mother Superior Catalina Serus of the Carmelite convent where Concepción Boullón Rubio lived claimed that she had no knowledge of Sister Concepción ever being ill and wondered, therefore, how she could have been miraculously cured by Escrivá de Balaguer's intercession. This disclosure cast further serious doubt on the authenticity of the miracle that guaranteed Opus Dei's Founder his beatification and also might tarnish the reputation of the postulator general, Father Flavio Capucci.

In Spain, Opus Dei outcast José María Ruiz-Mateos formed his own political party dedicated to fighting corruption. He had struck a deep vein of discontent in a country where 22 per cent of the active population was unemployed and 8 million lived below the poverty line. To help his campaign he acquired a Madrid radio station, Radio Liberty, and hosted a daily talk programme called 'The Sting of the Bee'. He also opened an office to investigate scandals that listeners brought to his attention.

Corruption had been the hallmark of González's thirteen years of government. A good example was the rise of the political candyman, Antonio Navalón. But even his fortunes took a turn for the worse after he was accused of bribing finance ministry officials with £3 million advanced by the fallen chairman of Banesto, Mario Conde, making him a fugitive from Spanish justice. But at least Navalón was still alive. One of the men he most admired, former justice minister Pio Cabanillas, was said to have disappointed his friends in Opus Dei, bringing God's vengeance upon him. He was photographed in the company of transvestites while attending a session of the European parliament in Strasbourg and accused of belonging to a paedophile network. He died of a heart attack in Madrid on 10 October 1991 and was buried before his son had time to return from the United States for the funeral.

Since then, Opus Dei's replacement for Rumasa, the Grand Tibidabo Company of Barcelona, had to be bailed out of trouble by Alfredo Sánchez Bella. 'I am not a member of Opus Dei; I do not have sufficient merit,' Franco's former tourism minister told *El País*.[1] He owned 18 per cent of Grand Tibidabo, whose chairman, Javier de la Rosa, a financial adviser to King Juan Carlos, was in prison on fraud charges. De la Rosa was the Kuwait Investment Office representative in Spain; his wife, Mercedes Misol, was a supernumerary, but Opus Dei claimed that de la Rosa himself was not a member.

Many believed that de la Rosa, along with another royal adviser, Manuel de Prado, had incurred Opus Dei's wrath. A major contributor to Opusian causes, de la Rosa was said to have disobeyed orders. Manuel de Prado, one-time Grand Tibidabo deputy chairman, had left his supernumerary wife for another woman and was drawn – unjustly, he insisted – into the de la Rosa scandal. The investigation of de la Rosa's misdealings led to the disclosure of allegations that he had attempted to bribe the King with a £60 million backhander from the Kuwaitis, seeking a royal nod for American warplanes to use Spanish bases during the Gulf War crisis. It was the first time the King's name had been linked to public scandal. Until the Spanish attorney-general decided to call off his investigation, rumour was rife that Juan Carlos would be forced to abdicate in favour of his son, Prince Felipe. Felipe's sister, the Princess Royal, was married to an Opus Dei supernumerary.

[1] *El País*, 17 November 1995.

The Madrid daily, *Dario 16*, reported without citing sources that the Pope was an accomplice of Opus Dei in its money-grabbing schemes:

'Why are you going to Italy?' de la Rosa was asked one day at the Zarzuela Palace.

The Catalan promoter, his eyes watering, lowered his gaze. 'It's a secret . . . but I'm financing an Opus Dei hospital for underprivileged children,' he explained confidentially.

In Rome, after discussing the project, the hospital director asked, 'Don Javier, do you want to come with me to the Vatican and see the magnificent work the Japanese are doing in the Sistine Chapel?'

Don Javier accepted. When they arrived at the Vatican, the director said, 'Wait here a moment while I go wash my hands.'

Off he went and, as if by miracle, a few minutes later another door opened and out came John Paul II in person. He walked slowly across the corridor towards Don Javier and in a low voice spoke his name: 'Señor de la Rosa, one thousand pardons, but the ways of the Lord are inscrutable. I can see you are an honourable and compassionate person. In this time of crisis the Church is again threatened with serious problems. I am counting on your help.'

The Holy Father then continued down the corridor . . . [1]

Should Papa Wojtyla's reign end before the millennium jubilee, Opus Dei's favourite to succeed him was rumoured to be Cardinal Ricardo María Carles of Barcelona. But these plans were upset when, on the basis of allegations made by an Italian hot money dealer, Riccardo Marocco, magistrates in Torre Annunziata, south of Naples, asked the Spanish authorities for permission to question Carles about allegations that he was linked to the laundering of astronomical sums of money through the Vatican bank for a ring of international traffickers. The ring's activities were alleged to include dealing in arms, strategic materials and precious metals. Among the strategic materials was an awesome commodity known as red mercury – described as 'cherry red and very dangerous' – used

[1] Isabel Durán and José Díaz Herrera, 'El Saqueo de España', as excerpted in *Dario 16*, 10 November 1995, pp. 6–14.

in the manufacture of a new generation of nuclear weapons of extremely high potency. The magistrates in Torre Annunziata were told by the Spanish justice, who had satisfied themselves there was not 'the slightest proof' implicating Carles, that their evidence against the cardinal was not serious.

Seven months later – in June 1996 – the investigation suddenly burst into new activity with the arrest on suspicion of twenty people in Italy and the launching of a dozen international warrants. An alleged former paymaster for the CIA in southern Europe, who claimed knowledge of the plot to poison John Paul I, was among those taken into custody. Police searched the home of Licio Gelli, apparently identified by several of the accused as one of the money laundering kingpins. The names of the Banda della Magliana and Camorra resurfaced. The alleged arms trafficking principally involved Croatia. It was claimed that Libya, with a clandestine armaments programme, was among the customers seeking red mercury.

The magistrates maintained their allegation against the Archbishop of Barcelona, claiming that he was suspected of helping launder at least $100 million through the Vatican bank.

The archly conservative Carles, who in the past had criticized Socialist ministers for their corrupt practices, denied he was involved, claiming instead that the allegations were the latest in a series of attacks by the enemies of Liberty against the Church. 'There are important financial interests behind these attacks from people who lose a lot of money when the Church defends ethics, morality and poor countries . . . The attacks are levelled at particular cardinals and have subsequently been proved false. Now it is my turn.'[1]

The Vatican leapt to his defence, with Navarro-Valls issuing a statement that 'no relations existed between the cardinal, the IOR and persons mentioned in the [Naples] investigation'.[2]

The situation was serious enough for John Paul II personally to intervene in an attempt to absolve his possible successor. He received Carles in a private audience that lasted almost an hour and named him to the governing board of the Holy See's Prefecture for Economic Affairs, under Cardinal Szoka.

---

[1] 'Barcelona cardinal rebuts corruption charges', *The Tablet*, 18 November 1995.
[2] 'El Vaticano defiende la inocencia del Cardinal Carles', *El País*, 10 November 1995, p. 17

'The meeting had great significance,' commented the Madrid daily *ABC*, 'because of the insidious campaign to which the Catalan prelate was subjected . . . The charges are demonstrably absurd and without foundation . . .'[1]

By then the Spiritual Wars had reached Geneva, city of Calvin, European headquarters of the United Nations, birthplace of the International Red Cross and now the home of Opus Dei's university of human rights, with the November 1995 slaying by *Gama'a al-Islamiya* of an Egyptian diplomat in an underground garage. Cairo charged that Ayman Zawahri, head of the militant Islamic hit squads operating from Europe, lived a comfortably financed under-cover existence in some Swiss mountain resort. But the Swiss authorities said they were unable to trace his whereabouts.

The FBI, meanwhile, seemed better informed. Headed by Opus Dei supernumerary Louis Freeh, it was investigating the bomb blasts that killed twenty-four Americans and wounded hundreds of others in Saudi Arabia. FBI analysts regarded the bombings as evidence that Islamic fundamentalism was gaining momentum in the Middle East. A group identified as the Islamic Movement for Change warned that all American and British 'Crusader' forces must leave the Muslim holy land or become the targets of a *jihad* decreed against the Saudi royal family and those associated with it.

Freeh also told a US Senate panel in March 1996 that 'sensitive sources' had informed the FBI that Hamas was raising funds in the US to pay for its suicide bombers. Freeh would not disclose who his 'sensitive sources' were, but one might legitimately ask whether they were related to Opus Dei's intelligence network.

With Felipe González's defeat in the 1996 elections, Opus Dei was back in power in Spain under the new prime minister, José María Aznar. Several of Aznar's Partido Popular friends were Opus Dei members and they naturally received cabinet positions. His 'Mister Clean', supernumerary Federico Trillo, an implaccable crusader against Socialist corruption, was named leader of the National Assembly. But also Aznar saw to it that senior Opus Dei people or close associates were appointed to key civil service positions. One example was the nomination of Alberto de la Hera

---

[1] 'El Papa recibió ayer en audiencia a monseñor Carles', *ABC*, Madrid, 21 February 1996.

as director general of religious affairs at the ministry of justice, which meant he controlled state subsidies to religious organizations as well as government relations with the Church hierarchy. Within weeks, other ministries also fell under the control of Opus-friendly civil servants.

Thus the Catholic Alliance in Europe that Pius XII had dreamed of founding as a bulwark against Communism had finally come about, with the Mediterranean powers of Spain, France, Italy and Croatia aligned through Opus Dei's influence to stem the tide of illegal immigration and co-operate on anti-terrorist measures. But also Opus Dei seemed determined to push through tighter controls on freedom of expression by banning excessive violence and blasphemy from state television networks and lobbying in favour of legislative support for the moral values set forth in John Paul II's encyclical, *Veritatis Splendor*. Former Spanish foreign minister Marcelino Orega-Aguirre, an Opus Dei member, was appointed to the European Commission in Brussels as the Community's audiovisual watchdog. He immediately made known his intention to bring higher moral standards to European programming.[1]

Opus Dei was vigilant in other fields as well. Archbishop Julián Herranz of the Council for the Interpretation of Legislative Texts ruled, for example, that mufti dress for priests was forbidden under Article 66 of a Congregation of the Clergy code of conduct. Article 66 specified that ordained members of the Church must wear clerical habits. A week later, a ruling by the Congregation for the Doctrine of the Faith, whose consultors included Opus Dei's new vicar general Fernando Ocáriz and his aide, theologian Antonio Miralles, declared that the Pope's ban on the ordination of women was an infallible part of Catholic doctrine and could not be disputed nor changed.

'We are among the most committed defenders of the notion that undebatable truth exists. Doctrine is not debatable,' claimed Monsignor Rolf Thomas, Opus Dei's former prefect of studies, known within the Prelature as *Il Gran Inquisitor*. Seen from the inside by a former Holy Cross priest, Opus Dei's prelates are

---

[1] Réseau Voltaire analysis: 'Le dessous des cartes – Depuis un an l'Opus Dei manipule l'opinion publique pour remettre en cause la liberté d'expression,' Paris, April 1995.

convinced that they possess the divine truth and by the same measure they are the 'inheritors' of the Templars.

'They feel assured that Opus Dei is no ordinary religious organization, and therefore not subject to the hierarchy of the Church. That same arrogance characterized the Templars – Christian warriors full of zeal, celibate and virile – and their determination to remain outside all control pushed them towards material ends. They acquired wealth in spite of their desire to remain poor. Their monastic zeal and obedience slowly transformed them, for extremely complex reasons, into a powerful economic and political force,' affirmed Father Felzmann.

'The Second Psalm was the Templar hymn. *Why do the nations conspire, and the peoples plot in vain?* Each celibate member of Opus Dei, man or woman, must recite the Second Psalm upon rising every Tuesday. "We are the children of God and we sing the Second Psalm." The Templars and Opus Dei sing the same psalm.

'In Opus Dei you find the same elitism as with the Templars, and this comes, I suppose, from that warrior mentality, from the idea that there is an enemy outside, and from a highly focused *esprit de corps*. In the long run, those who remain too long in that sort of atmosphere become paranoid. They have delusions of grandeur. They feel superior. They are the best, unique, and, at the same time, they believe there is an enemy stalking them. And so, because they are suspicious, they are reticent to be open and frank with the rest of the world.

'*Deus le volt!* We are God's chosen. These are not the words of the Founder. They are the words of the current Opus Dei leaders in Rome. I lived with them for four years. They told me with utter conviction, "*We have been chosen by God to save the Church.*" Some of them openly state that in twenty or thirty years Opus Dei will be all that remains of the Church. The whole Church will become Opus Dei because "We have an orthodox vision that is pure, certain, solid, assured of everything. The Founder was chosen by God to save the Church. Therefore God is with us."

'*Gott mit uns!* Think about it. That was the cry of the German Crusaders.'

The Lord is with us, and the Lord's counsel to kings is repeated weekly, after kissing the floor, by every Opus Dei numerary:

Now therefore, O kings, be wise;
be warned, O rulers of the earth.
Serve the Lord with fear,
with trembling kiss his feet,
lest he be angry, and you perish in the way;
for his wrath is quickly kindled.
Blessed are all who take refuge in him.[1]

[1] Psalms 2.10–11.

BIBLIOGRAPHY

Aarons, Mark & Loftus, John
Unholy Trinity – The Vatican, the Nazis and Soviet Intelligence
St Martin's Press, New York, 1991

Aburish, Said K.
The Forgotten Faithful: Christians of the Holy Land
Quartet Books, 1994

Artigues, Daniel
*L'Opus Dei en espagne – Son évolution politique et idéologique
(1928-1957)*
Editions Ruedo ibérico, Paris, 1968

Barber, Malcolm
The Trial of the Templars
Cambridge University Press, Canto edition, 1993

Berglar, Peter
Opus Dei – Life and Work of Its Founder Josemaría Escrivá
Scepter Publishers, Princeton, 1994
L'Opus Dei et son fondateur Josemaría Escrivá
MamE, Paris, 1992

Bernal, Salvador
*Msgr Josemaría Escrivá de Balaguer – Profile of the Founder of Opus
Dei*
Scepter, New York, 1977

Bowers, Fergal
*The Work – An Investigation into the History of Opus Dei and how it
operates in Ireland Today*
Poolbeg, Dublin, 1989

Bradford, Ernle
The Great Siege – Malta 1565
Hodder & Stoughton, London, 1961

Brenan, Gerald
The Spanish Labyrinth
Cambridge University Press, Canto edition, 1993

Brodhead, Frank, and Herman, Edward S.
The Rise and Fall of the Bulgarian Connection
Sheridan Square, New York, 1986

Bulajic, Milan
The Role of the Vatican in the Break-Up of the Yugoslav State
Strucna Knjiga, Belgrade, 1994

Calabro, Maria Antonietta
Le Mani Della Mafia
Edizioni Associate, Rome, 1991

Campo Villegas, Gabriel
Esta es Nuestra Sangre
Publicaciones Claretianas, Madrid 1992
Claretian Martyrs of Barbastro
Claretian Publications, Quezon City, Philippines, 1992

Carandell, Luiz
The Life and Miracles of Mgr. Escrivá
Editorial Laia, 1975

Casciaro, Pedro
Soñad y os quedaréis cortos
Ediciones Rialp, Madrid, 1994

Chadwick, Owen
The Christian Church in the Cold War
Penguin, London, 1992

Conde, Mario
El Sistema – Mi experiencia del Poder
Espasa Calpe, Madrid, 1994

Cornwell, John
Thief in the Night
Viking, London, 1989
Powers of Darkness Powers of Light – Travels in Search of the Miraculous and the Demonic
Viking, London, 1991

Cornwell, Rupert
God's Banker – The Life and Death of Roberto Calvi
Victor Gollancz Ltd, London, 1983

Ekaizer, Ernesto
José María Ruiz Mateos, el Ultimo Magnate
Plaza, Janes Editores S.A., Barcelona, 1985

Escrivá de Balaguer, Josemaría
  Conversations with Monsignor Escrivá de Balaguer
  Scepter Publishers, London, 1991
  Christ is passing by
  Four Courts Press, Dublin, 1985
  Friends of God
  Scepter Ltd, London, 1981
  The Way
  Four Courts Press, Dublin, 1985
Esposito, John L.
  The Islamic Threat – Myth or Reality?
  Oxford University Press, Oxford, 1992
Estruch, Joan
  Saints and Schemers – Opus Dei and Its Paradoxes
  Oxford University Press, New York, 1995
Evans, Joan
  Monastic Life at Cluny – 910–1157
  Archon Books, Hamden, Connecticut, 1968
Faricy, Robert and Rooney, Lucy
  Medjugorje Journal – Mary Speaks to the World
  McCrimmons, Great Wakering, Essex, 1987
Farmer, David Hugh
  The Oxford Dictionary of Saints
  Oxford University Press, Oxford, 1992 (Third Edition)
Ferrari, Giuliano F.G.
  Vaticanisme
  Perret-Gentil, Geneva, 1976
Fontán, Antonio
  Los católicos en la Universidad española actual
  Ediciones Rialp, Madrid, 1961
Fuenmayor, Amadeo de, Gómez-Iglesias, Valentín et Illanes, José Luis
  Itinéraire juridique de l'Opus Dei – Histoire et Défense d'un Charisme
  Desclée, Paris, 1992
  The Canonical Path of Opus Dei
  Scepter Publishers, Princeton, 1994
Gannes, Harry and Repard, Theodore
  Spain in Revolt
  Victor Gollancz Ltd., London, 1936
Garvey, J.J.M.
  Parents' Guide to Opus Dei
  Sicut Dixit Press, New York, NY 10165, 1989
Gibbon, Edward
  The Decline and Fall of the Roman Empire
  Everyman's Library, 1993 edition, London

Gilson, Etienne
The Spirit of Mediaeval Philosophy
University of Notre Dame Press, Notre Dame, 1991
Gondrand, François
At God's Pace – Josemaría Escrivá, Founder of Opus Dei
Scepter, London, 1989
Au Pas de Dieu
Editions France-Empire, Paris, 1991 (Third edition)
González Janzen, Ignacio
La Triple-A
Editorial Contrapunto, Buenos Aires, 1986
Grootaers, Jan
De Vatican II à Jean-Paul II: Le grand tournant de l'Eglise catholique
Centurion, Paris, 1981
Gutiérrez, Gustavo
A Theology of Liberation
SCM Press Ltd., London, 1974
Hammer, Richard
*The Vatican Connection – The Astonishing Account of a Billion
Dollar Counterfeit Stock Deal Between the Mafia and the Church*
Holt, Rinehart & Winston, New York, 1982
Hanson, Eric O.
The Catholic Church in World Politics
Princeton University Press, Princeton 1987
Hebblethwaite, Peter
John XXIII – Pope of the Council
Geoffrey Chapman, London, 1985
Paul VI – The First Modern Pope
HarperCollins, London, 1993
In the Vatican
Oxford University Press, Oxford, 1988
The Next Pope
Fount Paperbacks, London, 1995
Heikal, Mohamed
Illusions of Triumph
HarperCollins, London, 1992
Helming, Dennis M.
Footprints in the Snow
Scepter Publishers, New Rochelle, NY, 1986
Hersh, Seymour M.
The Price of Power
Summit Books, New York, 1983
Hiro, Dilip
Islamic Fundamentalism
Paladin, London, 1989

Hooper, John
  The Spaniards – A Portrait of the New Spain
  Viking, London, 1986
Kelly, J.N.D.
  The Oxford Dictionary of Popes
  Oxford University Press, Oxford, 1986
Kennedy, Paul
  The Rise and Fall of the Great Powers
  Fontana, London, 1989
Kepel, Gilles
  La revanche de Dieu – Chrétiens, juifs et musulmans à la reconquête du monde
  Seuil, Paris, 1990
  The Revenge of God – The Resurgence of Islam, Christianity and Judaism in the Modern World
  Polity Press, Cambridge, 1994
  Le Prophète et Pharaon – Au sources des mouvements islamistes
  Seuil, Paris, 1993
Kepel, Gilles (editor)
  Les Politiques de Dieu
  Seuil, Paris, 1993
Knight, Stephen
  The Brotherhood
  Grafton, London, 1993
John Paul II
  Crossing the Threshold of Hope
  Jonathan Cape, London, 1994
Johnson, Paul
  A History of the Modern World – From 1917 to the 1980s
  Weidenfeld & Nicolson, London, 1983
Lacouture, Jean
  Jésuites
  Seuil, Paris, 1991
Lernoux, Penny
  Cry of the People – The Struggle for Human Rights in Latin America – The Catholic Church in Conflict with US Policy
  Penguin, New York, 1991
Le Tourneau, Dominique
  L'Opus Dei
  Presses Universitaires de France, Paris, 1991 (Que Sais-je? series)
  What Is Opus Dei?
  Mercier Press, Dublin, 1989
Le Vaillant, Yvon
  Sainte Maffia – Le Dossier de l'Opus Dei
  Mercure de France, Paris, 1971

López Novoa, Saturnino
Historia de Barbastro
Imprenta de Pablo Riera, Barcelona, 1861 (republished 1984)

Malcolm, Noel
Bosnia – A Short History
Macmillan, London, 1994

Magister, Sandro
La politica Vaticana e l'Italia (1943–1978)
Riuniti, Rome 1979

Martin, Malachi
The Final Conclave
Stein & Day, New York, 1978

Meissner, W.W.
Ignatius of Loyola – The Psychology of a Saint
Yale University Press, New Haven, 1992

Messori, Vittorio
Opus Dei – Un'Indagine
Arnoldo Mondadori, Milan, 1994

Moncada, Alberto
Historia Oral del Opus Dei
Plaza & Janes, Barcelona, 1992

Moreno, María Angustias
El Opus Dei, anexo a una historia
Editorial Planeta, collection Textos, Barcelona 1976

Mumford, Stephen D.
American Democracy & the Vatican: Population Growth & National Security
Humanist Press, Amherst, NY, 1984

Oberlé, Thierry
L'Opus Dei – Dieu ou César?
Jean-Claude Lattès, Paris, 1993

O'Connor, William
Opus Dei – An Open Book
Mercier Press, Dublin, 1991

Olaizola, José Luis
Viaje al Fondo de la Esperanza
Ediciones Rialp, Madrid, 1992

Opus Dei
Testimonies to a man of God – Blessed Josemaría Escrivá (Volumes 1 & 2)
Scepter, London, 1992

Paulus Akademie
Opus Dei – Stosstrupp Gottes oder 'Heilige Mafia'?
NZN Buchverlag, Zurich, 1992

Péan, Pierre
V – Enquête sur l'affaire des 'avions renifleurs' et ses ramifications proches ou lointaines
Fayard, Paris, 1984

Pérez Pellón, Javier
Wojtyla, el último cruzado – Un papado medieval en el fin del milenio
Ediciones Temas de Hoy, Madrid, 1994

Perry, Mark
Eclipse – The Last Days of the CIA
William Morrow, New York, 1992

Preston, Paul
Franco – A Biography
HarperCollins, London, 1993

Previté-Orton, C.W.
The Shorter Cambridge Medieval History (Vols 1&2)
University Press, Cambridge, 1962

Raw, Charles
The Moneychangers – How the Vatican Bank Enabled Roberto Calvi to Steal $250 Million for the Heads of the P2 Masonic Lodge
Harvill, London, 1992

Rhodes, Anthony
The Vatican in the Age of the Cold War, 1945–1980
Michael Russell (Publishing) Ltd, Wilby, Norwich, 1992

Robinson, John J.
Dungeon, Fire and Sword – The Knights Templar in the Crusades
M. Evans & Co., New York, 1991

Rodríguez, Pedro, Ocáriz, Fernado and Illanes, José Luis
Opus Dei in the Church
Four Courts Press, Dublin, 1994

Ropero, Javier
Hijos en el Opus Dei
Editions B Serie Reporter, Barcelona, 1993

Runciman, Steven
A History of the Crusades
Penguin, London, 1991
The Fall of Constantinople, 1453
Cambridge University Press (Canto edition), 1990

Sainz Moreno, Javier
El Holding de las Mil Empresas
Madrid, 1992

Sastre, Ana
Tiempo de Caminar – Semblanza de Monseñor Josemaría Escrivá de Balaguer
Ediciones Rialp, Madrid, 1989

Scott, Martin
Medieval Europe
Longmans, London, 1964

Short, Martin
Inside the Brotherhood
Grafton Books, London, 1990

Solomon, Robert
The International Monetary System 1945–1981
Harper & Row, New York, 1982

Soriano, Manuel
Sabino Fernández Campo – La Sombra del Rey
Ediciones Temas de Hoy, Madrid, 1995

Steigleder, Klaus
Das Opus Dei – Eine Innenansicht
Benziger Verlag, Zurich, 1983

Tapia, María del Carmen
Tras el Umbral – Una vida en el Opus Dei
Ediciones B, Barcelona, 1994
Hinter der Schwelle – Ein Leben im Opus Dei
Benziger Verlag, Zurich, 1993

Thierry, Jean-Jacques
Les finances du vatican
Guy Authier, Paris, 1978

Thomas, Hugh
The Spanish Civil War
Penguin Books, London, 1990

Thomson, Ahmad
Blood on the Cross – Islam in Spain in the Light of Christian Persecution Through the Ages
TaHa Publishers, London, 1989
Dajjal – The King who has no clothes
TaHa Publishers, London, 1993

Torello, Juan B.
La Espiritualidad de los laicos
Ediciones Rialp, Madrid, 1965

Tosches, Nick
Power on Earth
Arbor House, New York, 1986

Urbano, Pilar
El hombre de Villa Tevere
Plaza & Janes, Barcelona, 1995

Valero, Samuel
Yauyos – Una Aventura en los Andes
Ediciones Rialp, Madrid, 1992

Vázquez de Prada, Andrés
El Fundador del Opus Dei – Monseñor Josemaría Escrivá de Balaguer (1902–1975)
Ediciones Rialp, Madrid, 1983

Velázquez, Flavia-Paz
Vida de María Josefa Segovia
Publicaciones de la Institución Teresiana, Madrid, 1964

Walsh, Michael
The Secret World of Opus Dei – An investigation into the controversial sect at the heart of the Roman Catholic Church
Grafton, London, 1989
John Paul II
HarperCollins, London, 1994

West, W.J.
Opus Dei – Exploding a Myth
Little Hills Press, Crows Nest, Australia, 1987

Willey, David
God's Politician
Faber & Faber, London, 1992

Woodward, Bob
VEIL: The Secret Wars of the CIA 1981–1987
Simon & Schuster, New York, 1987

Woodward, Kenneth L.
Making Saints – How the Catholic Church Determines Who Becomes A Saint, Who Doesn't and Why
Simon & Schuster, New York, 1990

Yallop, David
In God's Name – An Investigation into the Murder of Pope John Paul I
Jonathan Cape Ltd, London, 1984

Ynfante, Jesús
La prodigiosa aventure del Opus Dei – Génesis y desarrollo de la Santa Mafia
Editions Ruedo ibérico, Paris, 1970

DOCUMENTS

Almerighi, Mario
Ordinanza de rinvio a giudizio nel procedimento penale contro Flavio Carboni e altri
Rome, 24 March 1992

Calvi, Clara
Diaries – 1950–1982
Unpublished

Casanova, José V.
The Opus Dei Ethic: The Technocrats and the Modernisation of Spain
Paper presented at the Columbia University Seminar on Content and Method in Social Sciences, September 1981

Clark, Eileen
Opus Dei – An 11-year experience of the Women's Section
(Unpublished) February 1995

Congregation for the Doctrine of the Faith
Christian Freedom and Liberation
Rome, 22 March 1986

Fabbri, Gianvittore, Dr
Sentenza nella causa penale di primo grado No. 168/92 contro Flavio Carboni, Giulio Lena e Maria Paolo Hnilica
Tribunale di Roma, Prima Sezione Penale, 23 March 1993

Golias (Magazine)
Le Monde Secret de l'Opus Dei
Golias No. 30, Lyon, Summer 1992

Meunier, Robert, Dr
Reflections on Opus Dei
Unpublished

Moncada, Alberto
Catholic Sects: Opus Dei
Revista Internacional de Sociología, Madrid, December 1992

Opus Dei, Office of Communications
Response to 'The Inner World of Opus Dei' by John Roche
New York, NY (Undated)

Philips, Abu Ameenah Bilal
The True Religion
Islamic Da'awa and Guidance Center, Dammam

Picazo Moya, Francisco
Informe sobre la colonizacion por el Opus Dei, degeneracion y consiguiente fracaso de Pro Vida
Monóvar, 1 November 1988

Roche, John J.
The Inner World of Opus Dei
Oxford, September 1982

Shaw, Russell
Working for God the World Over
US Information Office of Opus Dei, 1981

Wojtyla, Karol (John Paul II)
L'Evangelizzazione e l'Uomo Interiore
CRIS Documenti 19, Rome, 1975
Il Coraggio di Confessare la Fede
CRIS Documenti 34, Rome, 1977

ENCYCLICALS

John XXIII
Pacem in Terris
11 April 1963
Paul VI
Gaudium et Spes
7 December 1965
Marialis Cultis
2 February 1974
John Paul II
Redemptoris Mater
25 March 1987
Tertio Millennio Adveniente
10 November 1994
Veritatis Splendor
6 August 1993

INDEX

Note: alphabetical order is word by word. Spanish names appear under the *first* element of the surname, as in 'Escrivá de Balaguer, Josémaría'. Most banks appear under 'Bank', 'Banco', 'Banque'